ISLAMICATE TRADITIONS IN SOUTH ASIA

Islamicate Traditions in South Asia

Themes from Culture & History

Edited by

AGNIESZKA KUCZKIEWICZ-FRAŚ

MANOHAR
2013

First published in India in 2013

ISBN 978-81-7304-975-0

Published by
Ajay Kumar Jain *for*
Manohar Publishers & Distributors
4753/23 Ansari Road, Daryaganj
New Delhi 110 002

Printed at
Salasar Imaging Systems
Delhi 110 035

Contents

Places & Images

People

Ideas & Notions

History & Language

Editor's Preface

Agnieszka Kuczkiewicz-Fraś

Perhaps no aspect of the history of South Asia provokes more discussion and disagreement than the evaluation of the role played by Islam in this part of the world. The Muslim presence and rule in South Asia were established firmly by the thirteenth century and flourished for the next five hundred years. The advent of Islam did not destroy the ancient civilisation of India, yet the mutual influences of Hindu and Muslim societies and their traditions were inevitable during centuries of their co-existence. This cohabitation has resulted in creating a unique phenomenon – the Islamicate[1] culture of South Asia.

Such an extraordinary, complex and in many aspects syncretic tradition calls for separate dealing in the immense field of

[1] The term "Islamicate" in the title of this book is used to refer to the phenomena influenced by Muslim tradition and presence but not restricted to the practice of Islam as a religion, i.e. "Islamic" in a strict sense of the word. In this sense the term "Islamicate" has been used by various authors, e.g. David Gilmartin, Bruce B. Lawrence, 'Introduction', [in:] *Beyond Turk and Hindu: Rethinking Religious Identity in Islamicate South Asia*, New Delhi: India Research Press, 2002, pp. 1-20 or Mukul Kesavan, 'Urdu, Awadh and the Tawaif: the Islamicate Roots of Hindi Cinema', [in:] *Forging identities: gender, communities, and the state in India*, ed. Zoya Hasan, Delhi: Kali, 1994.

studies on South Asia. Hence a number of publications, devoted to various aspects of this subject, has appeared during the last decades, and the present volume fits well into this tendency. Its main idea is to depict some of the Islamicate cultural traditions and influences understood today as an integral part of the civilisation of South Asia. The main issues discussed by the authors refer to the widely understood cultural environment of South Asian Muslims, including their language, literature, history, thought and traditions. The range of subjects has intentionally not been limited, as the aim of the editor was to show the multitude and variety of aspects of the Muslim presence in the Indian subcontinent's milieu as well as the vast spectrum of research conducted in this field in different academic centres of Europe, the United States and South Asia.

The fourteen articles collected in the volume are the result of academic investigation written by invited specialists in different fields, and cover a large array of themes. They vary from ones referring to a particular area of interest and study – such as linguistics, literature or history – to those more interdisciplinary in their character. Depending on what constitutes their focal point, they have been grouped into four sections, titled respectively: "Places & Images", "People", "Ideas & Notions", and "History & Language". Twelve contributions have been originally published in the yearly "Cracow Indological Studies" (2009, vol. 11), but for this edition they have all been scrupulously revised and amended. Two articles (by H. Trivedi and R. P. Das) were written specially for this volume.

The opening text of the volume, *Looking askance at Being: a note on Ghalib from a Hindi poet* by Ashok Vajpeyi, is a kind of tribute paid by an eminent contemporary poet writing in Hindi to another outstanding poet of the nineteenth century, who wrote in Urdu. Ashok Vajpeyi underlines Ghalib's role as the first modern Indian writer, at the same time paying attention to the fact that Ghalib's modernity had nothing to do with the West and was a realisation of the interaction which for centuries had existed between Indian[2] and Persian literary traditions. Vajpeyi

[2] For practical reasons, and also to accord with the usage of most contributions to this volume, "India" has been used synonymously with "South

enumerates the main determinants of Ghalib's modernity, namely placing an individual as such at the centre of the writer's attention for the first time in Indian poetic tradition and asking the most fundamental and crucial questions concerning the condition of man in his relation to God and the whole universe, the status of a poet involved in the extreme difficulties of his life, and the place of love in the face of indifference and hostility. According to Vajpeyi these factors draw "a totally new and intriguing contour in the geography that modernism in India sought to map out".

Real places and their images – be it a city, its part or a single piece of architecture – which exist in the authentic world as well as in the imagined space of people's memory: those are the connecting themes of three texts gathered in the first section of the volume. Using both philological and hermeneutical methods of analysing data, their authors try to extract and demonstrate legends of the past splendour of which those places are today silent and often forgotten witnesses.

The section starts with Daniela Bredi's article *Nostalgia in the re-construction of Muslim identity in the aftermath of 1857 and the myth of Delhi*, in the first part of which she characterises the post-1857 historiographical writing in Urdu by authors such as Sayyid Ahmad Khan, Shibli Nu^{c}mani, Amir ^{c}Ali and Altaf Husain Hali, whose output is replete with the nostalgia of the glorious Muslim past and is also an attempt to reconstruct the Muslim identity in a political and cultural dimension. Such a reflexive nostalgia, through poetry and prose, gave birth to the myth of Delhi which Bredi analyses in the second part of her text, focusing on the times of Bahadur Shah II's reign which "in the Indo-Muslim mind, became a Mughal garden undergoing its final spring before the autumn of the Revolt's aftermath destroyed it forever, or a Mughal candle flaring into its old brilliance before being extinguished for good". These complex times Bredi describes mainly through the famous work of Mirza Farhatullah Beg *Dillī kī āxirī šam^c*, where an imaginary last

Asia" here and in the following, with an older meaning not influenced by present-day circumstances and divisions in mind.

mušā^{c}*ira* in Delhi is recalled as a symbol evoking the old and splendid Muslim culture of the capital.

Five lyrical works – poetic images of India's Muslim past – written by Kunwar Narain are the subject of Renata Czekalska's observations (*Images of India's Muslim past in modern Hindi poetry – five poems on three cities by Kunwar Narain*). They all belong to one poetry collection titled *Ap'ne sām'ne*, published in 1979. Czekalska analyses the five works forming a kind of historical landscape, with their components, such as image, thought and word, evoking feelings of sympathy and empathy. She describes the content of these poetic reflections that call to mind the memories of probably the most turbulent times in the history of India – the years of Muslim invasion and domination. In the conclusion of her article Czekalska observes that Kunwar Narain in his poems not only presents the reader with a vast and picturesque panorama of historical places and events, but also proves to have the courage to tackle the difficult issue of the encounter of two great cultures, Hindu and Muslim, confirming at the same time that in his poetry history, tradition and the present are indivisible.

The last text in this section, *History preserved in names: Delhi urban toponyms of Perso-Arabic origin* by Agnieszka Kuczkiewicz-Fraś presents an analysis of Delhi urban toponyms of Perso-Arabic origin. The author's assumption that place-names are an important source of information regarding the people who have inhabited a given area, and that they are also very important land-marks of cultural and linguistic contacts of different groups of people, becomes a starting point for reflections on 90 toponyms connected with important historical objects of Delhi, such as mosques, tombs, shrines, forts, water reservoirs, towers, gates, palaces, gardens, etc. The author categorises and characterises them according to their etymological construction as well as their semantic value, more than once unveiling also the often forgotten or recondite true meaning of these names.

The second part of the volume, "People", consists of four contributions. A person and his or her individual endeavours remain the focal point of all of them. In the first text (*Zay Khay Sheen, Aligarh's purdah-nashin poet*) Gail Minault discusses the literary output of Zay Khay Sheen, or Zahida Khatun Sherwani (1894-1922), the daughter of Nawab Sir Muzammilullah Khan Sherwani who not only actively supported the Aligarh movement and Sir Sayyid Ahmad Khan, but was also a skilled poet in Persian. Minault depicts the writer as a woman who was brought up in a family which on the one hand was very progressive and supported education, also for women, and on the other very conservative, as the women of the family maintained strict *purdah* and were educated at home. Minault characterises Z-Kh-Sh as one who "remained hidden behind the four walls of the Sherwani compound", but who also had a lively intellect, was interested in the life and politics of her time, and energetically organised her cousins in support of education for poor children and girls, creating and publishing political poetry from a very early age.

The subsequent text, *Jihādī literature? Some novels of Nasīm Ḥijāzī*, is also devoted to a man of letters. Its author, Christina Oesterheld, examines the phenomenon of the extraordinary popularity of novels written by Nasim Hijazi (1914-96), who in his books continues a tradition current among Urdu writers engaged in the Muslim political and social reform movements of the nineteenth century, evoking the Golden Age of Islam, and aspiring to mobilise and consolidate the Muslim community. Hijazi's oeuvre has been often – and rightly, as Oesterheld states – judged as propagating a one-sided, militant *jihādī* image of Islam. But on the other hand, in some of his writings Islam is hailed as a religion and a political system which brings peace to the Arab Peninsula and to the world. Oesterheld discusses this very ambivalent picture of Islam and Muslims on the example of four chosen Hijazi's novels. She also emphasises that it is important to pay attention to this best-selling author who might have influenced the mindset of quite a number of young readers with his particular vision of Islam.

The figure to which the next text in this section has been dedicated is Fatima Jinnah (1893-1967), the younger sister of Muhammad Ali Jinnah, the founder of Pakistan, and its "Great Leader" (*Qāʾid-i Aʿẕam*). Kamila Junik describes in her article (*Between tradition and modernity: Fatima Jinnah*) the role of Jinnah's sister in the history and culture of Pakistan and she attempts to point out the reasons for Fatima's popularity which is almost as great as her famous brother's. The author describes Fatima first as the most dutiful sister and best friend of Muhammad Ali Jinnah and – since the death of Jinnah's wife in 1929 – also as the person taking care of his household, his closest companion and sometimes even advisor, and later, after the creation of Pakistan and due to her involvement in social actions – as the Mother of the Nation. In the article, Fatima is portrayed neither as an activist fighting for women's rights nor a feminist in her approach, but as someone always ready to serve a good cause, who did not have any political ambitions. Junik acknowledges Fatima Jinnah's contribution in the field of women's awakening, their development, education and participation in national affairs as "the most recognizable in the history of Pakistan".

The protagonist of the next article titled *Sir Sayyid's public sphere: Urdu print and oratory in nineteenth century India* is the great nineteenth century Muslim leader, reformer and educationist, Sir Sayyid Ahmad Khan (1817-98). David Lelyveld, the author of the article, ruminates on the concept of a "public sphere", trying to find the way in which it might apply to the Urdu language in the course of the nineteenth century. Asking what may have become of "some of the bits and pieces" that could be taken for the efforts to "formulate and promote a new form of collective consciousness among Indians in organized and ideologically articulate political and social movements", Lelyveld discusses some aspects of the career of Sir Sayyid based on his public utterances, in print as well as in speech, trying at the same time to place these publications and speeches in the wider context of his other enterprises.

The next section gathers four articles whose authors ponder on a particular idea or phenomenon. In the first of them titled *Power, culture and language of poetry: the transition from Vali to Ghalib*, Mehr Farooqi discusses the twofold tradition of Urdu poetry being created in Delhi in the eighteenth-nineteenth centuries. One component of this tradition was classical Persian verse, to which Ghalib frequently referred declaring his adherence to Bedil, considered as one of the eminent poets of the Indian school of Persian poetry (later known as *sabk-i-hindī* – Indian style). The other was the output of the Urdu-Hindi poets of the Deccan, and most of all the *dīvān* of Vali that reached Delhi at the beginning of the eighteenth century. Farooqi investigates the role and the significance of the reaction which the *dīvān* evoked within Delhi literary circles. Concluding, the author returns to the opinion expressed in the opening part of her essay, where she underlined the individuality of Ghalib, and states: "Ghalib worked in the same poetic tradition which was Mir's tradition, and which was Vali's tradition too. But he is so apparently different, and so thoroughly individualistic on the surface that most of us are led into the error of believing that he was doing something else".

The main aim of the next article, *The language of love: a study of the amorous and erotic associations of Urdu*, written by Tariq Rahman, is to document and discuss the presence of amorous and erotic themes in Urdu writings of the nineteenth century. The author refers to several statements which arose on the ground of the Hindi-Urdu controversy and were posed by those who advocated Hindi in the place of Urdu. The statements generally treat Urdu as the means of expression favoured by dancing girls and prostitutes, and serving as the idiom for propagating obscenity, decadence, backwardness and obsession with sex. Rahman attempts to answer the question whether the association of Urdu with sensuousness and eroticism in these statements was merely an assertion and a tactical manoeuvre directed against the spokesmen and supporters of Urdu (and possibly also against Muslims as such). On the other hand he reflects on the possibility that Urdu really did have such associations and wonders why – if that were true – there is so little mention about these phenomena nowadays. Making an assumption that the presence of certain ideological and political imperatives might have been the factor responsible for this silence, he tries to make them more understandable through documenting the erotic and amorous themes in nineteenth century Urdu literature.

The Urdu and Hindi languages and their literary traditions placed within the broader context of a comparative framework are in the focus of Harish Trivedi's musings. In his essay titled *Muslims and Hindus, Urdu and Hindi* the author tries to find out what and how much the two literary traditions have in common. In search of the so-called *gaṅgā-jamunī tahẕīb*, or 'composite' literary culture, Trivedi discusses the output of Hindu authors who throughout history wrote in Urdu, and of those who were Muslims but created their works in Hindi. Finally, he examines the attempts to read Hindi and Urdu together which sometimes, and mostly in the scholarly centres outside South Asia, have been undertaken by authors of textbooks and various reading materials as well as some literary critics. Concluding his ruminations, Trivedi stresses the fact that in the face of global English domination the old quarrel between Hindi and Urdu has lost its impetus and the common jeopardy "has now made bed-fellows of these old adversaries".

The fourth article contained in this section takes us further east. Rahul Peter Das in *Ḥasan and Ḥusain as the Sons of Muḥammad. A contemporary treatise from Bangladesh* presents an English translation of a most interesting as well as controversial text written in the form of a rebuttal by the head of a Sufi dargah in Thakurgaon in Bangladesh, purporting to prove that Hasan and Husain are not ᶜAli's but, in fact, Muhammad's sons. The line of reasoning is most intricate and has been strongly influenced by the sophisticated tradition of Urdu scholasticism, especially visible in those parts of the original text which extensively quote sources in Urdu (the rebuttal otherwise has been written in Bengali). The whole work was published in a small booklet from which Das translates the salient part. The translated text is accompanied by the translator's voluminous and informative notes, that make the rebuttal a great deal clearer and more understandable for the reader.

The buckle to fasten the three articles comprised in the last part of the book is history: the history of the Afghan people and the history of the Persian language in the South Asian context. André Wink, in his extensive study titled *On the road of failure: the Afghans in Mughal India*, presents the causes of consecutive waves of the Afghan eastward migrations, and their effects as well as the mechanisms that led to the creation of the first ever Afghan Empire – the Lodi Sultanate. Wink concentrates on the rivalry between the Afghans and the Mughals that in the course of centuries occurred mainly in two areas: North India and the Kabul Wilayat. He describes the struggle for power during the Lodi Sultanate, Sur Empire and Sher Shah's reign, the armed insurrection of the Roshaniyya movement led by the charismatic Bayazid Ansari, that arose on the ground of millenarian Islam and finally the rise and fall of the Durrani Empire, which ultimately resulted in the failure of the Afghan state. Wink's historical analyses are prefaced by an extensive introduction regarding the pastoral-nomadic economy of the region of Afghanistan, and a characterisation of Afghan tribal society.

The next two articles concern the historical presence of the Persian language in South Asia. In *Persian lexicography in South Asia*, Kinga Maciuszak traces back the history of Persian lexicography in this region as far as the thirteenth century. Following S.I. Baevski, she distinguishes three periods in the history of Persian lexicography on the Indian subcontinent and categorises the described dictionaries accordingly. The author enumerates over 50 dictionaries compiled in South Asia, giving basic data (date of compilation, full title, name of the author(s), number of entries, method of arrangement of the material included). In a more detailed manner, she describes over 20 of them, which she understands to be the most important. A list of printed editions of Persian lexicographical works in alphabetical order is included in the voluminous bibliography.

Tariq Rahman in his article *The learning of Persian in South Asia: the curricula and educational institutions for teaching Persian in South Asia*, discusses some aspects of learning Persian in the Indian subcontinent, focusing on the curricula of Persian and the ways (privately or in institutions of learning) in which the language was learned. The author discusses point by point the pedagogical material (basic primers or lexicons meant to teach Persian or Arabic through the medium of Persian, books about prose and composition, poetry, history and ethics, etc.). This is followed by a brief description of Persian literature created and taught in India, which, comprising mostly poetic works and rhymed tales (*dāstān*-s), was also a part of the traditional course of Persian studies. In the next part the author focuses on the learning of Persian by foreigners as well as on the role of educational institutions, both traditional – *maktab*-s or *madrasa*-s – and modern – established by the British. The article also provides some information about the teaching of Persian to females.

As can be seen from this short introduction, the variety of topics taken up and considered in the fourteen articles contained in this volume, as well as their geographical coverage and chronological range, is quite extensive. It remains the hope of the authors and the editor that they will serve well as a source of information and reference for students and specialists dealing with various aspects of Islamicate culture and traditions of South Asia.

Having the privilege to be the editor of this volume, I would like to express my deep gratitude to all the authors, who kindly agreed to contribute their texts, and to the Indian publisher of the book, Mr. Ramesh Jain, who offered his help and made it possible to bring it out in India.

* * *

The Roman transliteration used in the volume follows the systems developed for the Nagari/Bengali script and the modified Arabic script respectively. Since apart from English there are several other languages appearing in this volume, and variations in spelling are frequent in Urdu, Persian, Hindi, Bengali, Pashto and other relevant languages of all periods, any attempt to completely unify or standardise the methods of reproducing all original words and names in the Roman script remains an unrealisable idea. In addition, the authors themselves have employed different ways of English transcription for other languages, which partly also depend on the sources they use.

Trying to have the cake and also eat it, the editor hence decided to compromise and to leave the authors' Anglicized transcription of names unchanged in most of the cases, though and *ᶜain* has as rule been shown. However, single words, phrases, quotations and titles coming from Urdu, Persian, Hindi etc., have been transliterated according to the rules given in the tables on pp. 17-18. The systems adopted attempt to be exact, so that the reader should be able to reconstruct the original spelling of transliterated words or texts.

Nagari and Bengali

Vowels:

अ / অ *a*   आ / আ *ā*   इ / ই *i*   ई / ঈ *ī*   उ / উ *u*   ऊ / ঊ *ū*

ऋ / ঋ *ṛ*   ए / এ *e*   ऐ / ঐ *ai*   ओ / ও *o*   औ / ঔ *au*

* *a* + *i* and *a* + *u* are written as *aï* and *aü* to differentiate them from the diphthongs *ai* and *au* respectively

* *a* which is not pronounced is indicated by ', except at the end of a word

Consonants:

क / ক *ka*	ख / খ *kha*	ग / গ *ga*	घ / ঘ *gha*	ङ / ঙ *ṅa*
च / চ *ca*	छ / ছ *cha*	ज / জ *ja*	झ / ঝ *jha*	ञ / ঞ *ña*
ट / ট *ṭa*	ठ / ঠ *ṭha*	ड / ড *ḍa*	ढ / ঢ *ḍha*	ण / ণ *ṇa*
त / ত *ta*	थ / থ *tha*	द / দ *da*	ध / ধ *dha*	न / ন *na*
प / প *pa*	फ / ফ *pha*	ब / ব *ba*	भ / ভ *bha*	म / ম *ma*
य / য *ya*	र / র *ra*	ल / ল *la*	व / - *va*	
श / শ *śa*	ष / ষ *ṣa*	स / স *sa*	ह / হ *ha*	

Modifications:

क़ / - *k̲a*   ख़ / - *k̲h̲a*   ग़ / - *ga*   ज़ / - *za*   फ़ / - *fa*

ड़ / ড় *ṛa*   ढ़ / ঢ় *ṛha*   - / য় *ẏa*

Nasals: anusvāra ं / ং *ṃ*   candrabindu ँ *ṁ* / ˜ (depending on the author's choice)

virāma ्

Arabic script for Urdu, Persian and Arabic

ا	*a*	ش	*š*
آ	*ā*	ص	*ṣ*
ب	*b*	ض	*ẓ* (*ḍ* for Arabic)
پ	*p*	ط	*t̤*
ت	*t*	ظ	*z̤*
ٹ	*ṭ*	ع	*ᶜ*
ث	*s̱* (*ṯ* for Arabic)	غ	*ġ*
ج	*j*	ف	*f*
چ	*č*	ق	*q*
ح	*ḥ*	ک	*k*
خ	*x*	گ	*g*
د	*d*	ل	*l*
ڈ	*ḍ*	م	*m*
ذ	*ẕ* (*ḏ* for Arabic)	ن	*n*
ر	*r*	و	*v* (*w* for Arabic), *ū*, *o*, *au*
ڑ	*ṛ*	ہ	*h*
ز	*z*	ی	*y*, *ī*, *e*, *ai*
ژ	*ž*	ء	ʾ
س	*s*		

nūn-i ġunna (ں) in Urdu is indicated by a tilde ˜ above a preceding vowel or by *ṅ* (depending on the author's choice)

ʾalif maqṣūrah (ى) is given as *ą̄* } only in Arabic transliteration
tāʾ marbūṭa (ة) is given as *ah* in pausa }

Looking askance at Being: a note on Ghalib from a Hindi poet

Ashok Vajpeyi

Although one could find traces of the agony and turmoil of the nineteenth century in Ghalib, he hardly ever wrote directly about his time or contemporaneous events and developments. When he did so, it was in his prose, particularly in his letters but not in his poetry. He lived in his times as deeply, humanly and truly as any sensitive person could have. But his cosmic vision, his powerful apprehension of the angst of being and his sense of loneliness have a truly timeless dimension. Ghalib is not a poet of history, but of eternity.

All too often modernism in India is traced back to the nineteenth century and to the encounter we had with the West. In fact, to a large extent most of the Indian modernism or post-modernism is a West-propelled modernism.

In Ghalib another Indo-centric modernism had articulated itself which does not seem to have been adequately noticed. This modernism has nothing to do with the West and was a product of the inner dynamics of the cultural processes of India. It was a fruition of the centuries old interaction of Indian and Persian traditions. Ghalib could be located at the apex of this trend and in literature as indeed one of its best classics. In a manner of speaking he is our first modern.

If growth of the individual is a defining feature of any modernism, it is to be noted that the process of articulating such an individual in modern times starts with Ghalib.

In the Indian poetic tradition the individual as such becomes the centre of attention for the first time in Ghalib. An individual who has no support of any myth, no assurances or certainties of tradition nor the protective care of any community nor the patronage of any religion or God. It is an individual all by himself totally vulnerable, suffering from an acute angst of being, finding the world almost unreal and questioning almost everything. He has no home, no residence – he is on the road, *rāhguzār*, to use a Ghalibian image, all the time.

The central question that Ghalib asks with great intensity and agony relates to being. In fact he looks askance at being as it were: "Each place, each moment sings its particular song of not-being of being". He brought a new and disturbing sense of the angst of being to poetry in our country. In a way his entire poetry is a lament, a reproach: "to be or not to be". To him neither heaven nor hell sounds real: he insists "whatever happens must happen through one's being". He warns himself time and again, against the delusion of being trapped into the deceit of existence.

Indeed he treats the entire drama of being as a spectacle, *tamāšā*, which sometimes amuses and at other outrages him. He is drawn at one level towards the concept of oneness of all ("The One is only the One") and at another to the fragmentariness of everything whether of life, love or spirit.

At one point he asserts: "In the desire of the One to know its own beauty we exist" or that "...the sky bends unceasingly down to greet its own light" and at another "Hidden in this image is also its end. As peasants' lives harbour revolt and unthreashed corn sparks with fire".

Ghalib raises three key questions which exemplify his spiritual anxiety as well as artistic search. The first relates to the condition of man vis-à-vis God and this whole universe. The second relates to the status of the poet in the context of his extremely difficult life and complex, even abstruse expression. And the third is about the place of love in the face of indifference and hostility. The trio draws a totally new and intriguing contour in the geography that modernism in India sought to map out. One cannot recall any other Indian poet who, before Ghalib, might have raised the same kinds of questions and that too altogether.

Ghalib has a unique blend of the tragic and the comic. He had an unusual capacity to laugh at himself, to make fun of his love, poetry and desires. For him, many a time, he and the world are a laughable matter. In this again he was a true modern.

And yet his brand of modernism cannot be fully described without referring to his cosmic imagination. It is this imagination which leads him to ask "Am I not equal to the skies?"; to assert "On the page of the world I am not a word twice-written"; to feel "Like a shadow strange times have befallen us"; and to realise "For the raindrop, joy is in entering the river / Unbearable pain becomes its own cure".

In our dark times, as in his own, Ghalib is a poet both aglow and ablaze. He knows that he is "a green plant fed by poisonous water". He survives so gloriously and vibrantly in our midst.

Perhaps no one has in recent past spoken to us about our human predicament so movingly and yet so disturbingly. He felt "My words the darkened oil lamp on a stranger's unspeaking grave". Precisely because of his growing sense of uncertainty and darkening all around. Ghalib's words over the years appear so radiant and revealing.

He emerges as a colossus to whom all moderns and even the post-moderns could look back and feel forever grateful for his daring and despair, his innovations and questioning spirit, his dilemma of being and no-being. He looks askance at himself and his world and dares us to do the same.

Places & Images

Nostalgia in the re-construction of Muslim identity in the aftermath of 1857 and the myth of Delhi

Daniela Bredi

On 28 July 1859, Sayyid Ahmad Khan, scion of a noble family of Delhi, addressed a gathering of 15,000 Muslims in a mosque of his native city, to thank Queen Victoria for her proclamation of a general amnesty after the end of the so called "Mutiny" of 1857-8. The imperative of the day was to lead his defeated and demoralized community from a policy of opposition to the British to one of acquiescence and participation, in order to wean the British government "from its policy of suppression to one of paternalism".[1] Realizing that Indian Muslims, if they wished to participate in the political process, had to come to terms with Western political culture and make themselves acceptable to the new rulers, he started a process of re-construction of Indo-Muslim identity. In this process, Indo-Muslim intellectuals produced a large amount of writings based on a selection of images

[1] W.C. Smith, *Modern Islam in India*, London: Gollacz, 1946, p. 16.

of the past, building a specific Indo-Muslim "cultural memory".[2] Consciously or not, they reacted to the cultural trauma[3] of the abolition of the Mughal empire and their loss of status in the public sphere,[4] and re-constructed a common past for the imagined community[5] of the Indian Muslims, largely based on nostalgia.

Nostalgia can be defined as a longing for past, often idealized times, taken as the only alternative to modernity. In the words of J. Wu, it is

> a sentimental dream of returning to the past, to a time of supposed tranquillity and assurance, a time when we were more 'at home'. In its characteristic longing for an idealized past, the nostalgic mode is deeply implicated in our sense of identity, through which we link the past to the present and to the future, and through which we make sense of who we are and where we are going.[6]

In their identity-building effort, Modernist intellectuals, in order to meet the requirements of their co-religionists facing the challenge of the West, adopted a strategy of representation[7] involving a choice of various spatial and temporal elements, with long term cultural and political consequences.

---

[2] For the concept of "cultural memory" see J. Assmann, *La memoria culturale: scrittura, ricordo e identità politica nelle grandi civiltà*, Torino: Einaudi, 2003, p. 5 (*Das kulturelle Gedächtinis. Schrift, erinnerung und politische Identität in frühen Hochkulturen*, München, 1997).

[3] For the concept of "cultural trauma" see A. Tota, *La memoria contesa*, Milano: Franco Angeli, 2001, p. 15.

[4] For the concept of "public sphere" see J. Habermas, *Storia e critica dell'opinione pubblica*, Roma-Bari: Laterza, 2002 (*Strukturwandel der Öffentlichkeit*, Berlin, 1962).

[5] For the concept of "imagined communities" see B. Anderson, *Comunità immaginate – Origini e Diffusioni dei Nazionalismi*, Roma: Manifestolibri, 1996 (*Imagined Communities*, London-New York, 1983).

[6] J. Wu, "Nostalgia as content creativity: cultural industries and popular sentiment", *International Journal of Cultural Studies*, 2006, vol. 9, no. 3, p. 360.

[7] For this concept see L. Rofel, *Other Modernities. Gendered Yearnings in China after Socialism*, Berkeley: University of California Press, 1999, p. 35.

To begin with, Sayyid Ahmad Khan himself, who in his early historical writings had produced works dealing with Muslim India (*Āṣār al-ṣanādīd* in 1847; an edition of Abu 'l-Fazl's *Āʾīn-i Akbarī* in 1855; an edition of Barani's *Tārīx-i Fīrūz Šāhī* in 1862), later turned to the history of Arabia at the birth of Islam and to the biography of Muhammad. In 1870 he published his *Essays on the Life of Mohammed*, in English (*Xuṭbāt-i Aḥmadiyya* in Urdu) applying his peculiar kind of Westernized methodology, partly scientific and partly speculatively apologetic, to the history of Arabia at the birth of Islam and to the biography of the Prophet. This work was the starting point of modern historiography on Islam and set the pattern of modern Muslim apologetics.[8]

Later, Shibli Nuᶜmani was to give to Islamic historiography in Urdu a strong revivalistic color. The greater part of his work is essentially biographical and he concentrates on certain key developments represented by those whom he calls the "heroes" of Islam: first of all the Prophet and the caliph ᶜUmar, and then al--Ghazzali, Abu Hanifa, al-Maʾmun and Rumi.[9] If the life of Muhammad has for him a key position in the study of the doctrine, sociology, and ethics of Islam, the life of the second caliph constitutes the basis of Islamic polity, economic organization, and principles of coexistence with no-Muslim people. Principles of coexistence with no-Muslim people, in his historiographical perspective, is the main area of sensitivity, and therefore of apologetic concentration.[10]

While Shibli's cast of mind was essentially medieval, even if he was prepared to make compromises with the radical responses necessitated by the challenges of European scientific outlook, Amir ᶜAli, the chief polemicist of Islam in the last decades of the nineteenth and the first decades of the twentieth century, both in his explanations and apologia of Islam, followed Sayyid Ahmad Khan. His *Spirit of Islam* (1922) and *History of the Saracens* (1889) are a re-statement of the history of Islam for consumption in the West, and had a deep influence on the Western

[8] A. Ahmad, *Islamic Modernism in India and Pakistan, 1857-1964*, London: OUP, 1967, p. 39.

[9] *Ibidem*, pp. 77-8.

[10] *Ibidem*, p. 81.

educated Muslims in India. Though a Shi^ci, he emphasized the Sunni caliphate, and demonstrated a great admiration for the first two caliphs, Abu Bakr and ᶜUmar. Faced with the problem of the decline of Islam, the explanation he offered is based on the diagnosis of Shah Wali-Allah: the influx of extraneous elements in the Muslim creed, world view, and way of life.[11]

At the request of Sayyid Ahmad Khan, Altaf Husain Hali wrote his famous poem *Musaddas madd-o-jazr-i islām*, popularly known as *Musaddas-i Ḥālī*, in 1879. In lamenting the 'ebb' of Islam, he turned nostalgically to the glories of the past, appealing to the Muslims' glorious history in order to make them proud of their cultural heritage. As the first Urdu poem departing from tradition and conventionalized classicism, it inaugurated a cultural renaissance and a vogue for political romanticism. Revivalism and the political romanticism it generated, became the dominant trend in Urdu poetry, with the exception of the *ġazal*. Until the so called "Mutiny", nineteenth century Urdu verse had few political overtones. After it, there appeared a body of stirring poetry lamenting the fate of Delhi and the overthrow of Muslim culture as represented by the elite of that city. The most personal of these poems were the verses of the last Mughal emperor, Bahadur Shah II, whose *taxalluṣ* was Zafar, who had been dragged into the upheaval almost against his will. The ruins of Delhi became the symbol and the epitome of the ruin of the Islamic world, helpless against Western aggression because of its internal decadence.

The glory of the Arabs and the pristine purity of the first century of Islam were to become the focus of the reconstruction of Muslim identity in a political sense, giving credit, among other things, to the Salafi political project. Looking forward to regaining political significance through their adherence to a purified form of idealized Islam, as portrayed in the apologetic works of the Modernist historians, Indian Muslims, nevertheless, were made to regret the disappearance of the defeated Mughal culture symbolized by Delhi. Nostalgia here worked in both the senses of restorative nostalgia, leading to a reconstruction of nations or religious groups, and reflexive nostalgia, marked by an intense

11 *Ibidem*, pp. 86-97.

longing for the past.[12] Restorative nostalgia was to result in the notion of the Indo-Muslims as a separate nation, mainly through the ideas propagated by Muhammad Iqbal, whose poetry blends together the various currents of thought agitating the minds of his co-religionists – the backward-looking romanticism of the liberals, the socialist leaning of the young intellectuals, the desire of the militant Muslim Leaguers for a strong leader to restore the political power of Islam.[13] Moving from his early Indian nationalism through pan-Islamism, in 1930 he presented his proposal for the creation of a separate Muslim state in India; his mental journey highlighted in his essays – especially his *Six Lectures on the Reconstruction of Religious Thought in Islam* (1934) – and the whole of his poetry, Urdu and Persian.

Reflexive nostalgia, through poetry and prose, gave birth to the myth of Delhi.

Bahadur Shah II's Delhi, in the Indo-Muslim mind, became a Mughal garden undergoing its final spring before the autumn of the Revolt's aftermath destroyed it forever, or a Mughal candle flaring into its old brilliance before being extinguished for good.[14] But this symbol of the past Mughal glory, actually, owed its cultural renaissance to the British.

At the time of Lord Lake's conquest in 1803, in fact, Delhi had long lost his imperial centrality and importance, having undergone a century of invasions, plunders and massacres, famines. The replacement of the Marathas by the British did not alter the actual state of the Emperor's authority, illustrated by the popular verse "The 'King of the World', Shah ᶜAlam, / Rules all the way from Delhi to Palam". The imperial city that at the death of Aurangzeb, in 1707, had a population of close to two million people, in 1803 was reduced to a provincial capital of less than two hundred thousand, the imperial court deprived of its power

---

12 See S. Boym, *The Future of Nostalgia*, New York: Basic Books, 2001.

13 H.A.R. Gibb, *Modern Trends in Islam*, Chicago: University of Chicago Press, 1945, p. 61.

14 C.M. Naim, "Ghalib's Delhi: A Shamelessly Revisionist Look at two Popular Metaphors", *Annual of Urdu Studies*, 2003, vol. 18, http://www.urdustudies.com/Issue18/index.html.

and cultural role.[15] With the British becoming his master and protector, however, the Emperor, even if deprived of any semblance of overlordship, improved his financial condition. Shah ᶜAlam, an old and frugal man, at his death in 1806 was able to leave in the royal treasury five lakhs rupees. But his successors, whose number of dependants to support increased dramatically with the Pax Britannica,[16] never succeeded in having a parallel increase in their annual allowance.[17]

Under the British, whose system of government Ghalib praised in his letters and in a Persian poem he wrote in 1855 for Sayyid Ahmad Khan's edition of Abu 'l Fazl's *Āʾīn-i Akbarī* and that Sayyid Ahmad Khan did not include,[18] Delhi regained security and prosperity, and with the introduction of new ideas and institutions and new technologies, it rapidly became once again a vigorous cultural center. Social behavior did not imitate Western manners, but cultural life was deeply influenced by the institution of the Delhi College, a *madrasa* took over by the East India Company in 1825, with a staff of several Indian teachers and an English principal, where Western sciences were taught to all the students through the medium of Urdu. Complementing the College there was the Delhi Vernacular Translation Society, providing Urdu translations of scholarly books from Arabic, Persian and English for the College's students. Delhi's Renaissance, as Andrews called it,[19] was principally due to the Delhi College and to the printing press and Urdu newspapers. The true spread of the Urdu press occurred after the discovery of the technology of litho printing arrived in India. Much less expensive than the printing press, it could also use the professional calligraphers available and retain the aesthetic quality of the manuscripts. The first important Urdu newspaper, a weekly, was started in Delhi in 1837

---

15 *Ibidem.*

16 In 1848 the *salāṭīn*, or royal descendants depending from the Mughal were about 2,100 (in 1837 they were 800).

17 P. Spear, *Twilight of the Mughals*, Cambridge: Cambridge University Press, 1951, p. 38.

18 Naim, "Ghalib's Delhi", p. 11.

19 C.F. Andrews, *Zaka Ullah of Delhi*, Lahore: Universal Books, 1976, p. 40.

with the name of *Dihlī Axbār*, later *Dihlī Urdū Axbār*, edited by the grandfather of the first modern Urdu literary critic, Muhammad Husain Azad. The next important, *Saiyadu 'l-Axbār*, was started by Sayyid Ahmad Khan's brother in 1841. Between 1837 and 1857, there were at least five weeklies, two bi-monthly and one monthly in Urdu published from Delhi, and, of course, many other newspapers reached Delhi from other cities and were quoted by local journals. As Naim remarks, it is important to note that several people involved in the press had ties with the Delhi College; that these newspapers carried, besides news, informative articles on a wide range of subjects; that between 1835 and 1857 the press in British India was relatively free of governmental control and censorship. Equally important is to note that neither Bahadur Shah II nor any member of the Mughal house was in any way involved with the Delhi College nor the various presses and newspapers of the city. The court had its Persian weekly, but it was only a bulletin of the Emperor's daily activities.[20]

The presence of the Emperor was felt in Delhi only on occasions involving some public pomp and display. Mughal corteges paraded through the cities on festivities, and ceremonial durbars were regularly held in the Red Fort. Royal etiquette was imitated in the gatherings of the city's nobles, as it was all over India, but Bahadur Shah II never had any influence on the tastes and cultural orientations of the elite. Ghalib himself, his *ustād* after Zauq's demise, though keen on being recognized by the imperial court as the leading poet of his times, entertained a somewhat uneasy relationship with the King, and often found his duties as a courtier irksome.[21] Far more interested he was in widening his intellectual horizons through the opportunities offered by the British, such as the newspapers that he discovered while staying in Calcutta.[22]

As for Bahadur Shah II's religious role, it did not go beyond his regular participation in the two annual ᶜId ceremonies in the

---

[20] Naim, "Ghalib's Delhi", p. 18.

[21] R. Russell and Kh. Islam, *Ghalib – Life and Letters*, London: Allen and Unwin, 1969, p. 97.

[22] *Ibidem*, pp. 49-50.

Jama Masjid, the recognition of his position as emperor through the mention of his name in the Friday's *xuṭba*-s, and his symbolic position as the champion of Sunnism, to the extent that he had to conceal his personal Shiᶜite inclinations.[23] The *ᶜulāma*-s disdained the court, and held increasingly rigidly orthodox views which gained strength in Delhi. By the 1850s the tolerant Sufi ways of the King-poet and his court slowly came to look old-fashioned and outdated. Sufism and *ġazal* writing were the marks of court and high *šarīf* culture, but the rising Punjabi Muslim merchant class patronized the Islamic reformist movements, aiming at purifying society from all its un-Islamic accretions.[24] The Emperor's customary patronage of Hindu festivals and religious processions was criticized, as were seen with alarm and suspicion the establishment of a Christian presence in the walled city and the expansion of the Christian missionary activities.

In the eventful days of 1857, when Bahadur Shah II 'Zafar' acted, though reluctantly, as the symbolic head of the Uprising, he always dreaded a divide of Delhi down its religious axis. Since the city was almost exactly half Hindu, he clearly understood that it would be impossible to do without the support and consent of half of its population, and tried his best at opposing the *jihādī* faction of the insurgency. When Maulvi Muhammad Sayyid, one of the more strict mullah of Delhi, set up a standard of *jihād* in the Jama Masjid, in an effort to turn the Revolt into an exclusively Muslim holy war, he immediately ordered it to be taken down. Later, when Bakht Khan, one of the commanders of the rebels known for his 'Wahhabi' views, gathered the *ᶜulāma*-s and made them sign a *fatvā* of *jihād*, declaring it mandatory for all Muslims to fight the religious war under the head of the *jihādī*-s, Maulvi Sarfaraz ᶜAli, the King expressed his contrariety and alarm.[25]

---

23 *Ibidem*, p. 99.

24 See M. Pernau, "Multiple Identities and Communities: Re-contextualizing Religion", [in:] J. Malik and H. Reifeld, *Religious Pluralism in South Asia and Europe*, New Delhi: Oxford University Press, 2005, pp. 147-69.

25 W. Dalrymple, *The Last Mughal*, New Delhi: Penguin Books, 2006, pp. 228, 294.

His tragic part in the 1857 events, and his sad end in the exile of Burma, together with his fame as a poet, made him to be attributed a role he actually never played in pre-Mutiny Delhi, which, in the last years of his reign, was once again the largest pre-colonial city in India. No matter that the people in the Red Fort, Emperor included, had scarce resources and limited interests, with little evidence of creative energy in them, for in Old Delhi's beautiful gardens and traditional *ḥavelī*-s, almost untouched by Western imitation in their architectural structure, moved an incredible party of illustrious people. Shah ᶜAbdu'l ᶜAziz, Shah ᶜAbdu'l Qadir, Maulavi Mamluk ᶜAli, ᶜAllama Fazl-e Haq Khairabadi, Asadu'l-Lah Khan Ghalib, Momin Khan Momin, Muhammad Ibrahim Zauq, Maulavi Imam Bakhsh Sahbaᵓi, Mufti Sadru'd-Din Azurda, Navab Mustafa Khan Shefta, "Master" Ram Chandra, and Sayyid Ahmad Khan were all present in Delhi in the first part of nineteenth century. Since Europeans in Delhi were still relatively few, their importance in ushering in the new sense of security that made such a gathering possible, might be easily left aside in the construction of an imagined place embodying the final splendor of the Mughal age. But, with a few exceptions, almost everyone of the above mentioned personages had come to or did not emigrate from Delhi, because of the British. Sahbaᵓi, Mamluk ᶜAli and Ram Chandra taught at the Delhi College; Azurda and Fazl-e Haq served in the British administration, as did Fazl-e Haq's father and Sayyid Ahmad Khan; Momin, like Ghalib, received a pension from the British, and Shefta owed his estate to the new rulers. Only the poet Zauq and the two men of religion Shah ᶜAbdu'l ᶜAziz and Shah ᶜAbdu'l Qadir did not get any financial support from the British. Shah ᶜAbdu'l ᶜAziz, anyway, was successful in having back in 1807 a large land grant that he had lost twenty years earlier, by petitioning the British.[26]

With the rise of nationalism in India, in the thirties, in the public mind developed not only a tragic and romantic image of the last Mughal, but also a belief that he and his court actually presided over the effervescent social and intellectual life preced-

[26] Naim, "Ghalib's Delhi", p. 20.

ing the Uprising of 1857, and that only the Uprising's failure brought an end to that way of life and thought, and its imperial source.[27] The prevalence of this view can be seen in the works of writers as Rashidu 'l-Khairi, author of *Naubat-i panj roza* and *Dillī kī āxirī bahār*, Khvaja Hasan Nizami, who devoted several short books to this theme, ᶜArsh Timuri, who wrote *Qilᶜa muᶜallā kī jhalakiyāṅ*, Faizu'd-Din, author of *Bazm-i āxir*, Mirza Herat Dilavi, who wrote *Čirāġ-i Dillī*, Mirza Akhtar Gurganvi, who wrote *Savānniḥ-i Dillī*, Firaq Dilavi, who wrote *Lāl Qile kī aik jhalak*, and Mirza Farhatullah Beg, author of *Dillī kā aik yādgār mushāᶜira, 1261 Hijrī*, commonly known, and often published, as *Dillī kī āxirī šamᶜ.*

The "last candle of Delhi" provided the more frequently invoked metaphor for the age of Bahadur Shah II, and constitutes an emblematic example of the way reflexive nostalgia contributed to the re-construction of Indian Muslims' imagined past. Its author, Mirza Farhatullah Beg, was born in an old Delhi family in 1883, when Delhivallahs' self-confidence had collapsed together with the beautiful buildings of Shahjahanabad. These were destroyed after the repression of the Uprising by the British, who cancelled everything standing between the Red Fort and the Jama Masjid, and even the gorgeous harem apartments of the Fort, erecting in their place a line of barracks – an act that the great Victorian architectural historian James Fergusson, who certainly was no whining liberal, recorded in his *History of Indian and Eastern Architecture* as a "fearful piece of vandalism".[28] Farhatullah Beg, who in 1907 had to move to Hyderabad in order to gain his livelihood, and spent there his working life rising to a senior position in the state's judiciary, nurtured a lasting regret for his beloved birthplace. To sooth his pain of living in exile, he wrote several works evoking the old Muslim culture of Delhi, from his memory or his imagination, of which three deserve to be mentioned: *Nazīr Aḥmad kī kahānī, kučh merī aur kučh un kī zabānī*, *Phulvāloṅ kī sair*, and, obviously, *Dillī kī āxirī šamᶜ*. This last one, published for the first time in the review of the

[27] *Ibidem*, p. 7.

[28] J. Fergusson, *History of Indian and Eastern Architecture*, London: J. Murray, 1876, p. 594.

Anjuman-i Taraqqī-i Urdū, *Urdū Ādāb*, in July 1927, and re-published the following year by Khvaja Hasan Nizami under the title *Dillī kī āxirī šam*[c], gained him a place in Urdu literature. At a certain point, it was adopted as a textbook in various schools, and, as a textbook, it has been very much in demand in the last fifty years or so. For this reason it has been re-printed several times, often with many typographical mistakes. In 2003, Rashid Hasan Khan edited a critical edition published by the Anjuman-i Taraqqī-i Urdū (Hind), based on the original 1927 text.[29]

At the time in which Farhatullah Beg placed his fictionalized account, while the British were progressively depriving the Mughal Emperor of his prerogatives, removing his name from the coins, seizing complete control of the city of Delhi itself, and finally planning to remove the Mughals altogether from the Red Fort, the city's elite busied itself in every kind of entertainments: music, dance, sports, poetry. Delhi's nights were kept bright by the performances of famous musicians, singers and courtesans, whose beauty and coquettishness were celebrated. Nevertheless, owing to the Delhi's inhabitants' intoxication with the elegance of their Urdu language and their obsession with poetry, the biggest draw was not the *koṭhī*-s of the courtesans in Chauri Bazar but the *mušā*[c]*ira*-s, the contests of the poets. *Mušā*[c]*ira*-s were held weekly in the Ghaziu'd-Din Khan's *madrasa*, in the old Delhi College, and in the house of Mufti Sadru'd-Din Azurda, but those hosted in the Fort or in the nobles' residences added glamour to literary enjoyment. This is why the author set his *Dillī kī āxirī šam*[c], that purports to be one of the last great poetic contests held in Bahadur Shah II's Delhi, in the illuminated courtyard of a *ḥavelī*, whose decoration and arrangement is undertaken and paid for by the Navab-poet Zainu'l-[c]Abidin Khan [c]Arif.

Farhatullah Beg, while reading Maulvi Karimu'd-Din's *taẕkira*, *Ṭabaqāt-i šu*[c]*arā-i hind*, found that the author had hosted a *mušā*[c]*ira* at his place, on the 14 Rajab of AH 1261 under the direction of Navab Zaynu'l-[c]Abidin Khan, [c]Arif by *taxalluṣ*. Aiming at passing on to the future generations of Indian Muslims a portrait of the extraordinary cultural life of the pre-1857 Delhi

[29] Mirzā Farḥatullāh Beg, *Dillī kī āxirī šam*[c], Naī Dillī: Anjuman-i Taraqqī-i Urdū, 2003, p. 15.

that he idealized, he conceived the idea of describing a poetic contest fashioned according to the example of *Nairang-i xayāl* by Muhammad Husain Azad. He, besides being an author, was also a painter and a dramatist, and was fascinated by the thought of portraying the poets living in Delhi in those days, and bring them to life under the eyes of his future readers. Not that he knew exactly the physical details of them all, but he tried his best to get a documentation, supplying the rest by his imagination.[30] Concerned with the loss of old Delhi's memories, in the preamble, he says:

> Since 1857 many of these art-lovers passed away and the sons, left by themselves, were dispersed by the storm of the Mutiny, they went to stay where they found support, in Hyderabad or Rampur, deserting Delhi. Most of the nobles left their abodes as they had lost every hope to see Delhi again. And those who stayed back were ready to leave any time. Many actually left, and a time came when there was no inhabitant knowing where Momin's house was placed. In this way, now, with my exception, perhaps nobody knows the site of his tomb.[31]

For this reason, he tries to place his characters within the frame of the old Delhi, of which, of course, he was too young for having a direct experience, but about it had heard a lot, and whose remains he saw in his early days.

In Farhatullah Beg's work, it is Karimu'd-Din who tells the story of this extraordinary poetic contest, starting from the circumstances which brought him to promote it. Karimu'd-Din, the descendant of a family of men of religion, who had come from Panipat to Delhi attracted by its cultural life, had been a student of the Delhi College, and was the owner of a printing press. But his business was not successful as he hoped it might be, and he, though hardly inclined to poetry, decided to organize a *mušā^{c}ira*, whose proceedings he would then print and sell in order to improve his financial conditions, since everybody in town, from prince to poor, loved poetry.

---

30 *Ibidem*, pp. 28-9.
31 *Ibidem*, p. 28.

Farhatullah Beg, well aware of the existing cleavage between the religious minded and the nobles, puts this words in Karimu'd-Din mouth:

> I have never been versed in poetry, and I am not now. On the contrary, I have objections against reciting verses: it does not become learned men by profession. It is the people who are free from the worries of earning their daily bread that devote themselves to poetry, in order to enjoy themselves and give vent to their pains.
>
> I am an *ᶜālim*, like my father and grandfather, and therefore I am not inclined to frivolities of this kind, but what can't be cured must be endured, and I busied myself in organizing the *mušāᶜira*, even if, being poor and a newcomer in town, I was afraid that the poets I was going to invite to join in it might not be willing to have to do with me.

But Karimu'd-Din counted among his acquaintances a distinguished member of the *ašraf*, Navab Zainu'l-ᶜAbidin Khan, a poet under the pen-name of ᶜArif, and he went to ask his help. He describes ᶜArif as a nobleman in his thirties, extremely kind and well-mannered, though prostrate with illness. In fact, he died in 1852, inspiring to his friend and relative Ghalib, who adopted his children after his demise, the grief-stricken *ġazal*: *Lāzim thā kih dekho mirā rāsta koʾī din aur.*[32]

ᶜArif, moved by the wish to forget his illness for a while and to see all the major poets gathered together in a session, agrees to help Karimu'd-Din and arranges for him to be received by the King at the Red Fort, with the object to obtain his patronage. In this way the writer gets the chance to describe an audience with the Mughal Emperor, whom was to be greeted with seven low bows and the customary gift, *naẕr* (offering of fealty). The depiction of Bahadur Shah II is very detailed and appears clearly based on the coronation portrait by Ghulam ᶜAli Khan and the portrait by the Austrian artist August Schoefft now in the fort at Lahore, but the description of the inside of the Fort is somewhat wanting, as he says: "It was ages since I wished to see the inside of the Fort, and now that I got the opportunity I had not even the strength to look were I was going...". And then he gives a very

32 N. 66 of Ghalib's *Muravvaj dīvān*.

brief description of the bathroom in which he is introduced to the King's presence:

> Actually, it is not a bathroom, but a wonderful pavilion divided in two sectors, warm and cold. The warm sector is next to the Pearl Mosque, and the cold one faces the Jumna river. Its wall opening on the river is screened, for privacy, with screens made of fragrant herb. At the inside flows a water-course, and in its middle there are fountains from which gushes are spouting. It is not a bathroom, but a piece of Paradise![33]

The Emperor, seated in green[34] robes on a silver throne and with the poetry loving prince Mirza Fakhru seated at his feet, approves of the enterprise, takes the absolutely unusual decision not to establish a *maṭla^c*[35] and fixes the date for the 14 of Rajab (20 July), an auspicious day and a moonlight night. Navab Zainu'l-^{c}Abidin Khan takes upon himself the task of making all the required arrangements for the poetic contest and sends Karimu'd-Din to invite the major poets on his account. This provides the author with the opportunity to portray Zauq, Ghalib, Momin and others, set in the frame of their dwellings and surrounded by their friends and pupils. And when the day fixed for the *mušā^{c}ira* comes, Karimu'd-Din, who had to stay away from his place for more than a week in order to allow ^{c}Arif to set it properly, can hardly recognize the *ḥavelī* of Mubaraku'n-Nissa Begum, the widowed *bībī* of Sir David Otcherlony,[36] where he had his printing press cum residence. He says:

> Mubaraku'n-Nissa's house, starting from the gate, had been transformed in a gorgeous rose-garden, with lamps, lanterns, and chandeliers. From the main entrance to the internal hall there were so many lights that it was a feast for the eye. When I reached the interior I was stuck with stupefaction. My God! Was it my place or a

---

[33] Mirzā Farḥatullāh Beg, *Dillī kī āxirī šam^c*, p. 35.

[34] In Delhi green was the imperial color.

[35] Opening verse. In a *ġazal* an optional, but extremely common, introductory pattern-setting verse that has the rhyme (and refrain, if any) at the end of each two lines.

[36] See P. Spear, *The Nabobs*, London and Dublin: Curzon Press, 1980 (first published OUP, 1932), p. 93.

> king's palace? I looked around with wide eyes and exclaimed 'Bravo, ᶜArif, my friend! You did it! It does not look like the house of poor Karimu'd-Din, but a residence fit for an Emperor! You were right in saying that if you are not ready to spend up to two thousand rupees, you understand, you can't do anything!'. The house's walls, covered with fragments of mica and aluminium, were all glittering. The courtyard had been filled so as to raise it to the plinth of the house. On the wooden planks were spread white cotton rugs with carpets all around, and a row of big bolsters behind them. There was such a profusion of chandeliers, candelabra, wall lamps, hanging lamps and Chinese lanterns that the house was converted into a veritable dome of light. Everything was beautiful and in its right place... From the center of the ceiling hanged row upon row of jasmine garlands so as to form a canopy of flowers... Everywhere servants, folded handed, were standing in their spotless uniforms. The whole house was fragrant with musk, amber and aloes... Arranged in a row, at short intervals, along the carpets, were the huqqas, burnished and brightly polished... In sum, what can I say, it was a wonder to look at. I was like the Abu 'l-Hasan of The Arabian Nights. Wherever I looked, I remained spellbound.[37]

It seems obvious that the author's object is to induce in his audience admiration for old Delhi's lost world, and the residents of the Red Fort and the nobles are made to look like princes living in the rose-gardens of the *maṣnavī*-s. The *mušāᶜira*'s staging is quite accurate in its showing the importance of manners and etiquette in meetings attended by members of the royal family and nobility. Karimu'd-Din describes at length the place prepared for the poetic contest's president, Mirza Fakhru, acting on behalf of the Emperor, who was to seat under a small embroidered green velvet canopy, kept up with poles of precious metal, and lit up with silver lamps, upon an embroidered green velvet sofa, with big bolsters of embroidered green velvet. And, if the assigning of their places to the ordinary poets was a sensitive question because it required great care in order not to hurt their feelings, the accommodation of the Red Fort's residents had to follow the rules of the etiquette. He describes the prince's arrival as follows:

[37] Mirzā Farḥatullāh Beg, *Dillī kī āxirī šamᶜ*, p. 51.

> When he touched the ground, everybody rose to his feet and stood up still. Four green turbaned mace-bearers in uniforms of very fine green cloth with red sashes at their waists, carrying gold and silver maces and peacock feathers flabella in their hands, stood behind him on the elephant. As soon as Mirza Fakhru's foot touched the ground, the mace-bearers went to take position before him, and the flabellum-bearers behind him. They walked slowly up to the canopy, where Mirza Fakhru stopped to receive the greetings of all the present people. Then he looked around and said 'Do I have your permission?'. Everybody answered 'Please, please!', and he went under the canopy, greeted everybody, and sat down. All the rest of the people remained standing, waiting for his permission to sit down. He looked around and asked them to take their seats. Everybody bowed down and took their seats.[38]

Then the president, after saying the *fātiḥa*, starts the poetic contest, whose peculiarities he underlines in his address to the "Singers of the Delhi's garden":

> ...You know that this *mušāʿira* is quite unusual because it does not have a *maṭlaʿ*. You'll see that this is not its only peculiarity. In fact, not one but two candles will be made to pass around. While doing away with the *maṭlaʿ* was meant to free this competition from ostentation, thanks to the two candles, nobody will be bothered with the concern of precedence in reciting his poem. Besides, since the hearts of most of you are troubled by the thought of who will have the honour of doing the opening and closing of the poetic contest, this time I'll take both these tasks upon myself. The contest will open with His Imperial Majesty's poem, and the decision of who will recite the last verses will be mine. In this way no disagreement will arise.[39]

Karimu'd-Din goes on saying:

> At this proclamation a rummaging could be heard. The Fort's residents put away their quails[40] in their quail pouches and disposed of them behind the bolsters. The servants removed the water pipes and in their place put down spittoons, *pān*-boxes and trays with

---

38 *Ibidem*, p. 61.

39 *Ibidem*, p. 62.

40 The Red Fort's residents brought with them their birds, as the craze for quail and cock fighting was very strong at that time.

> coriander seeds in front of each guest, and went back to their places. In the meantime the personal representative of the Emperor, the World's Protector, arrived from the court with the King's *ġazal*, accompanied by several heralds. He went near to the candles, paid the due homage, and asked for permission to recite His Majesty's poem. Mirza Fakhru nodded and he took his seat. The heralds announced 'Gentlemen! Herewith will be given a reading of the admirable verses composed by His Majesty, Shadow of the Glorious, Second Lord of the Quran, God's skylark of the Kingdom and Empire. Be so kind as to turn your ears to them with reverence and attention'.[41]

From this point on the poets start their recitation, half singing, half reciting, applauding and expressing their approval to those they admire for their witty or subtle nuances, leaving the less accomplished to sink in silence. The candles are passed around at the sign of the contest's president and the versifying goes on until dawn, when it comes the turn of Ghalib and Zauq to bring the *mušāᶜira* to its climax. Of each one who is going to recite Farhatullah Beg provides a description, and highlights his poetic and human qualities and faults, faithful to his aim of making his verses alive and more appreciable. In fact, in his preamble, he had declared:

> Knowledge-lovers know and understand that, while reading somebody's works, if the reader has an idea of the author's features, way of moving, voice's timbre, manners, disposition, and even of the fashion of his clothes, his words leave a peculiar mark, and the pleasure of reading intensifies. Otherwise, reading a book without knowing anything about its writer, makes no more effect than a record on a gramophone.[42]

Probably because of his ability as a portraitist and play-writer, his anthology of more than fifty Delhi poets has been so successful, inducing in its readers a strong nostalgic feeling for those lost people, environment, and atmosphere. And, finally, when the *mušāᶜira* in which he epitomized the by-gone Delhi he cherished, comes to an end, it leaves in its reader a kind of melancholic

41 Mirzā Farḥatullāh Beg, *Dillī kī āxirī šamᶜ*, pp. 62-3.
42 *Ibidem*, p. 28.

mood. It creates a longing for an idealized society of culture and good manners, presided over by the Emperor, the hinge of the balance among the different sections and communities of his subjects, until these recognized him as such. The diverse audience he governed, in fact, responded to the Mughal amalgam of rituals and paraphernalia and virtually none questioned his divine sanction. Real rebels only, such as Shivaji, refused the Mughal political cultural as devised by Abu'l-Fazl in the *Āʾīn-i Akbarī*. Even when the capacity of the Emperor to enforce his own will and compel those who ruled in his name to obey him shrank to almost nothing, the role of the Emperor as the center and keeper of the sacred order on earth persisted in the minds of the people.[43] He was nothing more than a symbol, but until he was there, the members of the old elite could pretend to ignore the irreparable break-up of their *šarīf* world.

Farhatullah Beg's last *mušāʿira*, a veritable exercise in reflexive nostalgia, comes to an end when the two candles that had circulated among the poets are formally blown out and an herald proclaims: "The poetic contest is finished". In this way, the 'last *mušāʿira*' became in the popular mind the 'last candle'. The image of a last remaining candle, or flame, about to go evoked finality and doom, and, simultaneously, implied that the life in Delhi in the years before the 1857 Uprising was a miraculous recovery of a pristine Muslim/Mughal culture from its mortal illness, and not, as said before, the result of innovations introduced by the British. Those same British who were about to do away with the Delhi's Emperor in the belief that his reason of existence was no more, that he was an anomaly to be removed and not even the Muslims would object.[44]

The outcome of the so called Mutiny made absolutely clear to the Indians, and to the different sections of the old elite in particular, that change was substantial and could not be absorbed, nor incorporated in the Mughal political culture. Their world had undergone a dramatic, even if foreseeable, change and, in their need to find a newly defined identity, they could not attribute to

---

[43] M.H. Fisher, *A Clash of Cultures. Awadh, the British and the Mughals*, New Delhi: Manohar, 1987, pp. 11-12.

[44] *Ibidem*, p. 16.

the British a role in what they saw as the proof of the value of their culture. The cultural trauma had to be overcome, and the Delhi of the first part of the nineteenth century, with its sparkling cultural life, collection of poets and other talented men, and almost untouched architectural aspect lent itself admirably for selection as a privileged *locus memoriae*.[45] Works as Farhatullah Beg's and the like provided Indian Muslims with an imagined common past nearer, in time and space, than the Middle East of the historians and Muslim polemicists, and one that they might share with their fellow citizens, Indians of different communities.

In *Dillī kī āxirī šam*ᶜ, among the great poets like Ghalib, Zauq, Momin, Azurda, Azad, Dagh, Sahbaᵓi, Shefta, Mir, and the poet-princes of the royal house sit also Hindus (Lala Balmukhand Huzur, Sukhanand Raqb) and Christians (Alexander Heatherly Azad, George Peace Shor) freely mixing with Muslims. In Farhatullah Beg's imagined Delhi society, presided over by an Emperor whose mother was a Hindu, held true what Ghalib wrote in a letter to his friend Tufta: "My gracious friend, I hold all mankind to be my kin, and look upon all men – Muslim, Hindu, Christian – as my brothers...".[46]

---

45 In the sense of Pierre Nora's *lieau de memoire* in his *Realms of Memory: the construction of the French Past*, ed. L.D. Kritzman, tr. A. Goldhammer, New York: Columbia University Press, 1996.

46 Russell and Islam, *Ghalib – Life and Letters*, p. 226.

Images of India's Muslim past in modern Hindi poetry – five poems on three cities by Kunwar Narain

Renata Czekalska

vāpas lauṭā to dekhā
humāyūṁ ke mak'bare yā śāyad ḵutub ke parisar meṁ khaṛī
amīr ḵhus'ro kī ek nayī pahelī
joṛ rahī thī
kalāoṁ kī vaṃśāvalī meṁ ek aur kaṛī[1]

Five lyrical works – poetic images of India's Muslim past – written by Kunwar Narain are to be the subject of my observations. *Towards Delhi* [*Dillī kī taraf*], *The epoch of today* [*Āj kā*

---

[1] "When I returned I saw, / standing in Humayun's tomb or maybe the Qutab's precinct, / a new riddle of Amir Khusro / connecting / to the chronicle of the arts, another link". Kuṁvar Nārāyaṇ, *Ḵutub kā parisar* (*The Qutab's precinct*), [in:] *In dinoṁ*, Nayī Dillī: Rāj'kamal Prakāśan, 2002.

All English translations of titles of poems as well as of all the extracts from Kunwar Narain's poems quoted in this article, are by Apurva Narain. See: Kunwar Narain, *No Other World. Selected Poems*, translated by Apurva Narain, New Delhi: Rupa & Co., 2008 (henceforward *NOW*).

zamānā], *Passages* (*Fatehpur Sikri*) [*Rāste* (*Fateh'pur Sīkrī*)], *Soulless body* (*Fatehpur Sikri*) [*Anātmā deh* (*Fateh'pur Sīkrī*)], and *Lucknow* [*Lakh'naū*], belong to one poetry collection titled *In front of us* [*Ap'ne sām'ne*], published in 1979.[2]

The five works form a kind of historical landscape, in which the components such as image, thought and word evoke the feelings of sympathy and empathy. As for their content – these poetic reflections call to mind the memories of probably the most turbulent times in the history of India – the years of Muslim invasion and domination. They refer to three Indian cities which were of great importance during the times of Muslim rule in India.

However, before moving to some more detailed remarks about the poems, I believe it necessary to make a digression and recall a few historical facts.

2.

In the early eleventh century Muslim invaders arrived in India's northwest and by 1290 nearly all of India was under the domination of Muslim rulers. In the early sixteenth century the Mughals established an empire that stretched from the North-West Frontier to Bengal and down to the Deccan (present-day Andhra Pradesh). The Mughal dynasty in India was founded by Babur, who because of Timur's capture of Delhi in 1398, believed that he had an inherited claim upon northern India. His first serious expedition was launched in October 1525. Some forty years later it became evident that Babur's descendants were a new and established dynasty in northern India. The Persians referred to this dynasty as *muġul*, meaning 'Mongol' therefore they became known as the Mughal emperors of India. By the early sixteenth century the Muslim sultans of Delhi (an Afghan dynasty known as Lodi) were much weakened by threats from rebel Muslim principalities and from a Hindu coalition of Rajput rulers. The decisive battle against Ibrahim, the Lodi sultan, came on the plain of Panipat in April 1526. Babur was heavily outnumbered,

[2] Rāj'kamal Prakāśan, Nayī Dillī.

but his tactics secured his victory, which brought him the cities of Delhi and Agra. Babur's control was almost complete when he died in 1530, after just three years in India. His son Humayun tried to keep hold on the family's new possessions. His position in India was almost lost when in 1543 he went to Afghanistan to fight Sher Shah. Not until twelve years later, when civil war within India broke out, Humayun had a chance to return with almost no opposition. The victory at Sirhind in 1555, was enough to recoup the throne. But six months later Humayun died by an accidental fall down a stone staircase. His son Akbar was thirteen years old while inheriting the throne in 1556. Against all predictions, he established the mighty Mughal empire. In the early years of Akbar's reign, his inheritance was held together by an able chief minister, Bairam Khan. But from 1561 the 19-year-old emperor began to rule by himself. By marrying in 1562 a Rajput princess, daughter of the raja of Amber, he demonstrated that his intentions were to rule the two religious communities of India, Muslim and Hindu, in a new way – by consensus and cooperation, rather than alienation of the Hindu majority. In 1563 he abolished a tax levied on pilgrims to Hindu shrines. In 1564 he put an end to the *jizya*, or annual tax on unbelievers which, according to the *Qur᾿ān*, should be levied in return for Muslim protection. At the same time Akbar consequently extended the boundaries of the territory which he had inherited. In 1605 he was succeeded by his eldest and only surviving son, Jahangir. In spite of his inclination to alcohol and opium, the empire was now stable enough for him to preside over it for twenty-two years without much danger of upheaval. During the reigns of the next two emperors, Shah Jahan and his son Aurangzeb, the policy of religious toleration introduced by Akbar was gradually abandoned. In 1632 Shah Jahan brought back a stricter way of interpretation of Islam by issuing an order that all recently built Hindu temples should be destroyed. This decision, later followed by Aurangzeb's determination to impose strict Islamic rule on India, nullified most of Akbar's achievements. Moreover, Aurangzeb was obsessed with extending Mughal rule into South India. When he died in 1707, he left the empire larger but weaker than he had found it. Mughal emperors outwardly continued to rule for more than a century, but their prestige was low. As a result the empire fell into many small principalities whose existence greatly helped the British in gaining control over India, by playing rival neighbours off against each other. The empire lasted until 1858, when it was finally eliminated by the British.

3.

This is, in brief, the historical setting of the five poems by Kunwar Narain, selected as the basis of this article from among his works, which contain so-called Muslim references – or rather reminiscences of Indian Muslim past.

After these remarks, which were to organise the background and the context, let us look at these poems as we were looking at the artistic depiction of the soul of the poet, while he wanders the streets of the past and the present simultaneously. We can not only observe his reaction to history, seen through separate, individual images of places, people and happenings, but also perceive his reflections induced by remembering this turbulent but also interesting period of India's complex past.

4.

Out of the selected poems, the first two relate to Delhi, the Indian capital city, which has a long history, including its being the capital of several empires. Its earliest architectural relics date back to the Maurya Period (*c.* 300 BC). Since then the site has been a place of continuous settlement, and a lot of battles were fought to either keep or gain the rule over the city.

Towards Delhi is a poetic reflection on the city's troubled past. In the opening line the author pictures the common fate of all soldiers – always difficult to predict, no matter how brilliant the strategy.

But the reference to a collective action is very brief. Already in the second verse appears an anonymous human being, an ordinary man, who has to independently face his own fears and doubts, search alone for answers to the questions about the limits of responsibility for one's own actions as well as about the responsibility of an individual for the deeds of the human race. He also has to search alone for answers to the question about the meaning of life and death. Portraying in this way the solitude of a man in his search for his own place in history as well as in the universe, is one of the most characteristic features of Kunwar Narain's poetry. In this particular poem a reader comes across the most concise treatment of these fundamental existential issues, therefore – I believe – it needs to be quoted in full:

jidhar ghuṛ'savāroṁ kā rukh̲ ho
usī or ghisaṭ'kar jāte hue
maiṁne use kaī bār pahle bhī dekhā hai.

donoṁ hāth baṁdhe, maj'būrī meṁ, phir ek bār
kaun thā vah? kah nahīṁ sak'tā
kyoṅki keval do baṁdhe hue hāth hī
dillī pahuṁce the.[3]

The second poem related thematically to Delhi, *The epoch of today*, is of a different nature. The poet portrays the city in which he presently lives, but where he is also constantly accompanied by images of the past. In the first stanza comes the reference to *gulāmoṁ aur sultānoṁ kā zamānā*, or "the epoch of slaves and sultans", when around 1206 Delhi became the capital of the Delhi Sultanate under the Slave Dynasty. The first sultan of Delhi, Qutb ud-din Aibak, was a former slave who rose through the ranks to become a general, a governor and then sultan of Delhi. Qutb ud-din started the construction of the Qutb Minar,[4] a recognisable symbol of the city.

---

[3] "Whichever way the cavalcade turned / I have seen him go grovelling along / the same course many times before. // Both hands tied, helpless once again / who was he? I cannot say / for only two tied hands / had reached Delhi" (*NOW*, p. 57).

[4] To this structure Kunwar Narain dedicated the whole poem *K̲utub kā parisar* (*The Qutab's precinct*), a concluding fragment of which became a motto to this article.

The second stanza brings images from the remnants of the greatness of the Muslim past and the most crowded – even nowadays – part of the city:

aj cāṁdnī cauk meṁ baṛī bhīṛ hai
lāl ḵile se jāmā masjid tak[5]

The place is presently referred to as Old Delhi, but chronologically speaking it was the seventh subsequent ancient city, known in history as Shahjahanabad – the walled city built by Shah Jahan between 1638 and 1649, and designed by his daughter, Jahanara – the capital of the Mughal Empire during Shah Jahan's reign. It contains a number of significant architectural features, including the three mentioned in the discussed poem: the Lal Qila (or Red Fort), the Jama Masjid and the Chandni Chowk.

The Red Fort was originally referred to as *Qil^{c}a-e mubārak* (the blessed fort), because it was the residence of the royal family. Due to its architectural features, the Red Fort represents the pinnacle of Mughal creativity. But since it was here on 15 August 1947 that Jawaharlal Nehru unveiled the national flag, it is also a symbol of independent India. Jama Masjid (the "congregation mosque", or the mosque where *jum^{c}a* – the weekly Friday noon congregation prayers take place) is the common name of the Masjid-i Jahān-Numā (the "mosque – reflection of the World"). The courtyard of the mosque can hold up to twenty-five thousand worshipers. And, finally, the Chandni Chowk (originally meaning the moonlight square or market) is the major street in the walled city of Old Delhi. Crowded with shoppers and sellers, but also with the processions of the faithful (and at present also of tourists) going to and returning from the Jama Masjid.

The crowdedness of the place and the greatness of the monumental structures remembered in the second stanza is concluded by a puzzling action described below:

[5] "There is a huge din at Chandni Chowk / from the Red Fort to the Jama Masjid" (*NOW*, p. 57).

intazām kiyā jā rahā hai ki log khaṛe hoṁ ek pāṁv par kor'niś ke lie[6]

In antiquity, to 'stand on one's foot' was a figure of speech. Horace in his *Satires* ironically referred to Lucilius's productivity: "In an hour he used to dictate two hundred verses (…) while standing on one foot".[7] But in this poem, apart from an obvious reference to people tightly squashed in a crowd, the image evokes an association of basically a two-fold, or resting on two pillars, Hindu-Muslim structure of Indian civilisation. Considering one without the other could be compared to a person standing on just one leg.

And in the third stanza an image of *nikālī huī ek joṛā purānī āṁkheṁ*, or "a pair of ancient eyes", belonging to an unknown silent observer, brings about the appearance of an individual entangled in history, so typical for Kunwar Narain's poems. The silent observation does not mean a passive attitude, it rather means experience. It makes the observer equal with those, who are being watched and creates a distant view on the changeability of human fate.

5.

The next diptych of poems makes an elaborate reference to another landmark of India's Muslim past – Fatehpur Sikri.

Nowadays a city in Agra district in the state of Uttar Pradesh, historically it was constructed by Akbar in 1570 and served as the empire's capital from 1571 until 1585, when it was abandoned. The reasons why the capital was moved here from Agra remain unknown. A legend links the origins of the city with the Sufi saint, Salim Chishti, who lived as a recluse in the small town of Sikri, near Agra. When two sons of Akbar died, Salim

6 "arrangements are being made that the people may stand on one foot for the salute" (*NOW*, p. 57).

7 *in hora saepe ducentos (…), versus dictabat stans pede in uno* (1.4.9-10), see: S.J. Harrison, *Generic enrichment in Vergil and Horace*, Oxford-New York: OUP, 2007, p. 78.

predicted that the emperor would have another son, and indeed, the future emperor Jahangir, was born in 1569, actually in Sikri. The following year, Akbar, decided to build a palace and royal city in Sikri, to honour his *pīr*. As for the reasons of abandoning the city and moving the capital to Lahore – they remain even more obscure. There are some speculations that either the sources of water dried up or that Akbar needed to be closer to invading Persian and Afghan armies.

The left wing of the *Fatehpur Sikri* diptych, titled *Passages*, is a depiction of a city apparently deserted in great haste. A question comes in the opening of the poem:

ve log kahāṁ jāne kī jaldī meṁ the
jo ap'nā sāmān bīc rāstoṁ meṁ rakh'kar bhūl gaye haiṁ?[8]

But here, like in history, the question remains unanswered.

The three concluding lines of this poem are yet another characteristic example of one of the distinguishing features of Kunwar Narain's writing – his subtle sense of humour, based mainly on an unprecedented ability to observe as well as an exceptional acuteness of vision:

āścary, kī un betāb zindagiyoṁ meṁ
sabr kī guñjāiś thī!...
aur aisā sabr ki ab ye patthar bhī ūb rahe haiṁ.[9]

Soulless body, the right wing of the diptych, is an example of a three-dimensional landscape, structured with words. The picture captures an instant, seemingly without a past and beyond time. Nevertheless, the historical association is brought about not only by the direct reference to a certain historic place. Perception of the poem happens within a system of references, which functions differently for each reader. In other words, the text serves as a means of conveying an image moulded in imagination:

---

[8] "Where were those people in a hurry to go – / who left their belongings in the middle of the road and forgot?" (*NOW*, p. 45).

[9] "Amazing, that in those impatient lives / there was room for patience! / / And such patience that / even these stones are bored now" (*NOW*, p. 45).

muṁḍeroṁ ke kandhe hil'te haiṁ,
bharokhe bhāṁk'te haiṁ,
dīvāreṁ sun'tī haiṁ,
mehrābeṁ jamuhāī letī,
(...)[10]

In the first verse of the concluding stanza of this mysterious, poetic landscape a pond comes into sight (*tālāb ke sevār-ban meṁ jal kī par'chāiyāṁ cañcal haiṁ*[11]). Perhaps it could be the Anup Talab ("pond with no comparison"), with an island in the middle, on which the legendary musician Tansen is said to have performed?

But the most important, constructive element of this poem is time. Time which is not chronological but potential, only possible in the poet's imagination. Time which can take any form. Also a shape of a soulless beauty, amazingly desirable, resting on the carpet of greenery:

harī kāī ke k̲ālīn par ek anātmā deh leṭī hai
aur mīnāreṁ cāh'tī haiṁ
ki luṛhak'kar us'ke urojoṁ ko cūm leṁ.[12]

6.

Lucknow, placed here as the last part of the "urban quintet" found in *Apne sāmne*, is a deeply biographical poem (Kunwar Narain was educated in Lucknow and lived there for a significant part of his adult life), with some strong historical references which come as a natural consequence of the city's particular character.

Located in what was historically known as the Awadh region, its capital – the city of Lucknow – has always been a multi-

[10] "The shoulders of ramparts tremble, / Lattice windows stare, / Walls listen, / Arches yawn, / (...)" (*NOW*, p. 47).

[11] "Shadows of water swirl about in the pond's crusted grass" (*NOW*, p. 47).

[12] "a soulless body is lying on the carpet of green moss / and the minarets wish / that they tumble down and kiss its breasts" (*NOW*, p. 47).

cultural place. For long years it was a centre for education and Muslim culture. Courtly manners, beautiful gardens, poetry, music, and fine cuisine patronized by the *navāb*-s[13] – are well known, not only amongst Indians. Lucknow is popularly called the "The City of Nawabs". It is also known as the "The Constantinople of India".

But the city portrayed in the poem seems to have lost some of its old splendour and the observer seems to notice the changes that time has caused as well as some idiosyncrasies of its former dwellers:

adh'leṭe
adh'mare būṛhe-sā khāṁs'tā huā lakh'naū.
(…)

kisī murdā śānośaukat kī ḵabr-sā
(…)
kamān-kamar navāb ke jhuke hue
śarīf ādāb-sā lakh'naū,
(…)
kisī śauḵīn aur hāy kisī beniyāz kā lakh'naū[14]

The poem creates a certain kind of lyrical situation, in which some historically distant places, events and people meet together in a poem, in the moment of creation, in the moment of reading:

bārīḵ mal'mal par kaṛhī huī bārīḵiyoṁ kī tarah
is śahar kī kam'zor nafāsat,
navābī zamāne kī zanānī adāoṁ meṁ
kisī man'cale ko rijhāne ke lie
ḵavvāliyāṁ gātī huī nazākat[15]

---

13 *Navāb* – 'great, wealthy, of ground fortune'; a title adopted by the rulers of Awadh (during the time when it was an independent state).

14 "half-sprawled / half-stalled, coughing, old this Lucknow / (…) / / Like a tomb of dead magnificence, / (…) / Lucknow, like a hunched nawab, bowed, / like courtesies and greetings bestowed, / (…) / the Lucknow of connoisseurs and alas of bores" (*NOW*, pp. 53, 55).

15 "amidst ruins, the lament of some princess echoed, / like delicacies embroidered on a delicate dress, / the city's frail finesse, / like quawali-singing poise / to entice some fickle head" (*NOW*, p. 55).

Such a method of employing time close ups – practiced, among others, by T.S. Eliot – is a form of reflective analysis, carried out with the means of expression particular for lyrical poetry.

Travelling in time, the reader is taken through the city landmarks, *kāfī-hāus, haz'rat'gañj, amīnābād aur cauk,*[16] each metaphorically portrayed in a separate part of the poem. Each constituting different character and atmosphere, the distinctive features of Lucknow's culture and life. The associations call to mind an entire life-style, characterised on the one hand by refined cuisine, love for music, poetry and dance, and on the other – by leisureliness, decadence and extravagance:

nayī śāme-avadh –
das sekenḍ meṁ sam'jhāne-samajh'nevālī kisī bāt ko
kaṛīb do ghaṇṭe kī bahas ke bād sam'jhā-sam'jhāyā

(...)
bāzār –
jahāṁ zarūr'toṁ kā dam ghuṭ'tā hai,
(...)
bhāgābhāg –
jis'kī vajah nahīṁ,
mehaz ek (...) *ānā-jānā*[17]

Creating such an experience, living through it, and allowing the reader to partake in this life, is possible only in language. For it is the language which is the keeper of identity and memory of every nation, as well as of every human being. In this case it comes as a perfect means for the poet to express his sentiments and emotions as well as his sober way of perceiving reality, depicted in the concluding statement:

---

[16] "the Coffee house, Hazratganj, Ameenabad and Chowk" (*NOW*, p. 55).

[17] "Another Awadh twilight – / took two hours to take in and spell out / a trifle needing ten seconds to sort out / / (...) / Bazaars – / where wants run out of breath fast / (...) / hustle and bustle – / with no cause or aim, / just a come and go (...)" (*NOW*, p. 53).

yahī hai ḵiblā
hamārā aur āp'kā lakh'naū.[18]

7.

The five poems, taken out of the same volume, have one inspiration, connected with the biography of the poet, with his deep spiritual relationship with the way of life of the Indian Muslim community. For decades Kunwar Narain lived in a city believed to be the capital of Indian Muslim culture and the centre of the Urdu language.

Growing up and living in a mixed Hindu-Muslim community resulted in a biographical consequence, that not only are the references to both the traditions frequent in this poetry, but also that the poet continues literary traditions of both the languages, Hindi and Urdu, attaining a distinguishing and unique artistic syncretism.

Kunwar Narain's poems not only depict an incredibly vast panorama of historical places and events. They also prove that the poet boldly undertakes the difficult issue of the encounter of two great cultures: Hindu and Muslim, and that in his poems history, tradition and the present are inseparable.

[18] "This is Lucknow, Sir, / ours and yours" (*NOW*, p. 53).

History preserved in names: Delhi urban toponyms of Perso-Arabic origin

Agnieszka Kuczkiewicz-Fraś

Toponyms [from the Greek *tópos* (τόπος) 'place' and *ónoma* (ὄνομα) 'name'] are often treated merely as words, or simple signs on geographical maps of various parts of the Earth. However, it should be remembered that toponyms are also invaluable elements of a region's heritage, preserving and revealing different aspects of its history and culture, reflecting patterns of settlement, exploration, migration, etc. They are named points of reference in the physical as well as civilisational landscape of various areas.

Place-names are an important source of information regarding the people who have inhabited a given area. Such quality results mainly from the fact that the names attached to localities tend to be extremely durable and usually resist replacement, even when the language spoken in the area is itself replaced. The internal system of toponyms which is unique for every city, when analysed may give first-rate results in understanding various features, e.g. the original area of the city and its growth, the size and variety of its population, the complicated plan of its markets, habitations, religious centres, educational and cultural institutions, cemeteries etc.

Toponyms are also very important land-marks of cultural and linguistic contacts of different groups of people. In a city such as Delhi, which for centuries had been conquered and inhabited by populaces ethnically and linguistically different, this phenomenon becomes clear with the first glance at the city map. Sanskrit, Hindi, Persian, Arabic and English words mix freely, creating a unique toponymical net of mutual connections and references.

Words of Perso-Arabic origin (henceforth: PA) started to be used for naming places as soon as the first Muslim conquerors seized the city of Delhi and made it their capital, i.e. in the last decade of the twelfth century. Since then the amount of PA place-names was growing rapidly till the nineteenth century, when Muslim rulers in Delhi were replaced by the British government. They became especially frequent in these parts of the city which were one after another chosen by the Muslim rulers as their capital seats and for this reason were predominately inhabited by Muslims. These were successively: Aibak's Quṭb Minār complex, Tuġluqābād and Jahānpanāh – all in southern Delhi, Fīrūz Šāh Koṭlā and Purānā Qilᶜa – on the eastern bank of Yamuna and Šāhjahānābād – in the northern part of the city (present Old Delhi).

All of the Delhi urban PA toponyms can be generally divided and characterised: 1. according to their etymological construction; 2. according to their semantic value.[1]

1. Etymological typology:

a) toponyms created of one PA word (also compound word), e.g. Karbalā or Xvābgāh (with a separate category of hybrid compounds built of two etymologically different lexical units, e.g. Salīmgaṛh);

---

[1] Of course the two typologies presented here do not cover all the possibilities of describing PA toponyms – other important classifications could be made, for example according to their grammatical structure or according to their primary/secondary evaluation.

b) toponyms created of two or more words, of which at least one is PA (the other can be PA, Sanskrit, Hindi or English) – this group might be divided further in two:

b-1) those in which a PA word designates the category of the named object, like *masjid* or *darvāza*, e.g. Motī **Masjid** (H + PA) or Sabz **Burj** (PA + PA);

b-2) those in which a PA word is a distinctive part of the whole name, e.g. Ḥauẓ **Xāṣ** (PA + PA), **Fīrūz Šāh** Koṭ'lā (PA + H) or **Āzād** Road (PA + E).

2. Semantic typology:

a) toponyms connected with names:

a-1) of people, e.g. Bāġ-i **Bū Ḥalīma** or **Humāyūn** kā Maqbara;

a-2) of places, e.g. **Begampurī** Masjid or **Lahaurī** Darvāza;

b) toponyms created from common nouns, like names of colours (e.g. **Nīlā** Gunbad), precious stones (e.g. **Hīrā** Maḥal), real or wishful attributes of the named object (e.g. **Baṛā** Gunbad or Bāġ-i **Ḥayāt Baxš**) etc.;

c) toponyms created to commemorate:

c-1) historical events, e.g. Karbalā or Xūnī Darvāza;

c-2) legendary events, e.g. Pīr Ġāyib or Qadam Šarīf.

A detailed analysis of Delhi PA toponyms should probably require many months of work and a voluminous study. It is also highly possible that some place-names could never be explained. In this article I shall discuss PA names of chosen historical objects, which are Delhi's most significant land-marks and – due to being often used for creating secondary toponyms, like names of roads, squares, localities etc. – have become pillars of Delhi's toponymical framework.

These historical places have been divided into several semantic categories: 1. mosques; 2. tombs; 3. shrines; 4. forts; 5. water reservoirs; 6. towers; 7. gates; 8. palaces; 9. gardens; 10. other objects.

1. Mosques. As places of worship for followers of Islam mosques are the most obvious and crucial component of Muslim tradition. The number of Delhi mosques is difficult to estimate but certainly, there are more than sixty (Maulvi Zafar Hasan enumerates 69, some of them of no name), with a number still being used for everyday *namāz* (prayers). Mosques are quite often called after their founders' names but the essential part of every name of a mosque is P (A) *masjid*, *masjad* 'a mosque, temple, place of worship' [St. 1236].

Auliyā Masjid [Mosque of Saints] < P *auliyāʾ* (pl. of *valīy*) 'friends (of God), saints, prophets, fathers' [St. 122]. Located in the south-eastern corner of the Ḥauẕ-i Šamsī, this mosque is considered the most sacred by the Muslims. It is probable that the original structure, now obliterated, was built by Šams ud-Dīn Iltutmiš, *c.* 1191.

Begampurī Masjid [Begumpur Mosque] < P (T) *begam* 'a lady of rank' [St. 224]; H *pur* 'fortified town, castle, city, town; village…' [Pl. 234]. This magnificent mosque constructed *c.* 1375 is most probably one of the seven mosques built by Xān-i Jahān, the prime minister (*vazīr*) of Fīrūz Šāh Tuġluq (r. 1351--88) and named after Begumpur – a historical village situated in South Delhi District.

Čauburjī Masjid [Four-domed Mosque] < H *cau-* 'four (used only in comp.)' [Pl. 331]; P (A) *burj* 'a tower…' [St. 170]. The mosque, built in the fourteenth century by Fīrūz Šāh Tuġluq, derives its name from its architectural features of having 'four domes', which it once had.

Fataḥpūrī Masjid [Fatehpuri's Mosque]. The mosque was built in 1650 by one of Šāh Jahān's wives, Fataḥpūrī Begam (coming from the city of Fatehpur), after which it has taken its name.

Jamālī Kamālī Masjid [Mosque and Tomb of Jamali] < P *jamālī* 'amiable, lovable' [St. 370]; P (A) *kamāl* 'being complete, entire, perfect; perfection, excellence; completion, conclusion; integrity; punctuality' [St. 1047]. The name of the place comes from the two marble graves located there, one of which is that of Jamālī, which was *nom de plume* of Šaix Ḥāmid bin Faẓlullah Kanbo (d. 1536), a traveller and an eminent poet, known to have served the court of Sikandar Lodī (r. 1489-1517). Who Kamālī was remains a mystery.

Jāmi[c] Masjid [Congregational Mosque] < P (A) *jāmi[c]* 'who or what collects, (...) cathedral mosque, where the *xuṯba* is repeated on Fridays' [St. 351]. One of the largest mosques in India, built by Šāh Jahān in 1650, sometimes called **Masjid-i Jahān Numā** [World-reflecting Mosque] < P *jahān, jihān* 'the world; an age; worldly possessions...' [St. 380]; P *-namā, -numā* '(in comp.) showing, pointing out; an index' [St. 1425].

Khiṛkī Masjid [Mosque of Windows] < H *khiṛ'kī* 'a private or back-door; postern-gate, wicket, sally-port; a window, casement...' [Pl. 876]. It is located in the settlement of Jahānpanāh, the fourth city of Delhi and was founded by Moḥammad bin Tuġluq (r. 1325-51). The mosque's name comes from the perforated windows (*khiṛ'kī*-s), that decorate the upper floors.

Maxdūm Sabzvārī Masjid [Mosque of Priest of Sabzvar] < P (A) *maxdūm* 'a lord, master; the son of the house, the young gentleman, the heir; a Muhammadan priest; an abbot' [St. 1195]; P *sabzvār* 'name of a country in Persian Irāk; also of a town there' [St. 648]. Built in the fifteenth century, during the Tīmūr invasion of India. Nothing is known of the *ṣūfī* saint buried there.

Moṭh kī Masjid [Lentil Mosque] < H *moṭh* 'a kind of vetch, or pulse, *Phaseolus aconitifolius*' [Pl. 1086]. This mosque was built during the rule of Sikandar Lodī and has a legend attached to its origin. It is believed that one day Sikandar Lodī saw a grain of *moṭh* lying in the Jāmi[c] mosque which he held up and handed over to his wise and sagacious *vazīr*. The *vazīr* thought that as the grain had had the honour of being touched by the emperor, he should so arrange as to give it everlasting fame. He planted the seed and gradually, year after year, the seed multiplied so much, that it brought the *vazīr* a large sum of money, enough to build an imposing mosque, which thereafter was known as Moṭh kī Masjid.

Motī Masjid [Pearl Mosque] < H *motī* 'a pearl' [Pl. 1086]. It was built in the Lāl Qil[c]a complex by Aurangzeb in 1659-70 and was used by the emperor as his personal chapel. Motī Masjid derives its name from the pearl white colour of the mosque. Apart from this, a pearl (like other gemstones) designates an apparent preciousness of the religious structure. Therefore, naming mosques after generic names of precious stones was quite a popular practise in Mughal times.

Pahāṛī Vālī Masjid [Mosque on the Hillock] < H *pahāṛī* 'a small hill a hillock' [Pl. 282]. As indicated in its name, the mosque (of the late Mughal period) stands on a piece of hilly ground.

Qilᶜaᵓ-i Kuhna Masjid [Mosque of the Old Fort] < P (A) *qalᶜa, qilᶜa* 'a castle, fort (especially on the top of a mountain)...' [St. 984]; P *kuhna* 'old, ancient...' [St. 1067] is a grand mosque constructed by Šer Šāh in 1541 within the Delhi Purānā Qilᶜa [Old Fort] complex (the Persian and less used name of which is Qilᶜa-i Kuhna).

Quvvat ul-Islām Masjid [Might of Islam Mosque] < P (A) *quvvat* 'being strong, powerful; excelling in strength; power, force, vigour, strength, firmness; virtue, faculty, quality; authority' [St. 993]; P (A) *islām* 'yielding obedience to the will of God, resigning oneself to the divine disposal; (...) Islamism, Muhammadism; orthodoxy' [St. 59]. The oldest extant mosque in India; its construction was started in 1193 by Quṯb ud-Dīn Aibak, the founder of the Mamlūk dynasty and completed in 1197. It is also called **Masjid-i Ādīna** [Friday Mosque] < P *ādīna* 'Friday' [St. 30] or **Dillī Masjid-i Jāmiᶜ** [Delhi Congregational Mosque] < P (A) *jāmiᶜ* 'who or what collects, (...) cathedral mosque, where the *xuṭba* is repeated on Fridays' [St. 351].

Sunahrī Masjid [Golden Mosque] < H *sunah'rā* 'of gold, golden; gilded; gold-coloured' [Pl. 689]. In Delhi there are two mosques of this name. One is located outside the south-western corner of the Lāl Qilᶜa, and was built by Navāb Qudsī Begam in 1751. The other, situated near the Kotvālī in Šāhjahānābād, was built by a noble Raušan ud-Daula Ẓafar Xān in 1721. The domes of both the mosques were originally covered with copper gilt plates, from which they derive their names.

Zīnat-ul Masjid ᶜurf Ghaṭā Masjid [Mosque of Zinat, known as Cloud Mosque] < P (A) *ᶜurf* 'being known, public, notorious; known...' [St. 844]; H *ghaṭā* 'gathering of the clouds; mass of clouds, dense black clouds (on the horizon); cloudiness' [Pl. 930]. Built at the beginning of the eighteenth century by Zīnat un-Nisāᵓ Begam, the daughter of Emperor Aurangzeb, after whom the mosque has its name (cf. P (A) *zīnat* 'ornament, decoration, dress, beauty, elegance' [St. 635]). The popular name of the sanctuary is Ghaṭā Masjid [Cloud Mosque], because it was painted white with black stripes. This name may also come from its two extremely high (cloud-touching) minarets, which are the main features of this beautiful structure.

2. Tombs. Delhi, often called "a city of graves and mosques", is full of scattered tombs of emperors and saints, whose names appear in almost all toponyms of this class. The essential part of a name of a tomb is usually one of the following designations of this semantic category: P (A) *maqbara* 'a burying-ground, burial-place, sepulchre, graveyard' [St. 1290] – the word most often used to design a tomb, usually when we think of a room or small covered building (maybe a pavilion) which contains the grave; P (A) *mazār* 'visiting; a place of visitation; a shrine, sepulchre, tomb, grave; visitation, a visit' [St. 1221] – usually it means the particular building (maybe a pillared pavilion only) of the *dargāh* (shrine) containing the grave of a saint; it has religious rather than architectural significance; P (A) *qabr* 'burying; a grave, tomb, sepulchre, mausoleum, monument in honour of the dead' [St. 951] – a term usually applied to a grave with or without a tombstone over it; P *gunbad* 'an arch, vault, cupola, dome, tower; an arched gateway; a triumphal arch…' [St. 1098] – although the word itself does not have a meaning of a 'tomb', it is often used in this sense, being applied to the domed tomb structures. P (A) *turbat* 'earth, ground; a grave; a tomb; a mausoleum' [St. 292] – might be used instead of *qabr*.

Atga Xān kā Maqbara [Tomb of Atgah Khan]. Šams ud-Dīn Muḥammad Atga Xān was a general and a prime minister (*vaqīl*) in the Akbar's court. Killed by Adham Xān in 1562.[2]

Baṛā Gunbad [Big Dome] < H *baṛā* 'large, great, big, vast, immense, huge' [Pl. 151]. Baṛā Gunbad (built in 1490), located in Lodi Gardens, is a square domed tomb of an unknown but

---

[2] Cf. Abū 'l-Faẓl ᶜAllāmī, *The Āʾīn-i Akbarī*, vol. I, tr. H. Blochmann, ed. D.C. Phillott, Calcutta: The Asiatic Society, 1873; repr. 1993, pp. 337-8.

probably important person from the Lodi period, grouped together with the Friday mosque of Sikandar Lodī (Baṛā Gunbad Masjid) and a *mihmān-xāna* (guesthouse for pilgrims).

ᶜĪsā Xān kā Maqbara [Isa Khan's Tomb]. ᶜĪsā Xān Nyāzī, an Afghan noble who served Šer Šāh Sūrī and then his son Islām Šāh Sūrī, is buried in this tomb, built during his lifetime in 1547-8.

Ġāẕī ud-Dīn kā Maqbara [Ghaziuddin's Tomb]. This is a mausoleum built for himself by Ġāẕī ud-Dīn Xān (died in mid-1700), a nobleman and a general during the reign of Aurangzeb and his successors, and the father of the first Niẕām of Hydarabad.

Ġiyāṣ ud-Dīn Tuġluq kā Maqbara [Tomb of Ghiyasuddin Tughlaq]. This is a tomb and mausoleum of Ġiyāṣ ud-Dīn Tuġluq (r. 1321-5), the founder of the Tuġluq dynasty in India, which he built for himself.

Humāyūn kā Maqbara [Humayun's Tomb] has taken its name from the Mughal Emperor Naṣīr ud-Dīn Muḥammad Humāyūn, and was built for him by his wife Ḥamīda Bānū Begam in 1565-72.

Iltutmiš kā Maqbara [Iltutmish's Tomb]. This tomb was built in the Quṭb Mīnār complex by Šams ud-Dīn Iltutmiš himself, in 1235.

Imām Ẓāmīn kā Maqbara [Tomb of Imam Zamin]. Muḥammad ᶜAlī of Mašhad, known also as Imām Ẓāmīn, was a Muslim saint from Turkestan who came to Delhi during the reign of Sikandar Lodī. He built this mausoleum in his life time and was burried there after his death in 1539. His name could be translated as 'the protecting *Imām*' or 'one's guardian saint' (< P *imām* '...a head, chief, leader, especially in religious matters, antistes or reader in a mosque; prelate, patriarch, priest; a khalif...' [St. 97], *ẓāmin* 'a surety, sponsor, security, bondsman, bail...' [St. 798]; cf. Pl. 80).

Lāl Baṁgla [Red Bungalow] < P *lāl* 'a ruby; red' [St. 1112]; H (< E) *baṁg'lā* 'a thatched house, a bungalow...' [Pl. 172]. It is the name of an extentive enclosure, containing two small graves, supposedly being the resting place of Lāl Kunvār, the mother of Šāh cĀlam II (after whom the place is called), and her daughter Begam Jān.

Mazār-e Ġalīb [Ghalib's Grave]. It is also called **Mirzā Ġalīb kā Maqbara** [Mirza Ghalib's Tomb] and is a resting place of Mirzā Asadullāh Xān Ġalīb (1797-1869) – a great poet of Delhi, who wrote in Urdu and Persian.

Mubārak Šāh kā Maqbara [Tomb of Mubarak Shah]. This tomb is considered to be one of the finest examples of octagonal Sayyid tombs. Built around 1434, after the death of Mubarak Šāh Sayyid, the second ruler of the Sayyid dynasty.

Mubārak Xān kā Gunbad [Mubarak Khan's Dome]. It is the tomb of Muḥammad Šāh (d. 1445/6), the third king of Sayyid dynasty and the nephew and successor of Mubārak Šāh Sayyid.

Nīlā Gunbad [Blue Dome] < H *nīlā* 'dark blue; blue; livid' [Pl. 1168]. The monument (built in 1624-5), locally known as Nīlā Gunbad, due to the blue coloured dome, contains the remains of Fahīm Xān, the attendant of cAbd ur-Raḥīm Xānxānān, who lived during the reign of Jahāngīr.

Paik kā Maqbara [Tomb of a Messenger] < P *paik* 'a running footman; a carrier, messenger; a guard; a watchman; a footman, lacquey…' [St. 268]. It is a Lodi period octagonal monument of the fifteenth century. Nothing is known about Paik but the word literary means 'a messenger'.

Qabr-e Ṣafdarjang [Safdarjang's Tomb]. This splendid mausoleum was built in 1753-4 for Mirzā Muqīm cAbūlmanṣūr Xān, given a title of Ṣafdarjang, the viceroy of Avadh during the reign of Mughal emperor Muḥammad Šāh, by his son Navvāb Šujā ud-Daula.

Sikandar Lodī kā Maqbara (Sikandar Lodi's Tomb). The tomb of Sikandar Lodī, second ruler of the Afghan Lodī dynasty, supposedly was built by his son and successor Ibrāhīm in the year of Sikandar's death.

Šāh cĀlam kā Maqbara [Tomb of Shah Alam]. Šāh cĀlam was a saint who lived during the reign of Fīrūz Šāh Tuġluq, but nothing is known of him.

Šīš Gunbad [Glazed Dome] < P *šīša* 'a glass, bottle, flask, phial, cup, caraff, decanter; glass; a looking-glass; a cupping-glass…' [St. 775] (cf. H *šīš-* 'glass' [McG. 952]). This is a typical Lodi-period tomb, but none of the many people buried in it have been identified. The exterior of the structure is ornamented with blue glazed tiles in two shades, which gave the tomb its name.

Turbat-e Najaf Xān [Tomb of Najaf Khan]. Najaf Xān (d. 1782) was a Persian noble in the court of Mughal emperor Šāh ᶜĀlam II. For his admirable deeds the king made him *Amīru 'l-umarā*[3] with the title of Zūlfikār ud-Daula.

Xān-i Xānān kā Maqbara [Tomb of Khan-i Khanan]. ᶜAbd ur-Raḥīm Xān, also given a title of Xān-i Xānān (d. 1626-7), was the son of Akbar's prime minister Bairām Xān and an influential person in the courts of Akbar and Jahāngīr. He was also a known poet, the author of popular Urdū couplets, which he wrote under the pen name Raḥīm.

3. Shrines. Shrines, usually built over the grave of a revered religious figure (often a *ṣūfī* saint), are typical manifestations of South Indian Muslim culture. They are most often called *dargāh*-s, as many believe that these shrines are portals through which the deceased saint's intercession and blessing can be invoked (< P *dargāh* 'the king's court; a port, portal, gate, door; the lower threshold; a court before a palace or great house; a large bench or place for reclining upon; a mosque' [St. 513] > H *dar'gāh* 'portal, door; threshold; a royal court, a palace; a mosque; shrine or tomb (of some reputed saint, which is the object of worship and pilgrimage)' [Pl. 513]). *Dargāh*-s are often associated with meeting rooms and hostels, known as *xānqāh*[4] < P *xānagāh* (*xāngāh*), *xānagah* (*xāngah*) 'a monastery for Sofīs or Darwīshes; a convent, chapel; a hospice' [Pl. 443], and also usually include a mosque, schools (*madrasa*-s), residences for teachers or caretakers, hospitals, and other buildings for community purposes. Another term for a shrine is *naẕrīyat* or *naẕarīyat*, meaning verbatim 'a place of devotion; a place of offering' < P (A) *naẕr* 'vowing; devoting, presenting, dedicating to God; frightening, alarming,

---

[3] *Amīru 'l-umarā* 'prince of princes', 'chief of the nobles' – a title given by Eastern princes to their prime ministers (cf. St. 102).

[4] Cf. *k͟hān'k͟āh* 'a ṣūfī residential establishment; monastery' [McG. 235]; *xānqāh* 'convent, monastery, shrine' [STCD 282].

warning, inspiring dread of an enemy; a vow, promise made to God; a gift, anything offered or dedicated; a present or offering from an inferior to a superior' [St. 1394] + *-īyat*, which is an Arabic suffix of abstract substantives. A specific category of holy places, very common in India, attributed to various saints and held sacred by the general public, are so called *čillagāh*-s, usually secluded and lonely places where the Muslim saints indulge in prayer and meditation. The term comes from P *čilla*, *čila* 'a quadragesimal fast, the forty days of Lent, during which the religious fraternities of the East shut themselves up in their cells, or remain at home' [St. 398] + P *gāh* '...place (always in composition)...' [St. 1074].

Toponyms denoting shrines, similarly to those naming tombs, usually comprise the name of a particular saint.

Bhūre Šāh kī Dargāh [Shrine of Bhoore Shah] < H *bhūrā* 'brown; auburn (hair)' [Pl. 195] (cf. 'light brown, brownish; greyish...' [McG. 772]); P *šāh* 'a king (...); a title assumed by fakīrs...' [St. 726]. Xvāja Sadr ud-Dīn Šāh, who lived during the Jahāngīr's reign and is buried here, got his nickname because of his fair (H *bhūrā*) complexion.[5]

Čilla Nizām ud-Dīn [Nizamuddin's Residence]. The residence of thirteenth-century *ṣūfī* saint Ḥazrat Xvāja Niẓām ud-Dīn Auliyā, which is said to be the site where he used to fast and meditate (*čilla*), resembling the architecture of Fīrūz Šāh Tuġluq. Called also **Čillagāh-e Šarīf** [Saint's Residence] < P *šarīf* 'noble, eminent, holy; illustrious; a descendant of Muhammad...' [St. 743], by the disciples of the Chishti order in Delhi it is still regarded as one of the most sacred places in North India.

Čirāġ-i Dihlī kī Dargāh [Shrine of 'Lamp of Delhi'] < P *čirāġ* 'a lamp; light...' [St. 389]; *dihli* – a Persianized form of H *dillī*, which is the name of the city of Delhi [cf. St. 549]. The shrine entombs Šaix Nāsir ud-Dīn Maḥmūd (d. 1356), also known as 'Raušan Čirāġ-i Dihlī' ('Illuminated Lamp of Delhi'), a famous Chishtiyya *ṣūfī* of Delhi.

---

[5] More about this saint see: R.V. Smith, *The Delhi that No-one Knows*, New Delhi: DC Publishers, 2005, pp. 106-8.

Nazrīyat-e Pīr ᶜĀšiq Allah [Pir Ashiq Allah's Shrine] was built in 1317 by Sulṭān Quṭb ud-Dīn Mubārak Šāh Xaljī for a renowned Chishtiyya saint Šams ud-Dīn ᶜĀšiq Allah. Apart from his tomb in the *dargāh* there is a hill on which the *čillagāh* of Bābā Farīd, twelfth-century *ṣūfī* preacher and saint of the same Chishti order, is situated. It is a place of meditation for many *ṣūfī* mystics and saints.

Niẓām ud-Dīn kī Dargāh [Nizamuddin's Shrine] is the mausoleum of Ḥaẓrat Xvāja Niẓām ud-Dīn Auliyā, the world-famous Muslim *ṣūfī* mystic and saint of the Chishti order. The village that during the centuries sprang up around the shrine is also named after the saint (Niẓāmuddīn).

Quṭb ud-Dīn Baxtiyār Kākī kī Dargāh [Shrine of Qutb-uddin Bakhtiyar Kaki]. Khwāja Baxtiyār Kākī (d. 1235) was a renowned Muslim *ṣūfī* mystic, saint and scholar of the Chishti order. His shrine is the oldest *dargāh* in Delhi.

Šāh-i Mardān kī Dargāh [Shrine of Shahi Mardan] < P *šāh* 'a king, sovereign, emperor, monarch, prince' [St. 726]; *mardān* (pl. of *mard*) 'heroes, warriors' [St. 1212]. This shrine derives its name from Šāh-i Mardān [King of Heroes], which is a title of ᶜAlī (cf. P *shāh-i mardān* 'king of valour, Alī' [St. 726]). The name has been given to the enclosure of Qadam Šarīf, a structure which is believed to contain a footprint of ᶜAlī.

Xanqaʾ-i Šāh Ġulām ᶜAlī [Convent of Shah Ghulam ᶜAli]. The whole enclosure contains a mosque, a house, a Tasbīḥ Xāna (< P *tasbīḥ-xāna* 'a chapel, oratory' [St. 300]), a few apartments and four graves – among them there is that of Šāh Ġulām ᶜAlī, a well known thirteenth-century *ṣūfī* saint of Naqshbandi order.

4. Forts. Impressive Delhi forts stand as silent sentinels to the former glory of the mighty emperors who have ruled the city. Although some of them are now forgotten and partly ruined, once they marked the dawn of a new capital, portraying the desire of establishing a new kingdom. The names of the forts often refer to the names of their builders as well as contain a word denoting 'fort', being an exponent of this category. For this purpose one of the following is used: P *qalᶜa*, *qilᶜa* 'a fort (esp. one on a mountain or an eminence), a fortress, castle, citadel, fortification' [Pl. 794] < P (A) *qal^{c}at*, *qal^{c}a* 'a castle, fort (especially on the top of a mountain)...' [St. 984]; H *koṭ'lā* 'a small fortress, &c.; a place where the property of a temple is kept, and its affairs are managed' [Pl. 859] or H *gaṛh* 'a fort; citadel; castle' [Pl. 909].

^{c}Ādilābād Qil^{c}a [Adilabad Fort] < P (A) *^{c}ādil* '...one who gives partners to God, an idol-worshipper; just, equitable...' [St. 829]; P *ābād* 'a city, building, habitation...' [St. 3]. This small fort, known also as **Moḥammadābād** [City of Mohammad], was built by Moḥammad bin Tuġluq on the hills to the south of Tuġluqābād.

Fīrūz Šāh Koṭlā [Fortress of Firoz Shah]. Called also Fīrūzābād [City of Firoz], this fortress was built by Fīrūz Šāh Tuġluq in 1354 as the fifth city of Delhi and inherited the name after its constructor.

Lāl Qil^{c}a [Red Fort] < P *lāl* 'a ruby; red...' [St. 1112], called also **Lāl Ḥavelī** < P *ḥavelī* 'a house, dwelling, habitation; the districts attached to, and in the vicinity of, the capital of a province; government lands' [St. 434] or **Qil^{c}a-i Šāh Jahān** [Shah Jahan's Fort]. The Delhi Fort, built by Šāh Jahān in 1639-48, served as both a palace and a fortification for the Emperor. The fort is faced externally with red sandstone – hence its name.

Murādābād Pahāṛī Qil^{c}a [Muradabad Hill Fort] < H *pahāṛī* 'a small hill a hillock' [Pl. 282]. The fort was constructed in 1624 by Rustam Xān, the governor of Sambhal, and named **Rustam Nagar** < H *nagar* 'a city, town' [Pl. 1151]. Later it was re-named Murādābād after the name of Šāh Jahān's son Murād Baxš (cf. P *ābād* 'a city, building, habitation...' [St. 3]).

Purāṇa Qil^{c}a [Old Fort] < H *purāṇa* 'belonging to ancient or olden times, ancient, old, aged, primeval' [Pl. 236], known also under the Persian form of its name **Qil^{c}a^{ɔ}-i Kuhna** < P *kuhna* 'old, ancient...' [St. 1067]. It was the citadel of the city of **Dīnpanāh** [Asylum of the Faith] < P *dīn-panāh* 'support or prop of religion; a sovereign, defender of the faith' [St. 554]. Its construction was started *c.* 1530 by Humāyūn and continued by Šer Šāh Sūrī in 1540 after he defeated Humāyūn. Šer Šāh renamed the fort as **Šergaṛh** [Sher's Fort] (or Tiger's Fort, as his name Šer in Persian means 'a lion; a tiger' [cf. St. 772]).

Salīmgaṛh [Salim's Fort]. The fort was built by Islām Šāh Sūrī, also known as Salīm Šāh (after whom the fort is named), son and successor of Šer Šāh Sūrī, in 1546. It was constructed on an island of the river Yamunā. By the time of Salīm Šāh's death only the walls were completed, then the construction was abandoned. Later it was also called **Nūrgaṛh** [Fort of Noor], when Nūr ud-Dīn Jahāngīr built a bridge in front of its gateway (cf. P *nūr* 'light, rays of light' [St. 1432]).

Tuġluqābād [Tughlaq's Fort]. The fort situated on a hillock is a huge (stretching across 6.5 km), but dilapidated construction, built by Ġiyāṣ ud-Dīn Tuġluq, the founder of the Tughlaq dynasty. The construction began in 1321 and was completed in two years, but the fort was abandoned soon after its founder's death in 1325.

5. Water reservoirs. The large water tanks or reservoirs, built to supply water to the inhabitants of the city, are known as *ḥauẓ*-es < P (A) *ḥauẓ* 'a large reservoir of water, basin of a fountain, pond, tank, vat, cistern' [St. 434].

Ḥauẓ-i ᶜAlāᵓī [Ala's Tank]. It is a large tank, excavated by ᶜAlāᵓ ud-Dīn Xaljī (r. 1296-1316) in Sirī, the second city of medieval India, and named after him. In the fourteenth century it was renamed Ḥauẓ Xāṣ by Fīrūz Šāh Tuġluq.

Ḥauẓ -i Šamsī [Shams's Tank] is a water storage reservoir built in 1230 by Šams ud-Dīn Iltutmiš, the third ruler of the Sultanate of Delhi and named after him. As the legend narrates, a location for the reservoir was revealed to Iltutmiš by the Prophet Muḥammad in a dream. When the Sultan inspected the site the day after his dream, he reported to have found a hoof print of Muḥammad's horse. He then erected a pavilion to mark the sacred location and excavated a large tank around the pavilion to harvest rain water.

Ḥauẓ Xāṣ [Royal Tank]. P (A) *xāṣṣ*, *xāṣ* '...choice, select, excellent, noble' [St. 439]. In the fourteenth century Fīrūz Šāh Tuġluq re-excavated the old silted Ḥauẓ-i ᶜAlāᵓī and raised several buildings on its banks. Since then, the tank and surrounding area is known as Ḥauẓ Xāṣ, which can be translated as 'Royal Tank'.

6. Towers. A minaret, from which five times each day the voice of the *muᵓaẕẕin* calls thousands of followers to fulfil their religious duty, is the necessary component of every mosque, and as such – one of the most essential symbols of Islam. However, it rarely happens that minarets possess their individual names. Still, in Muslim times towers were quite frequently built, either as parts of fortifications or as separate constructions. There are two terms denoting 'tower' which appear in toponyms of this category: P *mīnār* 'a tower, turret, steeple, spire, minaret; an obelisk' [St. 1364] and P (A) *burj* 'a tower…' [St. 170]

ᶜAlāᵓ-i Mīnār [Ala's Tower] < P (A) *ᶜalāᵓ* 'being superior to, above…' [St. 860]. The unfinished tower in the Quṭb Mīnār complex is named after its founder, Sultan ᶜAlāᵓ ud-Dīn Xaljī who had started the construction of the tower twice the size of Quṭb Mīnār. It could not be completed because of the sultan's death.

Asad Burj [Lion's Tower] < P (A) *asad* 'a lion…' [St. 57]. Asad Burj is a part of the Lāl Qilᶜa fortification wall located in the south-eastern corner of the fort. It was damaged during the Uprising of 1857.

Čor Mīnār [Tower of Thieves] < H *cor* 'a thief, a robber, a pilferer…' [Pl. 450]. Built in the times of ᶜAlāᵓ ud-Dīn Xaljī, this tower has circular holes on the outside and it is believed that they might have been used for displaying severed heads of thieves, as a deterrent to robbers – which gave the tower its name.

Kos Mīnār [Milestone Tower] < H *kos* 'a measure of length equal to approximately two English miles (but varying in different parts of India), a league; a mile-stone' [Pl. 862]. The Kos Mīnār-s, which are several in Delhi and numerous along the main routes of northern India, were the milestones erected by the Mughal emperors between 1556 and 1707. They measure over 30 ft and the inspiration to build them was probably derived by the Mughals from Šer Šāh.

Muṣamman Burj [Octagonal Tower] < P (A) *muṣamman* 'octangular, eight-sided, eight-fold; an octagon' [St. 1173]. This octagon is one of the structures of Lāl Qil^ca, known also as **Burj-i Tila** [Golden Tower] < P *tila* 'drawn gold...' [St. 322], because its walls, built of white marble, as well as its cupola have been covered with gilded copper. This structure was used as *jharokhā* or 'showing place' (< H *jharokhā* 'loop-hole, eyelet-hole, lattice, window, casement, skylight...' [Pl. 403]), wherein the emperor appeared daily to his subjects.

Quṭb Mīnār [Tower of Qutb]. This tallest brick minaret in the world (72.5 m) was constructed *c.* 1200 under the orders of India's first Muslim ruler Quṭb ud-Dīn Aibak, after whom it has been named. The topmost storey of the minaret was completed in 1386 by Fīrūz Šāh Tuġluq.

Sabz Burj [Green Dome] < P *sabz* 'green...' [St. 647]. The name of this late sixteenth century octagonal tomb comes from the green tiles which originally covered it. During restoration in the 1980s the construction was re-tiled by the Archaeological Survey of India in a vivid blue colour and, for this reason, it is also known as **Nīlī Chatrī** < H *nīlā* 'dark blue; blue; livid' [Pl. 1168]; H *chatrī* '... a small ornamental pavilion generally built over a place of interment, or a cenotaph in honour of a Hindū chief, or a *faqīr*' [Pl. 458]. It is not known who built this monument or whose tomb it is.

Sohan Burj [Brilliant Tower] < H *sohan* 'beautiful, handsome, graceful, pleasing, charming...' [Pl. 703]. Probably built at the turn of the fifteenth century, the building does not resemble a tower at all. It could have been used as an assembly hall or a school (*madrasa*). It looks very much like a mosque, but is facing the wrong direction to be one.

Šāh Burj [King's Tower] < P *šāh* 'a king...' [St. 726]. It is an octagonal, three-storey building in the Lāl Qil^ca complex, a pavilion rather than a typical tower. In this building Šāh Jahān held secret meetings with princes and leading nobles.

7. Gates. Delhi for centuries was famous for its gates, although from the fifty two mentioned by William Finch[6] in his

[6] William Finch was an agent of the East India Company who travelled in India in the years 1608-11. Cf. R. Nath, *India as Seen by William*

description of the city, only 13 still exist and can be identified. A usual practice was to call them according to the name of a place of destination they were facing. A regular element of the name of each gate is P *darvāza* 'a door; a gate…' [St. 514].

ᶜAlāᵓ-i Darvāza [Ala's Gate] < P (A) *ᶜalāᵓ* 'being superior to, above…' [St. 860]. It is the main gateway from the southern side of the Quvvat ul-Islām Mosque, built by Sultan ᶜAlāᵓ ud-Dīn Xaljī in 1311 and named after him.

Dillī Darvāza [Delhi Gate] known also as **Alexandra Gate** (named so after Queen Alexandra of Denmark), in the south wall of the Lāl Qilᶜa, acquired its name as it faces the sites of the older cities of Delhi.

Lahaurī Darvāza [Lahore Gate]. Also known as **Victoria Gate** (named so after Queen Victoria), it is the most important and the most frequently used gate of Lāl Qilᶜa, in the centre of the West wall of the fort. The gate is named so because it faces towards the city of Lahaur.

Xūnī Darvāza [Bloodstained Gateway] < P *xūnī* 'bloody; a murderer' [St. 489]. Built by Šer Šāh Sūrī in sixteenth century, it was one of the gates of his city Šergaṛh, then called **Kābulī Darvāza**, as it opened on the road to Kabul. Because of the predominant use of red stone it was also called **Lāl Darvāza** < P *lāl* 'a ruby; red…' [St. 1112]. Its present name the gate acquired after the Uprising of 1857 since it was here that Captain W. Hodson shot two remaining sons of the last Mughal emperor Bahādur Šāh Ẓafar, imprisoned after the siege of Delhi by British soldiers. Local legend has it that during the rainy season blood drips from the ceiling (most probably it is rainwater that becomes slightly reddish after contact with the rusted iron joints of the gateways' ceiling).

8. Palaces. This category comprises residences of various kind, belonging usually to a royal personage or to a high dignitary, often large and splendid, used either for living or for entertainment, known generally as *maḥal*-s < P *maḥall*, *maḥal* 'de-

Finch (1608-11), Jaipur: The Historical Research Documentation Programme, 1990.

scending, lighting off a journey, staying, dwelling; place of abode; a building, house, mansion; a palace; a place, post, dignity, degree of honour, high station' [St. 1189].

Bhulī Bhaṭiyārī kā Maḥal [Palace of Bu-ᶜAli Bhatti]. It is one of the four hunting palaces (*šikārgāh*) built by Fīrūz Šāh Tuġluq. According to popular belief, its name comes from a man named Bū-ᶜAlī Bhaṭṭī, who is said to have occupied the building long ago. The name has gone through many variations over the years, hence its present corrupted form.[7] The other explanation of the name might be according to the word-for-word translation: 'Palace of Fair Woman Innkeeper' < H *bhūrā* 'brown; auburn (hair)' [Pl. 195] (cf. 'light brown, brownish; greyish...' [McG. 772]); *bhaṭiyārī, bhaṭhiyārī* 'woman who carries on the business of an inn-keeper; wife of a *bhaṭhiyārā*' [Pl. 183]. The mysterious innkeeper might have been a particular favourite of Fīrūz Šāh Tuġluq.

Hīrā Maḥal [Diamond Palace] < H *hīrā* 'diamond; adamant' [Pl. 1244]. A small marble pavilion in the Lāl Qilᶜa complex, built by Bahādur Šāh II who used to sit there and watch the river.

Jahāz Maḥal [Ship Palace] < P (A) *jahāz* '... a ship ...' [St. 380]. Built during the Lodi dynasty period (1452-1526) probably as a pleasure resort or an inn (*sarāy*) for pilgrims. It is called 'Ship Palace' because, located on the banks of Ḥauẓ-i Šamsī, it appears as if it was floating on the surface of the lake.

Kūšk-i Šikārgāh [Hunting Palace] < P *kūšk* 'a palace, villa; a castle, citadel' [St. 1062]; P *šikār* 'prey, game; the chase, hunting...' [St. 751]; P *gāh* '...place (always in composition)...' [St. 1074]. It is another hunting lodge built by Fīrūz Šāh Tuġluq. The other name of the place is **Kūšk-i Jahān Numā** [World-reflecting Palace] < P *jahān, jihān* 'the world; an age; worldly possessions...' [St. 380]; P *-namā, -numā* '(in comp.) showing,

[7] Such explanation of this name has been given by Sayyid Aḥmad Xān in *Āṣār us-ṣanādīd*, cf. R. Nath, *Monuments of Delhi. Historical Study*, Indian Institute of Islamic Studies, New Delhi: Ambika Publications, 1979, p. 38.

pointing out; an index' [St. 1425]. The palace was probably so named because of the astronomical observatory built in it.

Lāl Maḥal [Red Palce] < P *lāl* 'a ruby; red…' [St. 1112]. Presumably it is the other name for the **Kušk-i Lāl** (< P *kūšk* 'a palace, villa; a castle, citadel' [St. 1062]), a palace built by Ġiyāṣ ud-Dīn Balban before he ascended the throne. It is built of red sandstone which gave the palace its name. In the fourteenth century the famous Moroccan traveller Ibn Baṭṭūṭa stayed here during his visit to Delhi.

Mumtāz Maḥal [Palace of the Eminent] < P *mumtāz* 'chosen, distinguished, select, choice; eminent, excellent, illustrious; separate, distinct' [St. 1313]. It is the former harem of the Lāl Qilᶜa. According to popular belief, this palace was built by Šāh Jahān for his wife Arjumand Bānū Begam, also famously known as Mumtāz Maḥal.

Pīr Ġāyib [Vanished Saint] < P *pīr* 'an old man; a founder or chief of any religious body or sect' [St. 264]; P *ġāʾib* 'absent, latent, concealed, invisible…' [St. 880]. Supposedly it was originally a part of Kūšk-i Šikārgāh, built by Fīrūz Šāh Tuġluq in the fourteenth century. There are various interpretations whether it was used as a hunting lodge, or as an astronomical observatory. According to tradition, one of the rooms of the building was a *čillagāh* or the worshipping place of a saint, who suddenly and mysteriously disappeared. There is a cenotaph constructed in his memory and the whole building is known after him as Pīr Ġāyib.

Rang Maḥal [Palace of Colours] < P *rang* 'colour, hue' [St. 588]. The building is known also as **Imtiyāz Maḥal** [Palace of Distinction] < P (A) *imtiyāz* 'separation, distinction, discrimination' [St. 98]. The building, located within the Lāl Qilᶜa complex, was the largest of the apartments of the imperial seraglio.

Xāṣ Maḥal [Private Palace] < P (A) *xāṣṣ*, *xāṣ* '… private, for private use, personal, own, proper…' [St. 439]. Known also under the name **Čhoṭā Rang Maḥal** [Lesser Palace of Colours] < H *choṭā* 'little, small; less, lesser...' [Pl. 466]; P *rang* 'colour, hue' [St. 588], was a part of the Lāl Qilᶜa *zanāna* (women's apartments) and the residential palace of the chief ladies of the harem.

Ẓafar Maḥal [Palace of Zafar]. It stands in the centre of Bāġ-i Ḥayāt Baxš, a garden in the Lāl Qil^ca complex and is named after the *nom de plume* of Bahādur Šāh II, by whom it was built in about 1842 (cf. P (A) *ẓafar* 'accomplishing, succeeding in one's wishes, overcoming, conquering; victory, triumph…' [St. 825]).

9. Gardens. The construction of gardens since Babur's rule (1526-30) was one of the preferred imperial activities, becoming uncommonly popular during the times of the Mughal Empire. Some of them are kept well preserved and can still be admired in Delhi, although a traditional Persian word *bāġ* 'a garden; a vineyard…' [St. 148] in their names is more and more often replaced by the English word 'garden'.

Bāġ-i Bū Ḥalīma [Garden of Bu Halima]. Not much is known about Bū Ḥalīma and the origin of the garden locally named after the lady. Architecturally the enclosure-walls and the gateway of the garden by its style could be datable to the early Mughal period (sixteenth century). There is a dilapidated structure in the garden, containing a grave said to be of Bū Ḥalīma.

Bāġ-i Ḥayāt Baxš [Life-giving Garden] < P (A) *ḥayāt* 'life; life-time' [St. 434]; *baxš* (in comp., as part. of *baxšīdan*) 'a giver, donor; a distributor, or divider; a pardoner' [St. 159]. The garden within the Lāl Qil^ca complex, once a beautiful retreat and a favourite resting-place of the fort's inhabitants.

Bāġ-i Raušanārā [Roshanara's Garden]. This is one of the biggest gardens of Delhi, laid in 1650 by Raušanārā Begam, the youngest daughter of Šāh Jahān and named after her. Her tomb (Qabr-e Raušanārā), in which the princess was buried in 1671, is situated in the centre of the garden.

10. Other objects. This class comprises a range of toponyms which cannot be grouped under any of the above described categories, but are still commonly known and used for constructing secondary place-names.

Dīvān-i ^cĀm [Hall of Public Audiences] < P (A) *daivān*, *dīvān* 'a royal court…' [St. 555]; P (A) *^cāmm* '…the vulgar, common people, commons, commonalty' [St. 832]; cf. P *dīvān-i ᶜām* 'a public hall of audience' [St. 555]. It is an elegant arched hall in the Lāl Qilᶜa complex, where the emperor used to hear complaints or disputes of his people and meet dignitaries and foreign emissaries.

Dīvān-i Xāṣ [Hall of Private Audiences] < P (A) *daivān, dīvān* 'a royal court…' [St. 555]; P [A] *xāṣṣ, xāṣ* 'particular, peculiar, special, distinct; private, for private use, personal, own, proper; choice, select, excellent, noble' [St. 439]; cf. *dīvān-i xāṣṣ* 'a privy-council chamber' [St. 555]. It is a luxurious pavilion of white marble, a part of the Lāl Qilᶜa complex, where the emperor used to meet the highest and mightiest persons such as ministers and army chiefs as well as the most eminent and noble among the citizens.

Ḥammām [Baths] < P (A) *ḥammām* 'a hot bath; a Turkish bath; a bagnio' [St. 430]. The Lāl Qilᶜa royal baths complex is divided into three parts separated by corridors. One of the rooms, where the garments were removed, was called ᶜAqab-i Ḥammām (< P (A) *ᶜaqab* 'hinder part, rear' [St. 857]). The central chamber, entirely built of carved and inlaid marble, was known as Šāh-Nišīn [Seat of the Emperor] < P *šāh* 'a king…' [St. 726]; *nišīn* (in comp.) 'sitting, sitting down or along with…' [St. 1405]. The third apartment fixed with heating appliances was used for hot or vapour baths.

Ḥavelī Mirzā Ġalīb [Mirza Ghalib's House] < P *ḥavīlī* 'a house, dwelling, habitation…' [St. 434]. In this mansion the great Delhi poet Mirzā Asadullāh Xān Ġalīb spent the last phase of his life, from 1860 to 1869.

Karbalā [Karbala]. The Karbala is a large enclosure of Mughal times, surrounded by a wall built of rubble and containing a large number of graves. The name of the enclosure comes from Karbala, a place in Iraq where Imām Ḥusain (son of ᶜAlī), his followers and family members became martyrs in the hands of the army of the infamous Caliph Yazīd I [cf. St. 1021]. The places where the *taᶜziya*-s (namely the replicas or copies of the grave or tomb of Imām Ḥusain) are buried as a part of mourning observances are also called *karbalā*-s.

Nahr-i Bihišt [Stream of Paradise] < P (A) *nahr* '… a river, stream, flowing canal' [St. 1438]; P *bihišt* 'paradise; heaven' [St. 211]. It is a canal constructed inside the Lāl Qil^{c}a, passing from the Šāh Burj through the Ḥammām, Dīvān-i Xāṣ, Xvābgāh and Rang Maḥal.

Naqqār Xāna or **Naubat Xāna** [Drum House] < P *naqāra* 'a kettle-drum' [St. 1418] (cf. *naqār-xāna* 'a band of music' [St. 1417]) or P (A) *naubat*, *nauba* '… drums beating at the gate of a great man at certain intervals…' [St. 1431] (cf. *naubat-xāna* 'a watch-tower; a guard-house; the music-gallery' [St. 1431]). It served as a main entrance to the court of Dīvān-i ^{c}Ām. The name of the gate refers to the musician's gallery on the top of it, from which music was performed five times a day. It is known also under the popular name **Hāthiyān Pol** [Elephant Gate] < H *hāthiyāṁ*, pl. of *hāthī* 'an elephant' [Pl. 1215]; H *pol*, *paul* 'gate, door' [Pl. 281], it was at this point that all save Princes of royal blood dismounted from their elephants before entering further into the fort complex.[8]

Qadam Šarīf [Sacred Footprint] < P (A) *qadam* 'a foot; a footstep, track, trace' [St. 958]; *šarīf* 'noble, eminent, holy' [St. 743]. The structure (built in 1759-60) contains a footprint believed to be of ^{c}Alī and is held to be very sacred by the Shia community. It is a part of Šāh-i Mardān kī Dargāh.

Xvābgāh [Bedroom Suite] < P *xvābgāh* 'a bed, couch; a chamber, dormitory' [St. 479]. Xvābgāh is a part of another structure inside the Lāl Qil^{c}a, called **Tasbīḥ Xāna** (< P *tasbīḥ--xāna* 'a chapel, oratory' [St. 300]), namely the emperor's private apartments. The other part of this building was known as **Baiṭhak** (< H *baiṭhak* 'place where people meet to sit and converse, assembly-room, forum; reception-room' [Pl. 206]) or **Toša Xāna** (< P *toša-xāna* 'wardrobe; store-room' [St. 336]) and served as the king's sitting room.

[8] Cf. *Monuments of Delhi: Lasting Splendour of the Great Mughals and Others*, vol. I: *Shahjahanabad*, comp. by Maulvi Zafar Hasan, ed. J.A. Page et al., New Delhi: Aryan Books International, 1997 (1st edn. 1916), p. 11.

Concluding remarks

Almost half of the discussed toponyms (42 out of 90) have been created on the basis of personal names of people connected somehow with particular places. This tendency is observed predominantly in the names of burial places: almost all toponyms referring to graves and all referring to shrines (the most important element of which are graves of revered religious figures) comprise the name of a person laid there to rest (see the table below).

Semantic category of toponyms	Total number of described toponyms	Toponyms created on the basis of personal names
Mosques	15	4
Tombs	22	17
Shrines	8	8
Forts	7	4
Water reservoirs	3	2
Towers	9	1
Gates	4	1
Palaces	10	2
Gardens	3	2
Other objects	9	1
TOTAL	90	42

However, such constructions as towers, gates or palaces are rarely named after persons. Toponyms denoting them most often expose real or wishful attributes of the named object.

The 90 place-names, presented and discussed above, and connected with important Delhi historical objects are frequently employed for creating secondary toponyms, such as the names of roads (e.g.: Safdarjang Lane, Safdarjang Road, Gali Sheesh Mahal, Karbala Road, Purana Qila Road, Chauburja Marg, etc.) or names of localities, villages and apartments (e.g. Safdarjang Enclave, Qutab Vihar, Qutab Enclave, Hauz Khas Appartments, Hauz Khas Enclave, etc.). In the process of creating secondary toponyms the increasing role of English lexical elements is also worth noting.

BIBLIOGRAPHY

Delhi: City Map, New Delhi: Eicher Goodearth Ltd., 2005.

Fanshawe, Herbert Charles, *Delhi, past and present*, Delhi: Asian Educational Services, 1998 (1st edn. London, 1902).

McG. = McGregor, Ronald Stuart, *The Oxford Hindi-English Dictionary*, New Delhi: OUP, 2003 (1st edn. 1993).

Nath, Ram, *Monuments of Delhi: Historical Study*, Indian Institute of Islamic Studies, New Delhi: Ambika Publications, 1979.

Nath, Ram, *India As Seen By William Finch (1608-11)*, Jaipur: The Historical Research Documentation Programme, 1990.

Pl. = Platts, John T., *A Dictionary of Urdū, Classical Hindi and English*, Oxford, 1884 (repr. New Delhi: Munshiram Manoharlal Publ. 2000).

Rizvi, Saiyid Athar Abbas, *The wonder that was India*, Volume II, *A survey of the history and culture of the Indian sub-continent from the coming of the Muslims to the British conquest 1200-1700*, New Delhi: Rupa & Co., 2000.

Smith, Ronald Vivian, *The Delhi that No-one Knows*, New Delhi: Chronicle Books, 2005.

Sainty, Sarah, *Lost Monuments of Delhi*, New Delhi: HarperCollins, 1997.

Spear, Thomas George Percival, *Delhi. Its Monuments and History*, Updated and Annotated by Narayani Gupta and Laura Sykes, Delhi: OUP 1994 (1st edn. 1943).

St. = Steingass, Francis Joseph, *A Comprehensive Persian-English Dictionary*, London, 1892 (repr. New Delhi: Manohar, 2006).

STCD = *Standard Twentieth Century Dictionary Urdu to English*, compiled by Bashir Ahmad Qureshi, revised and enlarged by Abdul Haq, New Edition, Delhi: Educational Publishing House, 1999 (1st edn. 1980).

Monuments of Delhi: Lasting Splendour of the Great Mughals and Others, vols. I-IV, comp. by Maulvi Zafar Hasan, edited by J.A. Page et al., New Delhi: Aryan Books International, 1997 (1st edn. 1916-20).

People

Zay Khay Sheen, Aligarh's purdah-nashin poet

Gail Minault

Zay Khay Sheen, or Zahida Khatun Sherwani (1894-1922),[1] was the younger daughter of Nawab Sir Muzammilullah Khan Sherwani, Rais of Bhikampur in the Aligarh district of North India.[2] Sir Muzammilullah (1865-1938) was an important figure in the Aligarh movement. A follower of Sir Sayyid Ahmad Khan, he was a leading member of the Board of Trustees of Aligarh College, a champion of turning Aligarh College into a University, and politically loyal to the British connection. He was also a

---

[1] There are two basic sources about Z-Kh-Sh, a biography written by her cousin: Anīsa Hārūn Begam Šervānī, *Ḥayāt-i-Z-X-Š* (Hyderabad: Privately Published, 1954); and her collected poems: Z-X-Š [Zāhida Xātūn Šervānī], *Firdaus-i-Taxayyul* (Lahore: Dar ul Ishāᶜat-i-Punjāb, 1941).

[2] Secondary sources about her poetry, in Urdu, include: Šān ul-Ḥaq Ḥaqqī, "Z-X-Š", [in:] *Nukta-i-Rāz* (Karachi: ᶜAsri Kutub, 1972), pp. 283-307; M. Jamīl Aḥmad, *Tazkirah-i-Šāᶜirat-i-Urdū* (Bareilly: Qaumī Kutub Xāna, 1944), pp. 407-35; and [Dr.] Fāṭima Ḥasan, *Z-X-Š: Ḥayāt o Shāᶜirī kā Taḥqīqī aur Tanqīdī Jāʾeza* (Karachi: Anjuman-i-Taraqqī-i-Urdū Pakistan, 2007).

skilful poet in Persian, and had a string of alphabetical honors following his title as Khan Bahadur: LLD, KCIE, OBE, etc.[3]

The Sherwani clan of Aligarh district was distinguished in educational circles and produced a number of important figures, Habibur Rahman Khan Sherwani, Nawab Habib Yar Jung, was an Islamic scholar and an official in Hyderabad. Harun Khan Sherwani was a well-known historian of the Deccan (his wife is the biographer of Z-Kh-Sh). The clan had two main branches, the lineage of Bhikampur and that of Datauli, and practiced cousin marriage to an almost exclusive degree. The family tree presents a bewildering array of interlocking relationships.[4]

The Sherwanis were a family, therefore, that displayed an intriguing combination of the progressive and the conservative: They were supporters of education, whether Islamic or western, and promoters of education for women, although the women of the family maintained strict purdah and were educated at home. Their loyalist politics were manifested in civic service and membership in reform associations, along with resistance to the growing forces of anti-British activism before and after World War I.[5] Their marriage patterns kept the family properties intact, while taking a toll on the health of their increasingly inbred offspring.[6]

Z-Kh-Sh was a product of this large and intellectually vibrant family. Her mother died when she was very young. Her father, consequently, had a major role in Zahida's education and that of her siblings: an older sister, Ahmadi,[7] and a younger

---

[3] N.K. Jain, *Muslims in India: A Biographical Dictionary* (New Delhi: Manohar, 1983), vol. II, pp. 80-1; for Sir Muzammilullah's role at Aligarh, see S.K. Bhatnagar, *History of the MAO College Aligarh* (Bombay: Asia Publishing House, 1969), pp. 147-81, 231, 255, 258-9, 266-8, 289, 313-14, 327, 334, 344, 351-2; and Gail Minault and David Lelyveld, "The Campaign for a Muslim University, 1898-1920", *Modern Asian Studies*, 8:2 (April 1974), pp. 145-89.

[4] Sherwani family tree as an appendix to Šervānī, *Ḥayāt-i-Z-X-Š*.

[5] See e.g., G. Minault, *The Khilafat Movement* (New York: Columbia University Press, 1982).

[6] This is a generalization based on references to mental illness and early deaths in *Ḥayāt-i-Z-X-Š*, and Šān ul-Ḥaq Ḥaqqī, "Z-X-Š".

[7] Ahmadi's daughter married the son of Harun Khan Sherwani and Anisa Begam (see family tree appended to *Ḥayāt-i-Z-X-Š*); Ahmadi suf-

brother, Ahmadullah.[8] Their education began with a Bismillah ceremony at age four, initiating them into learning the Quran with an Aligarh Maulvi, Hafiz Ahmad Ali.[9] Once they had read the Quran, Sir Muzammilullah wanted his daughters to learn Persian, the mark of a cultured literary education, and he cast about for a capable governess (*mu*ᶜ*allima*), whom he found in Bhopal – recommended by the Begam of Bhopal herself – an Iranian woman, known as Farkhunda Begam Teherani. She was not only a native speaker of Persian, but an accomplished poet who introduced her pupils to the craft of writing, as well as reading, poetry.[10]

What was not known to either the Begam of Bhopal or to Sir Muzammilullah at that time was that Farkhunda was an alias. The governess had changed her name from Rakhshanda Khanum and started a new life in India after she had left Tehran under obscure circumstances. A former concubine of Nasiruddin Shah Qajar, she had apparently fallen afoul of political factionalism at the Qajar court. She nevertheless maintained a correspondence and exchanged poetry with the Shah even in exile, letters discovered among her papers at the time of her death many years later.[11] Becoming a governess to a landed family in Aligarh district must have been quite an alteration in her lifestyle, to put it mildly. In the description of the instruction that she offered the Sherwani daughters, there is little hint of her colorful past, though one supposes that she opened their eyes to the classics of Persian poetry and give them glimpses of the world outside Aligarh. During this period of their education, the two sisters began writing poetry both in Persian and Urdu. At about the age of ten, Zahida expressed her ambition to become a well-known poet:

fered from mental illness at the end of her life. Šān ul-Ḥaq Ḥaqqī, "Z-X-Š", p. 301.

[8] Ahmadullah died young, in 1916. M. J. Aḥmad, *Tazkirah-i-Šā*ᶜ*irat-i-Urdū*, p. 430.

[9] *Ḥayāt-i-Z-X-Š*, p. 23.

[10] *Ibidem*, pp. 24-5.

[11] *Ibidem*.

Aisī banūṅ maiṅ shāᶜirah jaisī koī na ho
Sārā jahān naẓm merī dekhtā rahe.

May I become like no other poetess
That the whole world may know my verse.[12]

Sir Muzammilullah also wanted his three children to learn Islamic theology and good Urdu expository prose, and he thus engaged the services of Maulvi Muhammad Yaᶜqub Israᶜili, from the family of the Imam of the Jumᶜa Mosque of Aligarh and associated with the Ahl-i-Hadith movement.[13] So Zahida and her sister and brother had both a Persian governess with a romantic and literary background and an Ahl-i-Hadith maulvi as a tutor in Islamic thought – all this in the first decade or so of the twentieth century, a time when in Aligarh the movement for founding a girls' school and women's normal school and the renewed effort to turn Aligarh College into a Muslim University were occupying public attention and preoccupying their father.[14]

During this time, Z-Kh-Sh started writing verses and articles, and sent them off to various women's magazines and other literary periodicals: *Xātūn* of Aligarh, *ᶜIṣmat* of Delhi, *Šarīf Bībī* of Lahore, and others.[15] She also became the organizer and ringleader of her generation of Sherwani cousins, starting a "Young Sherwanis' League" that met periodically (sometimes monthly, but also bi-annually), elected officers (she was the Honorary Secretary), collected dues, and had a formal list of aims and ob-

[12] Šān ul-Ḥaq Ḥaqqī, "Z-X-Š", p. 304; *Ḥayāt-i-Z-X-Š*, p. 33.

[13] *Ḥayāt-i-Z-X-Š*, p. 29.

[14] G. Minault, "Shaikh Abdullah, Begam Abdullah and *Sharif* Education for Girls at Aligarh", [in:] Imtiaz Ahmad, ed., *Modernization and Social Change among Muslims in India* (New Delhi: Manohar, 1983), pp. 207-36; and G. Minault and D. Lelyveld, "The Campaign for a Muslim University", *Modern Asian Studies*, 8:2 (April 1974), pp. 145-89. Though a supporter of women's education, Sir Muzammilullah, like Sir Sayyid Ahmad Khan before him, opposed sending girls out of the house to school, as witness his careful supervision of his girls' home education.

[15] For Urdu women's magazines in this period, see G. Minault, *Secluded Scholars: Women's Education and Muslim Social Reform in Colonial India* (New Delhi: Oxford University Press, 1998), pp. 105-57.

jectives that included starting schools for the children of Bhikampur and Datauli, and donating money to the drive for a boarding house for Aligarh Girls' School.[16] This organization, with its officers, rules, and fundraising showed that the Sherwani women (sisters and cousins), though maintaining strict purdah, were well aware of the burgeoning number of educational and social *anjuman*-s [voluntary associations] that were so much a part of public life among North Indian Muslims at the time.[17]

During this time too, Z-Kh-Sh became concerned with the fate of Muslims elsewhere, and wrote *naẕm*-s about the Balkan and Tripolitan wars and the Kanpur Mosque incident. Aligarh was a center of an effort to put together a Red Crescent Medical Mission to aid Turkey during the Balkan wars of 1911-13, and such Muslim leaders as Muhammad Ali and Shaukat Ali, Dr. Mukhtar Ahmad Ansari, and Hakim Ajmal Khan visited Aligarh College to raise funds both for the university movement and for the support of Turkey. In 1913 also, the Kanpur Mosque incident brought religion and politics together even more explicitly in a direct confrontation between Muslim publicists and the government. Her father opposed this religio-political activity as anti-British and "extremist" and hence detrimental to the cause of the Muslim University Movement, but the younger male Sherwani cousins surely reported to their sisters and female cousins about the excitement that these public meetings were generating in Aligarh. In 1913, Z-Kh-Sh wrote a *naẕm*, *ᶜĪd kī xušī meṅ ġamzadegān-i-Kānpur* ["Written on the Festival of *ᶜĪd* in Memory of the Victims of Kanpur"] and sent it to the newspaper *Zamīndār* of Lahore, which was edited by the poet and political activist, Zafar Ali Khan.[18] A relative clipped the published version from the paper and mailed it to Zahida. Her father opened the letter and was furious, calling her an "extremist" and ordering

16 *Ḥayāt-i-Z-X-Š*, pp. 42-4.

17 For various social and educational *anjuman*-s in this period, see G. Minault, *Secluded Scholars*, pp. 158-214.

18 On Zafar Ali Khan's political poetry, see G. Minault, "Urdu Political Poetry during the Khilafat Movement", *Modern Asian Studies*, 8:4 (October 1974), pp. 459-71.

her to stop "cursing the government", as it put him in a very delicate position.[19]

Quite aside from the fact that no one who read her published poems knew who "Nuzhat" (her pen-name) was, nor for that matter, who Z-Kh-Sh (another frequent alias) was, Sir Muzammilullah need not have worried. Zahida loved her father very much and delighted in his approval of her literary gift, but was so afraid of his disapproval that she had hidden from him the fact that she was publishing her poetry. When her political views veered toward Muslim political causes, and even nationalism, she stepped across a line (even in seclusion) that he could not tolerate. She was so upset by his anger that she stopped writing altogether for a while. Eventually, she resumed publishing her poetry without telling him (though he may have suspected it), an act that showed her considerable courage, not to mention her desire for self-expression.

In 1916, her younger brother, Ahmadullah, died suddenly, depriving her – not only of a beloved sibling – but also of her eyes and ears on the current events in Aligarh and the surrounding territory. Thereafter, Z-Kh-Sh's poetry takes on a darker tone that characterized some of her best known works. An example of her mature work, relatively speaking (it was written in 1918, when she was 24), was *Sipās nāma-i-Urdū* ["In Praise of Urdu"]. It was written to honor the occasion of the inauguration of Osmania University in Hyderabad, the only institution of higher education in India that used Urdu as its medium of instruction. The poem was read out at the inauguration, and apparently no one knew that its author was a woman. An excerpt:[20]

Ek laᶜl hūṅ gudṛī meṅ,
Ek čand hūṅ badlī meṅ;
Ek ḥusn hūṅ dehatī,
Ek phūl hūṅ ṣeḥrāʾī.

---

[19] *Ḥayāt-i-Z-X-Š*, p. 99; also Šān ul-Ḥaq Ḥaqqī, "Z-X-Š", p. 301.

[20] Z-X-Š, *Firdaus-i-Taxayyul*, p. 219; translation by the present author.

Hai xāk meṅ zar madfun.
Hai baḥr meṅ durr maknūn;
Hai šama^{c} teh damān,
Hai dašt meṅ šehnā'ī.

Zindān meṅ kyuṅ Yūsuf;
Pinjre meṅ kyuṅ bulbul?
Ye kaunsī ḥikmat hai;
Ye kaunsī danā'ī?

I am a ruby wrapped in a rag,
The moon in its darkened phase;
I am a rustic beauty,
A flower in the wilderness.

As is gold buried in the dust.
Or a pearl lost in the sea;
A candle under a cover,
Or in a void, the song of the shahnai.

Why was Yusuf enchained?
Why the nightingale caged?
Who gave the order?
What wisdom so ordained?

In his discussion of Z-Kh-Sh's poetry, Shan ul-Haq Haqqi devotes several pages to an analysis of this work, praising its powerful imagery and the parallels the poet draws between the status of Urdu – marginalized, ignored, hidden from view – and the status of women in her society. He also commends her development of a distinctive voice in *Sipās nāma* that, given time, she might have developed more fully.[21]

Dutiful daughter though she was, Z-Kh-Sh was also a lively intellect, interested in the life and politics of her time, and an energetic organizer of her cousins in support of education for poor children and girls. The product of an enlightened (for its time) literary education, and yet hemmed in by family custom and paternal opprobrium, she never left the various Sherwani

[21] Šān ul-Ḥaq Ḥaqqī, "Z-X-Š", pp. 284-5.

compounds and never married (the cousin that was intended for her died young and there was no one else within the family of appropriate rank or fortune).[22] The lively optimism of her earliest couplet (cited above) was replaced by a gloomy awareness of women's marginal status in her later verse such as *Sipās nāma*.

Z-Kh-Sh died young, succumbing to an unspecified fever (possibly tuberculosis) on 2 February 1922, at the age of 27.[23] Sajjad Hyder "Yildiram"[24] remarked in a remembrance of Z-Kh--Sh, published in the women's magazine, *Tahzib un-Niswan* of 22 February 1924, that: "She was a nightingale, now silenced, who was born in a cage, lived her whole life in that cage, and there drew her last breath".

> *Voh ek ᶜandalīb thī jo qafaṣ meṅ pedā huī, qafaṣ hī meṅ thī, aur qafaṣ hī meṅ dam thoṛ diʾā.*[25]

A few weeks before she died, Z-Kh-Sh had decided to support the Gandhian *svadešī* movement, and was in the process of transforming her wardrobe in order to wear *khādī* and thus to demonstrate her adherence to the nationalist cause.[26] But unlike her published poetry, this form of support for nationalism would remain hidden behind the four walls of the Sherwani compound.

---

[22] *Ibidem*, pp. 299-300, citing *Ḥayāt-i-Z-X-Š*.

[23] *Ḥayāt-i-Z-X-Š*, p. 153.

[24] Sajjad Hyder, a well-known Urdu litterateur, was also the first Registrar of Aligarh University, and the father of Qurrat ul-ᶜAin Hyder, a leading modern Urdu novelist.

[25] *Ḥayāt-i-Z-X-Š*, pp. 156-7; also cited in Šān ul Ḥaq Ḥaqqī, "Z-X-Š", pp. 303-4.

[26] *Ibidem*, p. 153.

BIBLIOGRAPHY

Aḥmad, M. Jamīl, *Taẕkirah-i-Šāᶜirat-i-Urdū* (Bareilly: Qaumī Kutub Xāna, 1944), pp. 407-35.

Bhatnagar, S.K., *History of the MAO College Aligarh* (Bombay: Asia Publishing House, 1969).

Ḥaqqī, Šān ul-Ḥaq, "Z-X-Š", [in:] *Nukta-i-Rāz* (Karachi: ᶜAsri Kutub, 1972), pp. 283-307.

Ḥasan, Dr. Fāṯima, *Z-X-Š: Ḥayāt o Shāᶜirī kā Taḥqīqī aur Tanqīdī Jāʾeza* (Karachi: Anjuman-i-Taraqqī-i-Urdū Pakistan, 2007).

Jain, N.K., *Muslims in India: A Biographical Dictionary* (New Delhi: Manohar, 1983).

Lelyveld, David, *Aligarh's First Generation: Muslim Ṣolidarity in British India* (Princeton, NJ: Princeton University Press, 1978).

Minault, Gail, *The Khilafat Movement: Religious Symbolism and Political Mobilization in India* (New York: Columbia University Press, 1982).

____, *Secluded Scholars: Women's Education and Muslim Social Reform in Colonial India* (New Delhi: Oxford University Press, 1998).

____, "Shaikh Abdullah, Begam Abdullah and *Sharif* Education for Girls at Aligarh", [in:] Imtiaz Ahmad, ed., *Modernization and Social Change among Muslims in India* (New Delhi: Manohar, 1983), pp. 207-36.

____, "Urdu Political Poetry during the Khilafat Movement", *Modern Asian Studies*, 8:4 (October 1974), pp. 459-71.

____, and David Lelyveld, "The Campaign for a Muslim University, 1898-1920", *Modern Asian Studies*, 8:2 (April 1974), pp. 145-89.

Šervānī, Anīsa Hārūn Begam, *Ḥayāt-i-Z-X-Š* (Hyderabad: Privately Published, 1954).

[Šervānī, Zāhida Xātūn] Z-X-Š, *Firdaus-i-Taxayyul* (Lahore: Dar ul Ishāᶜat-i-Punjāb, 1941).

Jihādī literature? Some novels of Nasīm Ḥijāzī

Christina Oesterheld

In the wake of the Muslim political and social reform movements of the nineteenth century, evoking the Golden Age of Islam turned into one of the favourite topoi of Urdu writers who aspired to mobilize and consolidate the Muslim community. Starting with the novels of ᶜAbd ul-Ḥalīm Šarār (1860-1926) and the poetry of Alṭāf Ḥusain Ḥālī (1837-1914) and continued by Muḥammad Iqbāl (1877-1938), the glorious past was used as counter-image to the desolate present. Images of vigour, bravery, self-sacrifice and the glorification of martyrdom are stock features of these literary works. Many of the texts deal with the conquest of Andalusia, the age of the Crusades or the early years of Islam. These settings were later adopted by several writers, among them the novelist Nasīm Ḥijāzī who was to become one of the most popular authors of Urdu. His works are available with several online booksellers and in regular bookstores. The Jahāngīr Book Depot in Lahore alone carries 21 titles by the author, some of which have seen up to 40 print runs. In Pakistan several of his novels were turned into successful films and TV serials. A film based on the novel *Xāk aur xūn* (Dust and blood, 1974) dealing with a village in eastern Punjab during the partition period was produced in 1979. In this story Ḥijāzī incorporated experiences of his own family which had migrated to Pakistan in 1947. The serial based on *Āxrī čaṭān* which was produced by Pakistan TV in the mid-1980s became very popular and is among the most frequently visited sites on video.google.com.

Several of Ḥijāzī's most famous novels are available online free of charge. Thus, for instance, until June 2008 *Dāstān-i mujāhid* which was published digitally on 26 January 2006 had been viewed by 8.409 readers and downloaded by 5.505, and *Āxrī čaṭān* which had been published on 12 September 2006 had been viewed by 5.377 readers.[1] An MA thesis was written on two of Ḥijāzī's novels[2] and an MPhil thesis on Iqbal's influences on him,[3] and a PhD thesis on his novels was submitted to the University of Karachi in November 2007.[4] Several audio books are based on his stories. One English translation is available online.[5]

Notwithstanding all this, he is not part of the literary canon of Urdu literature, a fact that can be attributed to his popular appeal as much as to the ideological underpinnings of his works. When he is mentioned at all in histories of the Urdu novel, he is often – and rightly so – accused of catering to the popular taste with his mix of adventure and romance, of too much proselytizing[6] and of idealizing his characters.[7] The most enthusiastic re-

---

[1] Figures as given by Iršād ᶜĀlam in "Urdū nāval, inṭarnaiṭ aur mutavvaqaᶜ qārī", *Urdū dunyā*, 2008, nr. 10:6 (Naʾī Dihlī), p. 31. The digitalised novels can be read and downloaded at http://www.kitaabghar.com and others.

[2] Yūsuf Bušrā, *'Xāk aur xūn' aur 'Āxrī čaṭān' kā taḥqīqī jāʾiza*, University of Bahawalpur, 1983.

[3] Ṭāhira Nāz, Allama Iqbal Open University, 2001.

[4] Mumtāz ᶜUmar, *Nasīm Ḥijāzī kī tārīxī nāvalnigārī kā taḥqīqī aur tanqīdī jāʾiza.*

[5] *Qāfila-i Ḥijāz*, transl. by Mohammad A. Qayyum, http://www.qayyums.com/maq/kafla.doc.

[6] Cf. Vaqār ᶜAẓīm, *Dāstān se afsāne tak*, Karāčī: Urdū Akādemī Sindh, 1966, p. 168.

[7] Cf. Suhail Buxārī, *Urdū nāvalnigārī*, Lāhaur: Maktaba Merī Lāʾibrerī, 1966, p. 128.

views of his works are to be found in popular Urdu digests, particularly in *Siyāra Ḍāʾijasṭ*. Literary histories of Urdu in English usually do not mention authors of his kind, and if at all he is referred to, then as an example of a literature which constructs a past that entirely belongs to conquerors and invaders.[8]

Why then should one bother to deal with this author? Are the sheer amount, distribution and popularity of his works reason enough to consider him worthy of attention? I think so. Popular culture has come into the purview of academic research on a wide scale since the 1960s, and recently the realm of the popular has also attracted the interest of some historiographers.

Nasīm 'Ḥijāzī' was born as Muḥammad Šarīf in Sujanpur/ Distr. Gurdaspur (India) in 1914. His family traced its ancestry to the Arab Peninsula (*Ḥijāz*) which enabled him later to attach the *nisba* Ḥijāzī to his pen name Nasīm ('pleasant breeze'). In 1938 he did his BA in History from Islamia College, Lahore. In the same year he started his work as a journalist and editor of several newspapers and journals which he continued until old age. He was actively involved in the Pakistan movement and especially in the struggle for Balochistan's accession to Pakistan. In an interview he declared that he had been a Pakistani by birth, even before the idea of Pakistan was developed, because already as a child he experienced the discriminative behaviour of Hindus toward the 'impure' and had come to detest any notion of untouchability.[9] His biographer Taṣadduq Ḥusain Rājā describes him as motivated by two missions – to gain Pakistan and, after 1947, to work for the stability of Pakistan and the introduction of an Islamic order in the country.[10] In the preface to *Āxrī čaṭān* he declared:

> As tragic as what happened in East Punjab may be, as instructive it also is. We are entering a decisive phase in the history of India.

[8] Cf. Mubarak Ali, "How many Qasims, Ghaznavis, and Ghoris do we need?", http://www.insaf.net/pipermail/sacw_insaf.net/2000/000508.html

[9] Mumtāz ᶜUmar, *Nasīm Ḥijāzī kī tārīxī*, p. 72.

[10] Taṣadduq Ḥusain Rājā, *Nasīm Ḥijāzī. Ek muṭālaᶜa*, Lāhaur: Qaumī kutubxāna, 1987, p. 8.

> At this stage a right step can take us to the highest peak and a wrong step can take us to the deepest abyss. If we like, we can wash away the blood of the martyrs of Eastern Punjab with tears of helplessness, or we can write the brightest chapter of Pakistan's history with their blood's ink.[11]

He made it very clear at the outset that the historical events were closely linked to later developments and that they were meant to teach his contemporaries a lesson:

> *Āxrī čaṭān* is a mirror of our past, and seeing the contours of our present in this mirror we will be able to mend our future. Otherwise history demonstrates that nature (creation; divine power? Urdu: *qudrat*) will never forgive a nation's political mistakes.
>
> In *Āxrī čaṭān* I have presented those young men to you which shouldered the burden of the great edifice of Pakistan.[12]

Nasīm Ḥijāzī published his first short story in 1936 and completed his first novel, *Dāstān-i mujāhid* (The story of a warrior for Islam),[13] in 1938, but it could be published in 1943 only. The second novel *Muḥammad bin Qāsim*[14] was written and published in 1945 after the author had received many enthusiastic letters from readers of the first novel, urging him to write a follow-up.[15] In 1947 he completed *Āxrī čaṭān* (The last pillar/bastion). The

---

[11] "Mašriqī panjāb ke vaqiᶜāt jis qadar alamnāk haĩ, isī qadar sabaqāmūz bhī haĩ. ham hindūstān mẽ apnī tārix ke ek faiṣla kun marḥale mẽ dāxil ho čuke haĩ. is marḥale par ek ṣaḥīḥ qadam hamẽ auj-i ṣuraiyā tak aur ek ġalaṯ qadam taḥatu-'ṣ-ṣarā tak pahũčā saktā hai. agar ham čāhẽ to mašriqī panjāb ke šahīdõ kā xūn bebasī ke ā̃suʾõ se dho lẽ aur čāhẽ to is xūn kī rošnāʾī se pākistān kā rošantarīn bāb likh ḍālẽ", *Āxrī čaṭan* (*AČ*), online edition, http://www.scribd.com/doc/7391590/Aakhri-Chataan-Part1-by-Nasim-Hijazi, p. 3.

[12] "*Āxrī čaṭān* hamāri maẓī kā ek āʾīna hai aur is āʾīne mẽ ham apne ḥāl ke xad-o-xāl dekh kar apne mustaqbil ko sãvār sakte haĩ, varna tārīx šāhid hai ki qudrat kisī qaum kī siyāsī ġalaṯiyā̃ muᶜāf nahī̃ kartī.

Āxrī čaṭān mẽ qaum ke un nau javānõ ko peš kartā hū̃ jinhõ ne apne kandhõ par pākistān kī ᶜaẓīmu-'š-šān taᶜmīr kā bojh uṭhāyā hai", *AČ*, p. 4.

[13] *DM*, Lāhaur: Jahāngīr Buk Ḍipo, 2005.

[14] *MbQ*, Lāhaur: Jahāngīr Buk Ḍipo, 2005.

[15] Preface to *MbQ*, p. 8.

present analysis will be based on these three novels as well as on his most ambitious and voluminous work *Qaiṣar-o-Kisrā* (The Emperors of Rome and Persia)[16] which was published in 1964. He completed this project after five years of writing, studying historical sources and travelling to the sites of the action. In an interview for Radio Pakistan he remarked: "The best moments of my life where those which I spent writing *Qaiṣar-o-Kisrā*".[17] He produced several more novels, often triggered off by contemporary events such as the secession of East Pakistan or the Soviet invasion of Afghanistan. His last novel which contained some autobiographical references appeared in 1991 under the title *Gumšuda qāfile* (Lost caravans).

A short outline of the four selected novels

The story of *Dāstān-i mujāhid* starts in the vicinity of Basra in the year 75 AH (694-5 CE). We watch the main protagonist Naᶜīm (= the *mujāhid* of the title) grow up into a brave soldier who is fully dedicated to the idea of *jihād* (holy war) and readily joins Muhammad bin Qāsim's campaign in Sindh. After a number of intrigues, fights and battles in Sindh, Turkistan and Spain, he finally kills his arch enemy Ibn-i Ṣādiq and returns fatally wounded to his village where he dies after instructing his son, nephew and grandson to continue the holy war. This fictional story is embedded in the historical setting of the Muslim campaigns under Valīd bin ᶜAbdu'l Malik (86-96 AH, 705-15 CE) and Sulaimān (96-9 AH, 715-17 CE). The eminent Muslim conquerors Muḥammad bin Qāsim and Qutaiba bin Muslim appear in some decisive battle scenes, but do not occupy the centre stage of the action.

Muḥammad bin Qāsim in a way is a sequence to the first novel, but, as the title suggests, here the focus is on the famous conqueror of Sindh who was recalled from India by Sulaimān and cruelly put to death in an act of revenge. The alleged cause of the campaign against King Dāhir of Sindh (92/3-6 AH, 711-15 CE), the abduction of Arab ships by Sindhi pirates, is dealt with

[16] *QK*, Lāhaur: Ḥijāzī Sanz, 1964.

[17] Taṣadduq Ḥusain Rājā, *Nasīm Ḥijāzī*, p. 307.

in great detail and provides the backdrop to the ensuing action. These passages are used to introduce a range of fictional characters who actually occupy more space than the hero of the novel. Special attention is given to the treachery and injustice with which the Sindhi rulers treat not only their Arab and Sri Lankan captives, but also their Sindhi subjects.

Āxrī čaṭān is based on the failure of the Abbasid Empire in Baghdad to unite forces with Khwarezm Shah to defeat the advancing Mongolian forces under Chengiz Khan and his successors which not only leads to the end of the Khwarezmid Empire but finally also paves the way for the gruesome sacking of Baghdad by Mongolian troops in 1258. In the centre of the novel are the Khwarezmid Sultan Jalālu-'d-Dīn and two Arabs (Ṭāhir bin Yūsuf and ᶜAbdu-'l-Malik) who are dedicated to Muslim unity and try to convince the caliph at Baghdad to come to the rescue of the Khwarezmid Empire because it is the "last bastion" (*āxrī čaṭān*, literally "last rock") of Islam against the Mongolian tide. But despite all their efforts, the caliph prefers to side with the Mongolians instead of supporting his Muslim rival. Sultan Jalālu-'d-Dīn is not able to save his empire and finally sets out alone from his camp to seek an honourable death. Ṭāhir bin Yūsuf and ᶜAbdu-'l-Malik find refuge in India where they serve the Delhi Sultan Iltutmish. Ṭāhir dedicates the last years of his life to his ultimate mission: the spreading of Islam.

Qaiṣar-o-Kisrā is a much more complex novel. The action is situated against the backdrop of the war between the Eastern Roman and the Sassanid Empires (602-30 CE). In the beginning the author draws a picture of Arab society which is torn by tribal rivalries, feuds and bloody revenge. The main protagonist ᶜĀsim tries in vain to put an end to the enmity between his and a rival tribe. After killing some of his own relatives he becomes an outcast and has to run away. He gets involved into the fights between the East Roman and Persian rulers and witnesses the bloodshed on the battlefield, the atrocities against civilians and the murderous intrigues of different contenders for power. These experiences make him long for peace and justice. He dreams of a just, merciful and truly humane ruler and a new Messiah. After many adventures and dramatic twists and turns ᶜĀsim marries a noble Christian girl and settles down in Constantinople. When he hears of the rule of Islam on the Arabian Peninsula, he embraces Islam, returns home and then joins the Muslim troops which are advancing against Damascus. He is convinced that the triumph of Islam will finally bring peace and a just rule to the whole region.

The general structure of the books

Nasīm Ḥijāzī wanted to reach out to a broad public, in particular to juvenile (male) readers. Commercial success was not his (primary?) concern. He was driven by a sense of mission which is corroborated by his journalistic writings. But to bring his messages home, he had to capture the readers and to uphold their interest. Hence he adopted some of the narrative strategies of his predecessors, albeit in a more sophisticated form. While his first two novels are still clumsy and tedious at places, his later work reveals somewhat refined literary techniques and highly developed stylistic devices.

The narratives usually progress chronologically with only a few flashbacks. Common to all books is an omniscient, impersonal narrator who occasionally also comments upon the events and provides historical information. The amount of such factual information is much greater in *Qaiṣar-o-Kisrā* than in the previous books. These passages deal not only with historical facts, but also with different ideologies and religious belief systems which are commented upon from the perspective of the author. With 736 pages, a great number of locations and characters and a good deal of ideological-philosophical musings, it is Nasīm Ḥijāzī's most ambitious novel and simultaneously the only book in which Muslims play only a marginal role in the action. They mostly appear as points of reference, as embodiments of the vision of a better world order.

All books under discussion have brave, courageous and righteous heroes who either are Muslims right from the start or embrace Islam in the course of the action. Most villains are non-Muslims, but there are a few exceptions to this rule, especially in *Muḥammad bin Qāsim* and *Āxrī čaṭān*. To create suspense and to save the course of the action from getting too predictable, the author had to construct a number of intrigues, unexpected turns and incredible coincidences. Not less incredible changes of heart are often needed to convey the right message, e.g. the overwhelming attraction of Islam which is exemplified by the conversion to Islam of Christian, Hindu or Buddhist characters.

Moments of great tension and dramatic action alternate with romantic episodes which, however, are brief and very chaste. Familial relations and love stories not only create the necessary amount of human interest and relief from the dramatic scenes. They are an indispensable part of the message in so far as they illustrate the right conduct in all forms of human relationships.

Despite the dramatic titles and the central role of heroic adventures, battle scenes are not depicted in graphic detail. In the first three novels, events on the battlefield are mostly summed up in a few sentences. *Qaiṣar-o-Kisrā* presents the horrors of war in much more detail, but here this was necessary to bring the message home.[18]

Short soliloquies are designed to allow insights into the character's feeling and thinking, but overall a third-person-narrative dominates. Dialogues are usually presented in the "modern" style, i.e. with the usual introductory phrases which were mostly absent in the "dramatic" dialogue style of most Urdu and Hindi novels of the late nineteenth century. The "dramatic style" is more evident only in *Āxrī čaṭān*. Indirect speech hardly ever occurs. Most characters are highly idealized or demonized stereotypes, but some of the main protagonists are depicted in more detail, undergo a change in the course of the novel and are less one-dimensional. The best example in this regards is ᶜĀsim.

The central ideas of the novels are conveyed predominantly through the actions, speeches, sermons and dialogues of the protagonists, to a lesser degree through commentaries of the narrator. Teaching through example and sermonizing thus complement each other. Occasionally we also find counter-arguments

[18] The proclaimed decadence of East Rome and Persia is demonstrated by the immoral and cruel conduct of their leadership. This is a common motif in Muslim literature on the period; cf. Jan-Peter Hartung, *Viele Wege und ein Ziel. Leben und Wirken von Sayyid Abū l-Ḥasan ᶜAlī al-Ḥasanī Nadwī*, Würzburg: Ergon Verlag, 2004, p. 132.

voiced by a character which are then refuted by another character (e.g. on the question of *jihād*), or inner conflicts expressed in inner monologues (e.g. Na^c^īm's dilemma concerning his relation with a girl whom he loves and who loves him, but who is to marry his brother). There is a good deal of repetition of the main teachings and the narrative patterns which, however, seems to have been happily tolerated by Ḥijāzī's admirers.

The language of the novels is laconic and matter-of-fact in the summarized reports of action, but highly emotional and metaphorical in those dialogues, speeches and letters which deal with the Islamic mission, Muslim bravery, the role of Muslim women, *jihād* and martyrdom. Here the author uses a number of conventional metaphors and images of Urdu poetry, albeit in a very stereotyped way throughout all the novels. The appeals for Muslim unity, courage, self-sacrifice which are voiced in speeches, Friday sermons and dialogues in the various novels are very repetitive. Nasīm Ḥijāzī time and again uses the same limited, but obviously powerful, repertoire of concepts and images.

Unlike most popular novels in Western languages, popular Urdu novels do not necessarily have a happy ending. Nasīm Ḥijāzī's books often end with the death of the main protagonist(s), but death in *jihād* is the guarantee of eternal life. Commenting on the smile of a dying Muslim hero, the narrator therefore remarks: "That smile which is bestowed only on those who are martyred in the way of God".[19] And when Ṯāhir condoles the grandmother of a young man on the death of her son, she replies: "He didn't die, he became a martyr/he was martyred".[20]

The image of Islam and Muslims in the three novels

It has to be noted right at the outset that Ḥijāzī does not present any new or original concept of Islam but is very close to the con-

---

[19] "vah muskurāhaṭ jo ṣirf xudā kī rāh mẽ šahīd honevālõ ko naṣīb ho saktī hai", *AČ*, p. 28.

[20] "vah marā nahī̃, šahīd huā hai", *AČ*, p. 260.

cepts of Maulānā Abū 'l-ᶜAlā Maudūdī (1903-79).[21] What concerns us here is how he transmits these concepts in his novels.

1. The concept of *jihād*

The dominant feature of the first three novels is the call for *jihād* (holy war).[22] The very titles of the books point to this central theme. *Jihād* here means armed fight for the supremacy of Islam. In *Dāstān-i mujāhid* a small boy who plays with a wooden sword tells his mother: "«I need a sword of steel. Get me one! I will go for *jihād*». Only those mothers can understand the joy of a mother on hearing these words of her little son who used to sing their sweethearts into sleep with the following lullaby: «O Lord of the Kaaba, let my dear son grow into a *mujāhid* and let his youthful blood water the tree planted by your beloved (Prophet)!»".[23] The *mujāhids* set out to invade foreign territories in the name of Islam. But, as the narrator stresses, their aim is not to conquer or oppress other people.[24] They come as "liberators" from unjust rule, oppression, discrimination and social inequal-

---

[21] When asked about influences on him, Ḥijāzī once replied: "If I may compare my literature to a stream of clear water, then I will have to admit that ᶜAllāma Iqbāl and Maulānā Maudūdī were the shores who kept me free from pollution and provided direction to my flow, and Maulānā Šiblī Nuᶜmānī showed me the fascinating glimpses of Islamic history which lent colour to my stories". Taṣadduq Ḥusain Rājā, *Nasīm Ḥijāzī...*, p. 339. Hijazi maintained close family relations with Maudūdī who is reported to have suggested the names of his two grandsons. Cf. Mumtāz ᶜUmar, *Nasīm Ḥijāzī kī tārīxī...*, p. 96.

[22] For the use of the concept of *jihād* on the Subcontinent in the nineteenth century, cf. Annemarie Schimmel, *Islam in the Indian Subcontinent*, Leiden: Brill, 1980, pp. 181-2, 209.

[23] "«...mujhe lohe kī talvār čahiye. Le do nā. maĩ jihād par jā'ũgā!» Kamsin beṭe ke mũh se jihād kā lafẓ sunne kī xušī vahī mā'ẽ jān saktī haĩ jo apne jigar ke ṭukṛõ ko lorī dete waqt yah gāyā kartī haĩ: Ai, rab-i kaᶜba! merā yah lāl mujāhid bane aur tere maḥbūb ke lagā'e hu'e daraxt ko javānī ke xūn se serāb kare", *DM*, pp. 9-10.

[24] Thus, when a Sindhi queen compares Muḥammad bin Qāsim with Alexander, he replies, that Alexander came as an emperor who wanted to subjugate people, whereas he (MbQ) does not believe in the rule of human emperors on God's earth (*maĩ xudā kī zamīn par insān kī bādšāhat se munkir hũ*), *MbQ*, p. 352.

ity. *Jihād* is thus inseparably linked to the proclaimed ideals of Islam: equality (*musāvāt*), the rule of God as against the despotism of human rulers, a new morality, and peace.[25]

These novels were written at the height of the struggle for Pakistan as a separate homeland for South Asian Muslims. There was considerable resistance to this concept in the territories on the Western fringes of British India (NWFP, Balochistan). Nasīm Ḥijāzī intended his books as a contribution to mobilize the Muslim youth to take part in the struggle. To this end, he on the one hand celebrated the spirit of sacrifice and the heroism of the *mujāhidīn* while at the same time stressing the noble aims of the struggle and suggesting a bright future in the envisaged Islamic state. Hence the promise of justice, egalitarianism, exemplary moral standards and "good governance" in an Islamic order. Thus, while agitating for *jihād* Naᶜim reminds his fellow Muslims; "It is our obligation to take the message of our beloved Prophet to every country of the world and to enact the law he brought with him among all peoples because this is the law that can establish equality between weak and strong nations and reinstall the oppressed and destitute people in their rights".[26] To fur-

[25] Addressing his troops, MbQ says: "The people of Sindh, who for years have been burning in the fire of cruelty and oppression, are waiting for those clouds of mercy from the western horizon which several years ago cooled down the fire temple of Iran. From their wounded breasts emanates the cry: «Oh let the warriors who with their blood watered the plant/sapling of equality, justice and peace in the garden of Adam snatch the sword of tyranny from the hands of the Sindhi ruler and let their horses trample down the thornbushes in which the sail of humanity and freedom is entangled»". (...sindh ke ᶜavām jo barsõ se ẕulm-o-istibdād kī āg mẽ jal rahe haĩ, ufaq-i maġrib se raḥmat kī un ghaṭāʾõ ke muntaẕir haĩ, jo āj se kaʾī baras pahle ātiškada-i īrān ko ṭhanḍā kar čukī haĩ. un ke majrūḥ sīnõ se yah āvāz nikal rahī hai ki e kāš! vah mujāhidīn jinhõ ne apne xūn se bāġ-i ādam mẽ musāvāt, ᶜadal aur inṣāf aur aman ke paudhe kī ābyārī kī hai, sindh ke ḥukmrān ke hāthõ se ẕulm kī talvār čhīn lẽ aur un ke ghoṛe un xārdār jhāṛiyõ ko masal ḍālẽ, jin ke sāth insāniyat aur āzādī kā dāman uljhā huā hai.) *MbQ*, p. 252.

[26] "Hamārā yah farẕ hai ki ham apne āqā aur maulā kā paiġām dunyā ke har mulk mẽ pahũčā dẽ aur jo qānūn vah apne sāth lāʾe the, dunyā ke tamām insānõ par nāfiẕ kar dẽ, kyõki yahī vah qānūn hai jis kī badaulat dunyā kī kamzor aur ṭāqatvar aqvām musāvāt ke ek vasīᶜ dāʾira mẽ lāʾī jā

ther highlight this progressive mission, Ḥijāzī went to considerable length to paint the despotic rule of King Dāhir and his allies in Sindh in the cruellest possible manner. This narrative can be interpreted as a warning about the future prospects of Indian Muslims under the rule of a Hindu majority. Social inequality, the discrimination of lower casts and "untouchables" and the concept of "impurity" are depicted as central features of Hindu society. Moreover, there is no adequate sense of shame and modesty which is amply demonstrated by the way in which Hindu women dress. Similarly, the atrocities committed by the Mongolian invaders of Muslim territories which are depicted in *Āxrī čaṭān* in a way mirror the horrors of the partition period in Eastern Punjab and are professedly used as a warning for contemporary Muslims.

Nasīm Ḥijāzī was by no means the first to call for *jihād* in the Indian independence movement. Abūl Kalām Āzād (1888-1958), the most prominent "nationalist" Muslim who opposed the Two-Nation-Theory, refashioned the theory of *jihād* in view of the aggressive expansion of European powers to legitimize modern anti-colonial struggles.[27] He "grasped the wider ethical meanings of *jihād* to make a forceful case for fighting colonial injustices".[28] "Following earlier scholars of Islam, Āzād identified three kinds of *jihād*: 1) verbal proclamations commanding good and prohibiting wrong, 2) giving property and goods for the cause and 3) the actual waging of war and fighting (*qital*)".[29] He propagated the concept of *jihād* in his Urdu weekly *Al-Hilāl* (The Crescent) which was read by Muslims in Bengal, the United Provinces and Punjab until it was closed down by the British in November 1914. "Article after article extolled the gallant Muslims resisting European aggression in the charred and bloodied

saktī haĩ jis kī badaulat maẕlūm-o-bekas insān apne kho'e hu'e ḥuqūq vāpas le sakte haĩ", *DM*, p. 67.

[27] Cf. Ayesha Jalal, "Striking a Just Balance: Maulana Azad as a Theorist of Trans-National *Jihad*", *Modern Intellectual History* 2007, nr. 4:1, pp. 95-107.

[28] *Ibidem*, p. 96.

[29] *Ibidem*, p. 100.

battlefields of Tripoli and the Balkans".[30] He dreamt of a united Muslim front under the Ottoman *xalīfa*. Āzād believed that "non-peaceful actions are needed for the sake of peace".[31] Āzād also reminded Muslims that "while others were masters of their own lives, the lives of Muslims were the property of God",[32] hence it was only natural to sacrifice these lives in the name of God.

Āzād explained the difference between temporary warfare/ political war (*ḥarb*) and *jihād*: While the first were waged to subjugate and slaughter people, or fought against people who broke treaties etc. (political wars of the Prophet), *jihād* was the direct opposite, fought with the purpose of establishing peace, tranquillity, and freedom.[33] Hence, "the true *jihādī* is moderate in his treatment of the vanquished and thinks only of winning God's favour".[34] The same arguments are again and again repeated in Nasīm Ḥijāzī's books. With Āzād he shared the strong belief in the ethical superiority of Islam. The rule of Islam is to be established to eradicate all causes for war and to attain a stable peace. However, like Āzād he, too, does not endorse the indiscriminate killing of non-Muslims, which is not sanctioned by Islam. The basic difference in their application of the concept of *jihād* is the attitude towards Hindus. Āzād in his presidential address to the Khilafat conference at Agra in 1921 stated that Muslims should fight for the removal of the illegitimate British government in India by uniting with their Hindu countrymen[35]. This stance was also advocated by the ᶜAlī brothers. "Referring to the Prophet's constitution at Medina in which Muslims and non-Muslims were

---

[30] *Ibidem*, p. 97.

[31] *Ibidem*, p. 99.

[32] *Ibidem*, p. 103.

[33] *Ibidem*; in Ḥijāzī's words: "We want safety and peace for ourselves and for all mankind, and the only way to peace in this world is Islam. This is the faith which extinguishes the differences between master and slave, black and white, Arab and Persian" (ham apnī salāmatī aur apne sāth dunyā ke tamām insānõ kī salāmatī čāhte haĩ aur xudā kī zamīn par salāmatī kā rāsta ṣirf islām hai. yah vah dīn hai, jo dunyā se āqā aur ġulām, gore aur kāle, ᶜarabī aur ᶜajmī kī tamīz miṭātā hai), *MbQ*, p. 332.

[34] *Ibidem*.

[35] *Ibidem*, p. 105.

described as one nation, Āzād asked Muslims to perform their religious duty by uniting with the Hindus".[36]

In contrast to this stance, Abū 'l-ᶜAlā Maudūdī in his book *Jihād fi'l Islām* (Jihād in Islam, 1927) identified the Hindus as the main enemies of Islam. When Nasīm Ḥijāzī started to write his novels, the Khilafat movement had long ended, and in 1940 the Two-Nation-Theory had become the basis for the Pakistan resolution of the Muslim League which demanded autonomy for areas with a Muslim majority. It seems that Ḥijāzī, who was a staunch supporter of Maudūdī, took the end of colonial rule more or less for granted and concentrated his efforts on the struggle for a separate statehood for Indian Muslims.

But although Ḥijāzī repeatedly stresses *jihād* as a duty for every (male) Muslim and mentions the reward for sacrificing one's life in the name of God in his novels,[37] it would be wrong to conclude that he wanted to call his fellow Muslims to arms against the Hindus. His purpose was political – to obtain a separate state for Indian Muslims where they would be able to establish a polity in accordance with the injunctions of *Qur'ān* and Ḥadīṣ. This view is in line with Maudūdī's "governance-oriented" concept[38] according to which the extrovert juridical aspect of religion is more important than the introvert spiritual dimension – although it has to be kept in mind that Maudūdī originally opposed the idea of separate statehood for South Asian Muslims. But Ḥijāzī fully agrees with Maudūdī as far as the question of an Islamic state as the basis for a truly Islamic way of life is concerned. Many statements by characters or the narrators of his novels confirm this stance. Thus the narrator comments on the situation of Baghdad under the late Abbasids in the thirteenth century where religious matters are left to the disputing, hair-

36 *Ibidem*, p. 106.

37 E.g., in *MbQ*, p. 337: "The blood of martyrs washes away all their sins" (šahīdõ kā xūn un ke tamām gunāh dho detā hai), or: "For a Muslim it is the greatest fortune/the most auspicious moment to die as a martyr for God" (musalmān ke liye zindagī kī sab se baṛī saᶜādat yah hai ki vah xudā kī rāh mẽ šahīd ho jā'e), *QK*, p. 731.

38 Cf. A.A. Maudūdī, *Al jihād fi'l islām*, Dihlī: Markazī maktaba-i islāmī, 1995 [1927], pp. 92-104.

splitting factions of the *ᶜulamā*: "This divide between politics and religion was the greatest cause of *fitna* (revolt, unrest) in Islam".[39]

There is much stress on the military aspect of Muslim power throughout all of Ḥijāzī's novels. Military leaders very often appear as the sole saviours of Islam as against the corrupt, decadent and cowardly civilian rulers. This tendency is very pronounced in *Āxrī čaṭān* where an old man says to a younger: "How fortunate is a nation whose men play with swords in their youth and in their old days are proud to take the horses of the younger generation by their reigns to lead them to the field of *jihād*!",[40] and where the heroine tells the hero: "Nobody can bring down the banner of a nation (*qaum*) which has warriors like you!".[41] Moreover, the unifying effect of military campaigns is stressed: "History is a witness that whenever Muslims left their homes to go for conquests, they never engaged in unnecessary mind-boggling about religious persuasions".[42]

Despite all the *jihād* rhetoric, there is not a single case of forced conversion in any of the novels. Outside military combat, not a single "infidel" is killed. The supremacy of Islam is constituted to create conditions for an implementation of Islamic ideals, but all conversions are inspired by the good example of the Muslim characters or by peaceful proselytizing, as done in India by Ṭ̈āhir in *Āxrī čaṭān*. Usually, these voluntary conversions are preceded by living with Muslims over a certain stretch of time, observing their daily lives and getting instructions from them about the basic tenets and injunctions of Islam. Thus the Muslim protagonists convince non-Muslims of the social and ethical superiority of the new faith by their own example and by religious instruction. Their words and deeds are in full accord.

---

[39] "siyāsat aur maẓhab kī yah taqsīm Islām ke liye sab se baṛā fitna thā", *AČ*, p. 42.

[40] "xuš baxt hai vah qaum jis ke afrād javānī mẽ talvārõ se khelte haĩ aur buṛhāpe mẽ apne baččõ ke ghoṛõ kī bāg pakaṛ kar unhẽ jihād kā rāsta dikhāte haĩ", *AČ*, p. 13.

[41] "jis qaum ko āp jaise sipāhī naṣīb hõ, us kā jhanḍā koʾī ṭ̤āqat sar nigũ nahĩ kar saktā", *AČ*, p. 241.

[42] "tārīx gavāh hai ki jis zamāne mẽ bhī musalmān futūḥāt kā šauq le kar gharõ se nikle, un mẽ iᶜtiqādāt ke bāre mẽ kabhī sar phaṭuval na huʾī", *AČ*, p. 59.

2. Ethics

In the *Qur'ān*, Muslims are expected to eradicate instability and injustice and to establish a just and virtuous society. This is a vision which the heroes of Nasīm Ḥijāzī's novels try to implement wherever they have their way. The best illustration of these principles is the conduct of Muḥammad bin Qāsim after his victory in Sindh. He is depicted as a paragon of magnanimity, tolerance, benevolence, human sympathy, and justice. Thus, he personally looks after wounded soldiers of the enemy, dresses their wounds and releases them into freedom once they are cured. He strongly prohibits any killing, plundering or molesting of women in the areas under his control. His behaviour stands in stark contrast to that of the Sindhi ruler whom he has displaced. Despite his glorious victories, his youth and his popularity, he remains utterly selfless and modest. And as a true, obedient soldier he obeys the order of Sulaimān though he knows that this will be his death sentence. He would have had all opportunity and means to escape, but he readily accepts his fate and refuses to rebel against the order of the caliph who, howsoever evil he may be, to him represents the sacred institution of *xilāfat* which he will serve to his last breath. Moreover, he hopes that this painful experience will teach Muslims a lesson and will lead to the election of a better caliph in the future.[43]

Nasīm Ḥijāzī, no doubt, added fictional details to the story, but as a whole he remained truthful to the historical character. With the stunning record of his conquests at a very young age, the reports of his exemplary conduct and his popularity among his own troops as well as the ordinary people of Sindh, Muḥammad bin Qāsim already had everything a legendary hero needed. A light touch here and there and some amount of exaggeration were sufficient to turn him into an exemplary leader. His tragic, premature end only adds to the fascination for this character.

Here we come across an important contradiction: Sulaimān is obviously wrong in his treatment of Muḥammad bin Qāsim, is unjust and acts against the wider interests of the Muslim community/polity, but Muḥammad bin Qāsim obeys his orders for the

---

[43] *MbQ*, p. 385.

sake of the unity of the empire and (temporary) political stability, thus holding the sanctity of the office of the *xalīfa* more important than the principles of right and wrong, just and unjust. This can be regarded as primacy of the political over the ethical principle. In this context it is important to note that Ḥijāzī strongly advocated a democratic process in the election of the *xalīfa* and denounced hereditary kingship as un-Islamic.[44] In the same vein, and following Maudūdī, he supported Fatima Jinnah in her candidacy against General Ayub in 1956 and condemned the military takeover by Ayub in 1958.

The conspicuous moral deficiencies of some Muslim leaders who appear in his works, most prominent among them the tyrannical Ḥajjāj bin Yūsuf, point to a lack of individual spiritual and moral perfection which Maudūdī's adversary Abū'l Ḥasan ᶜAlī al-Ḥasanī Nadvī (1914-99) deemed necessary for the mission of Islam. Nadvī saw "Islam as guidance for the whole humanity (and not just a social system for Muslims) and the individual (not the political domain) as the main target of the prophet's task".[45] This aspect is to some degree implemented in Ḥijāzī's exemplary "good guys", but it is inadvertently linked with the political supremacy of Muslims which is time and again stressed as the precondition for moral perfection and social harmony.

Another important topic is the interaction between women and men. All Muslim protagonists are shown to be without greed and lust. They never look at girls and women, but always lower the eyes when they encounter a female. Thus, the inhabitants of Debal (the then capital of Sindh) are astonished to see that the Muslim troops which have conquered the town cross the bazaars with their eyes cast down.[46] Girls and women are instructed to

---

[44] His view of democracy obviously corresponded to that of Maudūdī's "theo-democracy" (*ilāhī jumhūrī ḥukūmat*); cf. Jan-Peter Hartung, "Gottesstaat versus Kemalismus. Eine islamische Reaktion auf Mušarrafs Putsch in Pakistan", *Religion-Staat-Gesellschaft* 2000, nr. 1: 1, pp. 84-90.

[45] Ahmed Mukarram, "Some Aspects of Contemporary Islamic Thought: Guidance and Governance in the Work of Mawlana Abul Hasan Ali Dadwi abd Mawlana Abul Aala Mawdudi", PhD thesis, University of Oxford, 1992, p. 210.

[46] *MbQ*, p. 310.

stay away from men as far as possible, to cover their bodies and faces and to stick to "female/feminine" occupations.

Modesty is taught in all walks of life. The protagonists dress modestly, enjoy simple food, and denounce pomp and show. They prefer simple marriage ceremonies. Extravagant wedding parties, dowries and gifts are strongly discouraged – well in line with the teachings of reform Islam. Another quality which is time and again mentioned with regard to the Muslims – men and women alike – is dignity or acute sense of honour.[47] For the sake of adventure and romance, however, under the extraordinary circumstances of war Muslim girls are shown to come out of the confines of their houses and to meet male Muslim strangers. Otherwise there could be no love stories in the novels! But even on the battlefield, in hiding or under other untoward conditions, the Muslim heroes and heroines never trespass the boundaries of decency and morality. Their relationships have always to be sanctioned by marriage before they can become united.[48]

3. Culture and spirituality

Ḥijāzī's Islam is extremely austere. Singing, music and dance are strictly prohibited. These rules are established in an episode of *Dāstān-i mujāhid* where the Muslim protagonist Naᶜīm is saved and nursed back to health by Tartar tribesmen after he had been wounded on the battlefield. He is shocked to notice that men and women of the tribe mix freely and even sing and dance together. He starts to instruct the young girl who has nursed him (and fallen in love with him in the process) in the basic tenets of Islam and teaches her to behave bashfully and modestly, that is, he installs in her a sense of shame which she had been lacking. Similar patterns are followed in many other cases throughout the novels.

All Muslims in Ḥijāzī's books strictly observe the five daily prayers. They draw all inspiration form the *Qurʾān* as the word

---

47 In Urdu the adjective *ġayyūr* (high minded, very jealous in point of honour) is used.

48 It should be noted that ᶜAbd ul-Ḥalīm Šarār was not so particular about pre-marital relations in his historical novels!

of God. Their unshakable trust in God helps them to endure all hardships and tribulations and takes away the fear of death.[49]

The trust in God, however, does not relieve man from his individual and collective responsibility. Thus Muḥammad bin Qāsim exhorts his troops before the attack on Brahmanabad (Sindh): "The rewards of the Almighty are only for those nations who have coloured every page of their history with the blood of their martyrs".[50] In contrast to many contemporary Muslim ideologues, the characters and the narrator in the books under discussion do not blame others for the failures of Muslims. All defeats, problems and schisms are created by Muslims – either out of incompetence, ignorance and lack of faith or out of jealousy and greed for power.

Every Muslim is shown to have direct access to the word of God. There is no need for intermediaries. Mullahs and Maulavis, the traditional interpreters of the scriptures, come in for a lot of criticism. The main reason for this negative attitude is the divisive nature of their teachings. They are accused of having split the Muslims, thus weakening the Muslim community and playing into the hands of their enemies. Thus, Ṯāhir rebukes the representatives of the five warring factions (*firqa*-s) in Baghdad: "Don't tell me the theoretical problems which you have not been able to agree upon for the last five hundred years".[51]

---

[49] "The first condition for the faith of a Muslim is that he does not fear death..." (ek musalmān ke īmān kī pahlī šarṯ yah hai ki vah maut se na ḍare...) *MbQ*, p. 174. The outstanding Muslim commander Qutaiba bin Muslim says when asked about the extraordinary courage of Muslims: "...we don't fear death. Death for us is the message of a higher/elevated life. Once a person has developed the wish to live for Allah and the resolve to die for Allah, his heart will know no fear, not even of the biggest might" (...ham maut se nahī̃ ḍarte. maut hamāre liye ek aᶜlā zindagī kā payām hai. Allāh ke liye zinda rahne kī tamannā aur allāh ke liye marne kā ḥauṣla paidā karne ke baᶜd kisī šaxṣ ke dil mẽ baṛī se baṛī ṯāqat kā xauf nahī̃ rahtā), *DM*, p. 140.

[50] "Qudrat ke inᶜāmāt ṣirf un aqvām ke liye haĩ jin kī tārīx kā har ṣafḥa šahīdõ ke xūn se raṅgīn hai", *MbQ*, p. 333.

[51] "mere sāmne vah masāʾil bayān na kījiye jin par āp pā̃nč ṣadiyõ mẽ mutaffiq nahī̃ ho sake", *AČ*, p. 60.

Mystic elements in Islam are either not mentioned at all, or appear in a negative light. Thus, the most despicable, mean and inhuman character of *Dāstān-i mujāhid*, Ibn-i Ṣādiq, is introduced as a *nām nihād darveš* (a so-called dervish, i.e. member of a mystic order).[52] This may also mean that Ibn-i Ṣādiq only posed and dressed as a Sufi, but the expression remains ambiguous. Asceticism, escapism and renunciation of the world are strongly condemned, especially in *Qaiṣar-o-Kisrā*.

The overall impression while reading the novels is that being a Muslim dominates or even obliterates all other aspects of a person's identity. Cultural and social differences, where they are mentioned, are to be overcome. The image of Islam as it is presented here is that of a scriptural, unified and universal religious, political and social system.

Conclusion

In the present age with its obsession about militant Islam and a perceived "clash of cultures", Ḥijāzī's *jihādī* rhetoric is bound to create irritation among liberal Muslim and non-Muslim readers. Of course it would be naïve to believe that reading his novels would make anybody set out for *jihād*. Most readers probably turn to his books as a pastime, for the promise of adventure and heroism, to take part in a dream world of ideal characters, feel elevated by their gallantry and bravery and revel in the past glories of Islam, or just to escape, for a while at least, their pedestrian existence. But even then they might inadvertently be drawn into the net of the particular worldview which is presented in the novels. They may begin to accept the claims about the superiority of Islam and hence the need to establish an Islamic order, especially when these views correspond with the atmosphere of their upbringing and surroundings and with what they are taught in school textbooks. Ḥijāzī's books are recommended by certain groups, organizations and schools as a tool for indoctrination, and here one may perceive a real danger. When these books become part of a systematic Islamist instruction, with all their celebration of *jihād* and martyrdom they can perhaps develop a

[52] *DM*, p. 66.

dangerous dimension.[53] Their special appeal certainly lies in the simple patterns and solutions the novels seem to offer. Ḥijāzī's novels are very much in line with contemporary terrorist ideologies which dispense "entirely with old-fashioned concerns about the ritual and doctrinal details of Islamic practice".[54] With them he also shares the abstract notion of a global Islam/Islamic world in which Muslims have to fight in the defence of Islam wherever needed. Occasionally Ḥijāzī even appears to legitimize an individual call to *jihād* when the Muslim ruler of the territory in question fails to do so. This, too, can have dangerous implications in a situation where the proponents of an international *jihād* try "to wrest the jihad away from the juridical language of the state and make it a strictly individual duty that is more ethical than political in nature".[55] In a way, this runs counter to Ḥijāzī's concern for a very particular geographical space, namely Pakistan whose political stability is seriously eroded by a number of self-styled *jihādī* groups.

But the most negative aspect of the books may be something else. We learn about military campaigns, conquests and victories, but very little about life after the conquest. Most actions in the novels are destructive. We see how evil is destroyed, but we learn very little about how the envisaged life in equality, justice and peace is to be constructed and maintained. Even in the areas which have come under permanent Muslim rule, there is internal strife, power rivalry, greed, cruelty, injustice. With the exception of a few families, the ideal Muslim society is nowhere to be seen. The exemplary leader Muḥammad bin Qāsim is not allowed to fulfil his vision of a peaceful, just society which is governed by the ethics of Islam. Ḥijāzī conceived his novels also as a warning against the failures of Muslim societies, such as the lack of de-

---

53 For a discussion of the concept of *jihād* with regard to Pakistan, see Michel Boivin, "Jihad, National Process and Identity Assertion in Pakistan: the Dialectic of Metaphor and Reality", [in:] Saeed Shafqat (ed.), *New Perspectives on Pakistan. Visions for the Future*, Karachi: OUP, 2007, pp. 104-21.

54 Faisal Devji, *Landscapes of the Jihad. Militancy. Morality. Modernity*. London: Hurst & Co., 2005, p. 16.

55 *Ibidem*, p. 34.

mocracy, and particularly against the divisions among Muslims, but with his own narrow outlook on Islam he can easily be understood to endorse one specific rationalized version of Islam against all others. He expounds what C.M. Naim characterises as "a scriptural Islam that is exclusionary – filled with sectarian self-righteousness – and, far from being inspired by humility, is aggressively focused on having power and holding on to it".[56] We should not forget that sectarian violence in Pakistan (Muslims killing Muslims) is responsible for more deaths than any other form of terrorism in the country. Whatever the social, economic and ethnic reasons for these conflicts may be, the mobilizing ideologies used in them are based on religious concepts (purity of faith, finality of prophethood, a particular interpretation of the sharia etc.).[57] On the face of it, however, Ḥijāzī as many reformist writers preceding him stresses Muslim unity and propagates the basic tenets and social norms of Islam without entering into any theological disputes. He strongly condemns disputations between different sects and schools of Muslim jurisprudence as one of the main factors for the decline of Muslim power. He is very critical of the *ᶜulamā* who instigate hatred among Muslims and more often then not serve and legitimate unworthy worldly rulers.

In this regard, Ḥijāzī's books can also be read as a utopia of sorts. In his novels he constructs ideal spaces, however limited they may be, in which his notions of a truly Islamic way of living are realised. Thus his later works can also be understood as a critique of Pakistani realities. Although they are set in the past, their concern is the present and the future, and this certainly is part of how the readers relate to the books. In line with different traditionalist movements of the time, Ḥijāzī "sought to harmonise, albeit in different ways, the Muslims' everyday life with the

---

[56] C.M. Naim, "A «Hyper-Masculinised» Islam?", *Outlook India*, 16 January 2004.

[57] A revealing case study of Sunni-Shia militancy is Mariam Abou Zahab's "The Sunni-Shia Conflict in Jhang (Pakistan)", [in:] Imtiaz Ahmad & Helmut Reifeld (eds.), *Lived Islam in South Asia: Adaptation, Accomodation & Conflict*, Delhi: Social Sciences Press, 2004, pp. 135-48.

implications of the normative sources of Islam".[58] The books may be very attractive for the clear-cut, simple rules and the definite orientation they provide. The Pakistani writer and critic Anvar Sadīd called Ḥijāzī's novels "landmarks/signposts" (*nišān-i rāh*) for future generations.[59] The very positive evaluation of Ḥijāzī's works in the PhD thesis quoted above may serve as an indication of the ideological importance of this author in present day Pakistan. Mumtāz ᶜUmar reports how a delegation of the Islamic Student Federation (*Islāmī Jamīᶜat-i Ṭulabā*) came to meet Ḥijāzī. One boy kissed Ḥijāzī's hand and told him that Maulānā Maudūdī had organised them, but only Ḥijāzī's writings turn their spirits on.[60] In a special Nasīm Ḥijāzī number of the monthly *Siyāra* (1989) Naᶜīm Siddīqī wrote:

> Most of the young recruits in our army draw inspiring lessons about our glorious past from Nasīm Ḥijāzī's novels and go to confront death motivated by the selfless passion of martyrdom. A great number of youngsters in educational institutions highly appreciate his writings, innumerable female students (from middle schools to MA) learn about the message of Islam and its power by reading Nasīm Ḥijāzī, and actually the credit for the fact that Islamic *jihād*, an Islamic system and an Islamic movement are discussed with so much fervour in this country to a great deal goes to Nasīm Ḥijāzī.[61]

---

[58] Jan-Peter Hartung, "Affection and Aversion: Ambivalences among Muslim Intellectual Élites in Contemporary South Asia", *South Asia Research*, 2001, no. 21: 2, p. 201.

[59] "Nasīm Ḥijāzī: islāmī tārīx kā šaidāʾī", *Jasārat*, 9 March 1996, nr. 5.

[60] Literally: *hamārī ragõ mẽ daurne vālā xūn garm kartī haĩ*, Mumtāz ᶜUmar, *Nasīm Ḥijāzī kī tārīxī...*, p. 94.

[61] "fauj ke beštar naujavān Nasīm Ḥijāzī ke nāvalõ se apne šāndār māẓī zindagī afroz rivāyāt axẕ karte haĩ aur jaẕba-i šahādat ke liye bexud ho kar maut ke sāmne khaṛe ho jāte haĩ. taᶜlīmgāhõ ke kaṣīru-'t-taᶜdād naujavān us ke qalam ke qadr šinās haĩ, bešumār ṭālibāt (miḍal iskūlõ se le kar aim ai tak) Nasīm Ḥijāzī ko paṛh kar islām ke paiġām aur us kī quvvat se āšnāʾī ḥāṣil kartī haĩ, balki saččī bāt to yah hai ki is mulk-o-qaum mẽ agar islāmī jihād aur islāmī niẓām aur islāmī taḥrīk ke čarče zor par haĩ to is ḥālat ko paidā karne mẽ Nasīm Ḥijāzī kā baṛā ḥiṣṣa hai". Quoted in Mumtāz ᶜUmar, *Nasīm Ḥijāzī kī tārīxī...*, p. 468.

What Ralph Russell stated for Maudūdī could as well be applied to Ḥijāzī: the basis of the great appeal of his message for the urban lower middle class is that his "arguments, such as they are, confirm his supporters in the strong, unthinking prejudices they already hold".[62]

A phenomenon such as the huge popularity of Ḥijāzī's writings points to a major difference between popular literature in South Asia and in western languages. While popular reading matter in the west tends to be of an apolitical nature and, at least at the face of it, not to propagate any ideology (which means that the underlying ideology is implied, but not overt), didactic and openly ideological aspects are not so rare in popular Urdu fiction. One has to concede that nowadays Nasīm Ḥijāzī's novels are mostly located in the rubric of "juvenile literature" – a field in which normative features and appealing heroic role models are to be found in western languages as well. A clear distinction between good and evil and the preaching of a simple ethics is characteristic of many works of popular culture all over the world. And yet, the amount of direct indoctrination we come across in Ḥijāzī's works is quite extraordinary.

Although any "purpose" (*maqṣadiyat*) in literature is strongly condemned by the proponents of the priority of the aesthetic and the autonomy of art, committed literature as well as an overt didacticism are very common features in popular fiction of Urdu. Thus, popular literature deserves much more attention as a vibrant and ideologically loaded site in the system of public discourse in Urdu.

[62] Ralph Russell, "Maudūdī and Islamic Obscurantism", [in:] *How Not to Write the History of Urdu Literature*, Delhi: OUP, 1999, p. 222.

Between tradition and modernity: Fatima Jinnah

Kamila Junik

It seems indisputable that Fatima Jinnah is a very important figure in Pakistani society. She is a patroness of many girls' schools and colleges. Her name figures on institutions, institutes, organizations and even streets. She still enjoys great respect as a powerful woman leader. In this paper I will try to analyse the role of Fatima Jinnah in the history and culture of Pakistan, the reasons for her popularity which is almost as great as her brothers.[1]

Brother and sister

Fatima Jinnah (1893-1967) was born as the third girl out of seven brothers and sisters. From the childhood days she was Muhammad Ali's favorite sister and closest friend. After their father's death, she came under her brother's guardianship and stayed with

[1] Salahuddin Khan, compiler of *Speeches, Messages and Statements of Madar-i-Millat Mohtarma Fatima Jinnah (1948-67)* in the preface of the book described her as "the most respected person next to the Quaid-e--Azam". After: http://www.humsafar.info/litterature_on_fatima_jinnah.php, access: 6 January 2010.

him. Jinnah insisted on her education[2] and encouraged her to join the Bandra Convent in Bombay in 1902. In 1919 she was admitted to Dr. Ahmad Dental College at the University of Calcutta. Three years later she graduated as the first Muslim woman dental surgeon. Soon after that, with the help of her brother, she started up a dental clinic in Bombay where she practiced. However, in 1929 Jinnah lost his wife and Fatima gave up her career and moved back to his house. As a loyal sister she was ready to help him by taking care of the household. But this decision turned out to be the most important in her life. She became Jinnah's companion, friend and sometimes even advisor.

Those years were crucial for Jinnah's career, and equally dramatic for India. The fight for independence from British Raj – the fight for freedom – became a fact. The National Congress with its moderate tone towards the British seemed to overlook people's expectations. Many Indians insisted on taking up some action to remove the foreign government from the country. Soon the Congress had become very active in the independence movement. It produced great national leaders like B.G. Tilak, G.K. Gokhale, M. Gandhi and Muhammad Ali Jinnah who was its member since 1896. However, the Muslims seemed to be disappointed with the politics of the Congress and demanded a separate party to represent their interests. Their suspicion towards Congress dominated by Hindus led to the foundation of All India Muslim League in 1906. Jinnah initially avoided joining the new party and considered it too Muslim-oriented. He was deeply influenced by Western ideas of humanity and equality, but also recognized the British contribution to Indian law, education, and industry as beneficial. But soon he decided to take care of the Muslim minority and became not only a member of the League but also its president in 1919. He believed that the Congress and the League should act together and demand establishing self-government which would give India the status of a dominion in the British Empire. Yet the Hindu-Muslim alliance

[2] Jinnah acted against the will of the family who strongly opposed Fatima's studying in a British convent school. See: R. Malik, S. Awan, *Women Emancipation in South Asia: A Case Study of Fatima Jinnah*, Lahore: Centre for South Asian Studies, University of the Punjab, 2003.

never happened and Jinnah felt disappointed and disillusioned. He also objected to the idea of the Khilafat movement supported by Gandhi which was to lead, in his opinion, to the future division of the two communities. Besides, he engaged himself in the legislative assembly in Bombay and many other activities.

His sister's assistance was what he really needed at that time. She accompanied him on his trip to London in 1929. It was only then that she became politically active. Jinnah attended the Round Table Conference, and she took care of his health and well-being, but also supported him. In 1934 Muhammad Ali became convinced by the League leaders (i.e. Aga Khan and Muhammad Iqbal) to return to India. He started right away from the revitalization of the party. Fatima also engaged in this work. In 1938 by effort of Begum Shah Nawaz,[3] an important Muslim activist, the League's Women's Committee became established. Although Jinnah was against any divisions in the party, Begum Shah Nawaz insisted on creating a platform for Muslim women for whom taking part in mixed-sex gatherings and meetings could be difficult. Fatima Jinnah became an active member of the women's wing of the party. She made several visits to different Indian cities where she succeeded in founding branches of the Committee and a Student Federation. When the League decided to form the Women's Central Committee, Fatima became the leader of its Patna branch and worked there till 1947. She managed to convince a number of Muslim women to show interest in the Muslim League and organize themselves in provincial and central committees. As a result a large number of women attended the party's session in 1940. The formation of the All India Muslim Women Students Federation in Delhi was her personal achievement. Noor as-Sabah, a League worker, recalls her:

---

[3] Initially working for All India Women Conference, Begum Shah Nawaz decided to create a communal women's organization and take care of modernizing Muslim women's status in India by making them aware of their right to vote and be represented in the legislative assemblies. For further reading: G. Forbes, *The New Cambridge History of India*, vol. IV.2: *Women in Modern India*, New Delhi: CUP, 2000; R. Kumar, *The History of Doing: An Illustrated Account of Movements for Women's Rights and Feminism in India, 1800-1990*, New Delhi: Zubaan, 2002.

She easily managed the busy and tight schedule of the Quaid. She chaired the female processions of the League in the different areas in Delhi and used to address her counterparts in Urdu.[4]

In 1940 at a League conference Jinnah said it would be ruinous for India to keep those two different nations bound together. He claimed that the idea of a single state is a utopia and opted for a separate Muslim state. He emerged as a national leader – or Quaid-e-Azam as he was popularly known. In the elections in 1946 the League received almost 90 per cent of Muslim votes and announced the creation of Pakistan in the very near future. Fatima played her part in this fabulous result as she supported the campaign and managed to mobilize women to vote. As Jinnah once said, "No struggle can ever succeed without women participating side by side with men".[5] It was a powerful message to the nation.

The final stage of the freedom movement was most fierce. After the second world war the British were keen on giving India its independence. Jinnah's claim for Pakistan was opposed by Nehru, Gandhi and Maulana Azad as it would result in the division of the country. But it was too late to stop the wheels turning. 1947 saw India divided and the bloodshed and tears of many of its people. Jinnah became the first Governor General of Pakistan – a separate country. His idea was to create a modern, open-minded and secular state and unite different peoples. Fatima engaged in helping the refugees, homeless women and children. She established the Women's Relief Committee which provided basic aid and necessary items for the migrants. She also organized camps, shelters and financial support. Fatima frequently accompanied her brother on his numerous meetings where he addressed the nation and tried to convince people to act united and build the new country. Besides her, only a few people knew about Jinnah's illness and weak condition. He died a year after Pakistan was created and Fatima withdrew from political life.

---

[4] A. Jalal, *The Convenience of Subservience: Women and the State of Pakistan*, [in:] *Women, Islam and the State*, ed. D. Kandiyoti, New York 1991, [quoted after:] Malik and Awan, *Women Emancipation.*

[5] From a speech given at a public meeting.

Mother of the nation

The fight for women's rights began at the end of the nineteenth century when women zealously asked for access to education. The need to improve the status of women by letting them learn and gain qualifications became evident for reformists, such as Vivekananda, who believed that social reforms and the question of women were the priorities of the modern man. However, the educated Indians did not want to accept any British modifications in law or custom. As Geraldine Forbes claims, "they had little understanding for women's lives beyond those of women in their own families".[6] The emancipated women established their own organizations and took up the challenge of changing ancient social norms. Soon they became involved in the nationalist movement and took an active part in it.

The women's movement represented the issues of all Indian women and fought for their basic rights – such as forbidding child marriage, sati, securing property rights, etc. However, it was dominated by women related to male activists, the elite, and the Western educated, often upper class Hindu. A few years later, it was Gandhi who brought women into public life and gave them an important role to play in the non-obedience movement against the British. There were very few Muslim women engaged in those activities. Only a few shared Gandhi's convictions, many more either could not accept the Hindu-dominated ideology or were simply neglected by the political parties. The lack of representation, lack of women leaders was mainly a result of the different status of Muslim women or of Muslims in general. The common view of women was (and in some part still is) that they were incapable of making their own decisions and needed to be guided by their male relatives. Women's autonomy, freedom and independence would pose a threat to the proper Islamic order and were opposed by the conservatives. The traditional role of women was limited to fulfilling domestic duties and any appearance in public was largely criticized. The Islamic modernists, on the other hand, advocated education and liberation of women in terms of rereading and reinterpreting the traditional beliefs. They claimed

[6] Forbes, *The New Cambridge History of India.*

a distinction was to be made between custom and religion which were (and still are) commonly confused.

Fatima Jinnah was not the only lady engaged in the fight for the rights of women. The most active reformists were Aruna Asaf Ali, Lady Mirza Ismail, Lady Haroon, Begum Aijaz Rasul, Lady Fazli Hussain, Begum Muhammad Ali Johar and the already mentioned Begum Shah Nawaz. Initially they were members of the All India Women Conference and the National Federation of Indian Women – both initiatives and platforms for women to make other women aware of their rights as well as to convince them to stand up, get out of their homes and take action. Many of them later became members of the League's Women's Committee.

In comparison to those ladies, Fatima did not have any political ambitions. She was neither an activist fighting for women's rights nor a feminist in her approach. Her brother was the priority. Leaving politics to the politicians she busied herself with women, human rights and the edification of the backward classes. She believed in Jinnah's ideas and shared his dream of a strong, modern and educated society. Accompanying Jinnah on numerous occasions, meetings and tours, she showed her keen interest in his mission and supported him. As Sharif al Mujahid explains,

> People do not realize that just by accompanying Jinnah wherever he went during the 1940s, Fatima Jinnah was teaching Muslim women to stand shoulder to shoulder with men during the freedom struggle. Numerous pictures of the period show Fatima Jinnah walking alongside Jinnah and not behind him. The message was loud and clear and it was one both the brother and sister wished to convey to the nation.[7]

In a society in which women were kept inside the four walls of their homes, Fatima encouraged women to join their men in the struggle. This was a new way of thinking. Jinnah himself empha-

[7] *An enduring legacy*, Dawn, July 2003, [quoted after:] L. Kazmi, *Fatima Jinnah (1893-1967)*, http://www.jazbah.org/fatima.php, access: 9 January 2010.

sized the necessity of both men and women to strive together. In his words:

> No nation can rise to the height of glory unless your women are side by side with you. We are victims of evil customs. It is a crime against humanity that our women are shut up within the four walls of the houses as prisoners. There is no sanction anywhere for the deplorable condition in which our women have to live.[8]

Jinnah believed in progress and development by raising awareness in society. On the occasion of Sibi Darbar – the annual gathering of Baluch and Pakhtun leaders and chiefs – he asked Fatima to sit beside him. It was an unprecedented incident. "He was making a point: Muslim women must take their place in the history of Pakistan".[9]

Fatima was mostly concerned with female education. She used to encourage rich and enlightened men and women to sponsor study programs for girls and women. If the women were to contribute to the economic uplift of the country, they should gain knowledge and put it into practice. An important aspect to which Fatima felt very attached was the promotion of technical education. Having this as a purpose she delivered a number of speeches, addressed various institutions and established a variety of industrial homes.[10] After Jinnah died she resigned from public life. However, she continued meeting people especially on the anniversaries of her brother's birth and death, Islamic festivals and student gatherings at various schools. For this reason she was called Madar-e Millat or Khatoon-e Pakistan.

She returned to politics for a while when she was asked to contest the presidential elections in 1965 against Ayub Khan. The politics since the creation of the independent state drove the country deep into chaos. Nothing was left of Jinnah's ideals of

---

[8] From a speech given at a public meeting.

[9] A.S. Ahmed, *Jinnah, Pakistan and Islamic Identity: The Search for Saladin*, London: Routledge, 1997.

[10] R. Ahmad, "Fatima Jinnah's Concern for Women's Technical Education", *The Pakistan Development Review*, 2003, vol. 42: 4, part II (Winter), http://www.pide.org.pk/pdf/PDR/2003/Volume4/765-768.pdf, access: 8 January 2010.

democracy, brotherhood, freedom. Instead, Pakistan was led by self-centered politicians, trying to impose a regime. Fatima's opposition towards Ayub Khan's presidency coincided with the other parties' determination to remove him from his position. Moreover, she was the Quaid's sister, very respected and admired and – most important – a person who could revive Jinnah's ideas and bring them into reality. Her candidature raised the complex question of whether a woman could be the head of a Muslim state. After many debates Maulana Maududi, most eminent alim and founder of Jamaat-e Islami passed a resolution in which he promoted Fatima with regard to special circumstances, i.e. the need to restore the rights of people and order in the country. Fatima lost the election with 36 per cent of votes which showed the huge support she had in the country. In Riaz Ahmad's words, "though she lost, the way she fought the election in different areas of Pakistan and the speeches she delivered are a beacon of light for the future generations".[11] Her contribution in the field of women's awakening, their development, education and participation in national affairs makes her one of the most recognizable persons in the history of Pakistan.

BIBLIOGRAPHY

Ahmad, R., "Fatima Jinnah's Concern for Women's Technical Education", *The Pakistan Development Review* 2003, vol. 42: 4, part II (Winter), http://www.pide.org.pk/pdf/PDR/2003/Volume4/765-768.pdf, access: 8 January 2010.

____, *The Works on Madar-i-Millat Fatima Jinnah: An Evaluation*, http://www.nihcr.edu.pk/Latest_English_Journal/The_Works_on_Madare_Millat_Dr_Rriaz.pdf, access: 12 January 2010.

Ahmed, A.S. (1997), *Jinnah, Pakistan and Islamic Identity: The Search for Saladin*, London: Routledge.

Bielawski, J. (1980), *Islam*, Warszawa: Krajowa Agencja Wydawnicza.

[11] R. Ahmad, *The Works on Madar-i-Millat Fatima Jinnah: an Evaluation*, http://www.nihcr.edu.pk/Latest_English_Journal/The_Works_on_Madare_Millat_Dr_Rriaz.pdf, access: 12 January 2010.

Chandra, B., ed. (1989), *India's Struggle for Independence*, New Delhi: Penguin.

Desai, N., U. Thakkar (2001), *Women in Indian Society*, New Delhi: National Book Trust, India.

Forbes, G. (2000), *The New Cambridge History of India*, vol. IV. 2: *Women in Modern India*, Delhi: CUP.

Hasan, M., ed. (2003), *India's Partition. Process, Strategy and Mobilization*, New Delhi: OUP.

Husain, Z. (1994), *Demography and Partition of India*, Karachi: Royal Book Co.

Kazmi, L., *Fatima Jinnah (1893-1967)*, http://www.jazbah.org/fatima.php, access: 9 January 2010.

Kieniewicz, J. (1980), *Historia Indii* [A history of India], Wrocław: Ossolineum.

Kumar, H., ed. (2002), *Status of Muslim Women in India*, New Delhi: Sarojini Naidu Centre for Women's Studies.

Kumar, R. (2002), *The History of Doing: An Illustrated Account of Movements for Women's Rights and Feminism in India, 1800--1990*, New Delhi: Zubaan.

Lateef, Sh. (1990), *Muslim Women in India: Political & Private Realities 1890s – 1980s*, New Delhi: Kali for Women.

Malik, R., S. Awan (2003), *Women Emancipation in South Asia: A Case Study of Fatima Jinnah*, Lahore: Centre for South Asian Studies, University of the Punjab.

Other Voices from Pakistan, compiled by Pakistan-India People's Forum for Peace and Democracy, New Delhi, 1995.

Talbot, I. (2003), *Pakistan. A Modern History*, New Delhi: OUP.

Toczek, E. (1984), *Być muzułmaninem w Indiach* [To be a Muslim in India], Wrocław: Ossolineum.

Sir Sayyid's public sphere: Urdu print and oratory in nineteenth century India[1]

David Lelyveld

Many years ago Jürgen Habermas warned that the concept of a public sphere "cannot be abstracted from the unique developmental history" of Britain, France and Germany, especially since the eighteenth century; "nor can it be transferred, idealtypically generalized, to any number of historical situations that represent

[1] This paper, originally prepared for the "Vernacular Public Spheres Workshop" at Yale University, April 2007, combines several earlier presentations presented over several years at the Association for Asian Studies, the Salar Jang Museum, the Lockmiller Seminar at Emory University, and a later revision at the School of Oriental and African Studies, University of London. I am indebted to participants in the workshops and seminars, particularly Professors Ruby Lal of Emory University and Bernard Bate of Yale. I am also grateful to Professor Asghar Abbas of Aligarh Muslim University for providing me with publications of the Sir Syed Academy, to Ms. Jennifer Dubrow for sharing photocopies, and to Professor C.M. Naim for sharing his research on Sayyid Ahmad Khan's early publications. Further research for this paper was conducted in the British Library with on one semester sabbatical leave provided by William Paterson University.

formally similar constellations". He was careful to restrict his definition to a narrow "literary character of a public sphere constituted by private people putting reason to use".[2] In the market economy of early industrial capitalism, this realm of the public interposes itself between the bureaucratic state and the new domestic privacy of the nuclear family and claims autonomy in the formulation of cultural values and political goals for the society at large. Like Gramsci's analysis of the role of intellectuals, ideology, and civil society in modern Italy, Habermas's work was concerned with the content and social location of formal, discursive speech and writing in relation to dominating concepts of power and authority in particular times and places.[3] Intended to undermine the authority of such utterances, both Habermas and Gramsci claimed that there is a real authority to undermine. And for Habermas, as opposed to Gramsci, there was more than a hint of nostalgia for the era when intellectuals counted for something, before the evil day when the culture industry and the capitalist welfare state absorbed the democratic potentiality inherent, however ambivalently, in the public sphere.

It's easy, as usual, to say that India is another story. The state was foreign; the capitalists by in large foreign too, and also far away; the realm of family privacy, pretty much an undiscovered country. The question I would like to consider is what to make of some of the bits and pieces, many of them consciously adapted from British examples, that seem to resemble the model of the public sphere, the attempts to formulate and promote a new form of collective consciousness among Indians in organized and ideologically articulate political and social movements. What should we make of the small forays of the literate few into print capitalism, voluntary associations, political debates and

[2] Jürgen Habermas, *The Structural Transformation of the Public Sphere: An Inquiry into a Category of Bourgeois Society*, tr. Thomas Burger and Frederick Lawrence, Cambridge, Mass.: M.I.T. Press, 1989, pp. xvii-xviii [original German publication, 1962]. The term for "public sphere" in the German original is *Öffentlichkeit*.

[3] Antonio Gramsci, *Selections from the Prison Notebooks*, ed. and tr. Quintin Hoare and Geoffrey Nowell-Smith, New York: International Publishers, 1971, pp. 44-90, 206-46.

demands for a "public" role for Indians in the formulation of government policy? Are they, as Benedict Anderson suggested, deracinated "pilgrims" imitating the "modular" examples of their foreign rulers, adapting ideas and institutions that arose out of different conditions, leap frogging history in order to participate in an imposed present?[4] And whatever it took to get the British to pay attention to them, what relation could they have to the larger populations they claimed to represent and to lead for the sake of some idea of the general welfare?

How might the concept of a "public sphere" apply to the Urdu language in the course of the nineteenth century? As a very partial response, I propose to look at the long career of Sir Sayyid Ahmad Khan (1817-98), in particular, his public utterances, first in print and then in speech. The effort will be to identify for further research issues of social context as well as specific formats and technologies as they may have transformed the authority of the written or spoken word and the definition of actual or potential interlocutors and audiences.

Muslims and print

As a young man, before he came to prominence as an educational leader, religious reformer and political spokesman for a significant section of South Asian Muslims, Sayyid Ahmad Khan devoted himself to historical research and the preparation and publication of critical editions of Indo-Muslim historical texts. My present, very preliminary effort will be to ask questions about the physical appearance of these printed texts in relationship to their manuscript sources. How was "the art of the book" transformed by the processes of turning them into printed texts, and what do these transformations say about the authority of the text and its accessibility, perhaps, to new ways of reading and new reading publics? In what respects do Sayyid Ahmad's publications participate in an on-going tradition of Persianate literacy and to what extent were they altered by European textual conventions?

---

[4] *Imagined Communities: Reflections on the Origins and Spread of Nationalism*, London: Verso, 1983, pp. 106-23.

Large claims are sometimes made for the significance of printing in the modern history of India and the Islamicate world, first as absence, a symptom of "what went wrong";[5] then as "revolutionary" transformation with respect to religious consciousness, social identity, and the nature of authority. The category of printing refers not only to a range of technologies, developed first in China and Korea, then in Europe, but also to a set of institutions and practices now commonly bracketed as "print capitalism". Why Muslims and others over a period of nearly four centuries did not take up these technologies and practices, even when they were aware of them, has, in the eyes of some scholars, called for an explanation. Fairly elaborate arguments have been advanced about the nature of Islam and the Arabic alphabet, the alleged primacy of oral over written communication, the authority of face to face instruction, and the vested interest and aesthetic standards of calligraphers that are said to have made print technologies illegitimate or at least unappealing.[6]

The task of designing Arabic fonts for moveable type was taken up in Europe and by Europeans long before it took hold in the Islamicate world.[7] In India, the establishment of British rule in Bengal and surrounding areas in the late eighteenth century stimulated the first significant efforts to publish printed books. Christian missionaries, at first in the Danish colony at Serampore, then, after 1813, within territories under British rule, made vigorous efforts to reach new Indian audiences with books and pamphlets in Urdu and other Indian languages. William Jones, Francis Gladwin, William Kirkpatrick, and John Borthwick Gilchrist presided over the preparation and publication of text books and reference works in European formats, largely for British

[5] Bernard Lewis, *What Went Wrong? Western Impact and Middle Eastern Response*, Oxford: Oxford University Press, 2002, pp. 142-5.

[6] For example, see Francis Robinson, "Islam and the impact of print in South Asia", [in:] *The transmission of knowledge of South Asia*, ed. Nigel Crook, New Delhi: Oxford University Press, 1996, pp. 64-70; also Timothy Mitchell, *Colonizing Egypt*, Berkeley: University of California Press, 1991, pp. 133-4.

[7] "Maṭbaʾa", [in:] *Encyclopaedia of Islam*, 2nd edn., vol. 6, ed. C.E. Bosworth, E. van Donzel and Ch. Pellat, Leiden: E.J. Brill, 1991.

military and civilian officials. They also commissioned manuscript copies and later publication of works of historical and cultural significance. "As for the manuscript tradition itself", according to Jeremiah Losty, "it was (...) a victim of the interest of a few men like William Jones" and others, who "naturally collected manuscripts, being concerned to gather together the basic literature of India, and used the printing-press in Calcutta as the means of printing and, hence, widely disseminating India's ancient learning". By the mid-nineteen century, "a flood of Indian and Persian classics from presses throughout India" eliminated "the need to have works laboriously copied by hand (...), and the manuscript tradition itself (...) all but came to an end".[8]

The fact that printing developed in Europe and arrived in India under the auspices of Christian missionaries and imperial conquerors presumably made it strange, even suspect. The literary theorist Homi Bhabha quotes a missionary account of an incident in Delhi in 1817 when a group of Indians were supposedly struck with awe at the sight of a New Testament translation in "the Hindoostanee Tongue": "(...) never having heard of a printed book before, (...) its very appearance was to them miraculous". But if they felt that way, they nevertheless were unpersuaded by the missionary's arguments for Christianity and refused to be baptized. Since the book was printed, according to Bhabha's reading of the incident, it was bound up with the alienation of British rule. The creative response to the challenge, according to Bhabha's influential essay, was to "mimic" this foreign, imperial artifact "as the affect of hybridity – at once a mode of appropriation and of resistance, from the disciplined to the desiring".[9]

Not only a sign of foreign conquest, printing stands forth, according to some scholars, as part of the narrative of modernity, the domination of Europe over the entire course of human history: of science and technology, individual conscience, the nation

[8] Jeremiah P. Losty, *The Art of the Book in India*, London: The British Library, 1982, p. 150.

[9] Homi K. Bhabha, "Signs taken for wonders: questions of ambivalence and authority under a tree outside Delhi, May 1817", [in:] idem, *The Location of Culture*, London: Routledge, 1994, pp. 103, 120. Bhabha assumes, probably incorrectly, that the text was in Hindi, rather than Urdu.

state, the rise of standardized vernacular languages and much more.[10] When Aloys Sprenger, the Swiss physician and orientalist, was commissioned to prepare a catalogue of the libraries of the Nawab of Avadh in 1848, he prefaced his work by claiming that India was recapitulating the history of modern Europe. "After the Musalmans had, several centuries ago, entirely lost sight of the original idea of their religion, they are now beginning to make their sacred books intelligible to all. This must lead to results, analogous to those which the translation and study of the Bible produced in Europe". Furthermore, he claimed, the newly created audience, included women, had created a demand for "light literature" and "a spirit of liberality" and "general civilization".[11] Recently, Francis Robinson has asserted a more complex version of a similar view: the onset of print did create an "Islamic Protestantism" and "modernization", but it was as an act of resistance to European Christian rule, lead by ulama, that print came into its own among South Asian Muslims. By the 1820s, there emerged throughout India a powerful counter-missionary movement among Muslims, using similar techniques of printing as well as popular oratory.[12]

Whether or not one accepts the more sweeping claims for Europe or Euro-America as the model and standard for what might happen elsewhere, the historiography of European printing

---

[10] Most influentially are the classic works by Elizabeth L. Eisenstein, *The Printing Press as an Agent of Change*, single volume edn., Cambridge: Cambridge University Press, 1979; Lucien Febvre and Henri-Jean Martin, *The Coming of the Book*, tr. David Gerard, London: Verso, 1976. Febvre and Martin offered a more complex and less "revolutionary" view of the impact of printing.

[11] Aloys Sprenger, *A Catalogue of the Arabic, Persian and Hindustany Manuscripts, of the Libraries of the King of Oudh, compiled under the orders of the Govt. of India*, vol. 1: *Persian and Hindustany Poetry*, Calcutta, printed by J. Thomas, 1854, p. viii.

[12] Robinson, "Islam and the impact of print", esp. pp. 73 and 82. See also brief discussion and further references in my essay, "The colonial context of Muslim separatism: from Sayyid Ahmad Barelvi to Sayyid Ahmad Khan", [in:] *Living together Separately: Cultural India in History and Politics*, ed. Mushirul Hasan and Asim Roy, New Delhi: Oxford University Press, 2005, pp. 408-11.

can be instructive in raising questions about textualities in other cultural contexts. Most of the limited literature on the history of printing in India, at least with reference to Urdu, recounts the authors, titles, and types of texts – newspapers, novels, religious scriptures and disputations – and to some small extent the number and cost of such publications.[13] If one is to take European history seriously, as a guide to the significance of printing in India, one can do better. Print technologies and print capitalism in Europe were in fact considerably more diverse and uneven developments than many common characterizations would lead us to believe. The relationship between the elaborate conventions of the European manuscript and the early craft of printing, the so-called incunabula with their own special hybridities, reveal that the printed text was far from being the standardized and transparently authoritative artifact that are too casually associated with printing. The processes of producing, distributing and reading such texts, their various genres and formats, all had to be developed over time in a variety of cultural contexts. The economics and social networks of book production and consumption were

---

[13] There is one outstanding study of early print capitalism in Urdu (and also Hindi): Ulrike Stark, *An Empire of Books: The Naval Kishore Press and the Diffusion of the Printed Word in Colonial India*, Ranikhet: Permanent Black, 2007. See also Robert Darnton, "Book Production in British India, 1850-1900", *Book History* 2002, no. 5, pp. 239-62; *Print Areas: Book History in India*, ed. Abhijit Gupta and Swapan Chakravorty, Delhi: Permanent Black, 2004; Anindita Ghosh, "An uncertain 'coming of the book': early print cultures in colonial India", *Book History* 2003, no. 3, pp. 23-55, which deals primarily with Bengali. Some earlier studies that are more specifically relevant to Urdu include Muḥammad ᶜAtīq Ṣiddīqī, *Hindustānī axbārnavīsī (kampanī ke ᶜahd mẽ)*, Aligarh: Anjuman Taraqqī-e Urdū (Hind), 1957; Emmett Davis, *Press and Politics in British Western Punjab, 1836-1947*, New Delhi: Academic Publications, 1983; and Nazir Ahmad, *Oriental Presses in the World*, Lahore, Pakistan: Qadiria Book Traders, 1985, is exceptional in its attention to the technical history of printing. See also Graham Shaw, "Lithography v. Letter-Press in India: part II: Lithography and the Vernacular Book", *South Asia Library Notes and Queries*, 1994-5, no. 30, pp. 1-10. For a fresh look at "how printing did (rather than did not) spread among Muslims", see Nile Green, "Journeymen, Middlemen: Travel, Trans-Culture and Technology in the Origins of Muslim Printing", *International Journal of Middle East Studies* 2009, no. 41(2).

not necessarily so sharply divided between the era of the manuscript and the printed text, and there remained for many centuries significant areas of overlap between the unique version of a text and its mechanically reproduced ones. The details of the printing craft and physical appearance of a text, it has been argued, are constituents of its meaning, indications of how an utterance changes in transmission, not only what goes into creating texts but also what sort of activities can be considered "reading" them, what makes participation in any of the relevant roles associated with literacy accessible to some people and not to others.[14]

As in Europe, there is evidence of considerable continuity between the manuscript tradition and the introduction of print technologies to India. The nature of reading and writing in India at least during the Mughal era from the late sixteenth century had undergone a significant history of transformation before the introduction of print technology. For all the continuing authority of face to face mediation in the transmission of textual knowledge, Nile Green has shown a simultaneous world of bureaucratic, historical, epistolary and other literary texts that were collected, exchanged and read without the presence of personal interaction.[15] If the process of cutting the type fonts and assembling them for printing required a wholly different set of skills from the arts of calligraphy, the invention of lithography in Germany at the end of the eighteenth century opened up the possibility of reproducing hand written texts in ways that were more consistent with established practice. Abdul Halim Sharar's account of how the art of calligraphy thrived in the early days of lithography (*patthar kā chāpā*) in Lucknow after 1830, claims that it was at

---

[14] See Cyndia Susan Clegg, "History of the book: an undisciplined discipline?", *Renaissance Quarterly*, 2001, no. 54, pp. 221-45, for a recent review essay on the state of the field, and the *AHR Forum: How Revolutionary Was the Print Revolution?*, *American Historical Review* 2002 (February), no. 107(1), pp. 84-128. See among his many works Roger Chartier, *The Order of Books: Readers, Authors, and Libraries in Europe between the Fourteenth and Eighteenth Centuries*, tr. Lydia G. Cochran, Cambridge: Polity Press, 1994.

[15] Nile Green, "The Uses of Books in a Late Mughal *Takiyya:* Persianate Knowledge Between Person and Paper", *Modern Asian Studies*, 2010, no. 44, 2, pp. 241-65.

first uncontaminated by commercial motives. Only the finest calligraphers took up the new art, using the finest inks, the finest paper. No cost was spared: "(…) thousands of lamps of mustard-oil were lighted to produce the fine-quality lamp-black. Instead of aid, fine-skinned lemons were used and sponges took the place of cloth". Lucknow calligraphers became skilled in the art of making correction directly on the printing stone by writing the letters in reverse (*ulṭā likhnā*).[16]

Despite the looming spectre of British military and economic dominance, Lucknow, like Delhi, survived in the penumbra of Mughal courtly regimes until the upheavals of 1857. By that time, Sayyid Ahmad Khan, born and raised as a Mughal gentleman in a family closely attached to the Red Fort of Delhi and its surroundings, an employee of the East India Company for some twenty years, had managed to keep the colonial culture at bay by devoting his extra-curricular attentions to the study of Islamic theology and Mughal history. Well educated in Arabic and Persian, he did not know English. During those years Sayyid Ahmad participated in the introduction of printing to the cultural milieu of Delhi. Following the old Mughal pattern, his career took him to smaller towns and cities and extended his links to a more far-flung community, the so-called "service gentry," heirs to the literate officials, religious scholars and dispersed military families of the Mughal empire.

In cities, small towns and fortresses of the rural countryside, members of this "service gentry" lived off newly secured land revenue with occasional forays into "service" for the British or other holders of land and power. In the course of the nineteenth century, according to C.A. Bayly, "English education and new forms of communication greatly expanded the organization and self-consciousness of intermediate people between state and agrarian society". Bayly has argued, however, that "pre-colonial 'mentalities' and forms of organization (…) were active forces"

[16] ᶜAbd ul-Ḥalīm Šarār, *Guzaštā Lakhnau*, rpt. edn., Lucknow: Nasīm Book Depot, 1965, pp. 142-5; originally published in serialized form *c.* 1913-20; English edn. and tr. E.S. Harcourt and Fakhir Husain, *Lucknow: The Last Phase of an Oriental Culture*, London: Paul Elek, 1975, pp. 107-8.

in the social history of the colonial period.[17] In later work, Bayly has noted that the printing press, long ignored as a useful technology in an already complex and highly active "information order", suddenly blossomed forth in the 1820s and 1830s. He notes, however, that the content of printed texts closely resembled and complemented the religious, political, commercial and literary texts of long established oral and manuscript formats.[18]

Must we then identify the pre-colonial with the pre-modern and therefore the colonial with the rise of modernity: the familiar narrative of the mobilization of publics in the rising politics of the nation, with India, once again, consigned to an imperfect emulator of European history?[19] Instead, one can try to look more closely at the actual form and content of specific practices to see how people in India used technologies for their own diverse purposes, not only in response to the colonial situation but to the multiple histories that colonial rule could not wipe away.

The unread page (*varaq-e na-xunda*)

When Shiv Narayan Aram and Hargopal Tufta, two friends of Mirza Ghalib, the great Urdu poet, approached him in 1858 with a proposal to publish his Urdu letters, he refused. "Why should we let others read what only concerns us?" He had no objection to printing his poetry or his highly crafted *Persian* prose, if only as an insurance against the loss of hand-copied manuscripts. But

---

[17] C.A. Bayly, *Rulers, Townsmen and Bazaars*, Cambridge: Cambridge University Press, 1983, p. 195. Bayly identifies this so-called gentry with the late nineteenth century clientele of institutions like Aligarh and Deoband, having developed cultural styles and networks of communication which were separate from those of the predominantly Hindu merchants of the towns. Recognizing the variety of their local situations, some of which were quite insecure, he attempts to relate these variations to the emergence of "communal" politics.

[18] C.A. Bayly, *Empire and Information: Intelligence Gathering and Social Communication in India, 1780-1870*, Cambridge: Cambridge University Press, 1996, pp. 199-200, 238-43.

[19] This is the theme of Dipesh Chakrabarty's important book, *Provincializing Europe: Postcolonial Thought and Historical Difference*, Princeton: Princeton University Press, 2000.

casual, personal correspondence in a colloquial language was not something suitable for general distribution. Just a few months after the British reconquest of Delhi, the idea was offensive to this former court poet. Nor did he have any interest in accepting a British commission to write an Urdu textbook for schools in the North-West Provinces. But five years later Ghalib was somewhat more well disposed when "a man of high rank" came to him with a similar proposition regarding the publication of his Urdu letters. It turned out, however, that this person was merely acting as an intermediary for someone who was "only a dealer in books, concerned with estimating what he'll gain or lose, what he'll have to pay out and what he can save". Nothing came of the project. Then five years after that, just before Ghalib died, the first collection of his Urdu letters was in fact published.[20]

Sayyid Muhammad, who had published the first edition of Ghalib's Urdu *dīvān* in 1841, ran one of Delhi's first presses, which also published one of its earliest newspapers, the *Sayyid al-axbār*, founded in 1836 or 1837. When Sayyid Muhammad died in 1845, the press was taken over by his younger brother, Sayyid Ahmad, who continued the enterprise for eight more years while working as a *munṣif* for the East India Company. At the same time he prepared and published his history of the buildings of Delhi, *Ā̤ṣār us-ṣanādīd.* But in 1848-9, when the newspaper folded it had only thirty-nine subscribers.[21]

To call this "print capitalism" would be an exaggeration. In 1853 the total circulation of the forty vernacular newspapers in the North-West Provinces and Punjab was under two thousand. The three papers with circulations over 200 were taken on government subscription for use in the schools. For some time such government patronage was essential to the viability of a press, though one press, the Moostufaee Press of Lucknow and Delhi,

---

[20] Ralph Russell and Khurshidul Islam, *Ghalib: Life and Letters*, London: George Allen and Unwin, 1969, pp. 180-2 (translated from *Xuṯūṯ-e Ġālib*, ed. Ġulām Rasūl Mihr, Lahore: Panjab University, 1969).

[21] Muḥammad ᶜAtīq Ṣiddīqī, *Ṣuba šimāli-o-maġribī ke axbarāt-o--maṭbuʾāt (1848-1855)*, Alīgaṛh: Anjuman Taraqqī-e Urdū (Hind), 1962, pp. 103-4; Alṭāf Ḥusain Ḥāli, *Ḥayāt-i Jāvīd*, rpt. edn., Lahore: ᶜIšrat Publishing House, 1965 [1901], pp. 71-2.

was noted for having a successful distribution network of its own and, in the words of the British official who reviewed the so-called "native press" that year, "gets rid of a lot of trash, as well as succeeds in sowing the seeds of wickedness and vice". Presses that were notable for "scurrilous print" and "abuse of Covenanted servants" did not, of course, receive government patronage.[22] But even after the 1857 Revolt, British authorities admitted that they did not have the administrative resources to police "injurious publications". One British official noted that "the amount of Literature, good or bad, which finds its way into the Indian market, is to modern European ideas absurdly insignificant, and the 'general reading' Indian public forms such an infinitesimal fraction of the vast population, that direct influence of the few publications on readers, cannot be estimated by their number according to an European standard". He went on to say, however, "The thinking Indian public are a minority, but they are a most potent minority, (…) essentially hostile to European Science and Literature, as well as to Europeans and their Government. On them the political influence of treasonable or foolish publications is to be dreaded (…)".[23] It was not until 1870 that the law created severe obstacles to those who would try "to excite feelings of disaffection" for which a publisher could be fined, imprisoned or transported for life.[24]

From the Persian manuscript to the Urdu printed book

What follows will be a very preliminary presentation of some specific examples in the career of an individual, Sayyid Ahmad Khan, who was to become associated with "Islamic modernism" and a deliberate effort to integrate aspects of European cultural

[22] "Notes on the Native Presses in the North-Western Provinces, for the Year 1853", [in:] *Selections from the Records of Government: North-Western Provinces*, vol. IV, Allahabad: Government Press, N.-W.P., 1868, pp. 111-49.

[23] F.B. Outram, "Note on Native Periodicals and Presses – 1858", [in:] *ibidem*, pp. 152-3.

[24] Act XXVII of 1870 (Indian Penal Code amendment), quoted in Ram Ratan Bhatnagar, *The Rise and Growth of Hindi Journalism*, Allahabad: Kitab Mahal, n.d. [1947?], p. 98.

practice into the lives of a newly "imagined community" of Indian Muslims. This is not an attempt to present a comprehensive study of Sayyid Ahmad's printing enterprise, but rather to identify the range and development of printing technologies and aesthetic formats that he employed. It should be understood that a fuller examination of printing and other forms of communication in northern India and among Indian Muslims would present a much more various and complicated picture, but even this one series will suggest the multiple meanings of printed communications in different historical contexts.

Manuscript of the *Tūzuk-i Jahāngīrī* (India Office mss. Ethé, No. 2833)[25]

In addition to being one of Delhi's first publishers, Sayyid Muhammad was an accomplished calligrapher. Hermann Ethé, the learned orientalist who catalogued the Persian manuscripts in the India Office Library in 1903, describes in detail the "excellent Nasta'lik" and "splendid illuminated frontispieces", "fine gilt arabesques", "each page surrounded by a small gilt frame; gorgeous Eastern binding; size 12 $^{6}/_{8}$ in. by 8 $^{1}/_{2}$ in." of this "excellent copy" of the Emperor Jahangir's memoirs. The five page colophon starts by identifying the calligrapher, Sayyid Muhammad, and his distinguished lineage from the Prophet Muhammad and a long line of Mughal officials. Sayyid Muhammad says that he completed the work in July 1841, giving the Christian date, on the basis of two older manuscripts, one in the Mughal royal library, which was still extant, and another belonging to a private collector, Rajah Roghu Nath Singh; and that he did it for General Thomas Paterson Smith, with a view to preparing a printed version and English translation. A lithographed edition (*ba čhāpah sang*), he says, would be prepared by his brother Sayyid Ahmad,

---

25 Hermann Ethé, *Catalogue of Persian Manuscripts in the India Office Library*, Oxford: India Office, 1903, no. 2833, at http://www.archive.org/details/catalogueofpersi01greauoft; H. Beveridge, "Preface", [in:] *The Tūzuk-i Jahāngīrī or Memoirs of Jahangir*, tr. Alexander Rogers, ed. Henry Beveridge, rpt. edn., Delhi: Munshiram Manoharlal, p. 1968, p. xii. My initial interest in the colophon was spurred by a separate research project on the family history of Sayyid Ahmad Khan.

the *munṣif* of Fatehpur Sikri. According to an inscription on the inner flyleaf, General Smith presented the manuscript to the India Office Library in 1854.

In appearance, Sayyid Muhammad's handsomely illuminated manuscript has much in common with the lithographed publications that were just beginning to appear on the Indian scene, though the direction of influence will require further research. There is no title page and no punctuation or division into paragraphs, but there is a table of contents (*fehrist*) written in red. Consistent with older manuscripts there are corrections in red, rubrications, that may show links between older Islamic and European manuscript conventions. Also, the lines are justified, something that was more easily achieved in *nastaᶜlīq* than in *naqš*, the calligraphic style commonly used in moveable type. The fine waxed paper and multicolored gilt designs marking the separate chapters, were characteristic of older manuscripts, but the numbering of pages was presumably borrowed from printed models. It has been claimed that Indian *nastaᶜlīq* style is closer to printing than Irani styles.[26] If this is true, it isn't clear if this is a recent development in the wake of printing or a convergence of forms.

Manuscript of the *Tūzuk-i Jahāngīrī* (Bodleian Library ms., Sachau and Ethé, No. 221)[27]

Sayyid Muhammad completed the manuscript shortly before his death in 1845. Five years later, his younger brother, Sayyid Ahmad Khan, made his own copy in a similar format, "two illuminated frontispieces (…); each page framed with stripes in gold and other colors; different illustrations, coins, seals, a view of the black stone, etc. etc. (…); binding with green and gold". But there is a disparaging note here, aside from the "etc. etc."; the

---

[26] Golam-Hosayn Yusufi, "Calligraphy", [in:] *Encyclopaedia Iranica* 4 (fasc. 7), p. 711; available at http://www.iranica.com/newsite.

[27] *Catalogue of the Persian, Turkish, Hindustani, and Pushtu Manuscripts in the Bodleian Library*, ed. Eduard Sachau and Hermann Ethé, part I: *Persian Manuscripts*, Oxford at the Clarendon Press, 1889, no. 221, p. 118 [Elliot 406], at http://www.archive.org/details/catalogueofpersi01 bodluoft.

nasta^c*līq*, say the learned cataloguers, is "written by a very modern hand", a charitable way of commenting on the inferiority of the calligraphy, aggravated by a tendency to overlap or insert words over the lines. Aside from the modern style of the illustrations, other "modern feature included a table of contents coordinated with the numbered pagination. The colophon states that Sayyid Ahmad compared ten manuscripts from the library of Bahadur Shah, the *pādšāh* of Delhi, to establish this text. He had done the work for John Panton Gubbins.[28]

The fact that these copies were made for British officials raises questions about payment and patronage and to what extent Mughal and British practices in this regard resembled or diverged from each other.[29] There is no evidence, however, of money changing hands. One may also ask how the task of establishing a text based on comparative readings of alternative manuscript sources reflected contemporary European scholarship as opposed to earlier Islamic standards.

The era of lithography

Munshi Sayyid Ahmad Khan Dehlvi, *Jām-i Jam* ([Agra]: bi chāpa-e sang līthogrāfik [1840])[30]

Sayyid Ahmad Khan's first publication, written when he was twenty-one years old and printed a year later, was a lithographed chart of the Timurid dynasty, prepared at the behest of Robert

[28] S.A.A. Rizvi, "A Farewell Address in Urdu Presented to John Panton Gubbins by the Citizens of Delhi in 1852", *Bulletin of the School of Oriental and African Studies, University of London*, 1964, vol. 27, no. 2, pp. 397-407.

[29] For a good description of Mughal patronage of libraries and book production in the age of Akbar and Jahangir, see John Seyller, *Workshop and Patron in Mughal India: The Freer Ramayana and Other Illustrated Manuscripts of* ^{c}*Abd al-Rahim*, Washington: Artibus Asiae in association with the Freer Gallery of Art, Smithsonian Institution, 1999, Supplementum XLII, pp. 50-8.

[30] Edward Edwards, *A Catalogue of the Persian Printed Books in the British Museum*, London: British Museum, 1922, col. 98 at: http://www.

Hamilton, the Commissioner of Agra, where Sayyid Ahmad had just started his career in the East India Company service. The work starts with a preface that includes the kind of information about the author's family that was contained in the colophons of the Jahangir manuscripts. The chart itself goes from Timur to Bahadur Shah, filling in information under such headings as father's name, mother's name, *qaum* (they are all Chaghtai), various relevant dates (in the Hijri calendar), place of burial, and a brief comment.

***Āʾīn-i Akbarī*, ed. Sayyid Aḥmad Xān, ḥasb-e farmāʾiš Šaix Quṭb ud-Dīn va Muḥammad Ismāʿīl Saudāgarān-e Dehlī, dar Maṭbūʿa Ismāʿīlī... 1272 H [1855 CE]**[31]

As indicated on the title page, Sayyid Ahmad undertook the preparation of a scholarly edition of this late sixteenth century work on a commission from two Delhi merchants. Altaf Husain Hali, Sayyid Ahmad's biographer, states that Sayyid Ahmad was compensated by being presented, as a *naẕr*, an offering from an inferior to a superior, with the published books, valued at Rs. 1,600, although it isn't clear if this amounted to the full edition and how large that edition might have been. Of the three volumes planned for the book, only two, the first and the third, were published. Materials for the second were lost in 1857.[32] In any case,

archive.org/details/catalogueofpersi00brituoft. See also: *Maqalat-i Sar Sayyid*, ed. Muḥammad Ismāʿīl Pānīpatī, vol. 16, Lahore: Majlis Taraqqī-e Adab, 1965, pp. 2-3, 13-74. Cf. H.M. Elliot and John Dowson, *The History of India, as Told by Its Own Historians. The Muhammadan Period*, vol. 8, London: Trübner and Co, 1877, pp. 430-1. For the manuscript of this text, perhaps in SAK's own hand, see Charles Rieu, *Catalogue of the Persian Manuscripts in the British Museum*, vol. 1, London: British Museum, 1966, Or. 145, pp. 284-5, at http://www.archive.org/details/catalogueofpersi01brituoft (thanks to C.M. Naim). See also "Hamilton, Sir Robert North Collie, sixth baronet (1802-1887)", rev. Peter Penner, *Oxford Dictionary of National Biography*, Oxford University Press, 2004 (online edn, Jan 2008: http://www.oxforddnb.com/view/article/12125).

31 Edwards, *A Catalogue of the Persian Printed Books*, col. 55. For a facsimile edition see Abū 'l-Faẓl ʿAllāmī, *Āʾīn-i Akbarī, be taṣḥīh Sar Sayyid Aḥmad*, Alīgaṛh: Sar Sayyid Akaiḍmī, 2005.

32 A.Ḥ. Ḥāli, *Ḥayāt-i Jāvīd*, pp. 78-82.

the project was conceived as a luxury item and a highly limited edition. The book relied on extensive research, with much annotation and insertion of additional information based on variant manuscript and other sources, but it also exhibited the best traditional calligraphy and extensive illustrations.

In the tradition of Islamic manuscripts, annotations were inserted around the page, often sideways and upside down. On the other hand, Sayyid Ahmad took care with tables and charts to align them in ways more like those used in British official records. The illustrations were informative but relied on schematic line drawings at some distance from the Mughal miniatures of the past.[33]

Āṣār us-ṣanādīd, 1st edn. (Delhi: Maṭbū'a Sayyid ul--Axbar, 1847 ᶜisvī, 1263 H.)[34]

Among Sayyid Ahmad's most significant publications during his early years are two editions of an historical account and guide to Delhi. The press used to print them had been purchased by his older brother, Sayyid Muhammad, who died in 1841, the year he completed the *Tūzuk* manuscript. That press was destroyed in the course of the violent conflicts of 1857.

That first edition of *Āṣār us-ṣanādīd* may be counted as one of the earliest works of Urdu historiography, but it was clearly founded on earlier Persian prototypes, more an album (*mu-*

[33] Many of these illustrations were reproduced, without acknowledgement, in the English translation by H. Blochmann (Calcutta: Asiatic Society of Bengal, 1872 and later editions).

[34] J.F. Blumhardt, *Catalogue of Hindustani Printed Books in the Library of the British Museum*, London: 1889, col. 23. See facsimile edition, Sir Syed Academy publication, 1. Alīgaṛh: Sar Sayyid Akaiḍmī, Alīgaṛh Muslim Yūnīvarsiṭī, 2007. I am also indebted to C.M. Naim, "Syed Ahmad and His Two Books Called «Asar-al-Sanadid»", *Modern Asian Studies* 2011, no. 45, pp. 669-708. See also my essays, "The Qutb Minar in Sayyid Ahmad Khan's *Āṣār us-ṣanādīd*", [in:] *Knowledge Production, Pedagogy, and Institutions in Colonial India*, ed. Indra Sengupta and Daud Ali (Houndmills, Basingstoke, Hampshire, England: Palgrave, 2011; "Sauda Sulaf: Urdu in the Two Versions of Sayyid Ahmad Khan's Asaru's-Sanadid", *Annual of Urdu Studies* 2011, vol. 26, pp. 21-38 (<http://www.urdustudies.com/pdf/26/06LelyveldSauda.pdf>).

raqqa^{c}), guidebook, gazetteer and biographical dictionary (*taẕkira*) than historical narrative.[35] Interspersed throughout with long extracts of poetry, mostly in Persian, the Urdu style of the first edition is suffused with Persian language and rhetoric, not easily translatable into English and not, presumably, addressed primarily to a foreign audience.

Although this printed book partakes of some conventions of European publications, there is still some continuity with older Persian manuscript works in a similar genre. The illustrations in one copy at the British Library are hand colored.[36] The script is *nasta*^{c}*līq*, reproduced by lithography.

The title page recalls the ornamental rosettes (*šamsa*) of the Persian manuscript tradition, but as C.M. Naim has pointed out, there is commercial and publication information that one would not see on a manuscript:

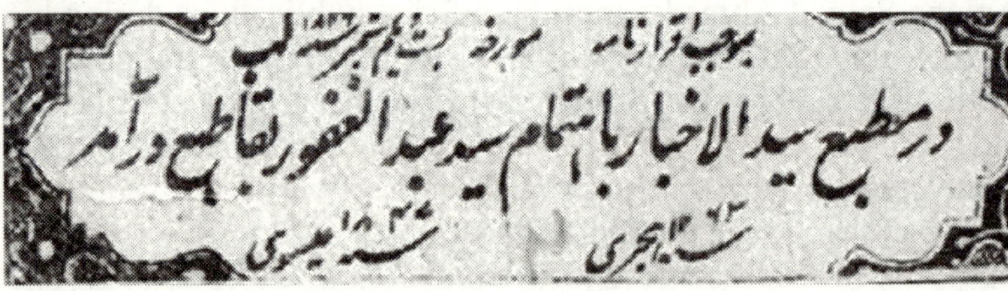

That is, "according to the contract (*iqrār nāma*) dated 1 September, 1846. At the press of Sayyid ul-akhbār, under the supervision of ^{c}Abd ul-Ghafūr, 1263 hijri, 1847 isvi". The text then starts off on the next page with an ornamental presentation of a *taqrīẓ* written for this book, as the heading states, by an eminent senior poet and intellectual of Delhi, Nawab Muhammad Ziya-uddin Khan, presented in four columns over the next four pages and ending with the inverted triangle common to the manuscript tradition. This is followed by the preface, with a new ornamental heading occupying one-third of the page and enclosing the

[35] Christian W. Troll, "Note on an early topographical work of Sayyid Ahmad Khan: *Āsār us-sanādīd*", *Journal of the Royal Asiatic Society*, 1972.

[36] J.F. Blumhardt, *Catalogue of the Library of the India Office*, vol. II, part II: *Hindustani Books*, London, 1900, no. 14109.c6.

bi'smi'l-lāh benediction. Below that comes the source of the book's title, a verse by ᶜUrfi Shirazi of Akbar's court:

> *az naqš o nigāre dar o divār šikasta*
> *āṣ̤ār padīd ast ṣanādīd ᶜajam rā*
>
> The marks and decorations of ruined gates and walls
> reveal traces of foreign [Persian] heroes.

Then comes a four page prose preface that ends with a dedication to the British commissioner of Delhi, a Persian *maṣ̤navī*-s, and a listing of the four chapters (*bāb*) that make up the book. Much of the body of the book is comments on landmarks of the city, presented in no particular geographical, historical or thematic order, and each illustrated with a lithographed black and white picture.

Āṣ̤ār us-ṣanādīd, 2nd edn. (dar maṭ̤ba'a sulṭ̤ānī vaqā'eᶜ qilᶜa-e muᶜallā, 1269 hijrī, muṭ̤ābiq 1852 ᶜisvī)[37]

During the years that intervened between the two editions of *Āṣ̤ār us-ṣanādīd*, Sayyid Ahmad was increasingly drawn into European ideas, methods and social relations. When Arthur Austin Roberts, the Collector and Magistrate of Delhi, travelled to England, he took a copy of the first edition with him to present to the Royal Asiatic Society. He returned with the idea of enlisting Sayyid Ahmad to help him prepare an English translation. In the process of discussing the work, however, Sayyid Ahmad was persuaded that it needed substantial revision with respect organization, chronology, and the accuracy of many of the details in the text.

The second edition has none of the illustrations of the first, but it contains extensive reproductions of inscriptions in a variety of Indic and Islamicate scripts, as well as tables, references and other scholarly apparatus. There is far less poetry, and the lan-

---

[37] J.F. Blumhardt, col. 23; facsimile edition, Sir Syed Academy publication, 2. Alīgaṛh: Sar Sayyid Akaiḍmī, Alīgaṛh Muslim Yūnīvarsiṭī, 2007; also available on google books under its English designation: Syud Ahmed Khan, *Asar-Oos-Sunnadeed: A History of Old and New Rules, or Governments, and of Old and New Buildings in the District of Delhi*, Delhi: Indian Standard Press, 1854.

guage is closer to the undecorated prose style that Sayyid Ahmad later used in much of his journalism. Responding to what purported to be the scholarly demands of some British officials, little was done to make the work attractive by Indian aesthetic standards.

Sayyid Ahmad Khan's shift to typography

Sayyid Ahmad Khan's publications before 1857 used lithography to reproduce handwritten texts.[38] After 1857 and the destruction of his brother's lithographic printing facilities, Sayyid Ahmad turned to moveable type to conduct a concerted campaign to reconcile British rulers and Indians, particularly Muslims, to each other. His publications in the years immediately after the rebellion, *Asbāb-e baġāvat-e Hind* (Causes of the Indian Revolt) and *An Account of the Loyal Mahomedans of India*, both of them printed by J.A. Gibbons at the Mofussilite Press, the first in Agra in 1859, the second in Meerut the following year. Printed in moveable type, they could accommodate both English and Urdu in the same format. Although the *Asbāb* was primarily an Urdu text, it contained marginal and interlinear English glosses and quotations. The *Loyal Muhammadans* text, intended as a serial publication, was presented in double columns, Urdu on the right, English on the left. Both were primarily intended for a British official audience.

> ***Syud Ahmud, The Mohomedan commentary on the Holy Bible*: *Taba'īn al-kalām fī tafsīr al-Taurāt va al-Injīl ᶜalá millat-i al-Islām*, Part First (Ghazeepore: Printed and Published by the Author at his private press, AD 1862, 1278 H)**

According to his biographer Altaf Husain Hali, Sayyid Ahmad drew on compensation and reward money that he received for

---

[38] An exception is *Taḥṣīl fī jarr al-ṣaqīl* (Āgrā ke yatīmoṅ ke chāpa-xāna meṅ [Agra Orphans Press], 1844) a short treatise on mechanics, translated from Persian to Urdu in accordance with the order of (*ba mubib hukam*) Padri John James Moore [?]; in Muḥammad Ismāʾīl Pānīpati, ed., *Maqālāt-i Sar Saiyid*, vol. 16 (Lāhaur, 1965), pp. 75-96.

siding with the British in 1857 to purchase a printing press from Rurki for the considerable sum of Rs. 8,000.[39] Posted in Moradabad at the time, he undertook the project of writing a commentary on the Bible as a way of defending Islam but also reconciling Christians and Muslims in the wake of the violence of the rebellion. When he was transferred to Ghazipur in 1862, he took along this expensive equipment and hired a staff to assist him in his various projects, including an Englishman to prepare the English text and a Jew from Calcutta to help him with the Hebrew. *The Mahomedan Commentary on the Holy Bible*, came out in two parts over the next two years, but was never completed. Using separate typefounts that Sayyid Ahmad had acquired for this purpose, it was printed multilingually in English and Urdu, with a good deal of Arabic and even some Hebrew. That was not something that would have been easy to achieve with handwritten lithography.

Toozook-i Jehangeeree, ed. Syud Ahmed (Allygurh: Printed at his Private Press, AD 1864, 1281 H)[40]

The colophon to Sayyid Muhammad's 1841 manuscript copy of Jahangir's memoirs had declared that a goal of the project was to enable the younger brother, Sayyid Ahmad, to publish a lithographed edition. Now, many years later, Sayyid Ahmad, recently transferred to Aligarh, returned to that text, but this time he used his own press with its moveable type in much the same format as the Bible commentary, even though this text was wholly in Persian. In a similar format was the *Tarīx-i Firūz-šāhī* of Ziya uddin Barani, edited by Sayyid Ahmad but completed "under the superintendence of W.N. Lees and Mawlavi Karbir al-Din" and printed by the Asiatic Society of Bengal in Calcutta.[41]

---

39 A.Ḥ. Ḥāli, *Ḥayāt-i Javīd*, pp. 118, 130. Rurki was a center for iron manufactures. See also Iftikhar ᶜAlam Khan, *Sir Sayyid aur Scientific Society* (Delhi: Maktaba Jamiᶜa, 2000), p. 15.

40 E. Edwards, *A Catalogue of the Persian Printed Books…*, col. 307.

41 Ziaa-i Barni, *The Tárikh-I Feroz-Sháhí of Ziaa Al-Din Barni, Commonly Called Ziaa-I Barni. Edited by Saiyid Ahmad Khán, Under the Superintendence of Captain W. Nassau Lees,... and Mawlavi Kabir Al-Din.* Calcutta: W.N. Lees' Press, 1862. [Available on google books].

One of the features of this and the other publications that issued from this press is that they were all done in a utilitarian moveable type font that eschews any hint of calligraphic (*xušnavīsī*) aesthetics. The work has clear divisions: a title page, a table of contents, a lengthy forward (*dībāča*) in Persian, and footnotes. There is only one illustration at the end of the book, a picture of Jahangir's tomb in Lahore. It is in black and white, and drawn according to European ideas of perspective.

With these two works Sayyid Ahmad's efforts as an historian of the Delhi and the Mughals came to an end. By this time, he had turned his attention elsewhere.

The Aligarh Institute Gazette and *Tahẕīb ul-axlāq*

When Sayyid Ahmad was transferred from Ghazipur to Aligarh in 1864, he brought the press with him. It was there the following year that he brought out his newspaper, *The Aligarh Institute Gazette*, the organ of the Aligarh Scientific Society, primarily in a bilingual format, this time closely resembling the layout of the official government gazette of the North-West Provinces. This publication remained for the rest of his life and beyond an important vehicle for the Muhammadan Anglo-Oriental College and what became known as the Aligarh movement.

In 1872 the total circulation of all vernacular journals in the North-West Provinces and Oudh was under six thousand. The journal with the largest circulation was the weekly *Aligarh Institute Gazette*. It had 381 subscriptions, but 100 of them were to the government, 38 to British readers, and 52 in exchange to other journals. That left 191 private Indian subscribers, all of them members of the Aligarh Scientific Society, sponsor of the journal since it first came out in 1866. The membership of the society had once been up in the four hundreds, but had declined. Members of the society were to pay Rs. 24 a year, plus Rs. 3 for postage, which entitled them to all the society's other publications as well, most particularly its Urdu translations and editions of historical and scientific texts. Non-member subscribers to the gazette had to pay Rs. 12, plus the same postage.[42] Small as the circulation was, it was distributed over a large territory, mostly from Lahore to Patna, but also Hyderabad and Bombay.

Although *The Aligarh Institute Gazette* was bi-lingual in double columns, many pieces were untranslated from the Urdu, in which case both columns would be in Urdu. The bi-lingual format was for the benefit of the gazette's British readers. One critic blamed the journal for wasting space by printing in English, for using "small and smudgy" typeface instead of lithography, and for "twisted and terse" language, a style that was partly imposed by the process of translating items from the English press.[43] But in its early years, perhaps because Sayyid Ahmad was posted in Banaras much of the time, the journal was not always in the good graces of the British authorities. "It affects considerable independence of speech, and apes the bluster of the English press," according to the annual report on publications for 1875. "The style is diffuse and unattractive". The report also noted that *The Aligarh Institute Gazette* and its sister publication *Tahẕīb ul-axlāq* were the targets of intense criticism from other Urdu journals, largely over Sayyid Ahmad's religious and social views.[44] If the press could command only a small circulation, it was nevertheless characterized by strong controversy and rivalry.

Tahẕīb ul-axlāq was explicitly in imitation of *The Spectator* and *The Tatler*, journals of the early eighteenth century London coffee house milieu, with a number of essays adapted from specific prototypes.[45] But, Sayyid Ahmad noted, there was a difference:

---

[42] *The Aligarh Institute Gazette*, vol. II (1867), on the first page of every issue.

[43] Wajid ᶜAli Khan, "Kardar namah", reprinted in *AIG*, XIII, 91 (12 November 1878); see reply in XIII, 98 (7 December 1878). (Thanks to Dr. Shafey Qidwai.)

[44] North-Western Provinces, General Proceedings, April 1875, no. 5 (U.P. Archives, Lucknow); see also *Selections from the Vernacular Press*.

[45] Muhammad Sadiq, *A History of Urdu Literature*, 2nd edn., Delhi: Oxford University Press, 1984, p. 343; A.Ḥ. Ḥāli, *Ḥayāt-i Jāvīd*, p. 163. Cf. Habermas, *The Structural Transformation*, p. 59.

> Steele and Addison were fortunate that their contemporaries used to read and appreciate their writings. But our misfortune is that our writings are regarded as anti-religious. To read them is to court perdition (…) It was not difficult for Steele and Addison to win over a thousand hearts. But to us it is extremely hard to captivate a single one (…) We do not say that by the help of this feeble organ we shall be able to do for India what Steele and Addison did in their days to England (…) 'We but try to begin; it is for Him to complete.'[46]

Journalistic "public" controversy in Urdu and commercial success or failure was a small scale matter. Probably more interesting are the ways that Sayyid Ahmad and his rivals came to represent time and community within the framework of their literary experiments. As Anderson argues, the form and concept of a newspaper rests on the shared, objectified experience of simultaneous stories of what could be a fairly far-flung population.[47] Anderson makes the same point about the novel, which Sayyid Ahmad is again said to have been instrumental in promoting. The first Urdu novel, "Deputy" Nazir Ahmad's *Mirāt ul-ᶜurūs* (The Bride's Mirror), published in 1869, the same year as Ghalib's letters, depicts private experiences, ordinary life and language, for a general, "public" audience to be read privately – or, at least, in school.[48] This echoses what Habermas says about Richardson

---

[46] Quoted in translation in Sayyid ᶜAbdu'l-Latif, *The Influence of English Literature on Urdu Literature* (London: Forster, Groom & Co., 1924), p. 117.

[47] Anderson, *Imagined Communities*, pp. 30, 37-8.

[48] *Mirāt ul-ᶜurūs*, rpt. edn. Delhi: Kutb Xānah Naẕīriya, n.d.; A.Ḥ. Ḥāli, *Ḥayāt-i Jāvīd*, p. 323; Frances W. Pritchett, "Afterword: the first Urdu bestseller", [in:] Nazir Ahmad, *The Bride's Mirror*, rpt. edn. of tr. G.E. Ward, New Delhi: Permanent Black, 2004, pp. 204-23; C.M. Naim, "Prize-Winning *Adab*: A Study of Five Urdu Books Written in Response to the Allahabad Government Gazette Notification", [in:] *Moral Conduct and Authority: The Place of Adab in South Asian Islam*, ed. Barbara Daly Metcalf, Berkeley: University of California Press, 1984, pp. 290-314; D. Lelyveld, *Aligarh's First Generation: Muslim Solidarity in British India*, Princeton University Press, 1978, pp. 56-8; in 1885, 14,000 copies were reprinted (*NWP and Oudh Gazette* II [1886], p. 911). Ralph Russell, in an excellent discussion of *Mirāt ul-ᶜurūs* denies that the work is a "novel", but

and Rousseau.[49] By 1888 it had sold more than 100,000 copies and been translated into five other Indian languages.[50]

For Sayyid Ahmad, however, English had become indispensable – even though he himself was never able to master it. In testimony to the Indian Education Commission in 1882, Sayyid Ahmad explained that he had abandoned his earlier belief in vernacular education, at least with respect to Urdu. It was, he claimed, virtually impossible to express oneself in Urdu without reliance on figures of speech and exaggerated expressions.[51] Sayyid Ahmad's shift from lithography to type, from decorated formats to plain ones, went along with changes in prose style, ideological focus and public activities, such as the creation of voluntary associations and, most of all, the Aligarh College.

Taṣānīf i Aḥmadīyah, vol. 7, part 1/ *Tafsīr al-Qur'ān*, vol. 6 (Aligarh: Aligarh Institute Press, 1335 Nabvi, 1312 Hijri, 1895 ʿĪsvī)

Even wholly Urdu publications, notably *Tahẕīb ul-axlāq*, the intellectual and literary journal of the Aligarh movement, maintained a format and typography that was similar to the *Aligarh Institute Gazette*. Most striking is Sayyid Ahmad's use of moveable type for an explicity religious text, namely his commentary on the *Qurʾan*. During his lifetime, he published six volumes over the space of fifteen years, from 1880 to 1895. The format of the Tafsir separated the scriptural text in a large, bold *nasx* typeface at the top of the page from the Urdu translation and commentary below, but assimilated them both to an image of rational

in terms of the arguments of Habermas and Anderson the work fits the model; "The Modern Novel in Urdu", [in:] *The Novel in India*, ed. T.W. Clark, Berkeley: University of California Press, 1970, pp. 118-22. Russell also points out that the novel was originally written before the announcement of the prize, for the private edification of the author's family; for a recent historical analysis see Ruby Lal, "Gender and *Sharafat*: Rereading Nazir Ahmad", *Journal of the Royal Asiatic Society*, 2008 (January), vol. 18, part I, pp. 15-30.

49 Habermas, *The Structural Transformation*, pp. 49-50.

50 Russell, "The Modern Novel in Urdu", p. 119.

51 Lelyveld, *Aligarh's First Generation*, pp. 206-7.

order, which was the point of Sayyid Ahmad's exegesis. A seventh volume, published posthumously in 1904 by the Mufīd al-ᶜĀmm Press in Agra, reverted to calligraphic lithography.[52] Even during his lifetime, Sayyid Ahmad published some of his religious as well as personal works with this press, which was notable for the beauty of its calligraphy and the clarity of its printing. It may not be possible to retrieve the spiritual experience of the typesetter and compare it to the calligrapher, but it is reasonable to conclude that Sayyid Ahmad, an indifferent calligrapher himself, wanted the act of producing the publication to reverberate with the technological processes of the modern world. Typography may have suggested impersonal, unambiguous standardization, something that could be read without benefit of an a personal intermediary. In the end, however, Sayyid Ahmad's use and style of typography turned out to be an idiosyncratic, personal statement of the man's quest to make religious inspiration relevant to the changing times.

Sayyid Ahmad's preference for moveable type over lithography was exceptional. Urdu publishing had overwhelmingly moved in the opposite direction since the introduction of lithography. The great commercial publishing houses, notably Nawal Kishor of Lucknow, relied almost entirely on lithography for its Urdu publications.[53] There is reason to believe that choosing typography over lithography was not a particularly wise economic calculation. Perhaps Sayyid Ahmad was stuck with his Rs. 8,000 investment, which lasted for nearly four decades, but one would still need to compare how much typesetters were paid as opposed to calligraphers.[54] Lithography, gradually replaced by photo-offset in the later twentieth century, maintained the role

---

[52] I have examined these volumes in the Rare Books collection of the British Library. The collection at Aligarh Muslim University has been scanned and now available on line at http://www.sirsyedtoday.org.

[53] See U. Stark, *An Empire of Books*; see also Brinkley Messick, "On the Question of Lithography", *Culture & History* [Copenhagen] 1997, vol. 15, pp. 158-76. Many thanks to Prof. Messick for providing me with a copy of his paper, which deals with Arabic legal texts from Yemen.

[54] For the expenses involved in operating Sir Sayyid's press, see Iftikhar ᶜAlam Khan, *Sir Sayyid aur Scientific Society*, pp. 38-41.

THE MOHAMMEDAN SOCIAL REFORMER

تہذیب الاخلاق

جلد دوم] یکم شوال سنہ ۱۳۱۲ ہجری سنہ ۱۲۲۵ [?] نبوی [نمبر ۱

نمبر ۱

عید

السلام علیکم عید مبارک ہو — وعلیکم السلام آپکو بھی مبارک ہو مصافحہ کیجیئے — اس سے مجھے معاف رکھو — مصافحہ کو عید کے دن مخصوص کرنا بدعت ہی — اگر بدعت ہی تو جانے دیجیئے — کیا آپ اسے بدعت نہیں سمجھتے ؟ — جناب میں تو نہ مصافحہ کو بدعت سمجھتا ہوں نہ معانقہ کو، بدعت دراصل اعتقاد سے تعلق رکھتی ہی — عید کے مصافحہ یا معانقہ کو کوئی سنت یا مستحب یا واجب نہیں سمجھتا — عید کا دن مسلمانوں کی خوشی کا دن ہی — کوئی آپس میں دوستوں سے ہاتھہ ملاکے خوش ہوتا ہی کوئی گلے لگ کے — اسکو سنت اور بدعت سے کیا تعلق ہی *

ایکی دفعہ تو عیدگاہ میں بہت کثرت سے لوگ تھے اور سب قسم کے لوگ بہت خوش معلوم ہوتے تھے آپ نے بھی دیکھا ہوگا — ؟ میں تو عیدگاہ نہیں گیا — مگر سب قسم کے لوگوں سے آپکی کیا مراد ہی — اور وہ سب کیوں خوش تھے ؟ *

حضرت — ہاں، پیر بڈھے تو اسلیئے خوش تھے کہ انکو توقع نہ تھی کہ انکی زندگی میں پھر رمضان آویگا اور اگر آویگا تو روزے بھی رکھہ سکینگے یا نہیں — خدا کے فضل سے انکی زندگی میں رمضان آیا اور انہوں نے روزے بھی رکھے فرض سے بھی ادا ہوئے اور قیامت میں بہشت میں جانے کا سامان ہوا *

علما اور زہاد اسلیئے خوش تھے کہ انہوں نے روزے رکھے — تراویح پڑھیں — اعتکاف کیا — ان کے مریدوں شاگردوں میں ان کا تقدس زیادہ بڑھا اور اگر اس میں سے کچھہ خدا نے بھی منظور کرلیا تو پھر کیا کہنا ہی چپڑی اور دو دو ادھر بندے خوش ادھر خدا خوش *

جوان اسلیئے خوش تھے کہ خدا خدا کرکے فاقوں کے دن کٹے — اب رات دن جو چاہو سو کھاؤ اور جو چاہو سو کرو چین سے رہو *

Tahẕīb ul-axlāq (March 28, 1895)

and aesthetics of Urdu calligraphy to dominate the field. Only very recently, over the last fifteen years or so, have computer fonts made calligraphy and calligraphers obsolete in India and Pakistan.

Type, however, made Urdu look somewhat more like English on the printed page in the late nineteenth century. By that time, for example, most government records, notably court cases and revenue regulations came in printed formats, not the cursive English calligraphy of the East India Company that perhaps had more in common to the chancery styles of Persian or Urdu. If one wanted to create an equivalence between Urdu and English, and to print them side by side, moveable type was more suitable than lithography. It should be noted that lithography was not the preferred method for other Indian scripts like Hindi, though it was used for a Hindi edition of *Ās̤ār us-ṣanādīd* that came out in 1876.[55]

Lekčarz-o-ispičaz

Hali, Sir Sayyid's biographer, devotes a section of his biography of Sayyid Ahmad Khan to "public speaking" – the word is transliterated – and public meetings (*majmūᶜa-i ᶜām*). A "speech" or "lecture" – again he uses the English words – has far more influence, he says, than the written word because people read individually in different settings and therefore have different responses, whereas "the effect of a speech [here, however, he uses the word *taqrīr*] falls upon the whole gathering collectively and simultaneously". Without mentioning the traditions of religious oratory, Hali claims that Sayyid Ahmad was the first person in Hindustan to introduce public speaking in a language other than English. (By Hindustan he probably means the region between Punjab and Bengal). Although there were some great Bengali orators, so far as he has heard, they all spoke in English. For Hali, who describes his own first experience of hearing Sayyid Ahmad speak in Lahore to an audience said to number over 10,000 in 1874, to raise funds for the Aligarh College, such ora-

55 *Saṃsāradarpaṇa*, Delhi: Gopal Malik, 1876. This is only a very approximate version, at best, of Sayyid Ahmad's work, though it is attributed to him. [OCLC: 32991055].

tory was a vivid, new experience. "Although public speeches now seem to be everyday things, Sir Sayyid's introduction of speechmaking was completely new to ordinary Hindustanis".[56]

The reason India had no tradition of oratory, Hali claims, is that under a *salṭanat* subjects have no right to express their opinions. Only by the grace of British rule was public utterance possible. But Hali ignores the *vaᶜẓ* delivered from the *minbar* of a mosque or the *malfūẓāt* of a Sufi *xānqāh*.[57] It is not that he excludes religious topics from his category of public speaking, because one of his chief examples is a wholly theological speech that Sayyid Ahmad gave in Lahore in 1884. The difference would seem to be the form and setting of these speeches, which make them into an entirely different genre of public utterance. In particular he emphasizes the informal and extempore nature of Sayyid Ahmad's oratory, never prepared in advance, relatively colloquial in language, and communicated as much in voice and facial expression as in words. Sayyid Ahmad, he says, had no training and no prototypes; he was just a natural orator.

Sayyid Ahmad's first recorded public utterance is a prayer (*duᶜā*) he offered in a Moradabad mosque in 1859 before an estimated twelve to fifteen thousand people. Marking the end of the Revolt, it was a formal statement of allegiance to British rule. The second was a Persian discourse on the value of studying European science, delivered at the home of ᶜAbd ul-Latif Khan in Calcutta. In 1864 in Ghazipur, first at the founding of a school, then of the Scientific Society, Sayyid Ahmad began to develop into the kind of public speaker that Hali describes.[58] In 1869, he travelled to London where he attended several public meetings,

---

[56] A.Ḥ. Ḥāli, *Ḥayāt-i Jāvīd*, pp. 193, 640-51.

[57] See references in D. Lelyveld, "Eloquence and Authority in Urdu: Poetry, Oratory, and Film", [in:] *Shariᵓat and Ambiguity in South Asian Islam*, ed. Katherine P. Ewing, Berkeley: University of California Press, 1988, p. 105. Cf. Patrick D. Gaffney, "Authority and the Mosque in Upper Egypt: The Islamic Preacher as Image and Actor", [in:] *Islam and the Political Economy of Meaning*, ed. William R. Roff, Berkeley: University of California Press, 1987, pp. 199-225.

[58] Sayyid Aḥmad Xān, *Mukammal majmūᶜa Lekčarz-o-Ispīčaz*, ed. Muḥammad Imām ud-dīn Gujrātī, Lahore: Maṭbūᵓa-i Musṭafaᵓi, 1900.

even though he did not understand English[59]. After that he made numerous tours along the major railway routes of north India and down to Hyderabad, all to raise money for Aligarh College.

A detailed account of his second tour of the Punjab early in 1884 was prepared by Sayyid Iqbal ᶜAli, a sub-judge of Bara Banki, who made it his mission to record as much as he could of Sayyid Ahmad's oratory.[60] Iqbal ᶜAli is highly conscious that they have crossed a linguistic boundary. He makes several remarks about how interesting it is to hear Punjabis speak Urdu and how difficult it is to understand what they are saying. (Bara Banki, as some of us know, has a particularly forbidding standard of linguistic perfection). Also travelling with Sayyid Ahmad was a zamindar from Aligarh district, a friend from Delhi, and Sayyid Ahmad's English-speaking nephew. At the station in Khanna, the first stop in Ludhiana district, and then at other stops along the way, they were met by members of local Islamic organizations, who accompanied them into Ludhiana itself. There a crowd that Iqbal ᶜAli guessed was over 800 overflowed the platform into the adjoining *maidān*. Among these Iqbal ᶜAli is careful to list the names of all the local notables and officials, including several Hindus and Sikhs, who were there to greet them. An Extra-Assistant Commissioner stepped forward and with both hands placed a garland around Sayyid Ahmad's neck, while others threw bouquets. The party then drove off to the house of the Nawab of Jhajjar. Among the people who came to see Sayyid Ahmad were strong opponents of his religious views who engaged him in serious and extended conversations.

That evening Sayyid Ahmad gave a "lecture" at the Ludhiana town hall to an audience that overflowed the room on to the verandas outside. Many had to leave for lack of space. After a brief introduction by the Nawab, Sayyid Ahmad stood up and in his own spontaneous words, as Iqbal ᶜAli puts it, "did the work of the *marṣ̤iya*-s of Dabir and Anis" – that is, drove the audience to sobs and tears. In the speech Sayyid Ahmad modulates skillfully

---

59 Ḥāli, *Ḥayāt-i Jāvīd*, pp. 153-5.

60 Sayyid Iqbāl ᶜAlī, *Sayyid Aīḥmad Xān kā Safar Nāmah-i Panjāb*, rpt. edn. Šaix Muḥammad Ismāᶜīl Pānīpatī, Lahore: Majlis Taraqqī-e Adab, 1973 [1884].

from a brief expression of Persianized politeness formulas to bits of Arabic piety finally to an intimate style in which he addresses his audience in the familiar *tum* mode. He starts by calling himself an insignificant traveller, unworthy of their gracious hospitality. Then he goes into a discussion of the concept of *qaum* or community. For Muslims it is not based on race (*nasl*) or country (*mulk*), but on individual submission to God. ("O Lord, make it so. Amen!") On the other hand, man has two aspects, human and divine. Religion, the divine part, is entirely between the individual and God; and no one else, neither family nor *qaum*, has the right to interfere.

In practical matters, however, there must be social cooperation. Here Muslims and Hindus are brothers, practically the same *qaum*, and differing Muslim sects must join together just as Hazrat ᶜAli joined the Khalifa Muᶜawiya to face the challenge of the Byzantine emperor. There is, to be sure, much that is virtuous among Muslims. They endow mosques, imambaras, khanqahs; they go on pilgrimage. But all this is finally self-regarding. It is all intended to prepare their individual souls for the day of judgement. What Sayyid Ahmad suggests is that if they work with their right hands for the end of days, let them at least use their left hands for the sake of others, for the sake of the *qaum*. A *qaum*, he says, is like a body of water: if there is no movement, no progress, it will dry up. What is required is not small, separate efforts in little localities. These are a mere drizzle and will bring forth no crop. Nor should they expect others, such as their British rulers, to do their work for them. The task requires the union of private, voluntary efforts for the mutual benefit of all Indian Muslims.

Then Sayyid Ahmad spoke of himself. For twenty-five years he has toiled for Muslim education. He has given up his home and moved to Aligarh, where he had no property or family, just because it was the most suitable place. He then describes the college, emphasizing the enforcement of prayers and theological education as well as the sense of unity among the students. Yet other Muslims have subjected him and his work to bitter attack. "Call me what you like, infidel, heretic, *naičari*. I am not asking you to intercede for me before God (…) Whatever I say is for the benefit of your own children."

The audience, Iqbal ᶜAli reports, cheered loudly and donated some fifteen hundred rupees to the Aligarh cause. The next day the party moved on to Jalandhar.

Conclusion: fragment of a public sphere

It would be appropriate to place the publications and speeches of Sayyid Ahmad Khan in the context of his other publications and his other enterprises; even more, it would be useful to see where these manifestations stand in the wider "information order" of Urdu and, alongside Urdu, Hindi, not to mention the other languages of India as well as the language of the colonial regime. Sayyid Ahmad Khan's publications and speeches cannot be described as commercial ventures. They relied initially on face to face relationships in which official British patronage loomed large, and even when they were touched by commercial motives, as in the case of the *Āʾīn-i Akbarī*, Sayyid Ahmad's compensation was masked in the terms of ritual exchange. In later years, Sayyid Ahmad's publications were supported by subscriptions that were broadly advertised as acts of public spirit, what would be called today non-profit activities. The names of the subscribers were usually printed in the publication.

In contrast, Sayyid Ahmad's friend and sometime critic, Nazir Ahmad, published *Mirāt ul-ᶜurūs* (The Bride's Mirror) in 1869, the "first Urdu bestseller".[61] First written for his daughters and circulated in manuscript among friends, this popular work of fiction became an enduring commercial success.

It would be more difficult to figure out how Sir Sayyid's various publications were actually read. The fact that most of them were produced typographically does not necessarily tell us what his readers made of them, either as occasions for liberation or domination or perhaps something else. "Your *Social Reformer* was constantly read to me by my fond father, who looked upon you as no less than a prophet of the nineteenth century", wrote Lala Lajpat Rai in an open letter to Sir Sayyid to express dis-

---

[61] See Frances W. Pritchett, "Afterword: the first Urdu bestseller", [in:] Nazir Ahmad, *The Bride's Mirror*. Rpt. edn. of tr. G.E. Ward (New Delhi: Permanent Black, 2004), pp. 204-23.

appointment over the latter's opposition to the newly formed Indian National Congress.[62] In this case, it seems, even a typographical text could be read aloud as part of a personal interaction.

The task now would be to identify Sayyid Ahmad Khan's audience or, more ambitiously, to analyse the conditions for the production and reception of his writings and those of his colleagues in the Aligarh movement. One might approach this sociologically, by counting of subscription lists, for example, and trying to locate these people according to indigenous or theoretical categories of groups and relationships. One might also consider this as a problem in rhetoric, a search for the "implied reader" in the text and relation of that text to other texts.[63] In either case it is important to consider the question over time, as part of a history that reaches ahead to later circumstances, interpretations, and uses.

---

[62] *Lala Lajpat Rai: Writings and Speeches*, Volume One, 1888-1919, ed. Vijaya Chandra Joshi (Delhi: University Publishers, 1966), pp. 1-25. "The 'Open Letters' originally appeared in the Urdu weekly Koh-Noor of Lahore" (<http://www.columbia.edu/itc/mealac/pritchett/00islamlinks/txt_lajpatrai_1888/txt_lajpatrai_1888.html#index>).

[63] Wolfgang Iser, *The Implied Reader: Patterns of Communication in Prose Fiction from Bunyan to Beckett*, Baltimore: Johns Hopkins University Press, 1974; cf. M.M. Bakhtin, "The Problem of the Text in Linguistics, Philology, and the Human Sciences: An Experiment in Philosophical Analysis", [in:] *Speech Genres and Other Late Essays*, tr. Vern McGee, Austin: University of Texas Press, 1986, pp. 103-31.

Ideas & Notions

Power, culture and language of poetry: the transition from Vali to Ghalib

Mehr Afshan Farooqi

As a very young man of perhaps not more than fifteen years of age, Mirza Asadullah Khan Ghalib (1797-1869) expressed his admiration for the Persian poet Bedil in a *šeᶜr*:

> Writing Rekhtah in the manner of Bedil!
> My God, Asadullah Khan! What an enormous
> Thing it is!
>
> *Ṭarz-e Bedil mẽ rextah kahnā*
> *Asadullah Xān qiyāmat hai*[1]

There is an untranslatable wordplay in the second line. *Qiyāmat hai* can be a phrase expressing wonder and admiration. It can also imply disapproval. But it can also mean, "It's very, very difficult". Its literal meaning is, "It's [as severe, as taxing as] the Doomsday". It is possible that the precocious adolescent meant

---

[1] This, and the following two verses are taken from the first version of Ghalib's *dīvān*, completed in 1816 when Ghalib was barely 18 years old.

all these things by *qiyāmat hai*, but it is certain that he was admiring himself for being able to tread the path that the great Indo-Persian poet Mirza Abdul Qadir Bedil (1644-1720) had walked with such distinction more than a century ago.

In an earlier ghazal, probably from a somewhat earlier date than the one from which I quoted above, the young poet alleviated his own doubts, as follows:

> Oh Ghalib, I have no fear
> Of going astray in poetry's journey:
> Bedil's pen
> Is the Guiding Staff of Khizir in poetry's vast
> And wild spaces.
>
> *Mujhe rāh-e suxan mẽ xauf-e gumrāhī nahī̃ Ġālib*
> *ᶜAṣā-e xiẓr-e ṣaḥrā-e suxan hai xāmah Bedil kā*

The youthful acolyte is conscious of the fact that poetry for him is not just drawing room art, to be mastered by bookish practice. The poetry that he wants to compose comes from a different world, from a *ṣaḥrā* in fact: a *ṣaḥrā* is a vast and lonely place, with some trees, some wildernesses, some trackless overgrown or barren roads to be discovered anew; and Bedil's pen/poetry functioning like Khizr's staff will save him from losing his way in that fascinating but dangerous space.

In yet another ghazal, the newly minted Master gave us reasons for exuberant confidence:

> Asad, poetry has everywhere
> Laid foundations for fresh gardens,
> The spring-inventing style of Bedil
> Does please my heart.
>
> *Asad har jā suxan ne ṭarḥ-e bāġ-e tāẓā ḍālī hai*
> *Mujhe ṭarz-e bahār ijādi-e Bedil pasand āyā*

Ignoring other wordplays, we must note the one in *pasand āyā* which means, "pleases me" and also "I have chosen for myself".

We must remember that these verses were written in the years immediately following the death of Muhammad Taqi Mir

(1722-1810), or maybe even during the last years of Mir's life.[2] Mir was then regarded as the finest and the greatest Urdu poet whose mastery had been acknowledged by Ghalib himself in this very *dīvān* from which I have been quoting. Ghalib wrote:

> What account should I give, oh Ghalib,
> Of the poetry of Mir whose divan
> Is nowhere less
> Than the garden of Kashmir?
>
> *Mīr ke šeᶜr kā aḥvāl kahū̃ kyā Ġālib*
> *Jis kā dīvān kam az gulšan-e Kašmīr nahī̃*

There seems to be a subtle but clear contradiction here: Mir's mastery is fully acknowledged by Ghalib, yet he doesn't choose Mir for his mentor and guide. He in fact has already started his poetic journey on the path of Bedil, and it's a conscious decision. There could be many answers to the question why Ghalib favors Bedil over Mir even though he admires Mir's poetry. A partial answer has been provided by his friend, pupil and first biographer Altaf Husain Hali (1837-1914) in his immensely influential *Yādgār-e Ġālib* (Ghalib's Memorial, 1897). According to Hali, Ghalib had a propensity for n o t doing things that were popular among his peers or even seniors. So he consciously veered away from the beaten track and wrote in a style that was obscure and highly Persianized. He chose themes that were far-fetched, subtle, and generally far from the common human experience as presented in Ghazal as a genre. According to Hali, Ghalib took a great risk in swimming against the current and earned scorn even derision from his peers. Hali even quotes an anecdote to illustrate Ghalib's penchant for the unpopular and the unusual: it seems that Ghalib had predicted (half jokingly) that he would surely die in the coming year. An epidemic quite fortuitously attacked Delhi in the next year, but Ghalib didn't die. On being asked by somebody about the apparent failure of his prediction, Ghalib is

---

[2] It is generally accepted that Ghalib wrote his first poem, a short *maṡnavī*, at the age of seven, that is, in about 1804.

reported to have replied that he didn't want to die at a time when all the world was dying.

The reason why Hali's explanation is only partly correct is because, there were at least two poets in Delhi in Ghalib's early youth who wrote in a style which has similarities to Ghalib. They were Shah Nasir (1755-1838) and his pupil Zauq (1788-1854). There was also, in Lucknow, Shaikh Nasikh (1777-1838) who acquired Shah Nasir's manner so much so that being the better known poet, he is credited as the inventor of that manner. All the three poets acknowledged Mir's undisputed mastery, and all three wrote in a non-Mir like, cerebral, non-emotive style that reveled in abstract or far fetched themes. Zauq imitated Nasikh's style, and Ghalib also wrote many ghazals which clearly show the influence of Nasikh, though he never admitted Nasikh's influence. Despite the fact that Ghalib was more cerebral, intellectually more sophisticated and stylistically more convoluted that any of the above three, there is a similarity, especially between Nasikh and Ghalib which cannot be wished away.

Hali's anecdote highlights Ghalib's individualism. Ghalib was an individualist, in as much as all great poets are in some sense or the other. But while Hali gives emphasis to the uniqueness of Ghalib, he also points out elsewhere in *Yādgār*, that Ghalib relied on Persian poet's usages and never deployed a word, phrase, or word-combination (*tarkīb*) that he didn't find in the pages of the acknowledged Persian masters of the past. If Ghalib was so dependent for his word-combinations on Persian poets then surely he was not as original (at least with words) as Hali makes him out to be. And Hali doesn't seem to have noticed this contradiction. Also, Hali seems to have failed to appreciate that Ghalib wasn't writing in isolation and that all poetry has to, and indeed does, learn from the masters of the past. This is especially true of Ghalib because he liked to see himself as primarily a Persian poet. Literary practices such as *istiqbāl* (salutation of poets and poetry), *javāb* (reply), *tatabbu*ᶜ (to walk after, or in the footsteps of someone), were common in Indian Persian poetics from the sixteenth century onwards, and Ghalib made unabashed use of these precedents. In his letters, Ghalib frequently refers to this or the other Persian poet whom he admires, or for whom, as in ᶜUrfi's (1550-8) case, he has unbounded and unconditional admiration. But he rarely claims to be doing something for which there was no precedent.

2.

There is no doubt that Ghalib comes across, even today, as very different from almost all other poets in the Urdu canon. But this could be much more a criticism of the canon than praise for Ghalib. It can be argued that by ignoring, especially under the influence of the powerful voices of Altaf Husain Hali and Muhammad Husain Azad, all those poets who were Ghalib's true predecessors in Urdu, the canon makers not only narrowed the canon down to a few poets but also managed to present Ghalib as something like a *sui generis* who didn't owe anything to anyone at all. This may also have had the effect of obscuring, or in fact fully occluding certain aspects of Delhi's cultural politics and history which could have a bearing not only on Ghalib's individuality alone, but also on the shift, or the departure from Mir that for most of us seems to characterize Urdu poetry of the nineteenth century.

Urdu literature did not begin in Delhi, though the language seems to have arisen in and around Delhi. The area which saw Urdu's birth in about the eleventh century is, in modern terms, much of Delhi's National Capital Region and some further parts of modern day Uttar Pradesh, Haryana and Panjab. At that time the language was known as *Hindī* or *Hindvī*, though these terms were also used to denote any local language. But since Panjabi already existed then, and was known by the name of *Panjābī* or *zabān-e Panjāb*, it is quite likely that contextually in eleventh century Panjab or other areas to the East, the language that we know as Urdu today was known as *Hindī/Hindvī*. Literature, if any happened to be composed in its first three centuries of existence, hasn't come down to us. We have, as is well-known, just two reports about the earliest Urdu literature. A century after the death of Masᶜud Saᶜd Salman (1046-1121) we are informed by Muhammad ᶜAufi, the first to write a *tazkira* (biographical dictionary) of Persian poets, that Masᶜud wrote a whole *dīvān* of

Hindvi verse. This was obliquely confirmed by Amir Khusrau (1253-1325) a century later. Khusrau also claimed to have written a few folios of Hindvi poetry for the delectation of his friends.

Nothing of the Hindvi poetry of Mas[c]ud or Khusrau survives. To all intents and purposes, Urdu literature was first written by the Sufis of Gujarat, and the first one to do so was Shaikh Bahauddin Bajan (1399-1526) who wrote, among other things, a verse account of a debate between the *sāṛī* and the *pešvāz*, the latter being a sort of loose full-dress gown favoured by women. There is no humor or satire in the poem, but it is clear from the language and the general air of the poem's "literariness" that the poet is not working in a vacuum. He describes his language as "Hindvi" and also as "Dihlavi". As time passes, the language is identified more often as "Gujri". We have no means of knowing how different, or how close to the Delhi register is the language of Shaikh Bajan. It certainly has elements that are recognizable even today in the Urdu spoken far away from Delhi in the eastern regions of modern eastern Uttar Pradesh and western Bihar. This suggests that Hindvi had already developed a register that was common to all the areas where it was spoken.

Hindi/Hindvi traveled further south, to the Deccan, in about the fifteenth century itself, and the first known Urdu poet there is Fakhr-e Din Nizami whose long *maṡnavī*, tentatively titled by scholars as *Kadam Rā'o Padam Rā'o* has been dated to the 1430s. The vocabulary of this poem, while retaining all the characteristics of Gujri, also shows a heavy undertow of Telugu and Kannada, while there are elements which seem more like Panjabi. It is obvious that a new register of the language is emerging. It is a register that is recognizable as Gujri-Dihlavi, but has much in it that is foreign to Gujri-Dihlavi. This is why early poets occasionally identify their language as Gujri or Hindi/Hindvi. There is a growing tendency to describe the language as "Dakani" or "Dakhini".

The Mughals arrived in strength in the Deccan by the seventeenth century, but not much change seems to have occurred in the language of Dakani/Hindvi. That is, no new characteristics identifiable as Dihlavi can be discerned in the poetry of, for example Nusrati (d. *c.* 1674) about whose language Lachmi Narain Shafiq Aurangabadi (1745-1806) wrote nearly a century later to the effect that on account of its heavy Telugu and other foreign components, Nusrati's poetry wasn't too popular among people of the North. Things changed when Aurangzeb and his armies came to the Deccan around the 1680's and the new city of Aurangabad sprang up within a very short time. Aurangzeb and his armies remained in Aurangabad until the emperor's death in 1707. The population and the language of Aurangabad was greatly influenced by the influx of the armies of the north. It must be remembered that until about the middle of the nineteenth century, the camp followers and hangers-on in the army exceeded the actual fighting force by a factor of ten. It was therefore natural for the Dakani-Aurangabadi register of Urdu to be colored by the Dihlavi register which too gained from its interaction with the Deccan.

Thus, by the last quarter of the seventeenth century there were at least four registers or idioms of Urdu/Hindi. (The language name *Urdū* didn't of course exist then). These four modes of Urdu/Hindi were:

(1) The Gujri register, which came increasingly to be again called *Hindī* in the eighteenth century;
(2) The Dakani register, which was now almost always called *Dakanī*;
(3) The Aurangabadi register, which was called *Dakanī* but which may also have been known by the name *Hindī/ Hindvī*;
(4) The Delhi register, whose name was *Hindī/Hindvī*, but the name *Rekhtah* too was not unknown. It must be remembered that this register was prevalent more or less throughout "Hindustan", that is, the entire land of India north of river Narbada (the Narmada in modern day Madhya Pradesh).

It must be noted that at that time none of these registers, and certainly not the Delhi register, had any privilege over the rest. More important, while Gujri, Dakani, and to a certain extent Aurangabadi had a written literature, Delhi (with one exception) didn't have any such thing in main line Urdu/Hindi/Rekhtah.

Delhi had some poetry in the "Rekhtah mode", that is, a sort of macaronic verse in which Hindi/Urdu was superimposed on the Persian template, or Persian was superimposed on the Hindi/Urdu template. The best and the most well known work in the Rekhtah mode is a long poem called *Bikaṭ Kahānī* (Dire Tale) by Muhammad Afzal who died in 1625.

The next important name in the Rekhtah mode is Jafar Zatalli (1659?-1713) who wrote quite a bit in main line Urdu/Hindi as well. His poetry and prose, though of great historical and literary interest, were entirely ignored in Delhi and elsewhere. While Zatalli found no imitators or admirers, his language shows that Hindi/Urdu in Delhi had reached an advanced stage of development. Zatalli's work is a storehouse of swear words, dirty words, abusive language, and sex related works whose repertoire has not been rivaled. As is well known, such words constitute a sub-language (not slang) which generally comes into being when a language has realized its possibilities in a large measure. Zatalli's work has much historical and literary value but he was regarded in his time as an insignificant writer mainly because he didn't write in any of the well known genres: *ġaẓal*, *qaṣīda*, and *maṣ̤navī*. His influence on the Urdu poetry of Delhi, or Urdu poetry anywhere, was zero.

3.

It is a paradox, not fully appreciated by the historians of Urdu literature, that Delhi had a vibrant and fully expressive local language in Hindi/Hindvi/Rekhtah before the end of the seventeenth century but it had no literature in that language. In fact, poets of Delhi tended to look down upon Hindi/Hindvi/Rekhtah and to believe that only Persian had the capability to permit composition of ghazals in it. This is borne out by a famous verse of Qiyamuddin Qaʾim Chandpuri (1725-95). He said:

> Qaiʾm, it was I who gave Rekhtah
> The manner of a ghazal. Otherwise

It was but a feeble thing
In the dakani tongue.[3]

We know that from Khusrau's times Delhi had prided itself on its Persian and the great linguist and lexicographer and Persian Sirajuddin Ali Khan-e Arzu (1688-1756) had declared Persian to be the language of the *Urdū-e Muᶜallā-e Šāhjahānābād* (that is, the Exalted City and Court of Delhi). Delhi's preference for Persian over Hindi may have been a sign of elitism, or even hubris. Indeed the large number of excellent local and trans-local Persian writers, especially poets, who could be found at any time in Delhi since at least the sixteenth century should have been enough to turn anyone's head. Qa'im's verse quoted above shows not a little of elitism and a substantial amount of contempt for Dakani. But the contempt may have been more political than literary. That is, it may have been assumed, not real, and its purpose could have been to make an important point in literary politics and it may have been more a symbolic expression of Delhi's centrality in the equation of literary power, a position that Delhi had almost lost on the political map of India. Mir, greatest of Urdu poets of the eighteenth century, had had not the least qualm in declaring in his *tazkira* of Urdu poets that no poet ever rose from the land of Deccan. In his own *tazkira* of Urdu poets, Qa'im had been more charitable about the poets from Deccan but he expressed his true opinion of Dakani poetry in the verse that I have quoted above. It can be said that this verse is the most famous one that Qa'im wrote and its fame is not because of any special literary excellence or felicity, but because of its explicit damning of Dakani poetry.

The literary politics behind the purdah of literary-linguistic contempt for Dakani originated in the year 1700 when a poet from Gujarat/Aurangabad visited Delhi. He is famous throughout Urdu history as Vali; his name may have been Muhammad Vali, or Vali Muhammad, or neither of the two, because other names

[3] Qā'im Čāndpūrī, *Kulliyāt*, vol. I, ed. Iqtidā Ḥasan, Lahore: Majlis Taraqqī-e Adab, 1965, p. 215.

too have been suggested.[4] He doesn't seem to have made a mark on the literary community of Delhi at that time, except that both Mir and Qa'im report long after the event that while in Delhi he visited Shah Gulshan, a respected local sufi and a minor Persian poet, who advised him to freely use the themes of Persian poetry that hadn't yet been introduced in Urdu poetry. According to Mir and Qa'im, and then by every Urdu scholar except Dr. Muhammad Sadiq and Shamsur Rahman Faruqi who believe that no such advice was given or taken, Vali took this advice to heart and revolutionized Urdu poetry.

Musahafi (1750-1824) has reported in his *tazkira*, called *Tazkira-e Hindī* (The Indian Tazkira, or the Tazkira of Hindi Poets, completed in 1794-5), that he was informed by Shah Hatam (1699-1783) that the *dīvān* of Vali arrived in Delhi in 1720 and in no time Vali's poetry became current on the lips of young and old. It must be noted that as against Mir and Qa'im, Shah Hatam was the nearest in time to Vali's visit to Delhi which was in 1700. And Hatam makes no mention of the incident of Shah Hatam. In fact, Hatam seems the only one to have freely acknowledged the achievement of Vali. The tribute of others seemed to have been somewhat double edged. Shortly after Mir and Qa'im, even Shah Hatam seems to have felt that if Delhi's primacy and supremacy in Urdu poetry was to be asserted and established, some distancing from Vali was necessary.

In 1755, Shah Hatam published a small *dīvān* of his ghazals, called *Dīvān Zāda* (Baby Divan). He wrote a prose preface for it in Persian in which he declared, clearly *contra* Vali, that he wrote in the language spoken by the *mīrzas* and *rinds* of Shahjahanabad, that is, the language used by the better class of people in Delhi. Further, he said that he was not in favour of using words from the Bhakha (that is, Braj Bhasha, this term at that time subsumed nearly all other *tadbhav* and many *tatsam*) words and phrases. He also spoke against relaxing the pronunciation of Persian and Arabic words to suit the metre, or in accordance with the common practice.

---

[4] A full discussion on Vali's name will be found in Jamīl Jālibī's *Tārīx-e Adab-e Urdū*, Delhi: Educational Publishing House, vol. I, *Qadīm Daur*, 1977, pp. 534-5.

It is not clear that the elements of language that Shah Hatam desired to exclude from poetry were actually archaic and were not to be found in the spoken language of Delhi. By asserting that he wrote in the language of the *mīrza*-s and the *rind*-s of Delhi, Hatam seems to have closed the door upon the language actually spoken by the greater majority of the citizens of Delhi. If the prose and poetry of Jaᶜfar Zatalli is anything to go by, the linguistic environment of Delhi at the beginning of the eighteenth century was much more earthy, much more spicy and salty, more colorful, much more given to the "coarser" things of life than the etiolated, if much more refined, salons of the *mīrza*-s and the *rind*-s of Shahjahanabad.

All these strictures hit the poetry of Vali more than anybody else. But the interesting fact is that the extant poetry of Hatam himself in no way conforms to Hatam's own prescriptions on the language of poetry. Regardless of what the friends and enemies of Urdu have made of Hatam's strictures these past two and a half centuries, the conclusion seems inescapable that Hatam wrote with an agenda in mind, and the aim of that agenda was to assert the primacy and supremacy of Delhi at the cost of Vali. Everybody freely acknowledged that Vali was the first Urdu poet in the new mode, but everybody also seemed to assert, or imply, that Vali's greatness was like a moon whose brightness came directly from the sun that was Delhi. Vali was essentially an uncouth Gujarati or Dakani, Shah Hatam "purified" or "reformed" Vali's language so that it became a tool worthy of the superior artists of Delhi.

We know that cultural and political change affects, among other things, the language of poetry. While poetry's language may not directly reflect the change, certain manifestations of it can be interpreted as the result of cultural and political change. But the changes that occurred in the political climate of Delhi during the eighteenth century seem to have had some paradoxical results. The case of Persian is an instance of this. Persian didn't lose its preeminent cultural status as the Mughal power began to wane. More Hindus were writing more Persian in India than at any time in the past. However, by the time we are in the middle of the century, Hindus take to writing in Urdu in large numbers and the first prominent Hindu names in Urdu poetry are from this period. Perhaps it was the prestige of Persian, coupled with the desire to gain distance from Vali which caused the poets of Delhi to advocate, at least in theory, the "correct" use of Persian words (for our purposes "Persian" subsumes Arabic, because almost all the Arabic words in Urdu arrived via Persian), the undesirability of framing compounds (*tarākīb)* of which one element was Hindi and the other, Persian, the desirability of not using any Persian compounds that did not occur in the works of "standard" Persian poets, the term "latter" almost always meaning native Iranian poets, or Persian poets in India who were first generation Iranians.

Denigration, or at least neglect, of the non-Delhi Urdu poets at the hands of the leaders and makers of literary taste in eighteenth century Delhi thus had far-reaching results for the course of Urdu poetry. Vali was often acknowledged as the first of the Rekhtah/Hindi/Hindvi/Urdu poets. It was even conceivable to see a thread of linguistic unity binding the Deccan and Delhi. Mir paid a left-handed compliment to Vali when he is said to have described him as a poet more famous than the devil himself, and he also acknowledged that the language of the Deccan was none other than Rekhtah.[5] We find the following *šeᶜr* in his second *dīvān*:

> It's not for nothing
> That I am so used to composing
> Rekhtah. I had a beloved once
> Who was from the Deccan.
>
> *Xū gar nahī̃ kuch yū̃ hī ham rextah kahne se*
> *Maᶜšūq jo apnā thā bāšinda Dakan kā thā.*

In spite of all this, we see very little direct appreciative mention of Vali in the poetry of Delhi after about 1750. Dakani poets of the eighteenth century do mention Vali often enough, and Vali comes through in their poetry as a substantial presence. Such is not the case with the poets of Delhi. The material empire had

[5] This sentence is not found in the extant copies of *Nikātuš Šuᶜarā*. Qa'im Chandpuri quotes it in his *Maxzan-e Nikāt*.

been lost, the poets of Delhi seemed to say, but the empire of poetry had been acquired.

4.

Mir died in 1810, the last to die of the great generation of Urdu poets in Delhi who learnt from Vali but who more or less marginalized Vali and established itself as the undisputed master of Urdu poetry and Urdu language. Mirza Muhammad Rafi Sauda (1706-81) was perhaps regarded more highly than Mir, but the two were seen as almost unscalable pinnacles of Urdu poetry. The language of both Sauda and Mir is not very far removed from the language of Vali, but the general impression that one gains from a page of Sauda or Mir is more that of difference than resemblance. Even so, they were not so much given to "correctness" of language (*pace* Shah Hatam above) as to what Urdu poetics calls *taṣarruf* (creative or masterly appropriation). Over the nineteenth century, Mir's reputation appears to have grown but he doesn't seem to have found any conscious imitator or follower among the poets who made their name in the first quarter of the century. Yet almost everyone of note, and Ghalıb not the least among them, paid lip service to Mir and some notable poets like Syed Muhammad Khan Rind of Lucknow even claimed to be his close follower.

Mir's greatest achievement in the area of poetic language had been his ability to use the language of common discourse as the language of poetry. It is not that he did not have special linguistic artifices, or "devices". It is that most of his effects and devices seem to have been executed without recourse to Persianism, and without using language in a specially heightened manner. His vocabulary was vast, but while he didn't stint in his use of rare or unfamiliar Persian words, he almost invariably let the balance of his vocabulary tilt in favour of Indic and commonplace words and he still managed to avoid words that were specific to Vali and some Delhi poets of the early eighteenth century, such as Muhammad Shakir Naji (1690?-1744?) and Shah Mubarak Abru (1683/5?-1733).

The poetry of Asadullah Khan Ghalib presents a radically different picture. As we saw at the beginning of this paper, Ghalib declared his allegiance to Mirza Abdul Qadir Bedil, the greatest poet of the style of Persian poetry which was later characterized as *sabk-i hindī* (Indian style). Bedil's poetry is difficult, mostly cerebral and mystic-sufistic, and it abounds with unusual words and phrases. A good number of the phrases and compounds that Bedil used were peculiar to him, for no other poet, and certainly not the Iranians, had ever used them. Ghalib's total devotion to Bedil suggests many things, but foremost among them is the obvious, though not often noted fact that an Urdu poet is swearing unconditional allegiance to a Persian poet. Mir and Vali did no such thing. In their own way they weren't slow in hinting, in fact, that they were as good as, if not superior to the Persian masters. Shah Hatam did say that he regarded the Persian poet Mirza Muhammad Ali Saʾib (d. 1665) as his teacher, but it was in regard to his Persian, not Urdu. In Rekhta/Urdu, Hatam clearly declared Vali his mentor.

The second point to be noted in regards to Ghalib's declaration of fealty to Bedil is that Bedil is an extremely difficult poet, as against Mir who was (rightly or wrongly) held as the master of simplicity and of direct, emotive discourse. And thirdly that Bedil is fond to excess of inventing remote themes and finding abstract images and metaphors, qualities which one finds in Mir but rarely. Ghalib is clearly placing greater value on the newness of theme and on the unfamiliarness of language in poetry.

Ghalib's adoption of the path of extreme Persianism, coupled with his preference for remote themes and abstract images and metaphors can be taken as a declaration of independence from both Vali and Mir. Mir and his senior contemporaries responded to the change signaled by the arrival of Vali by adapting Vali to their use and asserting Delhi's cultural eminence by not only accepting Urdu poetry as their own creation but also denying what was Vali's due. The emphasis on "correctness" of language and on implying, or even stating a hierarchy of languages in which Persian as written by Iranian authors stood above all else, and certainly above Urdu/Hindi/ Rekhtah was again a statement of power: it was Persian which gave value and validity to Urdu/

Hindi/Rekhtah, and this power was separate from and indifferent to the realities of political power.

The nineteenth century saw an event of great importance happening in Delhi, though Delhi itself, happy in its cultural and intellectual eminence, doesn't seem to have appreciated the full meaning of the event at that time. Shah Alam II had returned to Delhi in 1771, a full twelve years after his coronation in Bihar, in 1759. During much of the time from 1759 to 1771, Shah Alam was under the "protection" of the English at Allahabad. Now with his arrival in Delhi, unsupported by the English, Shah Alam reestablished in some measure the dignity and the pomp and circumstance worthy of the descendant of the great Mughal emperors of the past. The English naturally couldn't permit this state of affairs for any length of time. They retook Delhi in 1803, delivering in the process a comprehensive defeat on the Marathas who were in practical charge of the empire after the death of Mirza Najaf Khan in 1773.

The year 1803 saw virtual abolition of the Mughal empire. Culture and society in Delhi and elsewhere which were already changed substantially due to the impact of the Rohillas and the Marathas now underwent change faster than ever before. This change was wrought by the all pervasive presence of the English. Urdu writers responded to the new imperial situation but sporadically. However, it is possible to see Ghalib's excessive valorization of Persian as a symbolic, and maybe even subliminal resistance to the new order of things. It is also possible to see the rise of *xiyāl bandī*, that is, use or invention of abstract, far-fetched themes and intellectual appeal at the cost of emotive appeal in poetry (of which Ghalib himself is the supreme example) as a process of response to change and at the same time a continued assertion of the supremacy of Delhi and its perceived hegemonic role in the world of culture.

Ghalib worked in the same poetic tradition which was Mir's tradition, and which was Vali's tradition too. But he is so apparently different, and so thoroughly individualistic on the surface that most of us are led into the error of believing that he was doing something else. The fact is that just as Vali was sought to be marginalized by Shah Hatam and others, Mir was sought to be marginalized by Ghalib and his senior contemporaries, Shah Nasir and Shaikh Nasikh. The political situation of Ghalib was much more tragic, much more dire than that of any other poet in the eighteenth century. Ghalib's times had been tainted almost fully by the power of the English, and he seems to have felt the advent of the new order as a tragedy, and paradoxically, he seems also to have welcomed it. This again was an expression of his supreme individuality of mind.

The language of love: a study of the amorous and erotic associations of Urdu

Tariq Rahman

Bharatendu Harishchandra (1849-82), the father of modern Hindi literature (Dalmia 1997), said in his statement before the Hunter communion (1882):

> There is a secret motive which induces the worshippers of Urdu to devote themselves to its cause. It is the language of dancing-girls and prostitutes. The depraved sons of wealthy Hindus and youths of substance and loose character, when in society of harlots, concubines, and pimps, speak Urdu, as it is the language of their mistresses and beloved ones. The correct pronunciation of Urdu, with its *shin*, *ghain*, and guttural *kaf*, is indispensable, and one unable to twist his tongue into unnatural and unpleasant distortions is not a welcome or an agreeable companion. (Edn. Com. NWP 1884: 201)

Another respondent, Shiv Prasad, said that 'some of the women take up also amorous and vicious books, such as Mir Hasan ki Masnavi, Indarsabha, etc. etc' (*ibidem*, p. 327). Even books in Urdu translation, such as the *Alf laila* and *Qiṣṣa totā mainā*, were blamed for creating mistrust for women and obsession with sex. Thus in Upendra Nath Ashk's short story *Ceṭān kī mān*, Pandit Shadi Ram locks his wife in the house when he goes out because of his reading of these works. Both the respondents were supporters of Hindi against Urdu and the Hindi-Urdu controversy was going on during this period. Could it be that the association of Urdu with love and eroticism which they had brought up was merely an allegation? A stratagem to defeat the pro-Urdu lobby? An anti-Urdu (and possibly anti-Muslim?) prejudice? Or, could it be that Urdu really did have such associations in the minds of many members of the intelligentsia? And, if so, why is there so much silence about them nowadays? Does this silence itself indicate the presence of certain ideological and political imperatives which can be understood once the erotic and amorous themes are documented?

These are the questions which this article will attempt to answer.

The amorous and the erotic associations of Urdu

The major aim of this article is to document the presence of the amorous and erotic themes in Urdu writings of the nineteenth century. While scholars of Urdu are well aware of the erotic in the literature of the language, other scholars of South Asia would find it useful to have such a theme placed in a historical context. This is all the more necessary because the erotic associations of Urdu are suppressed by the Urdu-using community in both Pakistan and India in order to protect itself against charges of obscenity, decadence and backwardness. The construction of the modern, sanitized Urdu (Muslim) community needs re-examination and the restitution and acceptance of the erotic, rather than its suppression. Frances Pritchett, who has described this process through the works of Mohammad Hussain Azad (1830-1910) and Altaf Hussain Hali (1837-1914), two of the greatest critics of Urdu literature in the nineteenth century, argues that modernity, spearheaded by these two great trend setters, discredited the themes, values and ideas of the classical Urdu literature (Pritchett 1995) and one major area under attack, as it were, was the treatment of beauty, love and sex. However, despite the incisive analysis of scholars like Pritchett, the 'South Asian Victorians remain' and they not only 'view the *ġazal* through the special distorting lenses provided by Azad and Hali' as Pritchett says (*ibidem*, p. xvii), but also suppress the more overtly erotic associations of genres other than the *ġazal*. Indeed, while the *ġazal* 'continues to be vigorously alive' (*ibidem*, p. 189), partly because it is more amorous than erotic and also because it is possible to take advantage of its ambiguity to claim that the amorous symbolism is, in fact, mystical in nature, it is the other genres – *hazal*, *rextī*, *vāsoxt*, *sarāpā suxan*, *maṡnavī*, *naẕm* and the *dāstān* – which are in danger of being lost sight of by all except a few specialists of Urdu literature.

This article, then, brings out the erotic and amorous associations of Urdu writings in the late eighteenth and nineteenth centuries so as to question and deconstruct the puritanical, modern identity which the 'South Asian Victorians' – to use Pritchett's apt phrase – construct. Such themes have been mentioned in several contexts by several scholars who will be mentioned below but there is no attempt to explore the reasons why Urdu was associated with the amorous and the erotic during the period of our study. Moreover, the vast archive which is known to specialists of Urdu is scattered in many works and one advantage of this article may be that it is brought together here.

It should be mentioned at the outset, however, that the nineteenth century was a period of several themes in conflict the major ones being identity and religion but, because these non-erotic associations are very well documented, they will not be referred to in detail. To put the rest of the discussion in context they should be mentioned here, however. Very briefly then, Urdu became the symbol of the Muslim political identity in India during the Pakistan movement and helped 'imagine' or 'construct' – in Benedict Anderson's sense (1983) – both Muslim and Hindu 'nations' (Brass 1974: 45-6; King 1994). After Partition Pakistan's ruling elite used the symbol of Urdu to construct a Pakistani identity which would dominate and suppress the ethnic identities of the country, an attempt which the Bengali, Sindhi, Pashto-speaking and Balochi ethnic elites contested (Rahman

1996). Since these ethnic elites often espoused non-establishment, left-leaning views, Urdu came to be associated with official Pakistani nationalism and Islam. It is also associated with non-elitist schooling in Pakistan (the elitist one being in English) as has been brought out in several publications (Rahman 2004). However, the association with Islam was gaining in strength and salience since the nineteenth century when Urdu started replacing Persian and Arabic as the major language of South Asian Islam (Rahman 2006). In post-Partition India too Urdu remains a symbol of Muslim identity and is very much in evidence in Muslim minority politics (Farouqui 2006).

In view of the salience of these political and ideological identities of Urdu, it is ignored that from the late eighteenth century onwards till almost the end of the beginning of the twentieth century the language was associated with the amorous and the erotic as well as some other variables of Muslim identity – Islam, Muslim political aspirations in South Asia and education – which have been mentioned already. This particular association, with the amorous and the erotic, was primarily with Urdu poetry but, since the language was taught through literature, it extended to the language itself. The reformers of Muslim society, aware of this nexus, tried to break it and, instead, strengthened the association with Islam which, too, was formed during the same period. As the educated gentry (*ašrāf*) studied Persian texts till the middle of the nineteenth century, the British officials and the Muslim reformers made deliberate attempts to purge the curricula of them. The erotic and the amorous was associated with moral degeneration, decadence and blamed for backwardness and political defeat of the Muslim ruling elite. For the *ᶜulemā* (clergy) it was not only associated with all these but was also a great sin. Thus, in order to regenerate a powerful Muslim 'nation' (*qaum*) a new literature, chaste and moral, had to be created. This moral and political imperative and the steps taken to bring the amorous and erotic themes in Urdu literature into disrepute and create a culture shame and silence about them have been described in some detail in Rahman (2002: 499-515). Indeed, they continue to this date with the textbook committees excluding love poetry, even from the masters of the *ġazal*, out of the curricula and the Pakistan Television being squeamish about a married couple holding hands on the screen.

The erotic is excluded to such an extent from the officially constructed identities of Pakistani Muslims that the classics of Persian and Arabic, which are proudly owned as being Muslim heritage languages, are not taught in unexpurgated editions in Pakistani universities. Hardly any scholars touch the erotic as a subject of serious research though any writings on the subject become popular among that group of the intelligentsia of Urdu letters which can only be described as the equivalent of 'the Other Victorians'. For instance, Zamir Uddin Ahmad's study of the sexuality of the beloved (Aḥmad 1990) created a sensation and has had several reprints. Works of scholarship on such themes have been published by South Asians living, or at least publishing, in the West (notably Vanita and Kidwai 2000) but those published in Pakistan and India – a study of sexuality in the Urdu short story (Xān 2002) and boy-love in Urdu poetry (Az̤har 1995) for example – are superficial and lack analysis. This is hardly surprising considering that in Pakistan the construction of the Muslim identity suppresses the erotic, associating it with the decadent 'West' or the sensational nudity of Bollywood. And in India it is a theme which does not bear placing in a serious context either in Muslim politics or in the Hindutva one for both of which it is a stigma to be shunned. In short, the reformist discourse excludes the erotic and amorous for ideological and political reasons.

Such exclusion began in the nineteenth century and some of the reformist themes of the literature produced in Urdu during this period bears closer re-examination because it tells us what kind of associations existed in the minds of the educated public about much of Urdu poetry.

Reformist Urdu literature on the erotic theme

Nazir Ahmad's novel *Fasāna-e Mubtilā* (1887) begins with the following reflections regarding Urdu poetry:

> What is there in our poetry except love affairs (*ᶜišq bāzī*) and lack of manners (*be-tahẕībī*). Boys of respectable (*šarīf*) families learn

habits leading to corruption from this very school... (Aḥmad 1962: 64)

The protagonist, Mubtila, was taught Persian because it was assumed that one could not learn Urdu without knowing it but he was harmed by it, i.e. got conscious of his beauty (Aḥmad 1962: 78). Boys ogled the good-looking Mubtila making him narcissistic (*ibidem*, p. 83). Women – albeit after his family had rejected the match for their daughter – called him *hījṛā*, *zanxa* (effeminate, eunuch, hermaphrodite) (Aḥmad 1962: 92). He was always staring at the mirror at himself and was not interested in his plain wife (*ibidem*, p. 92). The author describes Mubtila's getting facial hair in a full page. He tells us how the youth's male admirers abandoned him and how he became lonely and sad (*ibidem*, p. 98). But now Mubtila turns to women and, of course, his taste for Urdu poetry becomes stronger. Among others, he praises Rind Lakhnavi's *sarāpā* called *Muraqqa^c-e xūbī* which describes and praises all parts of a woman's body as, indeed, do most poems of this genre (Moḥsin 1861?)

In *Taubat un-Nusūh* (1874), another novel by Nazir Ahmad, Nusuh, the protagonist who turns reformer after nearly dying of cholera, tells his wife that poetry is considered bad because the poets express the unclean (*nāpāk*) ideas of love and sensual gratification (*^cišq-o-^caiyāšī*) (Aḥmad 1964: 260). He finds his eldest son Kalim's books obscene (*fāḥeš*), removed from modesty (*ḥayā se dūr*), immoral and so on. So he burns them. This act is described by Frances Pritchett as 'a powerful, drastic act of cultural destruction' (Pritchett 1995: 187). The books which are burnt include the classics of Urdu poetry and were read by almost all educated people of the day though they are confined to specialists today.[1] The Persian ones are *Bahār-e dāniš* and even

[1] The following books were found by Nusuh in his son Kalim's room and burnt. They are mostly books of Urdu poetry, either the *ġazal* or erotic stories in verse. However, books other than poetry are also included. *Kulliyāt-e Ātiš* (*ġazal*); *Dīvān-e Šarār* (*ġāzal*); *Vāsoxt-e Amānat* (amorous story in verse with erotic description of female beauty); *Fasāna-e ^cajā^oib* (prose story in very Persianized Urdu); *Qiṣṣa gul-bakā^olī* (amorous story in verse); *Ārā^oiš-e maḥfil* (1801) by Sayyid Haider Baksh Haider. A tale (*dāstān*) originally said to be in Persian and rendered into ornate Urdu prose in

Inshallah Khan's *Daryā-e laṭāfat*. A 'good' boy – Bi Sahib's grandson – tells Salim, Nusuh's younger son, that the *Vāsoxt* is a dirty (*gandī*) book (Aḥmad 1964: 256). Later, Kalim meets the Sadr-e-Azam, a *maulvī* in Daulatabad state, who tells him in Arabicized Urdu that poetry is a corrupting influence and he considers it worthless (Aḥmad 1964: 323).

To take another example from literature, Abid Hussain, the protagonist of the novel *Šarīf zāda* by Mirza Hadi Rusva (1857-1931), was not like other youths of Lucknow who were notorious for debauchery. While most young men acquired the habit of falling in love and took to versification which enabled them to express lust in beautiful words, Abid Hussain worked hard (Rusvā n.d.: 534). Such works, products of modernist, reforming Muslims as they were, reinforced the association of the erotic with Urdu poetry in the public imagination.

Both the exemplars of modern Urdu literature, Azad and Hali, discredited the medieval world view which included the description of female and boyish beauty as a perennial theme. Hali argues against the description of boyish beauty because, in his view, it is unnatural. As for female beauty it is condemnable because if she is a beloved one is revealing one's vices and if a wife, it is shamelessness (Ḥālī 1893: 112-13). Besides these great names, other reformers too associated Urdu literature with eroticism. Mumtaz ᶜAli (1860-1935), a pioneer of Urdu journalism for women, wondered whether Mir Amman's *Bāġ-o-bahār*, that classic of Urdu prose for a century, was 'appropriate for either boys or girls' (Minault 1998: 83). Syed Husain Bilgrami, an in-

---

Fort William College. Like other tales it belongs to the fantasy world of magic, adventure, romance and necromancy; *Maṣnavī Mīr Ḥasan* (amorous story); *Vaqāʾeᶜ-e neᶜmat Xān ᶜAlī* – the author's full name is Nuruddin Muhammad Shirazi (d. 1710-11). The book is in Persian and it describes the victory of Bahadur Shah, son of Aurangzeb, over Golcunda (Hyderabad) in 1687; *Ġazliyāt-e Čirkīn* (scabrous poetry); *Hazliyāt-e Jaᶜfar Zaṭallī* (satirical and indecent verse); *Qaṣāʾid-e hajvia Mirzā Rafīᶜ Saudā* (satirical and highly polemical verse); *Dīvān-e Jān-Ṣāḥib* (*Rextī* poetry); *Indar sabhā* (amorous drama with descriptions of female beauty); *Dīvān Naẓīr Akbarābādī* (with couplets of Mian Hudhud) (some poems are erotic); *Vāsoxt* (the author is not specified but the *vāsoxt* is amorous and erotic at places); *Kulliyāt-e Rind* (mostly *ġazal*) (Aḥmad 1874: 253-5).

fluential man from Hyderabad, considered Urdu literature as 'coarse, pernicious, and unclean' being a product of decadent, aristocratic (*navābī*) culture (Bilgrami 1900). In short, there was an association of Urdu with the erotic and it was a source of anxiety for the reformers of the Indian Muslim society. The reformers dealt with it in various ways: modernizing literary norms in Urdu with reference to English literature (Azad and Hali); creating new reformist texts (Nazir Ahmad); purging the canon of classical Urdu literature to create a sanitized, highly puritanical, pedagogical model for the mass consumption of the Urdu-reading public, especially students; and abandoning Urdu for English literature or language-teaching without the literary component (educational decision makers; school and college teachers and even academics in universities).

But why did this association, disquieting as it was to people who wanted to break the British stereotype of Muslim sensuality and aristocratic (*navābī*) decadence, come into existence? Did it have any basis in reality? These are questions which the following sections will attempt to answer.

The place of the erotic in Muslim literature

Medieval literature in Muslim cultural languages – Arabic, Persian and Turkish – had an erotic content. This was natural, one part of life among many others, and was not the exclusive focus of the narrative. It was formulaic in the sense that beauty, both female and boyish, was described in certain fixed, conventional terms. Sexual desire was also described as the normal response to beauty. The sexual organs and intercourse itself were described in metaphorical, stylized, language though at places body parts were also referred to in words normally tabooed in society. This, however, was not in an erotic context as it is in pornography. The point is that, unlike the pornographer, the authors of classical literature in Muslim cultural languages were representing life – the whole of life that is – through certain conventional narrative devices.

Abdelwahab Bouhdiba, writing on the role of sexuality in Islamic cultures, suggests that eroticism 'is integrated in the Islamic view of the world and is situated at the heart, not at the periphery, of ethics' (Bouhdiba 1985: 127). Elaborating upon this theme he introduces the concept of *mujūn* which he explains as follows:

> Observe the ambiguous and equivocal richness of the root *ma ja na*, which signifies, according to the *lisān al-ᶜArab*, the density, the depth, the lack of shame, the frivolity, the gratuity, the art of mixing the serious and the lighthearted, pretended austerity, true banter. *Mujūn* is the art of referring to the most indecent things, speaking about them in such a lighthearted way that one approaches them with a sort of loose humour. In principle *mujūn* ought not to go beyond words. It is oneirism, collective experience and liberation through speech. (Bouhdiba 1985: 127)

The *One Thousand Nights and One Night* (*Alf laila va-laila*) is considered an example of a narrative with erotic passages of the *mujūn* genre. But the famous *Alf laila*, paradigmatic though it is, is not the only example of literature with a healthy, accepting, attitude towards the erotic. Almost all the classics of Arabic, Persian and Turkish literature have the same attitude.

The *Maṡnavī* of Mawlana Jalal-ad-Din Muhammad Rumi (1207-73), considered one of the most influential works in the Muslim world, and one which educated South Asian Muslims were acquainted with and held in high esteem, is said to embody the esoteric meaning of the *Qurʾān* (*hast Qurʾān dar zabān-e Fārsī* = is the *Qurʾan* in the Persian language). It is a six-volume work about the concept of the oneness of God (*tauḥīd*), redemption of the soul through mystical processes, the desire to seek union with the deity and other moral and spiritual themes. It is full of anecdotes, fables and aphorisms somehow related to the above deeply religious themes. And yet, in common with medieval norms of writing in the Muslim world, there are fables which would now be considered erotic and even obscene. The Mawlana also uses both the accepted, respectable words for the human anatomy and also ones which have earthy connotations and are tabooed in respectable writings today (collected in an appendix and defended against the charge of indecency by Iqbal 1956: 284-314). Modern Pakistanis would find them shockingly indelicate and teaching them to students of any age would be out of the question.[2]

Boy love in Muslim literature and society

The pervasiveness of boy-love in Persian and Turkish Muslim cultures is brought out, respectively, by Najmabadi (2005) and Andrews and Kalpakli (2005). Najmabadi makes the astute observation mentioned above, that the pre-modern beloved was a boy (*amrad*) who, like women (*zan*), belonged to the category of those who could be penetrated. Modernity changed this and Iranians became ashamed of this fact of their cultural past. The public space became hetero-socialized and male homosociality was heterosexualized during this era. Women's education too was seen in the light of this new female identity as it was in India (Najmabadi 2005: 196). The *amrad* disappeared from cultural imagination. Even the feminist reading of sexuality and gender identity has 'contributed to this historical amnesia by doing gender analysis without regard for the historical transformations of sexuality' (*ibidem*, p. 235). Such an analysis is required for the Urdu-using culture of North India where gender was perceived in the same way as in Iran. The role of the *amrad* in this culture, as expressed in the Urdu language, has not been fully analysed.

The lines along which the culture of eighteenth century Indian Muslim elite can be analysed is provided by *The Age of Beloveds* (Andrews and Kalpakli 2005). The authors contend that in the long sixteenth century – a period running from the late fifteenth century through the early seventeenth century (Andrews and Kalpakli 2005: 10) – the ideal beloved was an adolescent youth (an *amrad*) who also symbolized the absolute ruler as well

[2] European translators of the *Maṣnavī* were so embarrassed by the erotic content of some of the fables that Nicholson who translated it into English between 1925 to 1940 rendered them (133 out of 25,700 couplets) in Latin so that only a few scholars could have access to them. He considered them 'too outspoken for our taste' but now that they are perhaps no longer unsuitable for Europe, they are not acceptable in Pakistan. Even in 1956, when the Pakistani scholar Afzal Iqbal started writing his book on Rumi he was anxious to defend Rumi on the possible charge of sensuality (see Iqbal 1956: 284-314).

as the immanent deity in mystic love. During this period 'power relations of all kind, from the most personal (adult-child, husband-wife, lover-beloved) to the most public (courtier-monarch, patron-client, even empire-empire), were eroticized on a consistent pattern. That is, they were imagined in the forms, the language, and the metaphors of love' (*ibidem*, p. 28).

The authors contend that the *şehrengiz* (city thriller) was written as a catalogue celebrating the beauty of boys, generally artisan lads (*ibidem*, p. 40). This is common to Urdu poetry (*šahr āšob*) also. Then the gender of Ottoman literature is masculine and 'reflects and scripts the (adult) masculinity of public space' (*ibidem*, p. 54). This is true of Urdu culture again. The authors describe how, during this age, it was fashionable to be enamoured of boys, use the *ġazal* (in Turkish *gazel*) as a medium of communicating about the beloved and the use of certain literary practices and conventions for the above (*ibidem*, p. 90). This, again, is true for the Urdu culture. It needs to be investigated (for initial steps in this direction see Naim 1979: 120-42; Rahman 1990: 1-20).

It seems to be true that 'the traditional scripting of the erotic in the Persian tradition emphasized love between males and that it was important for literate Ottomans to see themselves as custodians and perpetuators of that tradition' (*ibidem*, p. 130). This is true of Indian Muslims who saw themselves as perpetuators of the Persian tradition. The two authors connect Ottoman sexuality with politics. They write:

> From our perspective, because the absolutist monarchy, and the society that it rules, is also phallocentric, its pedophilia (placing the object of desire in the role of child, either actually or structurally) is also fundamentally homoerotic (the hierarchy of domination is male on top of male). (Andrews and Kalpakli 2005: 269)

Decadence and loss of political power

One popular theory in modern Indian Muslim writings is that the decadence of society was a consequence of the loss of political power. However, one can explain the presence of the erotic in

Urdu literature with reference to history and convention without appealing to such theories.

A reading of texts from the medieval Indian period clearly shows that power was manifested in the possession of coercive ability which gave a person the ability to gratify himself (women were generally excluded from power) by possessing tangible and intangible goods (such as prestige). Among the tangible goods were sex objects – women and beautiful boys. Thus the Mughal rulers had large harems (Lal 1988) and a very active sex life. It was when political power was lost that people, especially reformers and apologists of this ruthless power, started propagating the theory that sexual excesses or promiscuity brought about the ruin of the Mughal (or other) empires.

Although Muslim political power was challenged by the eighteenth century in India, their cultural dominance was very much in place. Indeed, the British rulers themselves adopted the dress, etiquette, cuisine and the values – and sometimes even the religion – of the aristocratic Muslims becoming what William Dalrymple calls the 'white Mughals' (Dalrymple 2003). Thus, it was not a new breakdown of sexual norms but a continuation of older established patterns – established during the age of political power – which oft-quoted works like the *Muraqqa^c-i Dehlī* represent. The *Muraqqa^c*'s author, Dargah Quli Khan (1710-66) was a nobleman from Aurangabad who lived in Delhi from 1738 to 1741. He describes the capital of the declining Mughal empire as a place devoted to pleasures of all kinds. The public places were full of beautiful women and boys and the powerful indulged themselves with both (Xān n.d.). The descriptions of boy dancers and women who painted their bare legs as if they were wearing tight trousers may give one the feeling that Delhi was the most decadent of cities in the eighteenth century. But Paris and London, at the height of their colonial power, had all the pleasures which Delhi possessed (Bloch 1965: 217-52). Similarly the Lucknow of the Nawabs which Abdul Halim Sharar describes was not more profligate than, say, London, though, of course, the practice of having many women in the harem was reminiscent of medieval Muslim capitals at the height of their power. The social and literary norms for describing the sexual practices of European cities were, of course, different. But they were not any more virtuous even in Victorian England than Indian cities. Thus, the real reason why the erotic element in Urdu literature is condemned so unequivocally these days is not because such pleasures were found in certain urban centres or the rich indulged in them but because it is the product of a militarily defeated culture. And when one is defeated everything one does or possesses can be, and generally ***is***, condemned. The defeat is not easy to explain and the tendency of everyone, most of all the reformers of the defeated party, is to blame pleasure, especially sexual pleasure, for the defeat.

The erotic theme in early Urdu writings

The earliest specimens of the erotic in Urdu poetry go back to the time of Muslim power not to its decline. A certain poet called Qureshi wrote a *maṣ̤navī* called *Bhog bāl* in 1613 in Dakkani Urdu. It has twelve chapters describing sexual matters. Chapter 11, for instance, gives 84 positions for coitus (Šarīf 2004: 170).

However, since Urdu came into its own at the time of the decline of Muslim political power, probably the most obscene of the Urdu poets is also one of the earliest, at least in north India. This is Mir Mohammad Jafar Zatalli (d. 1713). He was a satirist in both Persian and Urdu and the obscene words he uses are not a part of the Urdu erotic tradition. Nor are they meant for evoking sexual pleasure. Instead, they are obviously meant to shock, outrage, express contempt and belittle others. Zatalli lived at a time of political instability after Aurangzeb's death. He responded to it by making fun of it. He was murdered, probably at the instigation of King Farrukh Siyar (r. 1713-19), in 1713 (see his works edited by Xān 2003). Zatalli created no tradition. His effect on Urdu literature is minimal. So it is not because of his use of obscenities that Urdu literature came to be associated with love and sex.

Another eighteenth century work is Sayyid Sirajuddin Aurangabadi's (1715-63) *Bustān-i xayāl* (written before 1783 when he stopped writing poetry). This is actually a *ṣūfī* narrative – major theme of both Persian and Urdu poetry – about finding the source of permanent bliss. The narrator loves a boy who is indifferent to him. Although another boy, the son of a chief (*sardār*), gives him attention, the narrator remains disconsolate. The beloved alternates between warmth and cold disdain till the narrator turns to God in whom he finds real love (Sarvarī 1998: 149-246).

Najmuddin Shah Mubarak Abru (1683-1733), a poet of Urdu, wrote a poem called *Advice for the adornment of a Beloved.* In this the narrator meets a beautiful boy who was, however, unsophisticated in the art of charming men. The narrator starts advising him how to behave like a 'beloved'. Above all, the boy must know when to stop behaving like a 'beloved' (*ma*[c]*šūq*) and become a lover ([c]*āšiq*) in his turn. So, when the hair on his face coarsens, he must 'then give up the desire to be adored/don't overdress or act coy any more'. That is when he must transit to the role of the lover and 'enjoy the company of beauteous ones' (Ābrū 1990: 298-308; available in English translation in Vanita and Kidwai 2000: 161-8).

But Abru's focus is not pornography; nor even erotica. He is discussing the norms of role-playing in a conventional society. Moreover, he is upholding decency because, like the behavioral norms enjoined upon the Greek boy (*eromenos* or *ephebos*) (Dover 1978: 16), there were certain forms of good behaviour expected from the *amrad* also. Abdul Halim Sharar also tells us that adolescent boys combed their hair in such a way on their foreheads that 'attraction like women was created in them also' (Šarār 2006: 261).

Modernity has changed the categorization upon which boy-love was based. The word homosexuality has now been imported in Urdu as *ham-jins parastī* (the worship of the same sex). In short, as Afsaneh Najmabadi puts it, 'the heteronormalizing dynamic of Iranian modernity' (Najmabadi 2005: 231), tends to bring in modern, Western categories of sexual identities in Pakistan as well. Though older attitudes persist residually in less Westernized parts of Pakistani society, there is considerable anxiety to wish away the presence of *hījṛā*-s (transvestites or eunuchs) in Pakistani cities and many people deny the presence of the boy-beloved in Urdu literature and, indeed, of anything but heterosexuals (most notably the President of Iran declared there are no homosexuals in his country in his visit to the USA in the end of September, 2007).

The pornographic minority

There were, to be sure, pornographers (*faḥḥāš-go*) also. They wrote poetry called the *hazal* or, more loosely, *kalām-e faḥḥāš* (obscene verse). One of them, Saiyid Imam [c]Ali Khan of Bilgram, writing under the pseudonym of Sahib-e Qiran, has left behind a collection of verse (*dīvān*) written in black in the *nasta[c]līq* script (Ṣāḥib-e Qirān, n.d). He flourished during the rule of Asif ud-Daulah as he has been mentioned in several couplets. At one place the *navāb* has been praised as a promoter of concupiscence (*šahvat*). Most of the verses are obscene and some mention the poet's exploits in the brothel. In some cases the names of prostitutes are also mentioned but mostly, like all pornographers, the poet is concerned with types of fornication. He even goes to the extent of creating an indecent parody of Amir Khusrau's famous poem with the refrain (*namī dānam če manzil būd / šab jā'e ke man būdam* = I did not know which place it was; the place I was last night…). According to Sharar, Mian Mashir, another *hazal-go*, perfected Sahib-e Qiran's style of using language idiomatically in this sub-genre (Šarār 2006: 122).

Another notable pornographic poet (*faḥḥāš-go*) is Kallan Khan who wrote under the poetic name of Bechaen (Bečaen n.d., No. 1401 RRL). Bechaen was from Rampur. He was a student of Jan Sahib of Lucknow who is well known for his *rextī* poetry. Bechaen was in the court of the Nawab of Rampur as well as the Maharaja Ranbhir Singh. His verses were collected together by Qudrat [c]Ali Qudrat in 1907-8. Out of all the *hazal-go* poets of the period, Bechaen's work is among the most pornographic. He writes mostly in Urdu but there are poems in Persian too.

Angiyā pe hāth ḍalā ye dilkā futūr thā
Merā quṣūr thā na tumhārā quṣūr thā

That the hand went on your brassiere was the fault of the heart
It was neither my mistake nor yours

Other verses refer to all sorts of sexual activities: anal sex, cunnilingus etc.

But perhaps the only pornographer with any influence was Sa^c^adat Yar Khan Rangin who wrote his *Dīvān-e amexta* as well as *Dīvān-e angexta* on erotic themes. Like the work of Sahib-e Qiran, Rangin's work is also full of obscenities and boastful exploits of copulation with prostitutes. It begins with praise for Satan which is not the usual pattern of Urdu pornographers who do not begin with the usual *bismillāh* (in the Name of Allah) but sometimes have merely *yā Šaiṭān ir-rajīm* (Oh! The Accursed Satan!) and most often no prefatory formula at all.

> *La^c^nat meṅ ko^ʾ^ī šarīk nahīṅ terā dūsrā jitne haiṅ raṇḍī-bāz tū unkā hai rāhnumā.*
>
> No one shares with you in the distinction of being the accursed one. Thou art the guide of all the world's womanizers.

Here too some prostitutes are mentioned by name but most remain anonymous. The *dīvān* ends with the praise of Satan as the provider of carnal pleasures.

The *Dīvān-e angexta* is about women's language which, according to the author, he heard during his womanizing days. Apart from the prostitutes themselves, he claims to have had access to married women (*xānagī*) from respectable families who formed occasional liaisons with men for fun or, possibly, some personal income. This language is called *Rextī* and Rangin is said to be the author of this genre of poetry which will be mentioned in more detail later (see Rangīn n.d., Inšā 1802: 86).

Elements of the *hazal* – couplets and even complete poems – are found interspersed in the works of some of the classical poets. Only a few, however, are mentioned as *hazal-go*: Mir Zahik, father of Mir Hasan, for instance, was one of them (Quraišī 1966: 9). These days they are either not printed or printed with blank spaces in their poetic collections.

The Rampur Raza Library has a large collection of *hazliyāt*. Out of these seven handwritten manuscripts, though all entitled *Majmū^c^a hazliyāt*, are all written by different people. One (No. 1411) carries the names of two authors: Miss Flora and Sharir or

Mir Hasan [c]Ali. Others are by Mir Ashiq Hussain Bazm (Bazm 1908; Nos 1403 and 1404); Agha Wasi [c]Ali Khan Lakhnavi Mazhar (d. 1912) (Maẓhar n.d.; No. 1407); Hayat Baksh Mustafa Abidi Rasa (d. 1913) (Rasā n.d.; No. 1409); Syed Javad Husain Amṛohi Shamim (d. 1915) (Šamīm 1915, No. 1410); Syed [c]Ali Husain (Ḥusain n.d; No. 1412).

An oddity among these kind of poets is Chirkin whose *Dīvān* (No. 100 RRL) falls in the sub-genre of the *hazal* but is distinctive in that he refers more to excretion than to sex. He is also one of the few, even among the *hazal-go*-s, to write on menstruation. Excretion is an obsession with him and even when he is mentioning sexual acts he brings in some allusion to excretion.

The other collections of the *hazal* use sex in order to continue the war of words between poets – or a hapless victim of a poet's satirical wit – through invective. Sex is used as a weapon; a device for insulting people; a means of embarrassing them. And this usage is based on the assumptions and values of a feudal society in which the crude use of power is a reality of life. This society was rigidly hierarchical and the male gender role was placed higher than the female one. Sexual acts outside the institution of marriage – in which case they were not discussed – were seen as conquests. For the male they brought honour; for the female, dishonour. And if a male (boy, eunuch or man) took the female role (of being penetrated) there was dishonour for him. It is in the context of these power relations and perceptions of reality that the world view of these anthologies of the *hazal* must be understood.

It is necessary to state, then, that the *hazal* – taking these collections as a whole – is neither part of erotica nor even of pornography. It is really part of satire (*ḥajv*) but it uses sexual invectives, tabooed words and acts in order to insult a person and continues to attack and humiliate its victims through sexual allusions and imagery. It yields no sexual pleasure, not even of the kind which pornography can and, of course, it is not erotic in any artistic sense of the word.

To give a few examples: Bazm narrates the story of a woman who has five lovers from the working classes – the lowest of the low in society, association with whom brings dishonour even if it is not of a sexual nature. Her husband, who cannot satisfy her, sees his insatiable wife's goings-on with all of them and is happy to yield to them himself as it is only a non-male, a passive homosexual, who can tolerate such disgrace. The purpose of the poem is to insult the man and his wife and not to excite lust. The poet sometimes names the butt of his insults – a certain Mazhar – who is said to be a passive homosexual and whose wife and daughter are sexually exploited by the poet (Bazm 1908).

Rasa insults a man called Samim boasting about taking his mother, wife and daughter. He even mentions bestiality but, again, to insult Samim whose sister is sexually abused by a bull dog. It is worth mentioning that the poetic collection does not begin with the usual *bismillāh*; it begins with *yā Šaiṭān ir-rajīm*. Rasa also mentions a European woman (*Mem*) called Flora by name (Rasā 1909). In short, the overall impression one gets from the *hazal* is that most of it is an extension of the *ḥajv* tradition rather than the erotic tradition in literature. It is also distinct, despite using sexual themes and obscene words, from the writings of pornographers such as Sahib-e Qiran, Bechaen and Sa'adat Yar Khan Rangin whose works are confused with the satirical *hazal*.

While the works of Rangin and maybe some other pornographers may have reinforced Urdu's association with the erotic, it was not the major factor in creating this association. Obscenity, after all, is a part of all languages and remains on the margins of all literatures. Much more was contributed to the creation of this association by the erotic sub-genres in Urdu which were not, however, pornographic.

The erotic genres of poetry

One of these, the *sarāpā suxan*, description of the female body, is beautiful. The other, the *rextī*, degenerates into the ridiculous, the frivolous and the misogynistic. The *sarāpā*, as mentioned above, is a collection of couplets on every part of the beloved's body starting from her hair to her heels. The breasts, buttocks, legs and vagina are all described through metaphors and poetic similes. The beauty is always described in formulaic terms without any attempt at individuation. Obscene words are never used but the poet does use the more sophisticated Persian words for body parts: breasts (*pistān*); buttocks (*surīn*) and so on. Examples are as follows:

Feet:

Aur jo hāthoṅ meṅ uṭhā lūṅ to ajab luṭf uṭhāʾūṅ
Phir jo vo luṭf uṭhānā tujhe biṭhā ke dikhlāʾūṅ (Jurʾat)

And if I lift the feet I would find a strange pleasure
And then to make you sit and watch that pleasure-taking

Breasts:

Gol-ubhre hue kyā us ke haiṅ pistān dono
Mast karne ko haiṅ maᶜjūn kī ḍibiyān dono (Himmat)

How rounded and raised are breasts both
To intoxicate, these are containers of intoxicants both

Buttocks & thighs:

Koh-e surīn dekho to sar phoṛo tum
Rāneṅ maxmal sī haiṅ xvāb-o-xuruš čhoṛo tum (Mahar)

And if you see the mountains of the derriere you would knock out your head
and the thighs are like satin – enough to make you leave all dreaming and thinking

Vagina:

Aur kyā is ke sivā kījiye midḥat us kī
Do hilāl ik jagah dekhe haiṅ qudrat us kī (ᶜAiš)

What other praise can I lavish upon it
Two crescent moons were seen at one place – God be praised!

The *sarāpā* is interspersed in the versified tales of the *maṣnavī* and the *vāsoxt*, especially the latter. The *vāsoxt* is a formulaic story of the narrator wooing a beautiful beloved who is described in detail. The beloved alternates between indifference and passion. The narrator takes revenge for her indifference by pretending to love somebody else who, in turn, is described much in the same conventional terms as the first beloved. The drama succeeds in bringing the lovers together again. Sometimes, however, the ending is tragic (see the work of Fida ᶜAli whose poetic name is ᶜAish; ᶜAlī 1829).

Among the books read by the Muslim gentlemen of India was the notorious Persian work, *Bahār-e dāniš* of Shaikh Inayatullah Kumboh (1608-71) written sometime between 1650-1, which was condemned by many Victorian British officers in various reports. These tales not only have erotic scenes but also feature a kind of defiant, and wayward, female sexuality which expresses itself by cheating the husband in a dare devil way. For instance, some of the women fornicate with a youth in the presence of their husbands. This book was eventually thrown out of the curricula but it was translated into Urdu, notably by Mirza Jan Tapish. He translated the Persian work during his stay in Fort William College Calcutta in 1802 (the history is in *Bāġ-o-bahār* which adds up to 1802 or 1217 Hijri). Modern translations purge out some couplets which are considered obscene but, in 1802, the work was acceptable to the authorities of Fort William College who are praised in it.

Another widely circulated tale (*dāstān*) was *Ṭalism-e hoš-rubā* or *Dāstān-e Amīr Ḥamza*. This was translated from Persian to Urdu by Munshi Syed Mohammad Husain Jah (1908-15). The stories of the great primal battle between good and evil – good personified by Amir Hamza and evil by the magician Afrasyab – have all elements of public entertainment: magic, war, deceit, trickery, sex and merrymaking. These tales were read out by professional story tellers (*dāstān-go*-s) who acted out the dramatic scenes and mimicked the actors' voices to create a riveting rendition which reached audiences which could not themselves read the seven thousand plus pages (in the present Sang-e Mīl edition). The tales describe scenes of drinking and female beauty every now and then. As in other works, the descriptions of women (*sarāpā*) are in the same formulaic terms as in Persian and Arabic literature: long black tresses, large dow-like eyes, full sensual lips, full breasts, narrow waist, curvaceous hips, rounded buttocks and sensual thighs. Sexual organs are described in metaphors, as is common in the *sarāpā*-s, and if body parts are named sophisticated Persian words are used for them. In the ambience the tales create, the erotic, as in other Muslim literature, is very much a part of life and it is life which the tales reflect. The *Ṭalism*, with its wide popular appeal, took the erotic expressed in the Urdu language to the literate public.

The *rextī* is written in a 'feminine' voice but this voice is satirical and mocking. It makes fun of the feminine, trivializing and vulgarizing it. It has already been mentioned that Rangin is credited with having pioneered it though, in fact, there are occasional poems in a pseudo-feminine voice from earlier poets. However, Insha's claim that Rangin invented it to induce women to such lewdness that he could seduce them (Inšā 1802: 86), is an exaggeration. In any case, this claim has been made by a comic character in *Daryā-e laṭāfat* called Mir Ghafar Ghaini and it is not possible to determine what truth value the author wishes to ascribe to it.

Rextī is coarse, facetious and licentious though hardly seductive. It provokes either disgust or risibility though hardly lust as erotica should (for study of *rextī* in Urdu with many examples see Mušīr 1974; also see Kāẓmī 1930).

The *rextī* presents a lustful, aggressive, rather high spirited woman. She is not idealized like the beloved of the *ġazal*. Instead, she is constantly being held to ridicule and has to hold her own against seducing men and scheming women. Very often she has a not-so-secret liaison with another woman: either a girl friend (*do-gāna*, *ilāʾičī*) or the nurse (the ubiquitous *annā*); and sometimes an older woman (*bājī*). However, because of the earthiness of these goings-on, the voice of the *rextī* is a full-blooded one; a real life one. In real life, however, there is much more than sex; the *rextī* has disproportionately large amounts of it. However, to be fair to the *rextī* poets, they do include much more of the daily lives of women than a mere erotica writer would (see Jān Ṣāḥib, n.d). Unfortunately, this glimpse into the lives of women has a slant towards the ludicrous. Its purpose is not to represent women but to ridicule them.

While the Urdu sources – Kāẓmī (1930) and Mušīr (1974) – merely give samples of *rextī* couplets along with literary appreciation modified by the presently mandatory condemnation of indecency – recent criticism in English engages with more complex dimensions of this unusual sub-genre of Urdu literature. Ruth Vanita and Saleem Kidwai (2000: 193) defend it on the grounds that it 'represents women stating that they prefer women to men when they have access to both' (*ibidem*, p. 193). Petievich argues that the new criticism, that of the Hindu right in India and the Islamists in Pakistan, have created a culture shame for the *rextī* because it was women's language and expresses lesbianism (Petievich 2001: 248). Moreover, according to Ruth Vanita the *rextī* was purged from the Urdu canon because it draws upon 'literary conventions and social actions drawn from non-Persianate and Hindu sources' (Vanita 2004). In short, being in ordinary Urdu (Hindustani), it was linguistically subversive during a period of hardening Muslim/Hindu identities. C.M. Naim, however, defends the more orthodox view that it is trivial, misogynistic and meant only for male titillation (Naim 2001).

While interpretations of the *rextī* in terms of identity, realism and the expression of lesbian feelings is new and interesting, it does not seem to be convincing at least for this writer. A full reading of the original sources reinforces the earlier view that the *rextī* was written by men and it was used to entertain men. Indeed, it is recited even now in all-male gatherings in Pakistan and India to make men laugh. It was a joke and, like all jokes, it created stereotypes and figures of fun. It was obviously a bawdy relief from the high minded, idealized, romantic love of the *ġazal*. But it was not even subversive of the universe of the *ġazal*. It merely confirmed its existence by pointing out that real people, in moods of banter, could exist on much lower planes where women were not the androgynous ethereal beings of the *ġazal*.

The *rextī* poets – Insha (1756-1817), Mir Yar ᶜAli Jan Sahib (1810-81), Nisar Husain Khan Shaida (b. 1868), Saiyed Sajid Sajni (1922-93) – have not been ranked high among Urdu poets for their *rextī* works at least. In Mirza Hadi Rusva's novel *Umrāʾo Jān Adā* (1905), the *rextī* poets are ranked as non-serious

(Rusvā 1905: 84). Some of the poets themselves have written of their work in terms of macho self-confidence expressed in terms of ridicule for the feminine. As Jan Sahib has it:

> *Qadr kyā nā mard janeṅ, mardu'e jo mard haiṅ*
> *Jān Ṣāḥib šād hote haiṅ vohī sun kar mujhe*

> The unmanly would never appreciate me; only men would who are real men
> And they, Jan Sahib, are entertained when they hear me

The 'real men' heard about women talking about their under garments, especially the brassiere (*angiyā* or *maḥram*) to the confidante: the nurse (*annā*) or a friend. The *angiyā* is a subject of great fascination. There are complaints about its being too light; too heavy; too gaudy and that the male lover (*mardu'ā*) has torn it to pieces or thrown it away. Sometimes she demands it as a present while at others she hides it from prying eyes of intrusive men. Sometimes the female friends – the words used by Rangin are *do-gāna*, *ilā'ičī* and *zanaxī* – are also sexual partners. In such cases they ridicule the men and indulge in tabooed pleasures. However, it is only rarely that this is expressed without ridicule and when it is, as in the *čapṭīnāma*-s of Jurrat, it is to provide sexual pleasure to men. Qalandar Bakhsh Jurrat (1748-1810), noted for salaciousness even in his *ġazal*, has written about two women, Sakkho and Mukkho, who complain against their husbands and invite all women who 'are given to clinging' (Vanita and Kidwai 2000: 222). They make love passionately as described below:

> When you join your lips to my lips,
> It feels as if new life pours into my being,
> When breast meets breast, the pleasure is such.
> That from sheer joy the words rise to my lips.
> The way you rub me, oh?...

(English translation by Vanita and Kidwai 2000: 223).

In such samples the passion dominates the ridicule. In most others, however, the dominating tone is satirical, marginalizing, ridiculing. Some couplets are as follows:

Rangīn qasam hai terī hī hūṅ maile sir-se maiṅ
Mat kholkar ke minnat-o-zārī izār-band (Rangīn)

Rangin I swear to you I am having my periods
Do not keep pestering me to open the band of my trousers

It seems to me that it was not because of the use of easy Urdu – the *dohā* remains respectable though of minor interest despite its use of 'Hindi' words even in Pakistan (see the works of Jamiluddin ᶜAli, Partau Rohila, etc.) and Nazir Akbarabadi's poems on the poor remain popular even today and are included in the curricula – that the *rextī* was purged. It was simply too unrestrained, non-serious, sexist and rambunctious. In an age of increasing puritanism when even the Persian classics were purged, it could not be countenanced by reformers wishing to assert the respectability of their literary legacy. However, it would not really be accurate to say that it was purged; it was never actually included in the canon of Urdu literature from the outset. It was a joke to begin with and remained one throughout its career. However, because it was quoted for fun in male gatherings as a joke, it may have contributed to the impression that Urdu was the natural language of erotica.

The *maṣ̤navī*, which is a love story in the medieval fairy tale tradition, has more erotic descriptions of feminine beauty and scenes of love-making than any other genre of canonical Urdu literature except the *vāsoxt* which, in a sense, is a formulaic *maṣ̤navī* in miniature.

There are, however, two traditions in the *maṣ̤navī*, like the *ġazal* but unlike the *vāsoxt*, that of 'earthly' and 'celestial' love (Suvorova 2000). The earliest *maṣ̤navī* were written in the southern centres of the Urdu language, the Deccan and Gujrat. The earliest one, called *Kadam Rāʾo Padam Rāʾo* is ascribed to Fakhruddin Nizami (1397-1462). It was written between 1421 and 1435 and it describes how the antagonist's soul takes over the hero's body and how he regains his true form (Jālibī: 1979). The early *maṡnavī*-s, both in the Deccan as well as Gujrat, had many elements from the indigenous culture and very often one of the lovers was a Hindu (Suvorova 2000: 1-44).

When the centre of Urdu literature shifted to the north, the masters of the *ġazal*, like Mir Taqi Mir (1724-1810), continued to write *maṡnavī*-s too. Mir, for instance, wrote eight *maṡnavī*-s of a romantic nature. Like his *ġazal*-s, they are more concerned with deep, romantic love than ephemeral lust. The erotic *maṡnavī*, still masquerading as a love story, came into its own in Awadh. Mir Hasan (b. 1727), born in Delhi but settled in Faizabad, is famous for his *maṡnavī*-s such as *Seḥr ul-bayan*.

The story is about Prince Benazir, and Princes Badr-i-Munir. They fall in love and Najmunnisa, the Vizier's daughter, advises her to yield to passion. Badr-i-Munir allows Benazir to make love to her. The scene of copulation is described in a formulaic manner (an early example being from Manjhan for the translation of which in English see Behl and Weightman 2000: 190).

This is true of most *maṡnavī*-s of Urdu – especially those written in Lucknow or under the influence of Lucknow's eroticism. According to Suvorova, "we come across similar more or less uninhibited descriptions of amorous intimacy in most of the Urdu *dastans* or «*dastan*-like» *masnavis*" (Suvorova 2000: 146).

The *maṡnavī*-s of Diya Shankar Nasim (*Gulzār-e Nasīm*) and of Tasadduq Husain Khan (Nawab Mirza Shauq; 1773-1871) (*Zahr-e ᶜišq*) are famous for their stylistic beauty. However, Shauq is an innovator in that he introduces realism in the *maṡnavī*. While the previous *maṡnavī*-s mostly described fairy-tale characters, this one describes the passions of the boys and girls of contemporary Lucknow.

In *Fareb-e ᶜišq* Shauq describes rendezvous with beautiful, veiled young ladies who are initially tricked by the lover into meeting them. The girl usually has a cunning maid servant who is bribed into making her palanquin-bearers leave her in a vacant house or garden. There the lover approaches her with seductive words and professions of ardour. She rejects him initially but eventually yields. When discovered the girl suffers and dies. However, in *Bahār-e ᶜišq* the lovers get married and in *Zahr-e*

[c]*išq* they both try to commit suicide though only the girl dies (Šauq n.d.).

Abdul Halim Sharar blames Wajid [c]Ali Shah's debauchery, or rather his advertisement of it, on his reading of Shauq's *maṡ-navī*-s (Šarār 2006: 96). As Suvorova points out, this is unproven and unprovable (2000: 218), but Shauq, as well as the Nawab, contributed to the association of eroticism with Urdu poetry, and indirectly with the language itself, at least with reference to Lucknow and its Urdu poetry.

Nazir Akbarabadi (1735-1830), often called a people's poet or a 'realist', has erotic appeal in many of his poems. Aditya Behl, in his insightful analysis of the poet, claims that 'Nazir's poems about sexual experience need to be viewed as expressive of an engagement with pleasure, a sensual sensibility' (Behl 2005: 194). Thus the poet, writing *naẓm* instead of the more restrictive *ġazal*, found it possible to situate sexual desire in stories of daily life in north India. Whether on a festive occasion – Eid, Shab-i-Barat, Holi, Divali or a fair (*melā*) – he mentions beautiful women and boys. Incidents like a storm are occasions for kissing or fondling a beauty and dreams, of course, are an excuse for describing them. In Nazir, because of the quality of realism, we get a sense of how forbidden pleasures made people yearn for them and act, even if in imagination, as thieves and robbers of delights (see *Kulliyāt-e Naẓīr*). Nazir uses words in common use, including obscene ones, which have been expurgated in modern editions so that there are blanks in many poems, especially those describing festive occasions. For instance, he uses the excuse of showing exotic pet animals to boys in order to take sexual advantage of them (*Biyā*, *Gilehrī kā bačča*, etc.).

The seductive charm of the Urdu *ġazal*

The *ġazal* contributed most to the image of Urdu as an amorous and erotic language. While the risqué Lucknow school of poetry with descriptions of women or seduction (*mu*[c]*āmala-bandī*) may be called erotic, even such descriptions do not use explicitly sexual words nor are they the major theme of the poetry which remains love. Indeed, most of the *ġazal* poetry is amorous rather than explicitly erotic but it is the *ġazal* which is associated with the amorous as well as the erotic in the public mind. One reason for this is the popularity and wide availability of the genre while the others are neither so easily available nor so often quoted as cultural icons. However, while the references are to the *ġazal*, there is an understanding – based upon allusions to other, less available genres – that there is a concealed, subversive literature in Urdu which is highly erotic and of which the *ġazal* is merely that tip of the iceberg which is visible.

Let us now look at the world of the *ġazal* through some examples. The beloved of the *ġazal* – whether the elusive deity, courtesan, veiled lady or adolescent boy – is beautiful but indifferent. The poet-lover's passion is, therefore, unrequited. Thus, the poet accuses the beloved of being cruel and faithless (*be-vafā*).

Čāra-garī bīmārī-e dil kī rasm-e šahr-e ḥusn nahīṅ
Varna dil-bar nā-dān bhī is dard kā čāra jane hai (Mīr)

It is not the custom of the dwellers of the city of beauty to give solace to anybody
Otherwise even an innocent beauty knows how to provide a cure for the disease of love

The beloved appears to favour the rival (*dušman*, *ġair*, *raqīb*). And Ghalib invests the situation with inimitable humour.

Maiṅ ne kahā bazm-e nāz meṅ čāhiye ġair se tahī
Sunke sitam ẕarīf ne mujh ko uṭhā diyā ki yūṅ

I asked the beloved that this gathering of charm should exclude the rival
upon hearing this she made me get up saying 'like this'
(present author's translation)

The lover is condemned to separation (*hijr*) from the object of his love. He cries, sighs and grows pale and ill with the pain of separation.

Čupke čupke rāt-din ānsū bahānā yād hai
Ham ko āb tak ^{c}āšiqī kā vo zamāna yād hai (Ḥasrat Mohānī)

Shedding tears night and day quietly I remember
the days of that love affair I remember

These themes – romantic love, separation, fidelity on the part of the lover, indifference and fickleness on the part of the beloved – were reiterated throughout the three-hundred year tradition dating at least from Vali Dakani (1667-1707) (even if the earlier one is not part of the common people's consciousness) of the Urdu *ġazal*.

The *ġazal* had a special place in the lives of educated people – both Hindus and Muslims – in North India. Even in other parts of India – Hyderabad, Murshidabad, Mysore, Lahore etc. – the Muslim elite enjoyed the *ġazal* as a distinctive cultural artifact. It was customary for educated, urbane men to learn several hundred couplets of the masters of the Urdu *ġazal*. These would be recited to make the conversation interesting. *Mušā^{c}ara*-s (poetry recitations) were common and are held even now even in the diaspora settled in the United States and Europe where Urdu poets are welcomed and people come to listen to them and enjoy the *ġazal* as well as the more recent genres of poetry. People played *bait-bāzī* in which one person recited a couplet. The other player had to recite a couplet in response beginning with the last sound (denoted by the letter of the Urdu alphabet) of the last line. This went on till one of the parties ran out of couplets. The other one was the winner. This has changed into *antākšarī* in Hindi where film songs, instead of the classical works of the Urdu poets, are used. However, if the official language of the songs in India is said to be Hindi it is that version of the shared language of North India and urban Pakistan which was called Hindustani and which is closer to the Urdu end of the linguistic spectrum. In any case the Hindi movie is strongly influenced by the amorous orientation of *navābī* Lucknow and, therefore, reminiscent of the link between Urdu and the life of love (Kesavan 1994: 255-6)

Very often couplet after couplet by the great masters were recited only for the pleasure of it. Such an evening and the special romantic atmosphere it created is described by E.M. Forster in his novel *A Passage to India* (1924) as follows:

> They listened delighted, for they took the public view of poetry, not the private which obtains in England. It never bored them to hear words, words; they breathed them with the cool night air never stopping to analyse; the name of the poet, Hafiz, Hali, Iqbal, was sufficient guarantee. (Forster 1978: 38)

This kind of enthusiasm for poetry was common. Every student of Aligarh Muslim University who has written memoirs has attested to it. Since the *ġazal* mentioned love and beauty repeatedly, Urdu itself came to be associated with romance and eroticism in the public mind. This image proved to be harmful for Urdu during the Urdu-Hindi controversy when some Hindu spokesmen said that they did not want their children to learn Urdu as, being taught through its literature, it would spoil them. This criticism is still repeated by the partisans of the indigenous languages of Pakistan who claim that Urdu, being nurtured in the decadent and effete culture of the *navāb*-s of India, is a decadent language.

The defeat of Eros

The reformers crusaded against the eroticism of Urdu in ways which have been described earlier (Rahman 2002: 508-15). They won and slowly Urdu started becoming associated with Islam and Pakistani nationalism in Pakistan. In India it remains associated with the Muslim identity. But this identity can be politically-oriented or a nostalgic throwback to the Mughlai past like Nur, the failed poet in Anita Desai's novel *In Custody* (1984). In the latter case there are some fading associations with romance and beauty but hardly the erotic. However, as the *madrasa*-s teach Urdu more often than secular schools in India, even the association with romance is fading away though the *ġazal* is still responded to among middle-aged, educated, urban people with much nostalgic enthusiasm. Mostly, however, in India Urdu is a matter of demands, protests and Muslim political mobilization at least in North India (see Farouqui 2006). In Pakistan it is a contested terrain – opposed by the supporters of ethnic identities as well as those of English (Rahman 1996) – and more often viewed as part of the Islamic-Pakistani identity than the language of love and longing.

Conclusion

In short, the nineteenth century witnessed battles, so to speak, for the soul of Urdu. It was a period of transition and the formation of new identities for groups of human beings (Muslims, Hindus etc.). Language was part of the construction of these identities. The Indian reformers' desire to purge the language of its erotic associations was motivated by their political agenda for the construction of a 'nation' which was respectable, serious and modern. They felt compelled to defend their culture and literature, and by extension the whole Muslim community, against the British and Hindu charge of concupiscence, decadence and lethargy of which the literature of Urdu, as known up to the reformist movement, seemed to be an obvious and painful reminder. This went hand in hand with the ideological imperative of emphasizing the Muslim identity which tended to push Urdu towards an Islamic orientation. As Muslim separatism needed it as a symbol of the Muslim political identity mobilized against a Hindu version of a similar but opposing identity, it took on new features of a strident nationalism which is perennial in Urdu textbooks in Pakistan. During the same century the new language – the older one being Persian – continued to express the medieval themes of redemption and spirituality of which the erotic was always a part.

During the same period Urdu produced all of its canonical literature in poetry which is predominantly associated with love and sometimes with the erotic. Thus the different, and often paradoxical, associations of Urdu kept in conflict with each other with the public mind responding alternately to different ones according to the demands of the situation and whether the occasion was public (when Iqbal's nationalistic and Islamic poetry was quoted) or private (when Ghalib's love odes were more appropriate). However, the public mode gained ascendancy and the amorous and erotic associations were suppressed in the wake of the political urgency and identity politics of the Pakistan movement and then the perpetual struggle the Pakistani ruling elite waged against the ethnic elites of Pakistan on the one hand and the Western and Indian 'Other' on the other. We now live in a highly politicized age when the amorous and the erotic are tolerated far less than ever before though, ironically, it is also the age of mass production of and easy access to commercial pornography through the Internet. So, although the beautiful aspects of the *ġazal* are moribund and still draw the ire of hardline Islamists as well as the Westernized professionals for their purported eroticism or romantic frivolities, a new generation of young people are being exposed to the commodification of the body in ways never imagined by even the most erotic poets of Urdu.

REFERENCES

Ābrū, Sirajuddin Šāh Mubārak, 1990, *Dīvān-i Ābrū*, ed. Moḥammad Ḥasan, New Delhi: Taraqqī Urdū Bureau.

Aḥmad, Naẕīr, 1962, *Fasāna-e Mubtilā*, Lahore: Majlis Taraqqī-e Adab.

____, 1964, *Taubat un-Nusūh*, Lahore: Majlis Taraqqī-e Adab.

Aḥmad, Ẓamīruddīn, 1990, *Xāṯir-e Ma^cṣūm*, Karachi: Aḥsan Maṯbū^cat.

^cAlī, Fida (^cAiš taxalluṣ), 1829, *Šola javālā: majmū^ca vāsoxt*, Lucknow: Naval Kišor.

Anderson, Benedict, 1983, *Imagined Communities*, London: Verso, 1991 ed.

Andrews, Walter G. and Mehmet Kalpakli, 2005, *The Age of Beloveds: Love and the Beloved in Early-Modern Ottoman and European Culture and Society*, Durban and London: Duke University Press.

Aẕhar, Šahdād, 1995, *Urdū ġazal meiṅ šāhid-bāzī*, Srinagar: Gulšan Publishers.

Bazm, Mīr ^cĀšiq Ḥusain, 1908, *Majmū^ca hazliyāt*, pp. 120, Mss No. 1403, Rampur Raza Library (RRL).

____, 1909, *Majmū^ca hazliyāt*, Mss No. 1404, RRL.

Bečaen, Kallan Xān, n.d., *Dīvān-e Bečaen*, Mss No. 1401, RRL.

Behl, Aditya and Simon Weightman with Shyam Manohar Pandey, 2000, *Mir Sayyid Manjhan Shattari Rajgiri, Madhumalati: An*

Indian Sufi Romance, trans. with introduction by A. Behl et al., New York: Oxford University Press.

Behl, Aditya, 2005, 'Poet of the Bazaars: Nazir Akbarabadi, 1735-1830', [in:] Kathryn Hansen and David Lelyveld (eds), 2005, *A Wilderness of Possibilities: Urdu Studies in Transnational Perspective*, New Delhi: Oxford University Press, pp. 192-222.

Bilgrami, S. Husain, 1900, 'Presidential Address at the Fourteenth Meeting of the Mohammedan Education Conference held at Rampur, December 1900', quoted from Minault 1998: 207.

Bloch, Ivan, 1965, *Sexual Life in England*, London: Corgi Edition.

Bouhdiba, Abdelwahab, 1985, *Sexuality in Islam*, trans. from French by Alan Sheridan, London: Routledge & Kegan Paul.

Brass, Paul, 1974, *Language, Religion and Politics in North India*, London: Cambridge University Press.

Čirkīn, n.d., *Dīvān-e Čirkīn*, Mss No. 1400, RRL.

Dalmia, Vasudha, 1997, *The Nationalization of Hindu Traditions: Bhāratendu Hariśchandra and Nineteenth-Century Banaras*, New York: Oxford University Press.

Dalrymple, William, 2003, *White Mughals: Love and Betrayal in Eighteenth-century India*, London: Harper-Collins.

Desai, Anita, 1984, *In Custody*, Harmondsworth: Penguin Books.

Dover, Kenneth James, 1978, *Greek Homosexuality*, New York: Vintage Books Edition, 1980.

Edn. Com. NWP, 1884, *Report by the North-Western Provinces and Oudh Provincial Committee with Evidence Taken Before the Committee and Memorials Addressed to the Education Commission*, Calcutta: Supt'd. of Govt. Printing.

Farouqui, Ather, 2006, *Redefining Urdu Politics in India*, New Delhi: Oxford University Press.

Flora and Šarīr or Mīr Ḥasan ᶜAlī, n.d., *Majmūᶜa hazliyāt*, Mss No. 1411, RRL.

Forster, Edward Morgan, 1978, *A passage to India*, Oliver Stalybran (ed.), Harmandsworth: Penguin Book.

Foucault, Michel, 1984, *The Foucault Reader: An Introduction to Foucault's Thought*, ed. Paul Rabinow, Harmondsworth: Penguin Books rpt. 1991.

____, 1976-84, *The History of Sexuality*, 3 vols, New York: Pantheon.

Ḥālī, Alṭāf Ḥusain, 1971, *Muqaddamah-e šiᶜr-o-šāᶜirī* [Urdu: Introduction to poetry and poetics], Lahore: Kašmīr Kitāb Ghar.

Ḥusain, Sayyid ᶜAlī, n.d., *Majmūᶜa hazliyāt*, Mss No. 1412.

Inšā, Inšā'allah Xān, 1802, *Daryā-e Laṯāfat*, compiled by Maulavī ᶜAbd ul-Ḥaq, trans. from Persian into Urdu by Paṇḍit Brajmohan Datātrya Kaifī, Lahore: Anjuman Taraqqī-e Urdū, 1988.

Iqbal, Afzal, 1956, *The Life and Work of Jalaluddin Rumi*, Islamabad: Pakistan National Council of the Arts, 1991.

Jāh, Muḥammad Ḥusain, 1908-15, *Ṯalism-e hoš rubā*, Lahore: Sang-e Mīl Publications.

Jālibī, Jamil (ed. & comp.), 1979, *Maṯnavī-e Kadam Rā'o Padam Rā'o*, Delhi: Educational Publishing House.

Jān Ṣāḥib, Mīr Yār ᶜAlī, n.d., *Dīvān-e Jān Ṣāḥib*, Lucknow: Ṣādiq Press.

Kāẓmī, Tamkīn, 1930, *Tazkirah-i rextī*, Hyderabad: n.p.

Kesavan, Mukul, 1994, 'Urdu, Awadh and the Tawaif: the Islamicate Roots of Hindi Cinema', [in:] Zoya Hasan (ed.), *Forging Identities: Gender, Communities and the State in India*, Colorado: Westview Press; edition used: New Delhi: Kali for Women, pp. 244-57.

King, Christopher R., 1994, *One Language, Two Scripts: The Hindi Movement in Nineteenth Century North India*, Bombay: Oxford University Press.

Lal, Kishori Saran, 1988, *The Mughal Harem*, New Delhi: Aditya Prakashan.

Maẓhar, Āġā Vaṣī ᶜAlī Xān Lakhnavī, n.d., *Majmūᶜa hazliyāt*, Mss No. 1407, RRL.

Minault, Gail, 1998, *Secluded Scholars: Women's Education and Muslim Social Reform in Colonial India*, New Delhi: Oxford University Press.

Moḥsin, Moḥsin ᶜAlī, 1861?, *Tazkirah-e sarāpā suxan*, no publication details.

Mušīr, Xalīlullāh Aḥmad Ṣiddīqī, 1974, *Rextī ka Tanqīdī Muṯālaᶜa*, Lucknow: Nasīm Book Depot.

Naim, Choudhri Mohammed, 1979, 'The Theme of Homosexual (Pederastic) Love in pre-Modern Urdu Poetry', [in:] M. Umar Memon (ed.), *Studies in the Urdu Ġazal and Prose Fiction*, Madison: University of Wisconsin, pp. 120-42.

____, 2001, 'Transvestic Words?: The *Rekhti* in Urdu', *The Annual of Urdu Studies* 2001, vol. 16, pp. 3-26.

Najmabadi, Afsaneh, 2005, *Women with Moustaches and Men Without Beards: Gender and Sexual Anxieties of Iranian Modernity*, Berkeley: University of California Press.

Petievich, Carla, 2001, 'Gender politics and the Urdu ghazal: Exploratory observations on *Rekhta* versus *Rekhtī*', *The Indian Economic and Social History Review* 2001, vol. 38: 3, pp. 223-48.

Pritchett, Frances W., 1995, *Nets of Awareness: Urdu Poetry and Its Critics*, Karachi: Oxford University Press.

Quraišī, Vaḥīd, 1966, 'Introduction', *Masnavīat-e Ḥusain*, vol. 1, ed. & comp. Vaḥīd Quraišī, Lahore: Majlis Taraqqī-e Adab.

Rahman, Tariq, 1988, 'Ephebophilia: The Case for the Use of a New Word', *Forum for Modern Language Studies*, vol. 24, no. 2 (April), pp. 126-41.

____, 1990, 'Boy-love in the Urdu Ghazal', *Annual of Urdu Studies*, vol. 7, pp. 1-20.

____, 1996, *Language and Politics in Pakistan*, Karachi: Oxford University Press.

____, 2002, *Language, Ideology and Power: Language-Learning among the Muslims of Pakistan and North India*, Karachi: Oxford University Press.

____, 2004, *Denizens of Alien Worlds: A Study of Education, Inequality and Polarization in Pakistan*, Karachi: Oxford University Press.

____, 2006, 'Urdu as an Islamic Language', *The Annual of Urdu Studies*, vol. 21, pp. 101-19.

Rangīn, Saᶜādat Yār Xān, n.d., *Masnavī maᶜa hazliyāt taṣnīf Saᶜādat Yār Xān Rangīn Dehlavī*, Oriental MSS Or. 385, 010 C.

Rasā, Ḥayāt Baxš Muṣṭafā Abedi, n.d., *Majmūᶜa hazliyāt*, Mss No. 1409, RRL.

Rūmī, Jalāl ud-dīn, 2006, *Masnavī Maulvī Maᶜnavī*, 6 vols, Original Persian with Urdu Translation by Qāẓī Sajjād Ḥusain, Lahore: Al-Faiṣal Našrān, 2006.

Rusvā, Mirzā Hādi, 1905, *Umrā'o Jān Adā*, Islamabad: Alhamra Publishing, 2000.

____, n.d., *Šarīf-zāda*, Lahore: Kitāb Ghar.

Ṣāḥib-e Qirān, Sayyid Imām ᶜAlī, *c.* 1811, *Muntaxab Dīvān Ṣāḥib Qirān*, Ms. No. 771, Delhi, Persian, OIOC, British Library, London.

Ṣāḥib-e Qirān, Sayyid Imām ᶜAlī Xān, n.d., *Dīvān-e Ṣāḥib-e Qirān*, Oriental MSS. Egerton 1040, Folio 49, 010C.

Sarvarī, ᶜAbd ul-Qādir, 1998, *Kulliyāt-i Sirāj*, Delhi: Qaumī Kaunsil Barā'i Farog̣-i Urdū Zabān.

Suvorova, Anna A., 2000, *Masnavi: A Study of Urdu Romance*, Karachi: Oxford University Press.

Šamīm, Sayyid Jāwad Ḥusain Amrohī, 1915, *Majmūᶜa hazliyāt*, Mss No. 1410, RRL.

Šarār, ᶜAbd ul-Ḥalīm, 2006, *Guzašta Lucknow: Hindustān meiṅ mašriqī tamaddun kā āxrī namūna* (2nd edn., comp.) M. Ikrām Čug̣tā'ī,

Lahore: Sang-e Mīl Publications; this is available in English as *Lucknow: The Last Phase of an Oriental Culture.*

Šarīf, Moḥammad Jamīl, 2004, *Dakan meiṅ Urdū še*ᶜ*rī Valī se pahle*, Hyderabad (India): Idārah-e Adabiyāt-e Urdū.

Šauq, Navāb Mirzā, n.d., *Masnavīat-e Šauq*, ed. Iṣrār Aḥmed Tabassum, Lahore: Tahliq Markaz, n.d.

Vanita, Ruth and Saleem Kidwai, 2000, *Same-sex Love in India: Reading from Literature and History*, New York: St. Martins' Press.

Vanita, Ruth, 2004, '«Married Among Their Companions»: Female Homoerotic Relations in Nineteenth-Century Urdu *Rexti* Poetry in India', *Journal of Women's History*, vol. 16, no. 1, pp. 12-52.

Xān, ᶜAbd ur-Rašīd, 2002, *Urdū afsāne meiṅ jinsī jazbat*, Srinagar: Gulšan Publishers.

Xān, Dargāh Qulī, 1993, *Muraqqa*ᶜ*-i Dehlī*, Persian with Urdu translation, ed. and trans. Xalīq Anjum, New Delhi: Anjuman Taraqqī-e Urdū.

Xān, Rašīd Ḥasan (ed. & comp.), 2003, *Zaṭal nāma: Kulliyāt-e Ja*ᶜ*far Zaṭallī*, New Delhi: Published by the compiler.

ABBREVIATIONS

OIOC = Oriental and India Office Collection, British Library, London
RRL = Rampur Raza Library, U.P., India

Muslims and Hindus: Urdu and Hindi

Harish Trivedi

One of the finest fruits of the devlopement of an Islamicate tradition in the Indian subcontinent is the Urdu language. Unlike the other languages of India, Urdu is replete with Arabic and Persian while, like the other Indian languages, it also shares in the inheritance of Sanskrit through its provenance partly from Hindi and, in the 'Deccan' or South, also from Gujarati and Telugu. Thus, while all languages are hybridized to some extent or the other, Urdu is nothing if not hybrid in its very essence and genetic code. In terms of its literature, it bears a direct genealogical connection with the major themes, literary conventions, and the numerous genres and forms that were already prevalent in Arabic and Persian, the major languages of Islam in Central Asia. While Arabic and Persian themselves had currency and influence in India since long before Urdu was born, they were regarded as largely foreign imports even during the years when Persian served as the language of command. Urdu, on the other hand, was born in India, is used only in the Indian subcontinent, and remains India's indigenous and living link with the Perso-Arabic literary cultures.

While Urdu's lineage and its genetic link with a larger pan--Islamic literary tradition has been a defining aspect of its identity, that does not make it an entirely or exclusively Muslim language, for two main reasons. Firstly, a number of non-Muslims, chiefly from the majority community of the Hindus, have also spoken Urdu while some have written in it as well, and secondly, a large number of the Muslims in the subcontinent do not know Urdu, for they speak and write in several other Indian languages such as, notably, Bengali, Panjabi, Sindhi and Kashmiri. And yet, as David Lelyveld sums the matter up at the end of a rich historical survey of the respective status of Hindustani, Urdu and Hindi since the late eighteenth century, reflecting in this regard a common perception also noted by Aijaz Ahmad, Urdu is 'almost universally identified as a language for a regionally unspecified Muslim population' in the subcontinent (Lelyveld 1993: 682).

The geographical region that Urdu occupies may not be identifiable in either India or Pakistan as a particular state or province (in the way that most other languages in India can be after the reorganization of state boundaries in 1956) but it is not difficult to locate it in somewhat broader terms. Since shortly after its reputed beginnings in the Deccan (the area around Aurangabad and later Hyderabad in South India), the terrain where it has flourished best as a literary language has been broadly the same as that in which Hindi has flourished equally and which is now sometimes called the Hindi heartland. The two languages have on the whole occupied the same turf and breathed the same air and, because of their close grammatical similarity, they have been described as sisters or, in a radical change of metaphor, as co-wives or co-concubines.

It has been claimed by some that the two are virtually the same language and by others that they are irreconcilably different and even opposed to each other. Beginning in the latter half of the nineteenth century and right up to the Partition of India if not beyond, they have often existed in a state of mutual contestation if not hostility. Their 'twinned histories' (Pollock 2003: 803) and intertwined fortunes have been recounted in rich historical detail from quite distinct points of view by several scholars, most notably Amrit Rai, Christopher King, and Shamsur Rahman Faruqi.

(Rai 1984; King 1994; Faruqi 2003). For what it is worth, I too have from time to time contributed my ha'penny worth to the debate (Trivedi 1984, 2003, 2004), but in the present essay I wish to view the relationship between Urdu and Hindi from a different point of view, as a matter concerning not generally language but more specifically literature.

It is commonly believed that the literature of a language embodies not only the finest specimens of its use but also the core and essence of the sensibility peculiar to that language, its unique imaginary. This remains broadly true not only of 'high' canonical literature but also, and perhaps more so, of popular and folk literature. The literature in a language is characteristic of its spirit and genius in a way that its functional uses may not be, and that is why while functional texts may be readily rendered from one language to another, and with increasing efficiency even by machines now, translation of literary texts presents a rather more complex challenge even to the best of human translators. To valorize literature in this manner in the present age of an apparently terminal crisis in the study of the humanities may sound like an elite predilection but that cannot undo the historical fact that such a predilection and preference, and assumptions about the value of literature, were commonly shared until fairly recently, through much of the history of the existence of these languages.

The specific questions I propose to ask in this essay about Urdu and Hindi literatures, as seen in a broadly comparative framework, are: what and how much do Urdu and Hindi literatures have in common? Are there any writers who are claimed equally by both languages, or any writers who wrote in both languages, either simultaneously or successively? More importantly, in order to interrogate the still abiding general impression that Urdu is a language of Muslims and Hindi that of Hindus, can we identify and highlight Hindu writers who contributed to Urdu literature and conversely Muslim writers who contributed to Hindi literature? What implications did such cross-over literary contributions have in terms of literature, religion and culture? Was there ever a 'composite' literary culture, a *gaṅgā-jamunī tahẕīb* as it is routinely called, a confluence of the two literary rivers, and what was its extent and its hey-day? And finally, after their twinned if also embattled history, where do these languages and their literatures find themselves today?

I. Hindus in Urdu

In terms of grammar, Urdu and Hindi are seen to be nearly identical and in terms of vocabulary too there is certainly common ground between them. It was precisely such common ground that was identified under the neutral term 'Hindustani,' especially in the period broadly between 1920 and 1947. (This was a new development, for in the eighteenth and nineteenth centuries, especially in British colonial usage, 'Hindustani' had meant effectively the same thing as Urdu.) There was significant variation in different estimates of just how wide this common linguistic ground was and what its capacity and capabilities were, but the idea of Hindustani was vigorously promoted by several well-meaning and idealistic champions, such as Gandhi, Nehru and Premchand, who wished to promote Hindu-Muslim harmony at the same time and by the same token. To this purpose, a Hindustani Academy was founded in Allahabad in 1927, and in 1942 Gandhi moved on from supporting the Dakṣiṇ Bhārat Hindī Pracār Sabhā (South India Society for the Propagation of Hindi), with which he had been closely associated since 1918, to found and begin to promote the Hindustānī Pracār Sabhā (Society for the Propagation of Hindustani), which was also supported, notably, by Rajendra Prasad, Abul Kalam Azad, Zakir Husain, Premchand and Tarachand.

As it happened, it was soon found by such newly established bodies that the language they were obliged to function in was Urdu as well as Hindi, alongside each other, but not a mixture of the two languages; their proceedings remained bilingual. Well-meaning efforts to yoke Urdu and Hindi together in this way actually served to exacerbate the relations between them and to show up if not also to widen the gap between them. Premchand reported how the annual convention of the Hindustani Academy, which he had gone to attend in Allahabad in 1936, failed even to elect a commonly agreed President; eventually, Maulana Abdul Haq was elected for the Urdu section and Pandit Ganganath Jha for the Hindi section (see Premchand's account cited in Rai 1982: 339-40).

As for producing literature in this mixed language, the project proved even more difficult to attain. It was found that as soon as one needed to go beyond the language of the man in the street to attempt to say anything more substantial or sophisticated, one necessarily had to take recourse to either Perso-Arabic vocabulary or Sanskritic vocabulary. When Premchand was challenged to name even one discursive book that had ever been written in Hindustani, he charmingly replied: 'if such a [mixed] language already existed, where would be the need for an institution such as this Academy?' (qtd. in Trivedi 2003: 979). Apparently, there still is no such book or such language. The journal *Hindustānī* published by the Hindustānī Pracār Sabhā from Bombay is published half in Hindi/Nāgarī and half in Urdu/Arabic script, and because the scripts are written in opposite directions, both the halves within the same covers can claim to be the front half, depending on how one holds the journal in one's hands. The website of the Sabhā operates in three languages, Hindi, Urdu and English, and its emblem is an open book with the Nāgarī letter 'a' written on the left-hand page and the Arabic *alif* on the right-hand page; the two languages are, quite literally, not on the same page (Hindustānī Pracār Sabhā: website).

So much for the future that never happened, but what about the past? Was there ever a stage when the language was more persuasively a mixed or common language? Was there ever a brave writer who could be said to belong to both the languages and stood astride the border between them (as Toba Tek Singh stood in the climactic scene of Manto's short story astride the newly drawn border between India and Pakistan)? Apparently not, and going back in history, even the probability of this having happened was drastically reduced by the fact that until Hindi switched to Khari Boli, beginning in the late nineteenth century but not completely until as late as in the 1920s (when the battle for Khari Boli was still being vigorously fought in public by its champions such as the poet Sumitranandan Pant), nearly all of Hindi literature had been written in Awadhi or Braj Bhasha. These were forms of Hindi which have far less in common even in terms of vocabulary and grammar with Urdu, which has always used Khari Boli structures.

There is therefore no Hindi poet of the older period, from Avadhi or Braj, who can even remotely sound like an Urdu writer or a writer readily accessible to Urdu readers. Conversely, perhaps the one older Urdu writer who is relatively accessible to Hindi readers is Nazir Akbarabadi (1735-1830), partly on the strength of his having written some poems on Hindu themes, such as those on the god 'Krishna Kanhaiya' or the festival of Holi. As for his diction and style, Mohammad Hasan says in an oblique and cryptic observation that he 'escaped [the] fate' of contemporary poets such as Abru and Naji who gave 'poetic language a new sophistication' in Urdu (Hasan 1973: 66-7) – that is to say, helped to make it more Persianized. The editor of a selection of Nazir's poetry in the Nāgarī script makes the more straightforward observation that 'no Urdu poet was more liberal in the matter of language' ('Kaif' 1995: 29). This relative judgment may be true enough yet, from a Nāgarī/Hindi reader's point of view, a simple line frequently alternates with a difficult one in Nazir's poetry as well:

Kah'te haiṁ jis'ko 'Nazīr' suniye tuk us'kā bayān
Thā vah muallim garīb, buz'dil-o-tarsanda jān.

('Kaif' 1995: 12; Hasan 1973: 69)

Similarly, there are not many writers of any significance who can be said to have written in both Urdu and Hindi. The one outstanding name here is that of 'Premchand' (Dhanpat Rai Srivastava, 1880-1936), who wrote exclusively in Urdu from *c.* 1902 to 1915, began gradually to move to Hindi by translating some of his own works from Urdu to Hindi, for the reason that he found ready publishers in Hindi while his works originally written in Urdu lay unpublished even though he was already regarded as the best Urdu writer of fiction of his generation. Thus, *Bāzār-e-ḥusn*, written in Urdu, was first published as *Sevāsadan* in Hindi in 1919 and only later in Urdu in 1922, and similarly, *Čauġān-e-hastī* was first published as *Raṅgabhūmi* in Hindi in 1924 and in Urdu in 1927. Not surprisingly, he soon began to write originally in Hindi. Beginning with *Kāyākalpa* (1926), he wrote all his novels originally in Hindi which were afterwards translated, often by nameless others, into Urdu: *Nirmalā* (1927), *Ġaban* (1929), *Karmabhūmi* (1933) and *Godān* (1936). The last named work, for example, was first published in Urdu under the title *Gau-dān* only in 1939 (see Rai 1982: *passim*).

Premchand himself gave two rather different reasons for moving from Urdu to Hindi. The first was that by 1915 he found that it was easier and more lucrative to publish in Hindi than in Urdu, and the second that even after he had established himself as the foremost writer of fiction in Urdu of his times, he felt that he was not really accepted in a largely Muslim literary culture: 'Has any Hindu ever made a success of writing in Urdu that I will?' (Rai 1982: 104). This private (but nevertheless unsettling) statement, in a letter to a dear friend, Daya Narain Nigam, who too was a Hindu and the editor of a major Urdu journal *Zamāna*, is however corroborated from the other side, as it were, by Muhammad Sadiq in his *History of Urdu Literature*: 'But this much will have to be admitted that Muslims continued to treat him [Premchand] more or less as an outsider. And yet the fact stands that he wrote Urdu with unusual distinction…' (Sadiq 1984: 439). The condescension implicit in that last observation is an unwitting attestation perhaps of the truth of Sadiq's preceding observation that Muslims treated him as an outsider, regardless of the quality of his contribution to Urdu.

As for the works themselves, Premchand's switch from Urdu to Hindi seemed to have had two major consequences. His own translation of *Bāzār-e-ḥusn* as *Sevasādan* offered illustrations of his numerous Hindu characters sounding (perhaps naturally) a little more Hindu in Hindi than they had in Urdu, with richer cultural connotations and resonances. And in terms of theme, his novels originally written in Hindi now took up themes which were part of the mainstream discourse in those nationalist times, though this trend had already begun with what is perhaps his pivotal transitional novel in this regard, *Čauġān-e-hastī/Raṅgabhūmi* (see Trivedi 1984).

Premchand remains the biggest Hindu writer to have ever written in Urdu, even if only for an early and apprentice part of his career and as a defector to Hindi afterwards. All the other Hindus who have ever written in Urdu are regarded as writers of far less eminence and perhaps none of them has a place in the front rank of Urdu literature. T. Graham Bailey in his history of Urdu literature found that of the 250 writers he had discussed in that history, only eight were Hindus. They are (i) Vali Ram, who apparently lived before the seventeenth century and wrote mainly in Persian, possibly because it is not even clear whether Urdu existed in those times; (ii) Daya Shankar 'Naseem' (1811-43) who died young; (iii) Nihal Chand Lahauri (no dates given) who called the Urdu he wrote in 'Hindi rekhta'; (iv) Lallu Lal (no dates given), who is anyhow 'more famous for his work in Hindi' at the College of Fort William; (v) Beni Narayan (no dates given) who was mainly an anthologist; (vi) Ram Chander, a nineteenth-century mathematician and translator but not a creative writer; (vii) Ratan Nath 'Sarshar' (1846-1902), an early fiction/'fasāna' writer; and (viii) Durga Sahae 'Suroor' (1873-1910), who also died too young to fulfill his promise but was rather like Nazir in writing on everyday subjects and in the fact that he 'liked simplicity and preferred vernacular Hindi words to those taken from Arabic and Persian' (Bailey 1928: 15, 60, 80, 83, 88, and 96 respectively).

This little cluster of just eight minor Hindu writers may be regarded as falling somewhat short of demonstrating a Ganga--Jamuni confluence, but that's how it seems to be, alas, in fact. In Muhammad Sadiq's much longer history, the additional Hindu names are equally minor if not a little more so: Tek Chand 'Bahar'; Javala Parshad 'Barq'; and Piyare [Pyare] Lal 'Ashob' (Sadiq 1984: 91, 317, 500). The one half-way major name is that of Brij Narain 'Chakbast' (1882-1926), who too died young, and was 'the [Urdu] poet of nationalism *par excellence*', who in his *Ṣubaḥ-e-vaṭan* composed elegies for Tilak and Gokhale, and whose political optimism was rather deflated by his 'despondency' at witnessing 'the growing estrangement between the Hindus and Muslims' (Sadiq 1984: 493-4).

A writer who had barely begun writing when Bailey's *History* was published, Raghupati Sahay 'Firaq' (1895-1986), could perhaps be regarded as a second major Hindu writer in Urdu after

Premchand. Unlike Nazir, he did not write about explicitly Hindu themes in his *ġazal*-s or other long poems but he did introduce certain images and allusions in them which have deep Hindu resonances:

> *Ādā mẽ khinčtī hai taṣvīr Krišn-o-Rādhā kī*
> *Terī naẓar ne fasāne Nal-o-Daman ke kahe.*
>
> Your manner paints a picture of Krishna and Radha,
> Your glance tells the tale of Nala and Damayanti.

Even more remarkable and new in Urdu were perhaps his *rubāᶜiyāt* in which he did provide vignettes of Hindu life by depicting, for example, attractive young women actually getting married under a palpably Hindu *maṇḍap* (ritual canopy) or holding a baby in their lap or celebrating the festival of *rakṣā-bandhan* or milking cows or churning milk to produce butter (Firāq 1990: 6-8) – the kind of images that had never before been seen in Urdu, where the inviolably virginal lady is always romantically distant and disdainful and far from such hum-drum and mundane activities as (perish the thought!) marrying or keeping house or doing anything domestic or even remotely useful. Firaq habitually expressed a robust contempt for modern Hindi literature and for Hindi language generally with the usual Urdu *hauteur*, but he also thought that Urdu literature needed to become less Arabicized and more Indian for the sake of its own future health:

> What is needed is nothing more, nothing less and nothing else than the Sanskritization of Urdu... If more and more Urdu writers are inspired by the life-giving influences of Sanskrit literature, Urdu literature will be cured of a split personality (Interview, qtd. in Trivedi 2008: 19)

Long before he made this recommendation in 1961, he had already in 1947 in the preface to his volume *Šabnamistān* declared that he wished that

> a grand vision of Indianness [*bulandtarīn Hindustānīyat*] should be made to suffuse Urdu poetry and literature, just as Germanness suffuses German literature, Russianness Russian literature, Arabianness [*ḥijāzīyat*] Arab literature, or Indianness the poetry of Bhavabhuti, Kalidasa, Bhartrihari or Tagore (qtd. in Trivedi 2008: 19-20)

Anyhow, Nazir, Premchand and Firaq Gorakhpuri are among the few writers who stand out in the history of Urdu literature for recognizing and registering in their works a wider empirical world and a cultural ambience which lay all around them, as distinct from the distant and unreal world of literary artifice and conventions which Urdu had inherited from Arabic and Persian. In their different ways, they came as close as Urdu writers have ever done to helping to ground Urdu language and literature in its local habitation and opening up a dialogue with its *doppelganger*, Hindi literature. Firaq (whom, incidentally, Premchand had encouraged to write and publish at the beginning of his career) recognized an affinity when he edited, with a highly commendatory introduction, a volume of Nazir's poetry in the Nāgarī script.

In his extensive selection running to 223 pages, Firaq included not only Nazir's poems on such themes as Krishna, Mahadeva, Holi and Divali, but also a generous proportion of his accessibly expressed philosophical meditations on the human condition, such as his poems on youth, old age, poverty, the various ways and circumstances of being a man ('Ādmīnāma'), death, Kali-yuga, the world being but a deception (*dhoke kī ṭaṭṭī*), the transience of this world, and two poems each titled 'Faqīrõ kī ṣadā' [The Voice of the Holy Beggars]. Firaq gave the volume the title *Naẕīr kī bāṇī*, the word *bāṇī* (from Sanskrit *vāṇī*, voice) connoting the 'verses, teachings (esp. of the *nirguṇī* sectarians and their followers)' (McGregor 1997: 724), as in a strand of the mainstream of Hindi *bhakti* poetry of which Kabir is the great exemplar. And he concluded his introduction to the volume by expressing the hope, which he said was encouraged by the signs that were emerging of a new (i.e., post-Partition) cultural awakening in India, that a fitting memorial to Nazir will be built one day and will become the venue of an annual festival that 'lovers of Hindi-Urdu in their lakhs will celebrate' (Firāq 1999: [16]).

To be accurate, the 'Hindi-Urdu' in the preceding sentence can in Hindi mean, according to the eight different ways of *samās* or combining words, either Hindi and Urdu (as separate languages) or Hindi and Urdu as a combined linguistic entity. Incidentally, this edition by Firaq published in Nāgarī may be the only one of Urdu verse so rendered which spends two pages explaining the Urdu linguistic conventions of combining words such as *ᶜaṭf* and *iẓāfat*, which constitutes another small piece of evidence to indicate that Firaq was here trying assiduously to build a bridge between Urdu and Hindi.

II. Muslims in Hindi

As for the Muslim contribution to Hindi, it is not only far more substantial than the Hindu contribution to Urdu but seems to have begun as soon as Hindi began – if not in fact a little earlier! For there were Muslims in India before there was Hindi, and some of them were already writing in forms of language from which Hindi would evolve. The earliest period of Hindi, as indeed of all older languages, is still chronologically a little hazy as being half-hidden in the mists of time but it is dated, in the comprehensively scholarly view of Rahul Sankrityayan, as extending from AD 760 to 1300 (cited in Caturvedī 1994: 24). This comprises in the earliest centuries of this era the religious traditions of the Siddha-Natha-Jain sects, and then, a stirring bardic epic of the resistance by the last Hindu king of Delhi, Prithviraj, to the Muslim invader, Muhammad Ghori who finally prevails. This epic, *Pṛthvīrāj Rāsau*, reputedly written by his court poet Chand Bardai (who accompanies his king in captivity to Ghori's capital and himself appears in the poem as an observer-participant) is the prime example of what Ramachandra Shukla, the foundational and still unsurpassed historian of Hindi literature, called an initial period of Hindi literature: *Vīr-Gāthā-Kāl*, the 'Age of Heroic Narratives' (Śukla 1940: 47-61). In alternative accounts, Chand Bardai lived and composed his epic much after the events he describes, probably in the thirteenth century, in which case he comes close to sharing the distinction of being the first major Hindi poet with a Muslim, Amir Khusro.

Khusro (1253?-1325) was mainly and substantially a poet in Persian, and of his few compositions in the local Indian language, the best-known are some punning comic-erotic riddles, *muk'rī*-s. He was apparently the first nativist among Muslim writers, for he recognized early that the local language of (north) India was a worthy vehicle of literary expression. His scant compositions in it are claimed by Urdu and Hindi alike, with different degrees of plausibility. Mohammad Sadiq says, accurately enough: 'The Urdu lines ascribed to Amir Khusrau, besides being all too few, have been unconsciously modified through generations of oral transmission...' (Sadiq 1984: 50). Brajratna Das, in his edition of *Khus'ro kī hindī kavitā*, makes the same point when he says that the little verses of Khusro that are still popular have through oral transmission changed substantially in diction: 'It is difficult to say that these are quite as they were written by Khusro' (Dās 1922: 12).

All that we can do then is to look at these verses as they have comes down to us. One of the most famous verses of Khusro runs as follows:

> *Gorī sovai saij par mukh par ḍāre kes.*
> *Cal Khus'ro ghar āpne, rain bhaī cahuṁ des.*
>
> (Dās 1922: 4)

As it happens, each word in this couplet can be traced back to a Sanskrit root and therefore belongs primarily to Hindi – except the name Khusro!

Apart from the issue of oral and therefore constantly modified transmission, another problem with making large linguistic claims on the basis of the meagre Hindi output of Khusro is that in neither Hindi nor Urdu do we get any verses in this Khari Boli form for the succeeding five hundred years or more. There is nothing by way of recognizable Urdu poetry until Vali Aurangabadi/Daccani (fl. *c.* 1700) while in Hindi all significant poetry is written in the different forms of Avadhi and Braj until the nineteenth century. In this sense, Khusro must be regarded as a false dawn for both these languages alike. A more substantial body of literature that was composed in Deccani/Dakhni in the sixteenth and seventeenth centuries by Muslim writers, is again claimed extraterritorially by both Urdu and Hindi though neither language knows quite how to assimilate this literature into the trajectory of its subsequent growth. It seems to come from a faraway time and place when neither Hindus nor Muslims had undergone the kind of cultural polarization which soon became a defining feature of their respective identities. In a way, Amir Khusro and the Daccani poets form a kind of no man's land between the two languages, an area hard to annex or cultivate.

Of the Muslim poets who began writing in what may be called the mainstream of Hindi and in fact helped to shape it, the earliest is Maulana Daud who composed his allegorical Sufi love-epic *Candāyān* in 1379. He came from a family long established in the small town of Dalmau near Rae Bareli (in the present Uttar Pradesh). The narrative form of his poem is the Persian *maṣ̤navī*, his cultural references are heavily Hindu, such as *dharm* (religion), *pāp* (sin), the river Ganga and the names and locations of his characters, his stanza pattern of several *caupāī*-s (long four-footed internally rhyming quatrains) punctuated by a *dohā* (rhyming couplet), is derived from Apabhramsha, his language is Awadhi, and his script is the Persian (McGregor 2003: 915-17). There quickly followed several more epics in a similar mould, including Sheikh Kutuban's *Mṛgavatī*, Sheikh Manjhan's *Madhumālatī* and above all, that supreme Sufi epic, *Padmāvatī* (1540), by yet another Muslim writer from the Awadhi-speaking area, Malik Mohmmad Jayasi. Few languages of the world have, right at the start of their literary history, as many as four allegorical epics to show for themselves, and this distinction of Hindi is enhanced by the fact that each of these four poets was a Muslim. What is even more remarkable is that a fifth epic that followed in the same language, and in the same *caupāī-dohā* metrical pattern, though on an altogether different theme, turned out to be what remains probably the greatest poem in all of Hindi literature, *Rām'carit'mānas* (1577) by Tulsidas – or as its more popularly known, the *Rāmāyaṇ* in Hindi.

The tradition of the Sufi love-epic or *premākhyān* continued to be enriched by several other Muslim poets including notably Usman, Sheikh Nabi, and Nur Mohammad. Somewhat earlier, a Muslim poet as great as any to have ever written in an Indian language, Kabir (1398-1518), and as different from the Sufi love poets as he was from Tulsidas, had sung of an abstract (*nirguṇa*) God whom he at times addressed as 'Rama'. He had been as scathing of Hindu religious practices as of Muslim observances and though tradition maintains that both the Hindus and the Muslims claimed him after his death, only Hindi has ever claimed him as a poet and not Urdu. Yet another strand of *bhakti* poetry, that centering on Krishna in which Mirabai and Surdas had written, also had some outstanding Muslim poets contributing to it. Indeed, one of the sweetest poets in the whole history of Braj bhasha poetry was Syed Mohammad Ibrahim (*c.* 1590-1680) who wrote under the name 'Rasakhan' (a mine of joy); his themes, as of numerous Hindu poets, were Krishna's childhood and his erotic encounters with Radha and other milkmaids. A later poet closely similar in theme as well as his adopted name was Ghulam Nabi Bilgrami 'Raslin' (i.e. 'immersed in joy'; fl. *c.* 1737).

A close contemporary of Tulsidas was Abdurrahim Khankhana 'Rahim' (1553-1626), whose worldly wise and wryly urbane couplets are regularly included in the Hindi school textbooks together with Rasakhan's verses, a sure indication of the canonical status of a poet. Rajjab Ali Khan was another *nirguṇa* poet but rather more directly didactic in intent. Mubarak (early seventeenth century) was a poet who belonged to the major poetic convention of *rīti* poetry, which had by and large come to succeed *bhakti* poetry, and was devoted mainly to highly formal and conventional poetry on erotic themes, as was Newəz. (Apparently, not one but three different poets with that Muslim name wrote in Hindi though not much is known about the other two.) Another notable poet in the *rīti* tradition was Alam (early eighteenth century), who reputedly was born a Brahmin but had converted to Islam on falling in love with a female dyer known as Sheikh Rangrezin who was herself a poet. (For engaging and insightful accounts of the life and works of all these poets, see Śukla 1940: *passim*; see also Razā 2011: 48-73, who mentions about ten more Muslim poets of significance in Hindi for this period.)

In the necessarily synoptic overview offered above of the three hundred years separating Maulana Daud and the Alam couple, at least 20 notable Muslim poets appear to have written in Hindi and to have contributed to each one of the major strands of development of Hindi poetry in this period. In fact, they represent between themselves each shade and nuance of Hindi poetry written between *c.* 1350 and 1700, and several among them belong to the very front rank of Hindi literature: Kabir, Jayasi, Rahim, and Rasakhan. This makes Hindi as 'composite' and 'secular' a literary culture as any Indian language can claim to be.

But then, something quite dramatic happens as the eighteenth century gets under way and this is illustrated as starkly as anywhere else in an anthology of Hindi poetry published in 1961. In the authoritative *Hindī kāvya saṅgraha* (An anthology of Hindi poetry) edited by Balkrishna Rao for the Sāhitya Akādemī which comprises 101 poets, fifteen of the first sixty-two are Muslim, up to Alam, but thereafter, among the subsequent thirty-nine poets, there is not a single Muslim. This constitutes an odd gap, a sudden silence, which nothing that happened before this point of time could have helped one anticipate. So, what happened?

There is perhaps never a sufficient explanation for unexpected historical developments, but it could be argued that there is a plausible enough explanation if we look just a little beyond the Hindi literary sphere. At the same time that Alam is writing in Delhi, there arrives in the capital city of the Mughals a poet from South India, from the 'deccan', called Vali Aurangabadi who would become known even better as Vali Deccani. He would come to be regarded as the first major poet in Urdu, predating Mir and Sauda and Momin. With him, Urdu poetry would have arrived in North India from the distant Deccan, and thereafter, both the Hindus and Muslims of India would have an option as to which language they would prefer to write in. And, as it turned out, virtually all the Muslim writers of North India would from now on desert Hindi, flock to the new literary medium of Urdu, adapt to its very different Perso-Arabic themes and genres, and identify with the language in all kinds of cultural ways. What was, and by and large remains, the Hindi heartland would have become what Ralph Russell calls 'the heartland of Urdu' as well (Russell 1999: 94). This common space from now on would be linguistically divided, segregated and compartmentalized into two parallel and mutually non-communicating literary cultures through much of the eighteenth and nineteenth centuries, and thereafter constitute an arena of bitter contestation until the coming of Partition and Independence. The historical fact of Partition and the establishment of Pakistan with Urdu as its official language, and the declaration subsequently of Hindi as the official language of India, would serve to cool down passions if not to settle the issue, with Urdu in India perceiving itself to be in a state of downward slide.

The decades after Partition would also bring about a new development with regard to the Muslim writers in North India. Premchand, a Hindu, had already noticed a downward trend in the circulation of Urdu by 1915, but by 1950, even Muslim writers would begin to notice this hard fact. Consequently, a generation of Muslim writers who had grown up in independent India would now return to Hindi, and begin writing in Hindi alongside their Hindu contemporaries just as they had before Urdu presented itself as an option in the early eighteenth century. The century and a half of the ascendance and dominance of Urdu as the literary language of choice for all Muslim writers and some Hindus as well, from about 1770 to 1947, would have well and truly ended; that chapter of our literary history would have closed. The future would mark a return to the past.

It is possible to theorize, or at least periodize, these developments in the mutual relationship between Hindi and Urdu. This would indicate the evolving Muslim preference for Hindi or lack of it, and also the fortunes of Urdu and its rise and fall in the Hindi/Urdu heartland. It could be suggested that from this point of view the Muslim contribution to Hindi falls in the following three chronological categories:

(a) The Pre-Urdu Period. This can be dated, as seen above, from *c.* 1350 to *c.* 1700. During this period, before Urdu came into existence as a literary language in North India, all Muslims wrote in the same local language, whether Awadhi or Braj, the two major forms of Hindi then dominant in literature, or in the less geographically rooted and more mixed variety of Hindi known as the Sadhukkari in which the *nirguṇa* poets often wrote.

In the early phase in which Muslim authors wrote the Sufi epics, there was no distinction between Hindu writers and Muslim writers in terms of form or diction.

(b) The Urdu Period. This can be dated as the period from *c.* 1700 to 1947. Not only did Urdu emerge as a vehicle of literary expression but it also gained considerable status and privileges after it was declared by the British government to be the official language of administration and judiciary in what are now the states of Uttar Pradesh, Bihar and Madhya Pradesh where not Urdu but Hindi was, and always had been, the language of the vast majority of the population (including the Muslims living away from the urban courts in the villages). The British may not have done this only or even mainly with a view to divide and rule, for an advantage that Urdu had over Hindi was that it was far closer to Persian, the previous language of command, and in the period following *c.* 1750, had tended to become more and more so. In any case, this turned out to be the period of the widest Muslim contribution to Urdu literature and the golden period of the rise of typically Urdu literary forms such as the *ġazal*, the *marṡiya* and the *qaṣīda*, of which there had been no tradition in Hindi.

(c) The Post-Urdu Period. This is the period after 1947. While a considerable amount of literature in Urdu was published in these years, a large number of Muslims had now begun writing in Hindi again in all the popular forms of modern literature: the novel, the short story, and the free-verse poem (as distinct from Urdu in which the *ġazal* still seemed to flourish and the *naẓm* too was often written in irregularly rhymed verse).

Among the Muslim writers who have written in Hindi after independence, the most notable perhaps are the novelists and short story writers Rahi Masum Raza, Gulsher Khan Shani, Asghar Wajahat, Abdul Bismillah and Manzur Ehtesham. Both Habib Tanvir and Safdar Hashmi stand out as among the most radical playwrights in Hindi. Among the Muslim poets writing in Hindi are Asad Zaidi, Ibbar Rabbi, Rizvan Zahir Usman, Shahanshah Alam and Sultan Ahmad, to name a sample from just one anthology (Zaidī and Nāgar 1994).

It is not possible to discuss here the various dimensions of the works of any of these writers but a couple of significant aspects may be noted. In Rahi Masum Raza's major work *Ādhā gāṁv* (1966), the villagers all speak a form of the local variety of Hindi, Bhojpuri, regardless of whether they are Hindus or Muslims; it is the young students from the Aligarh Muslim University, visiting the village in the run-up to Partition to propagate the cause of Pakistan, who speak in Urdu and they are promptly taken to task for doing so by a local resident: "...you have turned Urdu into something Muslim… After Pakistan is created, will you leave this Urdu behind or will you take it away with you?" (Razā 1966: 255). Gulsher Khan 'Shani' said in an interview that it was no coincidence that most of his short stories narrated 'the fears, tribulations, internal contradictions, sufferings, and paradoxes of the Indian Muslim community after Partition' (Śānī 1988: 14). And Manzur Ehtesham in *Sūkhā bar'gad* described with assured realism a Muslim young woman growing up in a small Indian town in a family which read only Urdu magazines and routinely mocked all Hindi words and the way of pronunciation of Hindi-speakers; the novel ends with the heroine deciding not to marry a person from Pakistan, and this at a time when a murderous communal riot, a veritable 'Karbala' was raging in India – for the reason that she wanted to bang shut the door on that option of Pakistan as a Muslim utopia and finally to feel at home in India such as it is (Eh'teśām 1986: 10, 231). In all these writers and in many others, the complexity of divided feelings about Muslim life and identity in post-Partition India is depicted with a candour and intimacy that might have been possible before perhaps only in literature written in Urdu. But now, Hindi is the apt and natural medium for such explorations by Muslim writers in North India; it is the primary language for them in which to fight their battles, to dream their dreams, to bare their souls, and to feel at home.

III. Reading Hindi and Urdu together

Urdu and Hindi are generally not taught together to the same students anywhere in India (and of course not in Pakistan, where

Hindi is hardly taught at all) while students in the few South Asia programmes in the USA are sometimes taught both the scripts, after which they divide into separate Urdu and Hindi streams for advanced courses. This pattern is adopted increasingly in the U.K. and in Europe too, though not in Russia, China or Japan. The textbooks or other study materials in print that are used are different and separate for the two languages, while the increasing use of films and other audio-visual materials serves not only to blur linguistic boundaries but also to dispense with the vexed issue of script.

However, Urdu and Hindi texts may be found included alongside each other in their respective scripts in a rare anthology: *Hindi and Urdu since 1800: A common reader*, in which the editors Christopher Shackle and Rupert Snell (who then taught Urdu and Hindi respectively at the School of Oriental and African Studies in London) put together twelve one-page texts each in Urdu and Hindi in their respective scripts. Passages were selected from a wide range of sources to instantiate the evolution of prose over a span of two hundred years in each language while, in an inspired editorial strategy, the passages were so chosen as also to address in some way or the other the issue of these languages itself and the relationship between them. Thus, the selection also possessed a metalinguistic thematic resonance.

The *Reader* provided two extensive and separate glossaries, one 'Hindi-English' and the other 'Urdu-English' (Shackle and Snell 1990: 181-98, 199-218). In the Urdu glossary, 654 out of 778 words, i.e. 84 per cent, were counted as having an Arabic, Persian or Perso-Arabic etymological source, while in the Hindi glossary, 418 out of 743 words, i.e. 56 per cent, were marked as being 'not only genuine S[anskrit] words but also the numerous neologisms coined from S[anskrit] roots and/or by analogy with existing S[anskrit] forms' – with the caveat that this made 'any attempt at computing the percentages of genuine S[anskrit] loans rather unreliable'. Thirteen words, i.e. 2 per cent, in the Urdu glossary were computed as derived from Sanskrit, while 110 words, i.e. 15 per cent, in the Hindi glossary were marked as being/derived from Arabic or Persian (Shackle and Snell 1990: 181, 199).

In another attempt to study Hindi and Urdu literary texts together, Christine Everaert offered a detailed stylistic analysis of three short stories each by eight modern writers, four from Hindi and four from Urdu, by comparing the original texts in Hindi or Urdu with their respective translations into Urdu or Hindi. Though her focus was mainly on morpho-syntactic, orthographic and phonological variations, she also quantified a large number of lexical changes including many that are predictable and necessary, but a few others that she called 'illogical', as when *sāhab* in Hindi is changed into *janāb* in Urdu, and *magar* in Urdu (which is Persian) is replaced in Hindi by *lekin* (which is Arabic) – presumably because one of the words in these pairs was mistakenly perceived by the translator to be more Urdu than the other! (Everaert 2010: 193).

In a comprehensive history of Hindi literature in sixteen volumes, *Hindī sāhity kā bṛhat itihās*, several whole chapters are accorded exclusively to discussing Urdu writers. For example, in Volume 8 which covers the 'Bhāratendu Kāl' (the Bharatendu Era), 'Saṃvat 1900-1950' (i.e., *c.* 1843-93), chapter 3 of Part III was titled 'Dakkhinī Hindī', which in this late period had not much to show for itself (Pāṇḍey 1972: 325-56), and the succeeding chapter was titled 'Urdū Sāhitya' which paid detailed attention to the differences between the Delhi school of Urdu poetry and the Lucknow school, showing that the latter sometimes degenerated to vulgarity and even obscenity (Avasthī 1972: 357-92). In the next volume, titled 'Dvivedī Kāl' [the Dvivedi Era), covering the period 'Saṃvat 1950-1975' [i.e. *c.* 1893-1918], a long chapter this time titled 'Urdū kā adab' by the eminent Urdu scholar Gopi Chand Narang surveyed the Urdu literature of this period with reference to as many as thirty-five Urdu writers, in a characteristically Urdu mode of literary discourse and with particular attention paid to the manifestation in some of the authors of patriotism and of a mixing of Hindi and Urdu dictions and styles (Nāraṅg 1977: 219-282).

This was a well-meaning inclusive gesture on the part of this monumental sixteen-volume history of Hindi literature, but whether it served, or even sought, to integrate Urdu literature with Hindi literature is much to be doubted; it seemed, rather, to want to accord a space to Urdu literature within the domain of Hindi literature, without any assimilationist agenda on the part of Hindi but wishing to signal anyhow the generous hospitality of Hindi. It is not known whether any such corresponding hospitality has been extended to Hindi literature in a history of Urdu literature.

Rather more illuminating in this respect perhaps, because of being more directly comparative, are the three or four closely argued and nuanced pages by Ramswarup Chaturvedi in a concise one-volume history of Hindi literature, in which he attempted a 'natural' comparison between Hindi *rīti* (convention--bound medieval) poetry and the Urdu poetry of the corresponding period. He pointed out that both of these simultaneous bodies of literature, as they flourished between 1725 and 1825, were similar in having been produced under courtly patronage, in free-standing short verses, with a liberal deployment of various figures of speech, and in close conformity with their respective classical conventions. On the other hand, they were dissimilar in that the Hindi poetry of the period depended for its effect on images and the Urdu poetry on inventive and idiomatic phrasing; the Hindi poetry depicted the joyous unfolding of the play (*līlā*) of god Krishna while the Urdu poetry inclined towards abstract philosophical speculation; and while the Hindi poetry depicted lovers in union, the lovers in Urdu poetry remained eternally separated (Caturvedī 1994: 69-72).

Among all the attempts so far made to take a composite or synthetic view of Hindi and Urdu literatures, probably the most ambitious and comprehensive is Madan Gopal's full-length history, *Origin and development of Hindi/Urdu literature* (1996). Madan Gopal was the author of literary biographies in English of several Hindi writers, especially those who wrote in both Urdu and Hindi including Bal Mukund Gupt and, more notably, Premchand. He was also the editor of *Premčand ke xuṭūṭ* (the letters of Premchand) in Urdu (1968) and of the complete works of Premchand in Urdu, the *Kullīyāt-e Premčand* in 24 volumes (2001-4; published by the Qaumī Kaunsil Barā'i Faroġ-i Urdū Zabān, i.e. the National Council for Promotion of the Urdu Language in India). He was a fully bilingual scholar of Urdu and Hindi (to say nothing of his competence in English), and if he leaned a little more towards one of these languages rather than the other, it may, on the evidence of the corpus of his scholarly and editorial work, be thought to have been Urdu.

In the 'Introduction' to his *History*, Madan Gopal identified a common 'base' of both 'Hindi and its Urdu variant', asserted that 'all the verbs used in spoken or written Urdu or Hindi language are the same', and that of the fifty-five thousand words to be found in a standard Urdu dictionary, 'forty thousand words are from Hindi' (Gopal 1996: viii, xiv). In his view, it was beginning in the 1860s, when 'the centre of Urdù' moved from Delhi and Lucknow to Lahore where Hali and Azad flourished and later Iqbal, that 'the cleavage between Urdu and Hindi became wider and wider', with Sir Syed Ahmad Khan playing an important role in the 1870s by opposing 'the introduction of Devanagari and Kaithi scripts in Bihar in place of the Persian Arabic script'(Gopal 1996: xiii). In line with this historical trajectory, it was only after treating of Ghalib (1795-1869) that Madan Gopal spoke, in his chapter-titles, consecutively, of 'A House Divided', 'Evolution of Urdu' and 'Growth of Hindi' (Gopal 1996: 117, 129, 137). Only thereafter do we get chapters titled in pairs, e.g. 'The Age of Awakening – I' and 'The Age of Awakening – II', 'Towards Progressivism – I' and 'Towards Progressivism – II', and 'Post Independence Literature – I' and 'Post Independence Literature – II' – of which the former treat of the literature in Hindi and the latter of the literature in Urdu.

This preferred pattern has its own peculiarities and inconsistencies if not contradictions and it involved Madan Gopal in performing some chronological contortions, as shown below. In common understanding, the house was divided and both Urdu and Hindi evolved and grew to be quite separate literary vehicles a generation or two before Ghalib was born in 1797, i.e. around 1750 or 1770. But then, Madan Gopal's different trajectory and time-line has its own logic and its own perception of the larger picture which may not be dismissed out of hand, in that it seems to emphasize not the moment of the split but rather, the beginning of an aggravated, sectarian and determinedly separatist consciousness of that split on the part of the Urdu-speakers, which had a clear political dimension and was to have enormous political consequences.

The novelty of Madan Gopal's historicization may unsettle our received wisdom (which itself comes in several widely variant versions, of course) but the shape of the wood that he delineated is given an internal cogency by the fact of his intimate familiarity with the individual trees that constitute that wood. His equally detailed knowledge and fine appreciation of the works of a considerable proportion of the authors he wrote about, from both sides of 'the divide', is sufficient warrant of his even-handed scholarship, as is the fact that he seemed to write directly out of the fullness of his personal knowledge, with no footnotes and quotations from primary texts often in his own English translations. What his book lacks in the protocols of academic rigour it makes up for in its candid enjoyment of its subject. Even a reader who disagrees with many of his 'findings' will come away the richer for having gained a finer understanding of what Madan Gopal sees as this partially common and partially divided literary tradition.

Another aspect of this book that authenticates its discourse, as it were, is the generous sample of the works by the major authors discussed in this book which is printed as an Appendix to the history, runs to 77 pages, and is printed in Nāgarī without any footnotes, glossary, or other explication of any kind, so that it may speak for itself. (This again goes to demonstrate Madan Gopal's close familiarity with Hindi and Urdu authors alike, a qualification that most of his readers may lack.) The selection of the authors here, and the order in which they appear, are in themselves sufficiently indicative of the view that Madan Gopal took of this literature. It may be worthwhile listing all the 38 authors who constitute the bilingual canon such as not put forward perhaps by any other historian of these literatures, though they appear in an idiosyncratically chronological order, according to Madan Gopal's broad understanding of the split. They are (as named, spelt and ordered in the book): Chand Bardai, Amir Khusro, Kabir, Tulasi Das, Surdas, Abdur Rahim Khan-i Khana, Malik Mohammed Jayasi, Keshav, Behari, Matiram, Bhushan, Dev, Padmakar, Muhammad Quli Qutubshah, Vali Aurangabadi,

Shah Zahiruddin 'Hatim', Muhammad Rafi 'Sauda', Mir Taqi 'Mir', Nazir Akbarabadi, Mohammad Momin Khan 'Momin', Sheikh Mohammad Ibrahim ['Zauq'], Mirza Aasadullah [Khan] 'Ghalib', Bahadur Shah 'Zafar', Khwaja Altaf Husain Hali, Bharatendu Harischandra, Mirza Khan Daag, Maithili Sharan Gupta, Jayashankar Prasad, Surya Kant Tripathi 'Nirala', Sumitranandan Pant, [Subhadra Kumari Chauhan], Mahadevi Verma, Sir Mohammed Iqbal, Braj Narain 'Chakbast', Harivansha Rai Bachchan, Ramdhari Singh Dinkar, Raghupati Sahai 'Firaq' Gorakhpuri, and Faiz Ahmed Faiz.

Most Hindi or Urdu readers may find themselves wondering just whose canon this is! How many of us have read even a couple of pages each of both Bhushan and Zauq, both Padmakar and Ghalib, both Hali and Maithili Sharan Gupt (even when a major poem of the latter was directly inspired by the *magnum opus* of the former), both Nirala and Faiz, or both Sumitranandan Pant and Firaq (who lived at the same time in the same city, Allahabad). It is an extraordinary, visionary achievement of Madan Gopal's to put them all within the same covers. Having said that, the order in which these poets appear (and there are no prose writers here) is to say the least peculiar. We get thirteen Hindi poets first, covering the period collectively from AD 1126 to 1835, followed by an almost equal contingent of eleven consecutive Urdu poets, from the collective period 1580 to 1916. It is as if Madan Gopal had climbed up to say the square numbered 74 when he was bitten by a snake and found himself back at say number 11 again and then had to climb another ladder altogether to say number 81, in a game of snakes and ladders (reputedly invented in India). Of the remaining 14 poets in his anthology, nine are from Hindi and five from Urdu, adding up to a total of 22 poets from Hindi and 16 from Urdu, of whom (just for the record!) 20 are Hindu and 18 Muslim. The poets represented by the largest selections here are Nazir Akbarabadi (102 lines), Ghalib (100), Tulasi Das (98) and Surdas (94) (Gopal 1996: 290-4, 299-303, 263-6, and 267-70, respectively). While the supreme canonical status of Ghalib, Tulasi and Sur as being among the greatest poets in their respective languages is unchallenged, it would appear that Nazir, though commonly regarded as a minor poet, is everyone's favourite in the specific context of a shared literary culture, and in this sense, he remains the lone totem pole of Hind-Muslim, Urdu-Hindi unity.

IV. Conclusion: beyond Urdu and Hindi

There has over the last couple of centuries been a sort of reversal of fortunes between Hindi and Urdu. While Urdu was the language of official preference in North India between 1837 and 1900 and thereafter in a diminished way until 1947 when it continued to be taught as a compulsory subject in all schools, Hindi has after Independence gained comparable advantages. This is demonstrated most tellingly perhaps by the fact that while advocates of Hindi had pleaded with and petitioned the British government through much of the latter half of the nineteenth century that the Nāgarī script may be permitted to be used alongside the Perso-Arabic script of Urdu as Hindi in the Nagārī script was the language of the majority of the population, it is advocates of Urdu who have in the latter half of the twentieth century and now into the twenty-first been pleading with the successive elected governments of the states of North India that Urdu in the Perso--Arabic script may now be granted the status of the official second language as it is the language of a minority of the population in these states. Such is the whirligig of time.

It is not clear whether any progress has been made in narrowing the gap between Hindi and Urdu. In fact, the opposite is probably true as Hindi and Urdu have both been required to fulfill the various duties and requirements of an official national language in India and Pakistan respectively, and have felt obliged not only to stand on their formal dignity but also to coin a whole range of new and uncommon terms for bureaucratic and technical purposes. This process has only served to affirm and even accentuate that fact that the classical basis of Hindi is Sanskrit and of Urdu, Persian and Arabic, and that it is from these respective roots that the two languages seek renewed vitality and sustenance when ramifying into new realms of vocabulary. These new words seemed invented and unreal in each language when they were first coined, but have found increasing acceptance with usage.

The project of Hindustani as a common language seems to have been given up for lost as having proved utterly utopian. The related project of a common script has, however, found partial and one-sided fulfillment, through editions of numerous Urdu poets being issued in the Nāgarī script, some of which have apparently sold better in India than Urdu reprints of these poets. This has succeeded so well that some prose works too, such as the early novels *Mirāt ul-ᶜurūs* and *Umrāᵓo Jān Ādā*, are now available in Nāgarī transcription.

However, all these texts carry a generous number of footnotes on each page glossing the unfamiliar Urdu words, and many more words could perhaps have been glossed as well which apparently seemed familiar to the Urdu-knowing editor but may not prove to be so to the common reader in Hindi. Some of these editions also carry a detailed editorial commentary in which works of Hindi poetry are cited by way of comparative elucidation and enjoyment; these include, for example, the editions of Ghalib by the Hindi writers Krishna Dev Prasad Gaur (better known as the humourist 'Bedhab' Banarasi) and Pandey Bechan Sharma Ugra, a novelist and short story writer. A major e-resource for Hindi literature, 'Kavita Kosh' (http://www.kavitakosh.org) similarly offers a generous representation of Urdu poets on its website, with about 200 poets listed also as 'shayars', which reflects the wide popularity of Urdu poetry among Hindi readers. Several Hindi poets, most notably Dushyant Kumar, have written a large number of successful *ġazals*, with the diction ranging from a kind of watered down Hindi or Hindustani to a quite Sanskritic register, as if the vocabulary was unaffected by the adopted form.

We may also need to stand back now and remind ourselves of certain broad parameters within which this complex history unfolded. For one thing, what we now refer to as Hindi and Urdu were a long time in the making, with Urdu growing away from its indigenous roots and distancing itself from the local elements until, paradoxically, these came to be seen as 'foreign' elements (Sadiq 1984: 183); correspondingly, it assimilated more and more of Persian vocabulary, idiom and thematic, which were apparently no longer seen as 'foreign'. The Urdu of today that is largely unintelligible to Hindi speakers is the result of this steady evolution which was apparently inaugurated by 'Hatim' (1699-1781) of the Delhi school and engraven as the incontrovertible standard by 'Nasikh' (?-1838) of Lucknow.

On the other hand, the Hindi of today became the preferred form and vehicle of literary and formal discourse only at the beginning of the twentieth century when it turned its back on Braj which had been the language of Hindi literature since the sixteenth century. The present khari boli Hindi brought Hindi syntactically closer to Urdu, which has always used khari boli structures, at a time, oddly enough, when the cultural and political differences between the two languages were perhaps at their widest. Always a Sanskritic language, Hindi earned a notoriety for 'Sanskritization' only later, after independence, when as the official language of administration and in radio broadcasts, it began to use unfamiliar Sanskrit-based neologisms in place of the hitherto prevalent vocabulary in English and also partly in Urdu, which had not been easy to understand either. In literary terms, modern khari boli Hindi is probably rather less Sanskritic than Braj was, or comparable languages such as Bengali or Marathi are, while it has a considerably larger stock of Perso-Arabic words than those other languages.

The script too became a badge of linguistic identity and an issue of contention only after the imposition by the British government in 1837 of Urdu in the Perso-Arabic script as the language of administration in the Hindi-majority areas and the script consequently began to impinge on a wide public domain in materially significant ways. This in turn led to the movement for Nāgarī, a campaign which achieved success in the provinces of Bihar and the Central Provinces (now Madhya Pradesh) almost before it had got going, in the 1880s, but which continued to be fought out and thus to aggravate feelings on both sides in the heartland of the United Provinces (now Uttar Pradesh), with the British government dragging its feet until conceding the demand finally in 1900. The almost non-negotiable identification of Urdu with its script is put in perspective by the fact that even before

Urdu was born, the four early Sufi love-narratives in Awadhi were all written in the Perso-Arabic script, and even in the post-Urdu period, so was Rahi Masum Raza's novel *Ādhā gāṁv*, which, as seen above, is not only written in Hindi but also has characters expressing some pointed anti-Urdu sentiments.

More importantly, our notions of 'Muslim' and 'Hindu' too have undergone considerable transformation over the centuries. Those great early epics in Hindi were all written by Sufis, a dissident or outlying form of Islam which had a higher threshold of sectarian tolerance. Anyhow, throughout the many centuries of Muslim rule, both Hindus and Muslims could be said to know their place and there was not much room for any kind of conflict other than armed rebellion – which too was often between one Muslim ruler against another. It was only after British rule began that Muslims and Hindus could vie with each other for relative preference or privilege, and this was aggravated after the 'Mutiny' of 1857 when the British first singled out the Muslims for punishment as having been the main perpetrators and then, following Sir Syed's influential intervention, conciliated them in order to balance out the claims of the Hindu majority. The separatist religious demand for Pakistan was based in part on the contention that the Muslims, who had for long ruled the Hindus, were not prepared to be ruled by them under a new democratic system in which they were forever going to be in a minority. As M.A. Jinnah forthrightly put it: 'Muslim India cannot accept any constitution which must necessarily result in a Hindu majority government' (Jinnah 1940: 88, rpt. in Pandey 1977: 88).

However, Islam had by then been in the Indian subcontinent for so long that the affiliation to Islam could not by itself remain the sole loyalty of all Muslims. Thus, there are more Muslims even now in officially secular India than in officially Muslim Pakistan, and furthermore, what happened in or to Pakistan after its creation underlines some competing loyalties as well. East Pakistan, which was as Muslim as West Pakistan and established on the same principle, broke away in 1971 mainly because of economic and political discrimination which, however, reached a flashpoint in the form of protest against the discrimination by the Urdu-speakers of West Pakistan against the Bengali-

-speakers of East Pakistan. In fact, the saga of the battle between Urdu and Hindi in the subcontinent is fully matched in intensity, significance and consequence by this relatively unsung conflict between Urdu and Bengali, perhaps because the latter came to a swifter culmination.

Ever since Bengal came under Muslim rule in the thirteenth century, Bengali has been spoken by Hindus and Muslims alike. Its native-speakers now number approximately 240 million (about 150 million in Bangladesh and 90 million in India), which makes it a much larger language than Urdu which is spoken as a first language by about 65 million people (about 50 million in India and about 15 million in Pakistan). *Allāhu akbar*, taken to be the cry of faith of Muslims everywhere, comes across with new cultural connotations when one sees it displayed in the streets of Dhaka as *Āllāh mahān* and *Āllāh sarbaśaktimān*.

Nor is Bengali the only other language of the subcontinent spoken in considerable numbers by the Muslim population. In fact, the regional language of the state is spoken by Hindus, Muslims and Christians alike in all the states of India except in the 'heartland,' with the minor exception of Andhra (where some Dakhni speakers may be able to speak also proper Urdu) and Karnataka (where a small number of Urdu-speakers is to be found in some parts of the state). Urdu is thus the one big glaring exception to the rule, the single aberration in the general linguistic paradigm in India. Of the total population of about 150 million Muslims in India, only 50 million speak Urdu, while the two-thirds majority, about 100 million, speak the same local language as all the non-Muslims. (The rounded off figures in this paragraph and the preceding one are culled not from official subcontinental sources but from neutral international sources such as Wikipedia and the CIA World Factbook, and are meant to be broadly indicative.) Anyhow, the exclusive and almost fanatical identification of Indian Muslims with Urdu, whether in their own eyes or in the eyes of non-Muslims, thus seems quite illogical and a gross misrepresentation of the facts and has always been so – which has, however, not prevented it from exercising a momentous influence on the history of the subcontinent.

Muslims have of course not only spoken but also written in virtually all the major languages of India. In a recent book, Jafar Raza has surveyed the contribution by the Muslim writers of India to the literatures of as many as twenty-seven languages of the subcontinent as well as to Arabic and Persian, and though such contribution is necessarily uneven across the many languages, it appears to have been particularly rich in Assamese, Bengali, Gujarati, Kashmiri, Malayalam, Marathi, Oriya, Panjabi, Sindhi and Tamil. Jafar Raza holds doctoral degrees in both Urdu and Hindi literatures and taught Urdu at the University of Allahabad, the city of the 'Ganga-Jamuna' confluence, and his wider pan-Indian account of Muslim literary activity is imbued with that spirit of harmony as well as a wry sense of historical circumstance: 'One does not know whether to call it the misfortune of Urdu or its good fortune that its early development took place at a time when the Mughal empire was breathing its last' (Razā 2011: 80).

For some time now, it has been said that Urdu in turn may be breathing its last. Fortunately, this is said by the champions of Urdu rather more than by its detractors, perhaps out of a sense of protective anxiety about its future. But the anxiety seems exaggerated if not misplaced when we remember that the cry that Urdu is dying or is in fact already dead has been raised for at least 150 years now. Raja Shiv Prasad 'Sitār-e Hind', a close ally of Sir Syed, was saying already in the 1860s that Urdu was dead, whereupon Bharatendu Harishchandra promptly ridiculed such scare-mongering by writing a *syāpā* or mock-lament for Urdu – which has sometimes been read quite out of its context as mocking Urdu itself (see Trivedi 2003: 973). In fact, there is a common threat now to the well-being of not only Urdu but all the Indian languages alike, which comes from the increasing ascendancy of English throughout the subcontinent and its growing hegemony. Before this urgent reality, the old battles that Urdu and Hindi fought with each other in the nineteenth and twentieth centuries seem to be truly history. English, a foreign language which too arose on the subcontinent as the Mughal empire went into a terminal decline, is now the language of command, and both Hindi and Urdu, together with all the other languages of India, are now equally threatened by its encroaching spread. In this sense, Urdu and Hindi have never been more alike than now and so much on the same side of the fence. The battle between Hindi and Urdu which was still being fought at the conferences of the Hindustani Academy in the 1930s has now given way to a struggle by Hindi, Urdu, and all the other Indian languages together to win a little space for themselves against the dominance of global English either in terms of international visibility and circulation or even at literary events within India such as the successive editions of the Jaipur Literary Festival. It is common adversity that has now made bed-fellows of these old adversaries.

REFERENCES

Avasthī, Mohan, 2029/1972, 'Urdū Sāhity', [in:] *Hindī sāhity kā bṛhat itihās*, vol. 8, ed. Vinay Mohan Śarmā, Vārāṇasī: Nāgarīpracāriṇī Sabhā, pp. 357-92.

Bailey, T. Grahame, 1928 (2008), *A history of Urdu literature*. Introduction by Muhammad Reza Kazimi, Oxford: Oxford University Press.

Caturvedī, Rām Svarūp, 1994, *Hindī sāhity aur saṃved'nā kā vikās*, 4th edn. Allāhābād: Lok Bhāratī Prakāśan.

Dās, Braj'ratna (ed.), 1922, *Khus'ro kī hindī kavitā*, Vārāṇasī: Nāg'rīpracāriṇī Sabhā.

Eh'teśām, Man'zūr, 1986 (rpt. 1989), *Sūkhā bar'gad*, Naī Dillī: Rāj'kamal Prakāśan.

Everaert, Christine, 2010, *Tracing the boundaries between Hindi and Urdu: lost and added in translation between 20th century short stories*, Leiden: Brill.

Faruqi, Shamsur Rahman, 2003, 'A long history of Urdu literary culture, part I: Naming and placing a literary culture', [in:] *Literary cultures in history: reconstructions from South Asia*, ed. Sheldon Pollock, Berkeley: University of California Press, pp. 805-63.

Firāq, Raghūpatī Sahāy, 1990, *Baz'm-e zindagī: raṅg-e śairī*, ed. Lakṣmīcandra Jain [in Nagārī], Naī Dillī: Bhāratīy Jñān'pīṭh.

____ (ed.), 1999, 'Nazīr Ak'barābādī', [in:] *Nazīr kī bānī*, Naī Dillī: Vāṇī Prakāśan.

Gopal, Madan, 1996, *Origin and development of Hindi/Urdu literature*, New Delhi: Deep & Deep Publications.

Hasan, Mohammad, 1973, *Nazir Akbarabadi*, 'Makers of Indian Literature', New Delhi: Sahitya Akademi.

Hindustānī Pracār Sabhā, 2012, http://hindustanipracharsabha.com/hps_hindi/index.php?option=com_content&view=article&id=46&Itemid=28. Accessed 6 January 2012.

Jinnah, M.A., 1940, 'Demand for Pakistan 1940', rpt. in *A Book of India: An Anthology of Prose & Poetry from the Indian Sub-Continent*, ed. B.N. Pandey. Calcutta: Rupa & Co., 1977, pp. 87-8.

'Kaif', Sarasvatī Saran (ed.), 1995, 'Jīv'nī' [Biography], [in:] *Nazīr Ak'barābādī aur un'kī śāyarī*, Delhi: Rajpal and Sons.

King, Christopher R., 1994, *One language, two scripts: the Hindi movement in nineteenth century North India*, Bombay: Oxford University Press.

Lelyveld, David, 1993, 'Colonial knowledge and the fate of Hindustani', *Comparative Studies in Society and History*, 35: 4 (October 1993), pp. 665-82.

McGregor, Ronald Stuart (ed.), 1997, *The Oxford Hindi-English Dictionary*, Delhi: Oxford University Press.

McGregor, Stuart, 2003, 'The progress of Hindi, part 1: The development of a transregional idiom', [in:] *Literary cultures in history: reconstructions from South Asia*, ed. Sheldon Pollock, Berkeley: University of California Press, pp. 912-57.

Nāraṅg, Gopī Cand, 2034/1977, 'Urdū kā adab', [in:] *Hindī sāhity kā bṛhat itihās*, vol. 9, ed. Sudhākar Pāṇḍey, Vārāṇasī: Nāg'rī-pracāriṇī Sabhā, pp. 219-82.

Pandey, Bishwa Nath (ed.), 1977, *A book of India: an anthology of prose & poetry from the Indian Sub-Continent*, Calcutta: Rupa & Co.

Pāṇḍey, Rām'nirañjan, 2029/1972, 'Dakkhinī Hindī', [in:] *Hindī sāhity kā bṛhat itihās*, vol. 8, ed. Vinay Mohan Śarmā, Vārāṇasī: Nāg'rī-pracāriṇī Sabhā, pp. 325-56.

Pollock, Sheldon (ed.), 2003, *Literary cultures in history: reconstructions from South Asia*, Berkeley: University of California Press.

Rai, Amrit, 1982, *Premchand: a life*, translated from the Hindi by Harish Trivedi, New Delhi: People's Publishing House.

____, 1984, *A house divided: the origin and development of Hindi/Hindavi*, New Delhi: Oxford University Press.

Razā, Jāfar, 2011, *Bhāratīy sāhity meṁ musal'mānoṁ kā av'dān*, Allāhābād: Lok'bhāratī Prakāśan.

Razā, Rāhī Masūm, 1966 (rpt. 1984), *Ādhā gāṁv*, Naī Dillī: Rāj'kamal Prakāśan.

Russell, Ralph, 1999, *How not to write the history of Urdu literature and other essays on Urdu and Islam*, New Delhi: Oxford University Press.

Sadiq, Muhammad, 1984, *A history of Urdu literature*, 2nd edn., revised and enlarged. [First published 1964.] New Delhi: Oxford University Press.

Sahai, Ratna (ed.), 1996 ?, *Muslims in India*, Produced for the Ministry of External Affairs [India] by FOLIO, New Delhi: Folio.

Shackle, Christopher and Rupert Snell (eds.), 1990, *Hindi and Urdu since 1800: A common reader*, New Delhi: Heritage Publishers, in association with the School of Oriental and African Studies, London.

Śānī [Gul'śer Khān], 1988, *Pratinidhi kahāniyāṁ*, Naī Dillī: Rāj'kamal Prakāśan.

Śukla, Rām'candra, 1940, *Hindī sāhity kā itihās*, Allāhābād: Indian Press.

Trivedi, Harish, 1984, 'The Urdu Premchand: the Hindi Premchand', *Jadavpur Journal of Comparative Literature*, vol. 22, pp. 104-18.

____, 2003, 'The progress of Hindi, part II: Hindi and the nation', [in:] *Literary cultures in history: reconstructions from South Asia*, ed. Sheldon Pollock, Berkeley: University of California Press, pp. 958-1022.

____, 2004, 'The anxiety of Hindustani', *The Yearbook of South Asian Languages and Linguistics*, ed. Rajendra Singh, Berlin/New York, pp. 267-73.

____, 2008, 'Foreword' [to:] *The selected poetry of Firaq Gorakhpuri*, tr. Noorul Hasan, New Delhi: Sahitya Akademi, pp. 15-22.

Zaidī, Asad and Viṣṇu Nāgar (eds.), 1994, *Yah aisā samay hai: sam'kālīn kavitā kā ek cayan*, Naī Dillī: Saf'dar Hāś'mī Memorial Trust.

Ḥasan and Ḥusain as the Sons of Muḥammad. A contemporary treatise from Bangladesh

Rahul Peter Das

In 1946, Muhāmmād Śām'sujjuhā[1] (14.2.1897-19.4.1971), of what is today the district of Thakurgaon (Ṭhākur'gā̃o) in Bangladesh, proclaimed himself the eleventh Caliph (*khālīphā*, A. *xalīfah*) of Islam,[2] and its last (*śeṣ*) Renewer (*mujāddid*, A. *mujaddid*), appointed to this rank by Allāh already in 1943. By his account, from 1942 until 1949 he received divine revelations through an angelic medium, set forth, after a preliminary work *Prem Pra-*

---

[1] Besides English, this study incorporates three other languages, namely Bengali, Arabic (= A.) and Urdu, each of these transliterated accordingly (cf. pp. 17-18). From the transliterated forms here, the language and script of the original are easily evident.

[2] This office he regarded as spiritual, not political. In the line of Caliphs referred to, the preceding ten are the four righteous Caliphs (A. *al-xulafā'u 'r-rāšidūn*), Ḥasan, and the first five Abbasid (A. *ᶜabbāsī*) Caliphs (until Hārūn ar-Rašīd). One more Caliph is to follow in the future, namely the Mahdī (Muḥammad bin ᶜAbdallāh).

saṅga Muẏāmālāh· ("Matter Concern[ing] Love") of 1942, in the *Bīthikā* ("Avenue"),[3] which – like most of his works – was published posthumously (in this case in 1979) by his son Muhāmmād Gulām Nāk·śābānd Ulubbī, the present Pīr of the Khilāphātī Khān'kāh· Śārīph in Thakurgaon founded by Muhāmmād Śām'-sujjuhā.

The *Bīthikā* was described by Muhāmmād Śām'sujjuhā as an explication of the *Qurʾān* and thus as being above the Ḥadīṯ. According to the doctrine prevailing at the Khān'kāh· today, however, it seems to be regarded as an explication of both *Qurʾān* and Ḥadīṯ, and thus ranking below both. Be that as it may, the status of Muhāmmād Śām'sujjuhā himself nearly approximates that of Muḥammad, the two being described as "as if one" (*yena ek'i*), i.e. neither one, nor separate. This is also demonstrated by the use of the same *ṣalawāt*[4] for both, namely *ṣallạ 'llāhu ᶜalaihi wa sallam.*[5] But this is not the place to go into doctrinaire issues connected with Muhāmmād Śām'sujjuhā and the *Bīthikā*, and also not his and the Khilāphātī Khān'kāh· Śārīph's history, the latter's contemporary status,[6] etc. Further particulars on these may be obtained easily from the study, in German, by Robert Siegfried;[7] a self-description by the Khān'kāh· is also to

---

[3] Cf. the Arabic terms *sunnah* and *ṭarīqah.*

[4] In Bengal mostly referred to as the *darūd* (in the Bengali script *dărŭd*).

[5] Abbreviated in the Bengali script as *sāḥ.*

[6] One point worth highlighting, though, is the very decided emphasis on Bengali as a sacred language and a language of discourse, the strained relations with much of the regional Islamic establishment (regarded as having deviated from the tenets of Islam to propagate a degenerate and narrow-minded form of this), and the emphasis on modern education including the natural sciences. It is, in this context, significant that in May 1971 six members of Muhāmmād Śām'sujjuhā's family and one of his main disciples were abducted and murdered by the Pakistani army and its local collaborators.

[7] Robert Siegfried: *Bengalens Elfter Kalif. Untersuchungen zur Naqšbandiyya Muğaddidiyyа in Bangladesh.* (Arbeitsmaterialien zum Orient 10.) Würzburg: Ergon Verlag, 2001. (This is the revised version of an M.A. thesis prepared at the Martin-Luther-Universität Halle-Wittenberg.)

be found on the internet.[8] A comprehensive description and analysis, as we now have for the Māij'bhāṇḍārī community of Chittagong,[9] is, however, still very much a desideratum.

One point of doctrine obviously considered extremely important is that Ḥasan and Ḥusain are not the sons of ᶜAlī, but of Muḥammad himself. This importance can be gauged from the fact that this tenet is found already in *Prem Prasaṅga Muẏāmālāh·* 33,1-4.[10] It is also found, though applied only to Ḥasan, in *Bīthikā* 11,1,5.[11]

It is not surprising that this tenet has lent itself to controversy. In April 1989, a 'Phur'phurā' Pīr,[12] Ābul Ān'sār Muhām-

---

[8] See <http://khilafateeislamnagar.com> (last consulted on 14.2.2012).

[9] Hans Harder, *Sufism and Saint Veneration in Contemporary Bangladesh. The Maijbhandaris of Chittagong* (Routledge Advances in South Asian Studies 20.) London/New York: Routledge, 2011. (This is the revised version of a habilitation thesis prepared at the Martin-Luther-Universität Halle-Wittenberg.)

[10] See Hāj'rāt Māolānā Muhāmmād Śām'sujjuhā Ekādaś Khālīphā sāḥ: *Prem Prasaṅga Muẏāmālāh·*. Is'lām'nagar, Ṭhākur'gão Roḍ, Dināj'pur: Āh·kār Muhāmmād Gulām Nāk·śābānd Ulubbī, 1983, pp. 230-3.

[11] *hāj'rāt Hāsān āḥ hāj'rāt Hābīber sāḥ putraï haïlen.* See Mār'hum Hāj'rāt Māolānā Muhāmmād Śām'sujjuhā Ekādaś Khālīphā sāḥ: *Bīthikā*. Is'lām'nagar, Ṭhākur'gão Roḍ, Dināj'pur: Āh·kār Muhāmmād Gulām Nāk·-śābānd Ulubbī, 1979, p. 369. Cf. also the commentary on this by Āh·kār Muhāmmād Gulām Nāk·śābānd Ulubbī: *Khālīphā Ha'te Yā Śikhechi (Dbitīẏa o Tr̥tīẏa Khaṇḍa)*. Ṭhākur'gão Roḍ, Dināj'pur: Āh·kār Ma. Ga. Ā. Jā. Mān'sūr Ulubbī 1981, pp. 127f.

[12] Phur'phurā (anglicised: Furfura) is a village in south-eastern West Bengal (India) with a famous Sufi shrine; it is an important pilgrimage centre for Muslims. In Bangladesh, however, "Phur'phurā" usually does not refer to this shrine in West Bengal or the Pīrs today associated with it, but to Pīrs and associations within Bangladesh itself claiming allegiance to the lineage of Phur'phurā. Most of these seem to propagate a rigid variety of Islam quite opposed to the Sufistic Islam propagated at Phur'phurā itself. The official website of the shrine in West Bengal clearly distances itself from those claiming to represent Phur'phurā located in Bangladesh (and not merely touring there from West Bengal); see the link <*"phur'phurā śarīph" nāmer apabyabahār prasaṅge:*> on <http://www.furfurasharif.com> (last consulted on 14.2.2012). The Pīr referred to here is not from West Bengal, but from Dhaka, namely from the Dārus Sālām (Phur'phurā Śarīph) at Mirpur, Dhaka (Mīr'pur, Ḍhākā). The website of this organization is at

mad Ābdul Kāh·hār Siddikī,[13] openly challenged those holding it as unbelievers (*kāphir*, A. *kāfir*). This he did in Thakurgaon itself, which was obviously a direct challenge to the Khān'kāh·. In answer, the Khān'kāh· published some short refutations in Bengali dailies, but its chief rebuttal was in the form of the booklet *Hāsān Husāẏ'n Nābīr Niśān* ("Ḥasan and Ḥusain are the Banners of the Prophet") by Muhāmmād Gulām Nāk·śābānd Ulubbī.[14] This seems to have been convincing, for Ābul Ān'sār Muhāmmad Ābdul Kāh·hār Siddikī is reported to have subsequently come to the Khān'kāh· and asked for forgiveness for his utterances.[15]

The rebuttal contained in this booklet has been translated into English below.[16] Robert Siegfried has already described the booklet and given annotated German translations of major portions of the rebuttal, but not of the whole text.[17]

The translation is as literal as possible, though the exigencies of English grammar and syntax at times made a few changes necessary, for instance the substitution of the historic simple present of the original by a past form. When anything is translated into Bengali from another language, only the Bengali translations are translated into English, not the originals translated into Bengali; the veracity of the Bengali translations themselves has not been checked. Note too that everything in the text, including Arabic and Urdu, is in the Bengali script, so that in some cases it is unclear what the underlying Arabic or Urdu actually is. And even when the wording of passages quoted in Urdu is clear,

---

<http://furfura.com> (last consulted on 14.2.2012) and clearly indicates its ideological orientation, already through its heading describing it as a "Symbol of Muslim Unity Free from Shirk & Bidyat".

13 The transliteration follows the name form as usually given in publications of the Dārus Sālām.

14 Hāj'rāt Muhāmmād Gulām Nāk·śābānd Ulubbī: *Hāsān Husāẏ'n Nābīr Niśān*. Is'lām'nagar, Ṭhākur'gā̃o Roḍ, Dinā̄j'pur: Ma. Ga. Ā. Jā. Mān'sūr Ulubbī, 1987.

15 This was related to me by Muhāmmād Gulām Nāk·śābānd Ulubbī himself when I visited the Khān'kāh· in December 1991.

16 All introductory and preliminary matter (clearly or most probably not by the author of the rebuttal) contained in the booklet has not been translated.

17 See *op. cit.* in note 7, pp. 88-100.

the orthography is not always so; cf., e.g., *huvā* and *hu'ā*, *gaye* and *ga'e*, etc. Since the originals quoted from have not been consulted, such possible inaccuracies were unavoidable.

Evident orthographic mistakes and misprints have been silently corrected and not remarked upon.

Now follows the translation of the rebuttal:

Ḥasan and Ḥusain are the Banners of the Prophet

When on the demise of Allāh's Messenger's[18] *ṣa*°[19] son Qāsim *ᶜa*°[20] the unbelievers gave Allāh's Messenger *ṣa*° pain by calling him childless, Allāh said: O Messenger *ṣa*°! (You are not cut off behind,[21] that is, sonless or without descendants.)[22] Definitely it is your enemy himself who is without descendants (Sūrah *al-Kauṯar*). The Messenger *ṣa*° said: Definitely this my son (Ḥasan *ᶜa*°) is a *sayyid* (Buxārī, *Miškāh* – p. 569). The Prophet *ṣa*° said: Definitely these (Ḥasan and Ḥusain *ᶜa*°) are my sons (*ibnaiya*) and also my daughter's (Fāṭimah's *ᶜa*°) sons (Tirmiḏī, *Miškāh* – p. 570). The Messenger *ṣa*° said: Among my descendants (*mina 'l-asbāṭi*) Ḥusain *ᶜa*° is a certain[23] lineage[24] (*sibṭun*) (Tirmiḏī, *Miškāh* – p. 571). *sibṭun* = lineage (*qabīlah*), son of the son, son of the daughter. *qabīlah* = that group, the people of which group are the sons of the same father (*Maẕāhir-i Haqq*, *Luġāt-i Kišorī*[25]).

---

[18] "Messenger" has been used to translate *rāsūl* of the original, whereas "Prophet" translates *nābī*.

[19] "*ṣa*°" stands for *sāḥ* in the Bengali script, the abbreviation (with the visarga as abbreviation sign) for *ṣallā 'llāhu ᶜalaihi wa sallam*.

[20] "*ᶜa*°" stands for *āḥ* in the Bengali script, the abbreviation (with the visarga as abbreviation sign) for *ᶜalaihi 's-salām*.

[21] *pichan kartita* (misprinted with a ṛ-sign under *rti*).

[22] Portions within round brackets are obviously the author's own explications.

[23] *anyatama*.

[24] Though *baṃśa* may also mean "offspring", "lineage" has been chosen in keeping with the following explanation of *sibṭ* and the further usage of *baṃśa* in the following.

[25] Also transliterated as *Kišvarī*.

From the Messenger *ṣa*° it is narrated that:[26] In the world Ḥasan and Ḥusain *ᶜa*° are my two flowers (Buxārī). In the book named *ad-Durr aṯ-Ṯamīn fī Xaṣāʾiṣ aṣ-Ṣādiq al-Amīn*[27] I have seen a narration of the Prophet *ṣa*° that: Mine and the prophets' *ᶜa*° Gathering will be on the same soil. There a certain[28] proclaimer will proclaim: Exult individually together with your respective offspring. By that[29] I shall exult together with my sons, that is, with Ḥasan and Ḥusain *ᶜa*° (*Nuzhat al-Majālis* – 2, p. 353).

It is to be known that from the flower the fruit arises. And in the fruit there is the seed. And in the succession of seeds that flower (lineage[30]) continues uninterrupted until the end of the world.

Question: The Messenger *ṣa*° has called the grandson son. He has said: I am the son of ᶜAbd al-Muṭṭalib (Tirmiḏī, *Miškāh*). Therefore, Ḥasan and Ḥusain *ᶜa*° are Allāh's Messenger's *ṣa*° grandsons.

Answer: He has not referred to the enatic grandson[31] in the sense of son, has he? In that sense he has referred to the agnatic grandson.[32] This very Ḥadīṯ proves that son = agnatic grandson = own lineage. Because, however far below[33] the son, the agnatic grandson, may be, through their intermediacy one's own lineage persists. Not through the intermediacy of the enatic grandson. Therefore, however far above the father, the father's father, may

---

[26] *barṇita āchen ye*. Note the respect form of the third person of the verb to refer to a matter connected with a person whom respect is due.

[27] This title seems to make the most sense, though it is not certain. The title as given in the Bengali original is: *āl· dārūl śāmīn phī khāsāẏesul sādekul āmin*. – I am grateful to my colleague Ralf Elger for his help on this.

[28] *janaika*.

[29] *tā̃te*, which could also be translated as "in this" or "through this". On the nasalised form of the pronoun, showing respect, cf. note 26.

[30] *baṃśa* (cf. note 24). The translation "lineage" has also been used for all subsequent occurrences of *baṃśa*.

[31] *dauhitra*, which refers to the daughter's son, who is thus descended through his mother, i.e. enatic.

[32] *pautra*, which refers to the son's son, who is thus descended through his father, i.e. agnatic.

[33] Incorrect *adheḥ* for *adhaḥ*.

be, they are the fount of one's own lineage. The Šarīᶜah says: Offspring produced by oneself by lawful means are one's own lineage. It is evidence that, when in the course of going on the Miᶜrāj, Allāh's Messenger *ṣa*° met Ādam *ᶜa*° in the first heaven, Jibrīl *ᶜa*° said: This is your father. Salute him. The Messenger *ṣa*° saluted. Then Ādam *ᶜa*° said: Thanks to (my) virtuous prophet son. Further, when in the second, third, fourth, fifth and sixth heavens he successively met the exalted ᶜĪsạ̄, Yaḥyạ̄, Yūsuf, Idrīs, Hārūn, and Mūsạ̄ *ᶜa*°,[34] they said after the words of salutation: Thanks to (my) virtuous prophet brother. And when in the seventh heaven he met Ibrāhīm *ᶜa*°, Jibrīl *ᶜa*° said: This is your father. Salute him. The Messenger *ṣa*° saluted. Then Ibrāhīm *ᶜa*° said: Thanks to (my) virtuous prophet son (Buxārī, Muslim). The Messenger *ṣa*° said: I have come to the world through the intermediacy of Ādam, Nūḥ and Ibrāhīm *ᶜa*° (*Šifāʾ* – 1, pp. 99, 100). The Messenger *ṣa*° said: In Arabia Allāh will educe[35] a person (the Mahdī *ᶜa*°) from my own[36] (*minᶜitrati*) (*Miškāh* – p. 471). *ᶜitrah* = offspring, one's own, those belonging to one (*Luġāt-i Kišorī* – p. 315).

It is to be known that at the end time the Xalīfah Mahdī *ᶜa*° will be lord[37] in the lineage of Ḥasan (*Miškāh*).

Question: Ḥasan and Ḥusain *ᶜa*° are not[38] the actual sons of the Messenger *ṣa*°. They are indeed his enatic grandsons. Has he called them sons out of love and affection or just in accord with[39] the language of local usage?[40]

---

[34] The numbers of heavens and prophets do not tally exactly because ᶜĪsạ̄ and Yaḥyạ̄ were, according to the tradition, both met in the second heaven.

[35] *ber kar'ben.*

[36] *āmār nija theke*, which could also mean "from me myself".

[37] *sāiẏid.*

[38] *naẏ* is used here, as well as in the first sentence of the answer, instead of the correct respect form *nan*.

[39] Here and in the following, "in accord with", rather than the more usual "in the sense (of)" or "as", translates *hisebe* in combination with "language".

[40] This translation accords with the question mark at the end of the sentence. Otherwise, the translation would have been: "He has called ...".

Answer: No, they are not his enatic grandsons. He has not said it[41] out of love and affection or in accord with the language of local usage. Rather, he has called them sons because they are indeed his real sons. Should they have in fact been enatic grandsons, then why should the Ḥadīṯ scholars *ᶜa°* say *ḥukman* in the commentaries on all those Ḥadīṯs? Look here,[42] the commentator of the distinguished *Miškāh*, ᶜAllāmah Nuwwāb Quṭb ad-Dīn Xān *ᶜa°*, says: *ḥukman jaise kih beṭe kā beṭā* – as the son of the son (*Maẓāhir-i Haqq* – 4, p. 648).

Further, is the Messenger *ṣa°* like you and me that he blurts out what comes to his mouth?[43] Rather, he knew: Be it correct or be it false, whatever it be – what I shall say, that will remain as evidence or ideal until the Resurrection. Mankind will go on following it. Should he bestow wrong teachings on mankind? Consequently in his case how can it be out of love and affection or in accord with language? Should he have spoken out of love and affection or in accord with language, then Ḥasan and Ḥusain *ᶜa°* would indeed not also state[44] their own identity in that sense. Why they?[45] Even ordinary persons too do not state that. Rather, whoever it be, tends indeed to state the own identity through the name of the own father, also not through the name of the mother. For not to derive[46] one's own identity from the actual father and grandfather is unbelief.[47] Look here, Allāh says: Do call them by the names of their actual fathers. Should one erroneously call by the names of the ones not actual no sin will accrue. But should one call intentionally, sin will accrue (Sūrah *al-Aḥzāb* – Āyah 5).

The Messenger *ṣa°* says: Heaven is prohibited for whichever person claims such a person as his father who is not his father (Buxārī).

---

41 *tã̄*. Cf. on this note 29.
42 Here and in the following, "look here" translates *ei ye*.
43 Literally: "…that [it] came to the mouth, and I said [it]".
44 Literally: "give".
45 I.e.: not only they.
46 Literally "give".
47 *kuphārī*.

The Messenger *ṣa°* says: Do not deny[48] from the identity of your actual father and grandfather. For he who has denied his own identity from the identity of the actual father has certainly committed unbelief (Buxārī). Now you yourselves say: Can a great person such as Ḥasan *ᶜa°* ever commit a forbidden act? Does he commit an act of unbelief? No, quite definitely not.

Look here, …[49] after His Eminence ᶜAlī's *ᶜa°* demise Ḥasan *ᶜa°* gave the Friday sermon: *maiṅ bašīr va naẕīr kā beṭā hūṅ. maiṅ sirāj-i munīr kā beṭā hūṅ. maiṅ iskā beṭā hūṅ, jo iẕn-i xudāwandī*[50] *se Xudā kī ṭaraf bulātā hai. maiṅ unkā beṭā hūṅ jinse Xudā ne najāsat ko dūr kar diyā, aur unko pāk kar diyā. maiṅ us ahl-i bait se hūṅ jinkī maḥabbat aur mavaddat Xudā ne apnī kitāb meṅ vājib kī hai. … is par Ibn ᶜAbbās*[51] *khaṛe huve, aur kahne lage – logoṅ! yah*[52] *tumhāre nabī ke beṭe haiṅ. unse baiᶜat karo. čunānčih logoṅ ne unse baiᶜat kī* (*Nuzhat al-Majālis* – 2, p. 349).[53]

ᶜAlī *ᶜa°* says: From the chest to the facial orb there was great similarity of Ḥasan *ᶜa°* with the appearance of Allāh's Messenger *ṣa°*. And of Ḥusain *ᶜa°* there was similarity with his nether region (Tirmiḏī, *Miškāh*).

---

48 On the evidence of the next line, this is elliptic for "deny [your identity]".

49 The ellipses here and further below are found in the original. Their function is unclear.

50 Read as *iẕn xudāwandī* according to the Bengali transcription (*ij·n khodāoẏāndī*).

51 In the Bengali script *Ib'ne Ābbās*, following the Persianised convention common in South Asia.

52 Singular form according to the Bengali transcription (*eh·*).

53 The translation of the Urdu text as reconstituted from the Bengali script runs: "I am the son of the bringer of glad tidings and the warner. I am the son of the radiant lamp. I am the son of this one who through the permission of providence summons towards God. I am the son of that one from whom God removed impurity, and made him pure. I am of those people of the house (= of that lineage) whose love and affection God has made binding in his own book. … Hereupon Ibn ᶜAbbās stood up, and began speaking: People! These are the sons of your Prophet. Swear them allegiance. Accordingly the people swore them allegiance."

The Messenger *ṣa°* says: If the man's seed is cast into the womb first, the woman's seed enters thereafter, then the offspring becomes like (the appearance of) its father. And if the woman's seed enters first, the man's seed is cast in thereafter, then the offspring becomes like (the appearance of) its mother (Buxārī, Muslim, *Miškāh*).

Question: Very well. If they are indeed the sons of the Prophet *ṣa°*, then how did it happen? Fāṭimah is after all the Prophet's *ṣa°* (own) daughter.

Answer: (a)[54] The fatwā̤ (written by me) through Allāh's command (in accordance with divine inspiration) on Ḥasan, Ḥusain *ᶜa°* being sons of the Prophet, namely: Once, at Allāh's will, during marital union two male seeds and two female seeds of the Messenger Muḥammad *ṣa°* were cast[55] into Xadījah's *ᶜa°* womb. Among them, only one female seed remaining manifest, the other two male and one female seeds remained concealed in that seed remaining manifest. Thereafter, a female seed of Xadījah *ᶜa°*, having entered her womb, united with the said manifest female seed of the Messenger Muḥammad *ṣa°*. As a result Xadījah *ᶜa°* conceived a female offspring. And in due time that offspring was born with the name Fāṭ̤imah *ᶜa°*. Therefore, now the three said seeds of the Messenger Muḥammad *ṣa°* remained concealed within Fāṭ̤imah *ᶜa°*. Thereafter, during some marital union of Fāṭ̤imah *ᶜa°* one male seed of the Messenger Muḥammad *ṣa°* remaining concealed within Fāṭ̤imah *ᶜa°* assumed manifestation in Fāṭ̤imah's *ᶜa°* womb. And at once an own male seed of Fāṭ̤imah *ᶜa°*, assuming manifestation, united with the said seed. And Fāṭ̤imah *ᶜa°* conceived a male offspring. In due time the offspring was born with the name Ḥasan *ᶜa°*. Due to being from the seeds of the Messenger Muḥammad *ṣa°* and Fāṭ̤imah *ᶜa°*, Ḥasan *ᶜa°* is their authentic son. Due to not being from the seed of ᶜAlī *ᶜa°* he is not his authentic son. Thereafter, during some marital union, at Allāh's will the other male seed of the Messen-

[54] "(a)", "(b)" etc. are here used for "(ka)", (kha)" etc. of the Bengali alphabet.

[55] Here and in the following lines, the finite verbal forms used for one or more of the seeds mentioned are respect forms. Cf. note 26.

ger Muḥammad *ṣa*° remaining concealed within Fāṭimah *ᶜa*° assumed manifestation in Fāṭimah's *ᶜa*° womb. And the female seed remained concealed in the said seed having assumed manifestation. And, quite simultaneously with that, an own male seed of Fāṭimah *ᶜa*°, assuming manifestation, united with the said seed. And Fāṭimah *ᶜa*° conceived a male offspring. And in due time that offspring was born with the name Ḥusain *ᶜa*°. For the said reason Ḥusain *ᶜa*°, not being ᶜAlī's *ᶜa*° authentic son, is the authentic son of the Messenger Muḥammad *ṣa*° and Fāṭimah *ᶜa*°.

It is narrated from[56] His Eminence Ibn ᶜAbbās[57] *ᶜa*°: The Messenger *ṣa*° says: Allāh created Ādam *ᶜa*°. And through the intermediacy of his spinal marrow made me come down on the earth. Thereafter, he made me come down in the spinal marrow of Nūḥ *a*° when he was on the boat. Thereafter, when Ibrāhīm *ᶜa*° was flung into the firepit, then I was present concealed in Ibrāhīm's *ᶜa*° spinal marrow. Thereafter, as long as Allāh did not bring me out through my father and mother, so long did I not desist from being transferred from successive great spinal marrows to successive holy wombs. My father and mother were never united in unlawful union (*Prem Prasaṅga Muẏāmālāh·* – p. 230[58]).

(b) *bah*[59] *rivāyat Jābir bin ᶜAbdallāh ᶜa° – Nabī ṣa° se rivāyat hai, kih Xudā ne mujhko aur ᶜAlī ko ᶜarš*[60] *ke sāmne do nūr banā kar paidā kiyā thā. Ādam kī paidāʾiš ke do hazār baras pahle se ham uskī tasbīḥ va taqdīs karte*[61] *haiṅ. phir jab Xudā ne Ādam ko paidā kiyā to ham donoṅ ko unkī pušt meṅ jāgūjī ba-*

---

56 *hate*. This marks Ibn ᶜAbbās as the originator of the following narration.

57 In the Bengali script *Ib'ne Ābbās*; cf. note 51.

58 In the edition of 1983 (see note 10), the passage alluded to here actually begins on p. 237. It may be that an earlier edition is meant, though I am unaware of any.

59 Because of the following Arabic title form, *bā* in the Bengali script is taken to stand for the Persian *bah* and not to simply mean "or" in Bengali ("Or the Narrative of Jābir …").

60 *ārāś* in the Bengali script, which could correspond to the plural *aᶜrāš*. This, however, is unlikely here; probably the Bengali form simply reproduces the pronunciation.

61 Misprinted in the Bengali script as *kāẏ'te* (for *kār'te*).

nāyā. phir ham pušt-i pākīzah[62] *aur šikam-i pāk*[63] *se muntaqal*[64] *hote rahe. yahāṅ tak kih hamko ᶜAbd al-Muṯṯalib kī pušt meṅ ṭhahrāyā. phir vah nūr judā ho kar ᶜAbd al-Muṯṯalib meṅ pahunčā. aur do ṣalāṣ uskī ᶜAbdallāh meṅ gaye. aur ek ṣalāṣ (tihāʾī) Abū Ṯālib meṅ āyā. phir vah nūr mujhse aur ᶜAlī se Fāṯimah meṅ ā kar mujtamaᶜ huvā. pas Ḥasan aur Ḥusain ᶜa° Rabb al-ᶜĀlamīn ke do nūr haiṅ*[65] (*Nuzhat al-Majālis* – 2, p. 347).[66]

(c) It is narrated from[67] the Mother of Faḏl: Ḥusain *ᶜa°* is a piece of flesh cut from the body of Allāh's Messenger *ṣa°*. And his son (Baihaqī, *Miškāh*). Allāh's Messenger *ṣa°* says: Fāṯimah *ᶜa°* is a piece of my body (Buxārī, Muslim, *Miškāh*).

(d) That is, His Eminence Ḥusain *ᶜa°* is arisen from the *sarkār-i do ᶜālam* (*Irphān*[68] – November-December 1978 English era – p. 100).

It is to be known that, if the *kašf* and *ilhām*[69] of the Sufis, in which there is the chance of an error arising, correspond to the

---

62 According to the Bengali transcription read as *pušt pākīzah* (*puś·t pākijā*).

63 According to the Bengali transcription read as *šikam pāk* (*sekām pāk*).

64 According to the Bengali transcription read as *muntaqil* (*muntākīl*).

65 Singular *hai* according to the Bengali transcription (*hāẏ*).

66 The translation of the Urdu text as reconstituted from the Bengali script runs: "In accordance with the narration of Jābir bin ᶜAbdallāh – From the Prophet there is the narration that: God brought forth me and ᶜAlī, creating (= as) two lights in front of the throne [of God]. Since two thousand years before the creation of Ādam we performed his glorification and sanctification. Further, when God created Ādam, then he made us both of wakeful spirit (= cognisant) in his back. Further, we went on being transferred through immaculate backs and pure stomachs. Thus far that [God] caused us to stay in the back of ᶜAbd al-Muṯṯalib. Further, that light arrived in ᶜAbd al-Muṯṯalib having been divided. And two-thirds of that went into ᶜAbdallāh. And one-third (a third part) came into Abū Ṯālib. Further, that light, having come from me and ᶜAlī into Fāṯimah, was brought together. Consequently, Ḥasan and Ḥusain are the two lights of the Lord of the Worlds."

67 *hate*. Cf. note 56.

68 This is a Bengali periodical.

69 As in the context of Sufism these two words are technical terms, they are left untranslated.

opinion of the learned persons[70] of the Ahl-i Sunnah,[71] then they are true (*Maktūbāt-i Mujaddidī*[72] – 1, 112th maktūb).

(e) Now-a-days the science of medicine says: Operating on the body of a male truck driver of the capital Baku of the province Azerbaijan of the Soviet Union, an embryo of developed shape has been removed from his lung. After operation due to difficulties of breathing, the surgeons could see an embryo in the cavity of the driver's lung. The hair of the embryo was matted, the teeth fully developed; there were eyes and a backbone. The reason for being so: the driver was to have been a twin child of his mother. But one embryo entered into the other. And was stuck there upto forty years (*Māsik Gaṇa Sbāsthya* – 1st year, 4th number, Āśbin, Bengali year 1387 – p. 62).

Now I say that if the mentioned driver had, not being a man, been a woman, and the embryo, not being stuck in the lung, had become stuck in her womb, then that embryo would indeed have been the sister or brother of the female driver. If the mentioned embryo had been born after the marriage of the female driver, would it then have been the actual offspring of her husband himself? It would only apparently have been identified as the offspring of her husband himself.

(f) What is[73] narrated in the *Qur'ān* and Ḥadīṯ is actual truth. May that be comprehensible to our knowledge or not be comprehensible, we have brought belief to it (*ᶜaqā'id* book).

Question: All these are esoteric matters. It is not appropriate to divulge them to the populace. Should one divulge, people might fall into confusion. They might become corrupt in faith. Consequently what is the use of divulging?

---

[70] Here and in the following, "learned person" translates *ālīm* of the original. Note that the plural of this is throughout formed by the addition of Bengali suffixes; *ulāmā* or *ulemā* is not used.

[71] Though this usually refers to Sunnis, the term is left untranslated as it may have been used, or understood, in a broader or a narrower sense.

[72] According to the Bengali transcription read as *Maktūbāt Mujaddidī* (*māk'tubāt mujāddidī*).

[73] *āchen*. On the respect form cf. note 26.

Answer: If Allāh orders someone to divulge, what then is his duty? Is not divulging an obligation for him then?

Look here, see: (a)[74] Xaḍir[75] *ᶜa°* says: Oh Mūsā̤, I have not done all these deeds (breaking the boats, slaying the boy and repairing the orphans' wall without wages) based on my own inclinations (Sūrah *al-Kahf*).

(b) Imām Mujaddid[76] *ᶜa°* says: Since the deeds of these great persons *ᶜa°* are connected with Allāh, hence the supererogations of others are obligations for them (2, 55th maktūb).

(c) Allāh says: Oh Messenger *ṣa°*, say: If you[77] wish to love Allāh, then pledge allegiance to me. Then Allāh will love you (Sūrah *Āl ᶜImrān* – Āyah 32). From this it can be understood: loving Allāh's Messenger *ṣa°* is, verily, loving Allāh. And it is Allāh's love arising for the created being that is the fulfilment of that desired by the created being. But the arising of love for the Messenger *ṣa°* indeed depends upon his apperception.[78] The more someone is able to know him, the more does his love for him establish itself. With this very import indeed, due to the particularities of the circumstances of the times, the subject of Ḥasan and Ḥusain *a°* being the Prophet's sons has today gained manifestation.[79] The Messenger *ṣa°* says: These (Ḥasan and Ḥusain *a°*) are my sons and also the sons of my daughter. Oh Allāh! Definitely I love these. Therefore, do you too love these. And love him who loves these (Buxārī, Tirmiḏ̣ī, *Miškāh*).

(d) Imām Mujaddid *ᶜa°* says: Why the general public?[80] Even distinguished persons are incapable of understanding its meaning. Nevertheless, disseminating it was not forbidden for the prophets *ᶜa°*. And the fear of an error by the public did not become a hindrance to it (1, 172nd maktūb).

---

[74] Cf. note 54.

[75] Probably better known as Xiḍr.

[76] I.e. Aḥmad Sirhindī.

[77] Plural.

[78] This translates *paricaẏ* here, as more fitting than the translation "identity" otherwise used.

[79] *prakāś pelen*. On the respect form cf. note 26.

[80] I.e.: not only the general public.

(e) On the day of Resurrection, a bridle of fire will be applied to the mouth of him who conceals knowledge in spite of it being known (Abū Dāwūd, Tirmiḏī, Ibn Mājah, *Miškāh*).

Question: These new words can be heard only from your[81] mouths. Before this it has indeed not been heard from anyone else's mouth. Neither indeed has any learned person said such words.

Answer: The assessment of whether the matter is new or old is not subject to anyone's inclination. What scripture calls new, that indeed is new. And what it calls old, that indeed is old. So I say: Whether the matter be new or old, the selection of that is examined by means of the scriptural touchstone, and is settled only by the veracious scales of extremely religious, very knowledgable scriptural authors.[82] Therefore, it is a great offence to raise the insinuation of newness against an ancient Šarīᶜah rule. Alas! What is not new in the darkness of ignorance! Even Allāh's 'doctrine of being one',[83] which is an eternal truth and primordially ancient, was appearing quite new in era after era with the appearance of new prophets *ᶜa*°. The people were saying: We have never heard such words.

The matter is, that as the very first it was Imām Abū Ḥanīfah *ᶜa*° who did bring forth the *maḏhab.*[84] Before him there was no *maḏhab* at all. As the very first it was ᶜAbd al-Qādir al-Jīlānī *ᶜa*° who brought forth the *ṭarīqah.*[85] Was there any *ṭarīqah* before him? Haven't they said new words? Look here, listen! The Messenger *ṣa*° says: For this community Allāh will, at the beginning of each century, send such a person who will reform the religion (Ḥadīṯ).

Allāh's favourite never brings a new Šarīᶜah. Rather, he brings such an understanding of the *Qur'ān* and Ḥadīṯ as is com-

---

81 Plural.

82 Incorrect *gāner* for *gaṇer*.

83 *Āllāh·r 'ekatbabād'*. What is meant is, most probably, the doctrine of Allāh being one.

84 This term is left untranslated, as a technical term.

85 This term too is left untranslated, as a technical term.

pletely unknown (*aṭ-Ṭabaqāt al-Kubrā* – 1, p. 6, Mujaddid-i Alf-i Ṣānī[86] – p. 6).

Therefore, in accord with *waraṯatu 'l-anbiyāʾ*[87] the learned persons of the Muḥammadan community[88] too vary in prestige amongst themselves.[89] Each learned person is not of the same rank. The work of all and sundry learned persons is not of the same sort. "The learned persons are the successors of the prophets *ᶜa°*" (*Miškāh*).

Finally, let me say this, that once ᶜUmar *ᶜa°*, preparing to kiss the Black Stone, said: Oh stone! I know you are definitely only a piece of rock. Nevertheless, I am kissing you for the reason that the Messenger *ṣa°* has kissed you. Once a person asked ᶜAbdallāh bin ᶜUmar *ᶜa°* about giving the Black Stone a kiss. He answered: (I do not know anything.) Only this, that I have seen Allāh's Messenger *ṣa°* touch and kiss (Buxārī, *Miškāh*).

Consequently, if in imitation someone should indeed have called Ḥasan and Ḥusain *ᶜa°* Messenger-sons, what is the fault in that? Where is unbelief?[90] Rather: beautiful.[91] Quite unquestionable[92] faith.

Look here, the dictionary too says: *sayyid* = *payġambar ᶜalaihi ʾṣ-ṣalātu wa ʾs-salām kī āl* (*Luġat-i Fīroz* – p. 800). *āl* = *aulād* (*Luġāt-i Kišorī* – p. 38). *aulād* = lineage, son, daughter (*Luġāt-i Kišorī*). *ᶜalavī*[93] = *vah šaxṣ, jo ḥaẓrat ᶜAlī kī aulād se to*

---

86 The Persian name form is used here to accord with the name in the Bengali script: *Mujāddid Āl'phisānī*.

87 In the Bengali script *oẏārāsātul āmbiyā*.

88 *mūhāmmādī ummāt*. Note that *is'lāmī, mus'lim* or *musal'mān(ī)* is not used. This peculiar usage is found several times in publications of the Khilāphātī Khān'kāh· Śārīph, and clearly emphasises, though subtly, adherence to what is regarded as the true creed of Muḥammad.

89 *eke apar hate maryyādāśīl*.

90 I.e.: Where is [it] unbelief (*kuphārī*)? = What is unbelief about that?

91 I.e.: It is, rather, beautiful.

92 Assuming *muhākkik* to be a mistaken reproduction of *muḥaqqaq*.

93 In Bengali script: *ālābbī*.

ho, magar ḥaẓrat Fāṯimah se nah ho[94] (*Fīroz* – p. 571, *Kišorī* – p. 326).

Look here, Mr. Muhāmmad Hāsān Ālī Caudhurī, M.A. (Dhaka), B.E.S. says:

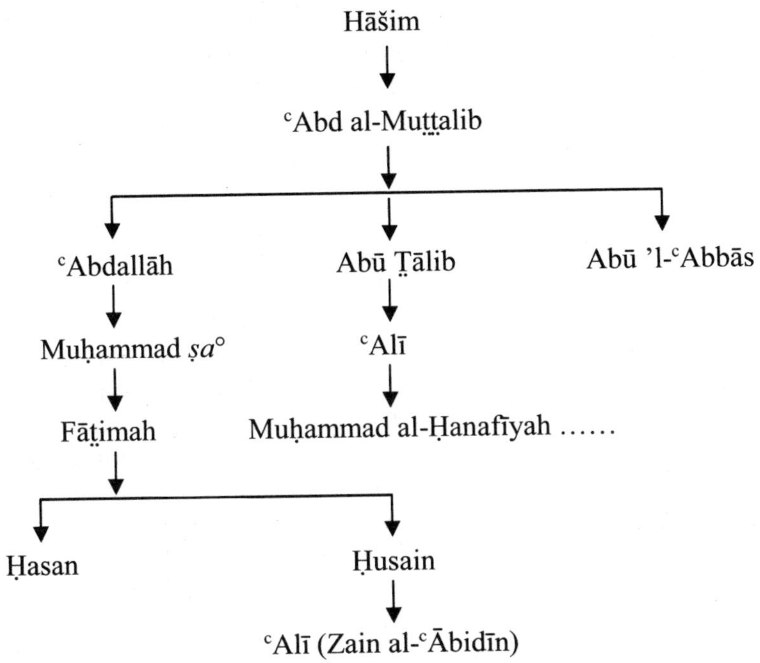

(*Is'lāmer Itihās (ucca mādhyamik o snātak śreṇī)* – p. 346)

Question: It is indeed found in the Ḥadīṯ, but it is not, after all, found so openly in the *Qur'ān*.

Answer: (a)[95] The Mother of Ya^{c}qūb *^{c}a*° said to ^{c}Abdallāh bin Mas^{c}ūd *^{c}a*°: You allegedly execrate all those ladies who for enhancing their beauty wear tattoos, pluck the hair of the fore-

---

94 The translation of the Urdu text as reconstituted from the Bengali script runs: "That person, who forsooth be of the offspring of His Eminence ^{c}Alī, but not be of Her Eminence Fāṯimah".

95 Cf. note 54.

head, etc. In answer ᶜAbdallāh *ᶜa°* said: Should I not execrate those whom Allāh's Messenger *ṣa°* and Allāh's book have execrated? The Mother of Yaᶜqūb *ᶜa°* said: I have indeed read[96] the *Qur'ān* from beginning to end, but I do not in fact find that in it which you are saying. ᶜAbdallāh *ᶜa°* said: If you would read the *Qur'ān*, you would certainly find it. Have you not read in the *Qur'ān*: "Accept that which the Messenger *ṣa°* indicates to you,[97] and abstain from that which he forbids"?

The Mother of Yaᶜqūb *ᶜa°* said: Yes, I have quite definitely read that in the *Qur'ān*. ᶜAbdallāh *ᶜa°* said: From that which I am saying, the Messenger *ṣa°* has quite definitely forbidden (Buxārī).

(b) Definitely that which Allāh's Messenger *ṣa°* has made prohibited corresponds to that which Allāh has made prohibited. Yet all this is not in the *Qur'ān* (Ḥadīṯ).

(c) Allāh says: *allaḏīna 'stajābū lillāhi wa 'r-rasūli*[98] – Through this it is clearly proven that what the Messenger *ṣa°* has indicated, that is also Allāh's indication. May that be in Allāh's book, or may it not (*Maᶜārif al-Qur'ān* – 2, p. 359).

(d) In the *Qur'ān* are only the sole words: maintain the *namāz*, deliver the *rukūᶜ*, and perform the *sijdah*. But these here rules and regulations of the *namāz*, these are in fact not mentioned in the *Qur'ān*. Are all these not parts of the *namāz* because of this? Will the *namāz* be valid without all these? Look here, listen. The Ḥadīṯ is the explanation[99] of the *Qur'ān* itself. Without the Ḥadīṯ it is not possible to grasp the *Qur'ān*. Allāh says: And upon you[100] I have made the *Qur'ān* descend for this reason, that you will relate to humans that which has been made to descend for them (Sūrah *an-Naḥl* – Āyah 44). The Messenger *ṣa°* says: At the end time a group of people will appear; they will

---

[96] Or "recited" (*paṛechi*), as *paṛā* can also mean "recite", especially in connection with texts regarded as holy. Thus also in the following.

[97] Plural.

[98] Given in the Bengali script as *āllājī nās'tāsābu* [sic] *lillāhi oẏār rāsūl*.

[99] Though *byākhyā* has been translated by "commentary" farther above, "explanation" has been chosen here because this seems more fitting, and also to differentiate it from *ṭīkā* (printed *ṭikā*) "commentary" in the following.

[100] The respect form is used.

believe the *Qur'ān*, but will not believe the Ḥadīṯ. And the Ḥadīṯ is, however, the most excellent explanation of the *Qur'ān* (Commentary of the *Miškāh*). The Messenger *ṣa*° says: He who is averse to the Sunnah (Ḥadīṯ) is not among mine (Buxārī, Muslim).

Question: But the *Qur'ān* says: Muḥammad *ṣa*°, is not the father of anyone among your[101] men.

Answer: Very well. If it be so, then who were Qāsim, Ṯāhir, Ṯayyib, Ibrāhīm *ᶜa*°? Are they not, respectively, the sons of Muḥammad Allāh's Messenger *ṣa*° born of the wombs of mother Xadījah and mother Māryah *ᶜa*°? Yes, they were indeed his sons (Ḥadīṯ).

Therefore, it can be understood that the meaning of the Āyah should be: "Muḥammad *ṣa*° is not the father of anyone among your contemporary men." This Āyah descended in the context of Allāh's Messenger's *ṣa*° marrying Zaynab bint Jaḥš *ᶜa*°, the divorced wife of Allāh's Messenger's *ṣa*° adopted son Zayd *ᶜa*°. In that context Allāh said in that Āyah: An adopted son is not the actual son. The wife of an adopted son is not prohibited for the foster father. Accordingly, for Allāh's Messenger *ṣa*° Zaynab *ᶜa*°, the divorced wife of his adopted son Zayd *ᶜa*°, is not prohibited, but rather, admissible (Tafsīr and Ḥadīṯ books). It is necessary to know that the said Āyah descended in the second Hijrī year. And Ḥasan and Ḥusain *ᶜa*° attained birth in the third and fourth or fifth Hijrī year respectively (*Saṃkṣipta Is'lāmī Biśbakoṣ* – 2, pp. 343, 556 and 563).

Therefore, on the import of that Āyah Ḥasan and Ḥusain *ᶜa*° are not those contemporary men.

Dear readers!

You will also find the matter of Ḥasan and Ḥusain *ᶜa*° being Prophet-sons in the books translated into Bengali mentioned below. Those who wish to, please look it up. The books are as follows: (a)[102] Buxārī, translated by Maulānā[103] Mr. Śām'sul Hak, published in 1964 English era – 5, p. 424, (b) Buxārī, by courtesy

---

[101] Plural.

[102] Cf. note 54.

[103] The Arabic form has been used here and in the following.

of the Saudi embassy, Dhaka – 3, pp. 17,18, (c) *Miškāh*, translated by Maulānā Phāj'lul Kārīm – 4, from p. 1935 upto p. 1943, (d) *Māsik Mādīnā* – December 1979 English era, 9th number – p. 9, (e) *Irphān* – November-December 1978 English era – pp. 80, 100, (f) *Irphān* – December 1979 English era, 11th number – p. 7, (g) *Saṃkṣipta Is'lāmī Biśbakoṣ* – 2, p. 556, (h) *Sirr al-Asrār*[104] – 1, p. 4, (i) *Miftāḥ al-Jannah* – p. 9.

Concluded

104 For this and the following, the Arabic name form is given here.

History & Language

On the road of failure: the Afghans in Mughal India

André Wink

Whosoever's star is declining takes the road of failure of his own accord, and soon receives the retribution of his evil thoughts.
Abū 'l-Faẓl, *Akbarnāma*, III, 510

The origin of the name Afghans is unknown – it is known to the Afghans themselves only through the medium of the Persian language. Their own name for themselves is Pashtuns or Pakhtuns, while in India they have generally been known as Pathans. All of these names, attempts to prove otherwise notwithstanding, refer to the same ethno-linguistic group. In Babur's memoirs they make their appearance as a tribal and mostly pastoral-nomadic people whose original homeland in the Sulayman mountains was called Afghanistan. These mountains, like most of the other lands that make up modern Afghanistan, were then considered to have been part of Khurasan, or were simply referred to as Sarhadd, 'the frontier'

Like their Turko-Mongol rivals, the Afghans were originally 'frontier' nomads and as such they had much in common with them. In the sixteenth century they became each other's main antagonists in their attempt to establish dominance in Hindustan, even though, ironically, both ethnic groups had a radical aversion for the climate of the Indian plains – in particular the hot season.[1] 'We suffered from three things in Hindustan', wrote Babur, 'One was the heat, another the biting wind, and the third the dust'.[2] Having first come to Agra in the hot season, in an especially hot (*xailī garm*) year, Babur faced widespread defection of his men – Turks, Mongols, and Afghans – while 'many began to sicken and die as though under the influence of a pestilential wind'.[3] Similarly, Elphinstone recorded of the Afghans that 'almost all of them are (...) impatient of hot climates; and when on campaigns in India, the approach of summer used to thin their armies by desertions, even in the vigorous reign of Ahmad Shah [Abdali]'.[4] During Ahmad Shah Abdali's campaign of 1763, 'his army, composed of Afghans, Uzbeks, Baluchis, and other natives of cold climates, suffered great hardships during the first part of the march, and he lost an incredible number of men from heat before he arrived at Multan'.[5] In another instance, in 1756, when Ahmad Shah Abdali marched straight to Delhi and the Afghans passed the whole summer in India, 'as they were becoming extremely

---

[1] For the medieval Turko-Mongol nomads, see A. Wink, *Al-Hind: The Making of the Indo-Islamic World*, 3 vols. (Leiden, Boston and New Delhi, 1990-2004), II, p. 77; idem, 'India and the Turko-Mongol Frontier', in: A.M. Khazanov and A. Wink (eds.), *Nomads in the Sedentary World* (London, 2001), p. 226.

[2] Zahiruddin Muhammad Babur, *Bāburnāma: Chaghatay Turkish Text with Abdul Rahim Khankhanan's Persian translation, Turkish Transcription, Persian Edition and English Translation by W.M. Thackston, Jr.*, 3 vols. (Department of Near Eastern Languages and Civilizations, Harvard University: Sources of Oriental Languages & Literatures XVIII, ed. Ş. Tekin & G.A. Tekin, Turkish Sources XVI, 1993) (henceforward *BN*, with folio pagination), 300.

[3] *Ibidem*, 294b-296.

[4] M. Elphinstone, *An Account of the Kingdom of Caubul*, 2 vols. (1815; rpt.: Karachi, 1992), I, p. 327.

[5] *Ibidem*, II, p. 297.

sickly, Ahmad found it necessary to retire to his own dominions'.[6]

Like Turko-Mongol nomads generally, Afghans appear to have been deeply attached to their own homeland and habitat. This attachment took a variety of forms. The Durrani Afghans, for instance, developed a special reverence for Qandahar – which locality contained the tombs of their great ancestors.[7] The Durranis, regarding themselves as superior to other Afghans, never went to India as merchants or soldiers of fortune, and rarely settled out of their native country; even in the comfortable circumstances in which they found themselves in Kashmir in the later eighteenth century, 'their fondness for their own country' prevented them from remaining long.[8] In the earlier centuries, it was widely observed that career opportunities in India attracted primarily the more common run of Afghans because tribal chiefs of consequence preferred the autonomy they enjoyed at home to serving a sovereign in India. Afghans did not easily take to a sedentary life anywhere; for them, agriculture was and remained at most a supplement to pastoral nomadism.[9] As true nomads, Afghans have always regarded peasants who invested a great deal of time and energy in agriculture as somewhat pathetic – fit to be conquered but not emulated. Successful Afghan agriculturists would be landlords but not cultivating peasants and commonly seem to have preserved a preference for a pastoral habitat.

Under these circumstances, there had to be powerful incentives for Afghans, as for pastoral Turko-Mongols, to move deeper into the Indian subcontinent. It is well known that Babur himself had little choice and that he conquered Hindustan by default, when Samarqand had been irretrievably lost to him. The reason why, over the centuries, so many Afghans migrated to India more often than not had to do with simple economic necessity. Afghans (or at least Afghan men) typically regarded not

[6] *Ibidem*, p. 289.

[7] *Ibidem*, p. 126.

[8] *Ibidem*, p. 239.

[9] J.T. Arlinghaus, *The Transformation of Afghan Tribal Society: Tribal Expansion, Mughal Imperialism and the Roshaniyya Insurrection, 1450-1600* (unpublished PhD dissertation, Duke University, 1983), pp. 80-1.

only cultivating land but all manual labour as beneath their dignity. It was disgraceful to them to engage in crafts like carpentry or stone cutting, while shopkeeping and moneylending, in their view, was best left to Hindus. Without sufficient land at their disposal – and peasants to work it – Afghans therefore had no choice but to quit their country.[10] In the western parts of modern Afghanistan, where marriages were late and land was plenty, emigration to India was for this reason relatively rare; but in the eastern parts it was common during long periods.

Redundant Afghans thus poured forth into India. When population outstripped resources, entire tribes would sometimes migrate in order to be able to maintain kinship solidarity; or branches of tribes would conquer adjacent lands. Tribes were also driven off their lands by more powerful rivals and these could disappear from their homelands almost without trace and end up in India or on the Indian borderlands. One of the main reasons why many members of the Lodi Afghan tribes migrated to India in the fifteenth century – in their case mostly as individuals and families – was probably the growing power of the Ghilzai Afghans on the Ghazna plateau.[11] As with the Turko-Mongol nomads on the steppes, it can be speculated that necessity, when it became the main motivation for the migration of Afghan nomads to India, was caused by overpopulation.[12]

The pastoral-nomadic economy of Afghanistan and Kabul

Medieval Afghanistan was a (semi-)arid and in many places cold country, a wild assemblage of hills, mountains covered with perennial snow, and wastes unmarked by enclosures even in the cultivated parts, destitute of roads or navigable rivers and canals, with only a few towns at great distance from each other, and, above all, overwhelmingly poor. Astride of what Babur describes as some of the 'most worthless mountain zones in the world',[13] this land has been the habitat of genuine pastoral nomads of both

10 M. Elphinstone, *An Account of the Kingdom of Caubul*, II, pp. 34-5.
11 Arlinghaus, *Transformation of Afghan Tribal Society*, p. 167.
12 *Ibidem*, p. 126.
13 *BN*, 141b.

local and remote origins since ancient times. As it was still known to Babur, medieval Afghanistan was an area to the south of Kabul on both sides of the Sulayman mountain range, extending down to the Indus river, and generally mentioned together with Bangash, Bannu, and Dasht. This was the southern part of what modern scholarship has referred to as 'Indo-Khurasan' and, with less precision, the 'Indo-Iranian frontier', i.e. the middle part of the Makran-Pamir shatter zone running from the Makran coast on the Arabian Sea to the Pamir Knot and the Karakorum Range in Central Asia.[14] Located in the southern part of the country of Roh, this (semi-)arid and mountainous region to the west of the Indus and south of the Hindu Kush, containing only a modest amount of land for agriculture, was and still is eminently suitable for pasturing large flocks of sheep and goats. With Baluchistan and parts of Sind and Rajasthan, Afghanistan's pastoral and mixed pastoral-agricultural economy was the closest approximation to be found in South Asia to the purely nomadic economies of the arid zone of Persia and the much vaster open spaces beyond the Hindu Kush mountains which historically were known as Turan, the steppe lands of the Turko-Mongol world.

The ethnogenesis of the Afghans in this area is an obscure and entangled process that took place over centuries and involved successive waves of nomadic migrations into and through the Afghan homeland. What stands out is that the medieval Afghans shared in a common nomadic culture – called *kūčī* or *pūyanda* – supplemented with rudimentary agriculture, hunting and gathering, highway robbery, and a long-distance peddling trade between India and Khurasan along the routes of their annual migrations.[15] The summer pastures or *yailāq*-s of the Afghan nomads were in the upland portions of southern Indo-Khurasan: the Sulayman mountain range and the Ghazna plateau.[16] On some of the relatively well-watered and fertile soil near their summer pastures they planted wheat and barley. After the autumn harvest they brought their flocks of sheep and goats

---

[14] Arlinghaus, *Transformation of Afghan Tribal Society*, pp. 4-6.

[15] *Ibidem*, pp. 39-40, 69.

[16] *Ibidem*, pp. 69-70.

down from the mountains and the plateau to the winter pastures or *qišlāq*-s at lower altitudes in the other subregions of Indo-Khurasan. Among the various trajectories of Afghan nomadic migration, the most important were those to the Derajat in the Indus river valley, the Kabul river valley, and Qandahar.[17] The Derajat was a natural winter grazing area for Afghan nomads. Especially below Kalabagh, the snow-fed Indus river inundated a wide area and when the river retreated in the fall and winter it left the flood plains moist and rich with grasses. Many of the Afghan nomads who followed the routes from the Ghazna plateau to the Indus river flood plains engaged in trade or hired themselves out as camel drivers.[18] Those who migrated between the Ghazna plateau and northern Indo-Khurasan had their winter pastures at lower altitudes along the Kabul river, in such tumans or 'districts' as Nangrahar or Lamghanat. Here the Afghan nomads, by Babur's time, had taken control of the trade along the Khyber route, between the Panjab and Khurasan and Turan. The third trajectory of Afghan nomadic migration, between the Ghazna plateau and the relatively low and snow-free valleys around Qandahar (of the Arghandab, Tarnak and Arghastan rivers) is known to have been followed regularly throughout the medieval centuries, and in Babur's time was especially favored by the Ghilzais, who tended extremely large flocks of sheep, but as a rule did not engage in trade.[19]

The pastoral nomads of medieval Afghanistan, then, kept large herds of sheep and goats, as well as some camels and horses (on which more below), where grazing land was sufficient, supplementing pastoralism with agriculture where possible, and engaging in peddling trade mostly where their nomadic migration patterns coincided with trade routes. This was a fundamentally pastoral-nomadic society in which kinship was the main organizing principle of tribes – not territory – and in which there was no place for chiefs or kings.

Medieval Afghanistan was, in other words, not a kingdom. Yet, in spite of this, it was a fairly clearly delineated territory. Its

---

[17] *Ibidem*, pp. 70-1.
[18] *Ibidem*, p. 70.
[19] *Ibidem*, p. 71.

southern boundary, approximately along a line drawn from Dera Ghazi Khan on the Indus river through Quetta and beyond, was the scorched deserts of Baluchistan and the Makran. The latter were a land of even greater scarcity, although not without some agriculture in enclaves (like the Kij valley). Baluchistan-Makran had a largely pastoral-nomadic economy based on sheep, goats and camels, as well as some black cattle and small horses of poor quality, and a population of tent-dwelling Baluchis and Brahuis whose extreme poverty and weak social organization appears to have put them at a disadvantage vis-à-vis the Afghans who dominated the (semi-)arid tracts and fertile river valleys to their north. Medieval Afghanistan was separated by the Koh-i-Safed or 'White Mountain' range (also known in Pashto as Spinghar) from northern Indo-Khurasan, which comprises the Kabul river basin with its numerous mountain valleys and fertile lands with abundant water from perennial streams, supporting intensive agriculture in addition to relatively limited pasture lands. Northern Indo-Khurasan was made up of three subregions: Kabulistan, the upper part of the Kabul river watershed; Lamghanat, the central part of the Kabul river basin, separated from Kabulistan by the Jagdalik pass; and Peshawar, divided from Lamghanat by the Khyber pass and including the Peshawar plain as well as the valleys to the north drained by the Swat river and its tributaries and the valleys of Tirah to the southwest of Peshawar.[20] As a whole, northern Indo-Khurasan was an environment which favored sedentary agriculture rather than pastoral nomadism. Prior to the beginnings of Afghan conquests and settlement in this area in the fifteenth and sixteenth centuries, its dominant ethnic groups were Tajiks, Turks, and Mongol Hazaras in the west, and Dardic peoples, Pashai-speakers, and Kafirs in the east.[21] Northern Indo-Khurasan resembled the extremely mountainous northern region of the *kohistān*-s – both were divided, to a large extent, into territorial rather than tribal units, under a stratified lineage system that favored the formation of mini-states and village republics. Afghan conquest and settlement, accompanied by the emergence

[20] *Ibidem*, p. 10.

[21] *Ibidem*, pp. 13, 17, 39, 144; G.S. Robertson, *The Kafirs of the Hindu-Kush* (1896; rpt.: Delhi, 1998).

of Afghans as a dominant landlord stratum and sedentarization, changed this picture considerably.[22]

There was one fundamental difference between medieval Afghanistan and Turko-Mongol Turan. The pastoral-nomadic economy of medieval Afghanistan had a very limited potential for horse-breeding. In Afghanistan, as Elphinstone put it, 'the great stock of the pastoral tribes is sheep, and those of the kind called in Persian *Doomba*, and remarkable for tails a foot broad, and almost entirely composed of fat'.[23] Goats were also common in all the mountainous parts of the country, and by no means scarce in the plains.[24] Afghan nomads who lived near the deserts had camels, while the poor used bullocks and asses, and almost every man had a horse; but in general the horses of the Afghan dominion – even in its much extended eighteenth- and nineteenth-century version – were 'not remarkably good'.[25]

To be sure, the broad region in which the Sulayman mountains are situated had been known for its horse-breeding populations of 'Ashvakas' in ancient times. But these appear to have been eclipsed by the Turko-Mongol horse-warrior revolution of medieval times. Some excellent horses continued to be bred in Bannu and Daman, and between the Jhelum and Indus rivers.[26] Very good horses were produced in Herat as well, and some of these were carried to other countries, although (at least under Afghan rule) few or none to India.[27] Almost no horses were bred at Kabul, and those bred at Qandahar were not exported. Most tellingly, the vast majority of the horses of the Afghan army in the early nineteenth century came from the Uzbek territories ('Uzbek Tartary' in Elphinstone's words) and the Turkman country along the Amu Darya or Oxus river.[28]

---

22 Elphinstone, *An Account of the Kingdom of Caubul* is evidence that by the early nineteenth century the process of settlement had advanced further and that pastoral nomadism was by then even more confined to what he calls the 'western Afghans' (see esp. I, pp. 302-4; II, pp. 84-7).

23 *Ibidem*, I, p. 190; and see II, p. 117.

24 *Ibidem*, I, pp. 190-1.

25 *Ibidem*, I, p. 189; II, p. 117.

26 *Ibidem*, I, p. 189.

27 *Ibidem*, I, pp. 386-7.

28 *Ibidem*, II, p. 272.

It is, hence, somewhat paradoxical that in the course of the medieval centuries Afghan traders acquired a near monopoly of the trade in horses between Turan and India, and that this trade became one of the driving forces of Afghan migration to India. According to Babur, every year seven, eight or ten thousand horses were brought to Kabul by Afghan traders (*saudāgarān*), and these included both 'thoroughbred horses' (*aspān-i tapčāq*) and 'trade horses' (*aspān-i saudā*).[29] Great numbers of excellent horses were sold annually by Afghan traders in India under the name of 'Kabul' and 'Qandahar' horses, but these were almost all from Balkh, a province of Turkistan, or from Bukhara and the Turkman country.[30] Afghan traders bought these horses cheap, when they were thin and in bad shape, and would then fatten them up in and around Qunduz, or near Parwan and Charikar, or in the Wilayat of Kabul – which, although it lay in the midst of mountains, had some good pastures where 'the grass agrees with horses, and there are few flies [in spring and summer]'.[31]

Overall, the pastures of Afghanistan and Kabul 'could scarcely be compared to those of Farghana and Mughalistan'.[32] The summer pastures or *yailāq*-s of the mountainous regions or *kohistān*-s on both the eastern and western sides of the Wilayat of Kabul were of two sorts. The *kohistān*-s of Andarab, Khwast and the Badakhshan region were covered with juniper, had many springs, and were soft, rolling and hilly, with mostly good 'clump grass' (*bütägä oti*), and their *yailāq*-s were like those of Hissar, Khuttalan, Samarqand, Farghana, and Mughalistan in the sense that they could be used to graze both sheep and horses, albeit on a much reduced scale. The lower *kohistān*-s, with their rocky hills and peaks, of Nijrao, Laghmanat, Bajaur, and Swat had many jalghoza, oak, olive, and wormwood trees, and plentiful and high grass that was useless for sheep and horses. The *kohistān*-s to the west, of Dara-i-Zindan, Dara-i-Saf, Gurzuwan, and Gharjistan had grasslands of a single type which was suitable

---

29 *BN*, 129, 148b.

30 Elphinstone, *An Account of the Kingdom of Caubul*, I, pp. 383; II, pp. 180, 182.

31 *BN*, 130, 141b.

32 *Ibidem*, 140b.

for sheep and horses, but mostly only in the glens. And the *kohistān*-s of Ghur, Karnu and Hazara were similar to these western mountains, with all the grasslands in the glens, and few trees and no juniper, but suitable for sheep and horses. The other *kohistān*-s of Khwaja Isma'il, Dasht, Duki, and Afghanistan, Babur concludes his survey, were all very low, with little grass and water, treeless and ugly, 'worthy of their inhabitants' but not noteworthy as good horse-breeding country.[33] Whenever Babur and his men raided the nomadic inhabitants (*sahrānišīn*) of any of these territories just described – Afghans or otherwise – he came away with or imposed a tribute of very small numbers of horses, and mostly just a lot of sheep (*gosfand*).[34] In one celebrated raid of 1507-8 on the Ghilzai Afghans – then camping between the Ulabatu and Qayaqtu rivers – Babur and his five or six thousand 'galloping horsemen' took over a hundred thousand sheep, more than in any other of his raids, but no horses at all.[35]

Afghan nomads, as the evidence shows, raised huge numbers of sheep, and not many horses, whereas the Turko-Mongol nomads of the steppes raised both huge numbers of sheep and excellent horses. The Afghans, of course, were not the only pastoral nomads in the areas that now comprise modern Afghanistan. Competing with them for space, there were numerically important fragments of medieval Turko-Mongol nomad tribes. These went by a variety of names, and the ethnic boundaries between them – and between them and the Afghans – are far from always clear and, moreover, appear to have been in constant flux. Turko-Mongol nomads in origin, none of these groups entirely abandoned pastoralism in this environment; nor did they entirely lose their mobility and warlike character. But many of them sedentarized and took up agriculture; and in so far as they preserved pastoral nomadism, they – like the Afghans – specialized largely in sheep-raising, and either abandoned horse-breeding altogether or limited themselves to the production of small, hardy breeds of ponies suitable for transportation purposes and carriage only and not for warfare.

33 *Ibidem*, 141.

34 *Ibidem*, 140, 144b, 145, 161b, 196b, 204, 245.

35 *Ibidem*, 203b.

The most frequently mentioned ethnic group of this kind were the Hazaras – a pastoral-nomadic population of Turko-Mongol origin whose name is Persian for a 'one thousand' unit in Chingis Khan's army.[36] According to Abu 'l-Fazl, the historian of Akbar's reign, the Hazaras were the descendants of a Chaghatay army sent by the Great Khan Möngke (r. 1251-9) to assist his brother Hülegü under the command of his son Nögödar.[37] Enigmatically, the Hazaras are often mentioned together with 'Nögödaris'. The latter became best known, after the middle of the thirteenth century, as one of a number of dissident anti-Ilkhanid Mongol groups that were active on the Indo-Khurasani frontier for quite a while.[38] Nomadic warbands of Mongol origin operating under a nephew of Chaghatay who was also known as Nögödar are again mentioned in this area in the first two decades of the fourteenth century and these too could have been the predecessors of other groups of Nögödaris.[39] If there was any relationship between some of the Hazaras and the Nögödaris it is not at all clear what it was. Other Hazaras appear to have been moving independently to India's north-west frontier from areas like Balkh, Qarshi and Pyrmurgh during Chingis Khan's conquests. Their origins are also murky, especially so since at some stage they began to intermarry extensively with the Persian-speaking sedentary population. From very early times they seem to have been moving, with their sheep and whatever other animals they brought along, into the area that was later named after them – the Hazarajat, around Bamiyan, to the west

---

[36] Cf. A. Wink, *Al-Hind*, II, pp. 209, 191, 210; H. F. Schurmann, *The Mongols of Afghanistan: An Ethnography of the Moghols and Related Peoples of Afghanistan* ('s-Gravenhage, 1962); S.A. Mousavi, *The Hazaras of Afghanistan: An Historical, Cultural, Economic and Political Study* (New York, 1997); K. Ferdinand, 'Ethnographical Notes on Chahār Aimāq, Hazāra and Moghol', *Acta Orientalia*, 1964, vol. XXVIII, 1-2, pp. 175-201; E.E. Bacon, 'An Inquiry into the History of the Hazara Mongols of Afghanistan', *Southwestern Journal of Anthropology*, 1951, nr. 7 (3), pp. 230-47.

[37] H. Blochmann (transl.), *The Āʾīn-i Akbarī*, 3 vols. (New Delhi 1977-8), II, p. 406.

[38] Cf. Wink, *Al-Hind*, II, p. 210.

[39] *Ibidem*, III, p. 120.

of Kabul. This was an area that, according to some historians, was almost depopulated by the massacres of Chingis Khan.[40] In the fifteenth and early sixteenth centuries the Hazaras are still found all over the map – nomadizing with their sheep, in fast-moving military formations of cavalry, or migrating to India in search of employment on an individual or family basis. Sultan Husayn Mirza, the Timurid ruler of Herat, is on record to have brought under control (*ẕabṭ*) an unprecedented number of turbulent 'Hazaras and Nögödaris' in Ghur and Zamindawar in the 1480s.[41] According to Babur, there were 'Turks, Mongols, Aymaqs and nomad troops (*ahšām*, lit.'tented tribes'), Afghans, and Hazaras which filled Kabul and Ghazna with evil and tumult (*šarr-o-šor*)'.[42] 'Hazaras and Nögödarīs of whom some speak Mongolian (*bazabān-i muġūl*)' and 'Hazaras and Afghans who are nomads (*sahrānišīn*, 'dwellers in the wasteland') in the western mountain zone (*kohistān*) of the Wilayat of Kabul'ī[43] 'strongholds and dwellings' (*maʾman-o-maskan*) of 'the tribe (*qaum*) of the Nögödaris and Hazaras' in the mountain zones (*kohistān*) of Karnu and Ghur in the Lamghanat and Peshawar districts, and 'Hazaras' in the valleys of Ghurband, to the east and north of Kabul;[44] 'Turkman Hazaras' with their flocks and herds of sheep and horses, corrals and tents in the *qišlāq*-s of the Khush valley;[45] and 'Hazaras' in Bamiyan.[46] Later in the sixteenth century, Abu 'l-Fazl wrote in the *Āʾīn-i-Akbarī* that the 'Hazaras and Afghans' were the two chief pastoral-nomadic tribes of the Mughal sarkar of Kabul, and he located the Hazaras in the area

[40] A. Janata, 'Die Bevölkerung von Ghor: Beitrage zur Ethnographie und Ethnogenese der Chahar Aimaq', *Archiv für Völkerkunde* 1962/3, Bd. XVII/XVIII, p. 126.

[41] *BN*, 172b; Jalāl al-Dīn Humāʾī (ed.), *Habīb al-siyar fī akhbār-i afrād-i bashar* of Xvandamir, 4 vols. (Tehran, AH 1333), III, pp. 150, 276; IV, pp. 170, 293.

[42] *BN*, 187b; Babur also wrote that many tribes and clans (*ayāl-o-ūlūs*) had come to Kabul from Samarqand, Hissar and Qunduz, and that it was a military (*saif*) rather than a civilian city (*qalam*) (144b).

[43] *Ibidem*, 131, 137b, 140.

[44] *Ibidem*, 128, 135b.

[45] *Ibidem*, 160, 195-7.

[46] *Ibidem*, 162.

'from Ghazna to Qandahar and from Maidan (slightly southwest of Kabul) to the confines of Balkh', estimating their number to have been more than a hundred thousand families or 'households', all possessing horses, sheep and goats.[47] Throughout the sixteenth century, and long afterwards, Hazaras and Nögödaris are mentioned in the Mughal chronicles. Substantial numbers, running in the tens of thousands, of 'Hazaras', 'Hazaras and Afghans', and 'Hazaras and Nögödaris and others' fought in the armies of the Timurids and their rivals, mostly as cavalry (sometimes also as infantry) next to Afghans, smaller numbers of Baluchis, and sometimes regiments of Arabs as well – in Kabul and adjacent Wilayats but also deeper into the subcontinent.[48] By the later sixteenth century however the 'Hazarajāt' or 'Bamiyan' had become identified as 'the Hazara country'.[49] This is where they remained; early in the nineteenth century the Hazaras had become practically confined to the latter area. Elphinstone estimated their number between 300,000 and 350,000.[50] Their rugged country, in the eastern Paropamisan mountains between Kabul and Herat, was unfavorable to agriculture due to the sterility of its soils and the severity of the climate, and hence produced little grain.[51] The Hazaras still lived mostly off their flocks of sheep, bred oxen, and produced a 'very strong and useful breed of ponies' for export.[52] Their economy, in other words, was still predominantly pastoral, although they had also adopted agriculture and their mobility was quite diminished. But the Hazaras, in

---

[47] Blochmann, *The Āʾīn-i Akbarī*, II, p. 406. Masson confirms in the early nineteenth century that 'the Hazaras would also seem to have held the country from Karabagh to Ghazni, but have been (…) expelled (…) [by the Afghans]' (Ch. Masson, *Narrative of Various Journeys in Balochistan, Afghanistan and the Panjab, 1826 to 1838*, 4 vols. (1842; New Delhi 1997-2001), II, p. 224).

[48] *BN*, 251b, 250, 293b; *AN*, I, 209, 229, 230, 234, 240, 257, 285, 301; II, 126, 186, 279; III, 364, 652, 669, 776, 822.

[49] H. Beveridge (transl.), *The Akbarnama of Abu-l-Fazl*, 3 vols. (New Delhi, 1979) (henceforward *AN*, with folio pagination), I, 293; II, 126; III, 822.

[50] Elphinstone, *An Account of the Kingdom of Caubul*, II, p. 213.

[51] *Ibidem*, p. 208.

[52] *Ibidem*, I, p. 189.

the early nineteenth century, lived mostly in villages of twenty to two hundred thatched houses, sunk in the slopes of the hills, each defended by a high tower capable of containing ten to twenty men, with only some still living in 'Tartar tents'.[53] Their language, by then, was a dialect of Persian, with as yet a considerable sprinkling of Turkish and purely Mongolian words, and they had all converted to Shiᶜism. They differed from the Afghans in every possible way, except that they too now raised mainly sheep. With no account of their origins, a tradition declared them the offspring of Mongols. They were still referred to as Mongols by others, and they were often confounded with the Mongols and Chaghatays who resided near Herat, although they could not comprehend the latter's language.[54] The Hazaras had 'strong Tartar features', let their women go unconcealed and had a reputation for prostitution, due to a custom called *kuri bistan* or 'wife lending' which Elphinstone ascribes to their Mongol heritage.[55] Living extremely simple lives, they amused themselves with bare back horse races, archery, singing and poetry, and were regarded as 'very passionate, fickle and capricious'.[56]

The other frequently mentioned ethnic group of non-Afghan pastoral nomads in sixteenth-century Indo-Khurasan are the Aymaqs, more precisely the Chahar Aymaqs or 'Four Aymaqs' (the word is simply a Turko-Mongol term for 'tribe' and is often used in Persian in combination with *ahšām* ['tented tribes']).[57] The history of the Aymaqs is perhaps even more obscure than that of the Hazaras. They are first mentioned in Babur's memoirs, and their modern descendants, who live in the Paropamisan mountain range to the west of the Hazaras, are ethnographically among the least well-known peoples of Afghanistan.[58] Babur mentions Ay-

[53] *Ibidem*, II, pp. 208, 210.

[54] *Ibidem*, II, pp. 202-3.

[55] *Ibidem*, II, pp. 208-9. Wilfred Thesiger, visiting the Hazaras in the mid-twentieth century, doubted the existence of *kuri bistan* and thought it was a fabrication, but affirmed that the Hazara women were 'not very chaste' (*Among the Mountains: Travels through Asia* (London, 2000), p. 75).

[56] Elphinstone, *An Account of the Kingdom of Caubul*, II, p. 210.

[57] *BN*, 145b.

[58] G. Mandersloot, *Firozkohi: Een Afghaans Reisjournaal* (Rotterdam, 1971), pp. 7, 87.

maqs (T. Aymaqlar) among the nomads (*sahrānišīn*) of the Wilayat of Qunduz, on the northern side of the Hindu Kush, as well as among those of other parts of Khurasan, and of Samarqand, in and around AD 1505, next to the Nögödaris and Turkish nomad tribes such as the Yilanchuq and Qaqshal.[59] He also mentions them as one of the *qaums* living in the glens and plains of the Wilayat of Kabul, together with Turks and Arabs (the latter possibly brought there by Timur);[60] with other Turkish nomads in the summer pastures (*yailāq*-s) of Ghurband;[61] as a wandering (*kūč*) tribe in the winter pastures (*qišlāq*-s) of Lamghanat;[62] to the west of the Hazaras, in the summer pastures (*yailāq*) of Yay, Astarob and adjacent regions, as well as in the Koh-i-Saf.[63] He recalls that during one of those years he had induced Aymaqs by means of promises and enticements to migrate and come to Kabul from the other side of the Hindu Kush but that, since Kabul was too confined a territory and did not provide adequate summer and winter pastures for the herds of 'these Aymaqs and Turks' they had asked for and received permission to cross back to the other side, to Qunduz and Baghlan.[64] Babur then observed that 'if left to their own devices, nomads (*sahrānišīn*) would have no desire for Kabul'.[65] In the sixteenth century, many Aymaqs appear to have continued their nomadic existence, breeding sheep and horses, to the north of the Hindu Kush, 'in Turan', and in Badakhshan, Kahmard, and around Balkh.[66] Close to the Uzbeks, they often served in their armies, but they also fought on the Timurids' side and became renowned in Mughal India as superior horsemen, with some Aymaq leaders entering the Mughal nobility. Most Aymaqs however ended up in what became the new Aymaq homeland in the western Paropa-

---

59 *BN*, 125b, 140.

60 *Ibidem*, 131; L.W. Adamec, *Historical and Political Gazetteer of Afghanistan*, 6 vols. (Graz, 1972-85), VI, pp. 37 ff.

61 *BN*, 136.

62 *Ibidem*, 145.

63 *Ibidem*, 162b, 184b.

64 *Ibidem*, 237b.

65 *Ibidem*.

66 *AN*, I, 276, 289, 299; II, 124, 187; III, 154, 444-5, 567-78, 583, 723, 790.

misan mountains. Elphinstone mentions them there and nowhere else, estimating their number to have been between 400,000 and 450,000 in the early nineteenth century.[67] At that time the Aymaqs still lived almost entirely in tents (mostly of the Mongol type called *xargah*, although some had taken to the black Afghan tents) grouped together in ordus or camps, keeping many sheep but also rearing 'a small, but active and hardy breed of horses, of which many are exported'.[68] Their country was less mountainous than that of the Hazaras, and it had wide and grassy valleys in places, but there were steep and inaccessible fortresses where all visitors had to be drawn up with ropes. The few villages in the valleys where wheat, barley and millet were cultivated, were all inhabited by Tajiks.[69] The Aymaqs' headdress was more often a cap of black lamb-skin than a turban.[70] Unlike Afghans, they ate horse-meat.[71]

Afghan tribal society

In the fifteenth and early sixteenth centuries, the economy of the Afghans and other pastoral-nomadic populations of the Kabul Wilayat and its Kohistan extensions was thus primarily based on sheep raising, while horse breeding was limited, and agriculture and trade were supplementary activities for the pastoral-nomadic populations themselves and practiced full time only by sedentary, Persian-speaking Tajiks and other peasant populations settled in villages scattered or clustered throughout much of the area. The Afghans typically lived in black tents and shared a common *kūčī* or *pūyanda*, that is to say nomadic, culture that set them apart from peasants and townspeople alike and remained an essential part of Afghan tribal life until recent times.[72] Afghans who lived in villages continued to share in this culture, engaging in agricul-

67 Elphinstone, *An Account of the Kingdom of Caubul*, II, p. 208.
68 *Ibidem*, p. 206.
69 *Ibidem*, pp. 204, 206.
70 *Ibidem*, p. 206.
71 *Ibidem.*
72 Arlinghaus, *Transformation of Afghan Tribal Society*, pp. 22, 41, 79.

ture in a distinct and less laborious fashion.[73] Such Afghans still lived in tents or mat huts during the part of the year they spent in their *qišlāq*-s or winter pastures, while Tajiks did not spend any part of the year in tents or mat huts.

Being pastoral and nomadic, the basic organizing principle of Afghan tribal society was not territory but kinship. Tribal ideology valued kinship solidarity and respect for lineage elders above all else, and promoted individual freedom, hospitality, generosity, and bravery. Each tribe or *ūlūs* constituted 'a complete commonwealth within itself'[74] and consisted of segmentary lineages, also called *ūlūs*, which were theoretically all descended from a single ancestor. Unlike Tajiks who identified with a town, village or region, Afghans defined themselves in kinship terms and knew the genealogies of their patrilineal descent groups going back six or seven generations. This was the reason Afghan tribal society knew of no chiefs or rulers and was fundamentally egalitarian, a kinship of equals.[75] Leadership was in the hands of maliks or khans – the natural heads of lineages and tribes – but effective power and authority rested with tribal councils or jirgas. A famous saint among the Yusufzai Afghans is said to have left his tribe this blessing and curse, 'That they should always be free, but that they should never be united'.[76] Throughout history, the Afghan tribes did not develop kingdoms or chiefdoms in Afghanistan itself, with the exception of the Ghilzais and Durranis (or Abdalis) in the eighteenth century. Even in the eighteenth century, Ahmad Shah Abdali required less exertion to conquer all neighboring kingdoms than to subdue his own countrymen.[77] Moreover, in the Kingdom of Kabul the government was remarkably moderate towards its own subjects; more specifically, the Persian practice of blinding or maiming the common people was unknown among Afghans.[78]

73 *Ibidem*, pp. 80-2.
74 Elphinstone, *An Account of the Kingdom of Caubul*, I, p. 210.
75 Arlinghaus, *Transformation of Afghan Tribal Society*, p. 90.
76 Elphinstone, *An Account of the Kingdom of Caubul*, I, p. 231.
77 *Ibidem*, p. 233.
78 *Ibidem*, p. 248.

The tribal customary law of *Paštunvali*, embracing the notion that it was every man's right and duty to do himself justice, included hospitality (*melmastyā*), revenge (*badal*), and giving refuge (*nanawatai*).[79] Any violation of this code would result in a deeply dreaded loss of honour, and the invocation of shame or *peġor*, insult, humiliation, castigation, and instigation. *Paštunvali*, as a tribal code, was fundamentally at odds with Islamic religious law, and purda, the concealment of women, was traditionally not part of it and only developed at a later stage when the Afghan nomads moved from open-air camping grounds into the seclusion of towns. Hospitality did not extend beyond the lands of the tribe, and particularly the most pastoral tribes were prone to robbery – although not normally murder, or wanton cruelty – of strangers and trespassers with whom they had no genealogical relationship. Especially the Afridi, Shinwari and other Afghans of the Khyber pass were notorious for the rapacity with which they attacked caravans coming through their lands; and so were all tribes of the Sulayman mountains.[80]

Even within the tribes there was constant discord about *zan*, *zer* and *zamīn* (women, wealth and land).[81] The slightest occasion would give rise to a dispute; extreme jealousy prevailed. The tribesmen lived in constant fear of violence and never went about unarmed. This characteristic feature of Afghan life is what outside observers like Elphinstone referred to as the 'turbulence of the tribesmen' or 'a state of anarchy', what nowadays journalists often refer to as the 'lawlessness' of the frontier.[82] Masson says that 'the Khaibaris, like other rude Afghan tribes, have their maleks, or chiefs, but the authority of these is very limited; and as every individual has a voice on public affairs, it is impossible to describe the confusion that exists amongst them'.[83] It was the same 'clannish spirit' that made Afghan unity difficult or impossible to achieve, even though it did not preclude an interest in the

---

[79] *Ibidem*, p. 220; Arlinghaus, *Transformation of Afghan Tribal Society*, pp. 101-8.

[80] Wink, *Al-Hind*, III, p. 90; *BN*, 131b, 132, 139, 213b.

[81] Arlinghaus, *Transformation of Afghan Tribal Society*, p. 102.

[82] Elphinstone, *An Account of the Kingdom of Caubul*, II, pp. 21, 23.

[83] Masson, *Narrative of Various Journeys*, I, p. 163.

honour of the Afghan name – as the verses of the Pashto poet Khushal make clear. In practice, lineages cooperated at the lowest level necessary to meet an outside challenge; tribal alliances were ad hoc, and tribal confederations were the exception in Afghan history and disintegrated at the first opportunity.[84] Afghan nomads rarely paid taxes in kind or in services, even after they sedentarized.[85]

When moving against the peasant societies of the plains and valleys of northern Indo-Khurasan, or against the Sultanate of Swat, Afghan tribal organization could be turned into an advantage. Their pastoral economy, kinship solidarity and egalitarianism gave the Afghans mobility and allowed them to concentrate large numbers of men against local, stratified societies of sedentary peasants (often presided over by an alien elite) which were organized to defend only small areas.[86]

Tribal Afghans, however, were no match for the imperial Mongols at any time in their history. There were three reasons for this. The first is that the Mongols – as much as their sixteenth-century offshoots like the Uzbeks and the Mughals – had long broken the kinship solidarity of their tribes and were unified under a central command structure headed by individual khans. The Mongols thus operated on a higher level of military organization than the tribal Afghans. 'All Tartar tribes' Elphinstone rightly observed, 'conferred (...) much power on the chiefs,' and this was 'the great difference' between their government and that of the Afghans.[87] Among the Uzbeks of Bukhara, such centralized leadership was 'the result of a long exertion on the part of the government, which is stated to have from ancient times practiced the policy of dividing and mixing the various tribes under its authority, and of keeping the great men from all employments that might give them influence over the people with whom they

---

[84] Arlinghaus, *Transformation of Afghan Tribal Society*, p. 101.

[85] *Ibidem*, p. 198; Elphinstone, *An Account of the Kingdom of Caubul*, I, pp. 219, 229-30, 265, 337, 408, 410; II, pp. 26, 30, 71, 104, 111, 157, 170, 180, 245, 259, 266.

[86] Arlinghaus, *Transformation of Afghan Tribal Society*, pp. 41, 44, 78, 128, 222-3.

[87] Elphinstone, *An Account of the Kingdom of Caubul*, II, p. 188.

are connected by birth'.[88] The Uzbek state was, moreover, a conquest state which retained its military organization, in a country that was flat, and hence unfavorable to the preservation of the independence of tribes or small groups.[89] The same basic pattern was found among the Aymaqs, Hazaras and Mughals. The Aymaqs were organized under chiefs who had all the rights of absolute monarchs, inhabiting strong castles, some of them with palaces where they maintained small courts, private armies and retinues, while levying taxes from their tribes.[90] The Hazara tribes had their own Sultans, whose power was absolute, and some of whom also lived in castles with their retinues.[91] The Mughals under the Timurid prince Babur were a predatory organization which represented something between a chiefdom and a state or emerging empire with better disciplined troops under a single and much superior leadership against which the Afghans were ineffective, except when operating against very small numbers or within mountain fastnesses.[92]

The second reason is that the Mongols, unlike the Afghans, were a horse warrior people, and had perfected the art of mounted archery, while they also possessed siege engines and had become acquainted with artillery at an earlier stage. The Afghans rode horses which were not inferior, and they had infantry bowmen, and chain mail, but they were not mounted archers like the Turko-Mongol peoples of the steppes. When, between 1540 and 1565, the Yusufzai Afghan tribal confederation reached the peak of its power in the Peshawar area under Khan Kaju, they were still no more than an assembly of 'one hundred thousand spearmen'.[93] In a famous passage, Babur describes how the Af-

88 *Ibidem*, pp. 188-9.

89 *Ibidem*, p. 189.

90 *Ibidem*, p. 205.

91 *Ibidem*, pp. 211, 213.

92 Cf. Arlinghaus, *Transformation of Afghan Tribal Society*, pp. 43, 78, 129, 161, 223.

93 *Ibidem*, pp. 217, 220, 225, 254. Manucci wrote about the Yusufzai in the later sixteenth century, when they were attacked by Akbar: 'He [Akbar] determined (...) to make war against the Pathan tribe, which dwells on the other side of the Indus River, to the west, up to the boundary of the Kabul kingdom. There are in these regions several princes, all of whom

ghans of Bajaur had never seen firearms (*tufak*), betrayed no fear of matchlocks, and even made fun of these with obscene gestures when they first encountered them.[94]

The third reason that the Mongols prevailed is that they and their sixteenth-century descendants, operated with a brutality, ferociousness and ruthlessness that was unknown among the Afghans. The tribal Afghans were generally lambasted by Timurid Turks, Persians and Indians alike as rude, unrefined, obtuse, and lacking in vision, but their 'code of war' was not brutal in the way that of the Mongols was.[95] According to one sixteenth-century author, Badauni, 'it was the code (*tora*) of Chingis Khan to massacre or make slaves of all the inhabitants [of a conquered region] (…) to destroy utterly many towns and villages and sweep everything clean and clear (…) to value God's creation as if it were but radishes, cucumbers and leeks'.[96] Another sixteenth-century historian, Muhammad Haydar Dughlat, wrote of the nomadic Chaghatay Mongols of an earlier time that 'they were as wild as the beasts of their mountains'.[97] Timur saw himself as part of the same Turko-Mongol tradition of ferocious, bestial steppe warriors that brooked no opposition. As Babur wrote, 'havoc and destruction have always emanated from the Mongol nation (*az ūlūs-i-muġūl*)'.[98] Babur, of course, saw himself as a Turk and a Timurid prince of much greater refinement than his nomadic ancestors and his attitude towards them

---

dwell in the midst of mountains. They are a very ferocious people, of fair complexion, and all adherents of the Mahomedan faith. One of these princes alone can collect three hundred thousand lancemen, all barbarous, uncouth, and unruly, for they do not make much use of cavalry' (W. Irvine (transl.), *Mogul India or Storia do Mogor by Niccolao Manucci*, 4 vols. (Delhi, 2005) (henceforward *Manucci*), I, p. 135).

94 *BN*, p. 217.

95 Wink, *Al-Hind*, II, pp. 117, 193; III, pp. 134-5; *BN*, 226b, 227; Elphinstone, *An Account of the Kingdom of Caubul*, I, pp. 324, 326, 374.

96 G.S.A. Ranking et al. (transl.), *Muntakhab-at-Tawarikh of Al--Badauni*, 3 vols. (New Delhi, 1990) (henceforward *MT*), II, p. 50.

97 Muhammad Haydar Dughlát, *The Tarikh-i-Rashidi; a History of the Moghuls of Central Asia; an English version*, transl. and ed. D. Ross and N. Elias (1898; rpt.: New York, 1970), p. 153.

98 *BN*, 64b.

reflects this. At the same time, it is undeniable that Babur dealt with the Afghans of his time with the same unspeakable brutality that had been characteristic of the Mongols for centuries. Babur's autobiographical writings are full of episodes in which he describes himself as remorselessly engaged in massacres of the Afghans, torturing them to death, impaling them, and routinely beheading them, leaving behind towers of their skulls (*kalla-menār*), while taking captive their women and children.[99] It was only in the later sixteenth- and seventeenth-century Mughal empire that such conduct became less common, although even then the 'Tartar' code of warfare was still practiced, notably by the Uzbeks. One Uzbek warlord in Mughal service, Abdullah Khan, for instance, in 1619-20, with his 12,000 horse and 20,000 foot, destroyed many 'rebel' towns in the Kalpi-Kanauj area, taking some 200,000 women and children as slaves to be sold in Persia, and erecting some 260 pillars made of almost ten thousand heads of the massacred men.[100] Even as late as the early nineteenth century the nomadic Uzbeks adhered to these brutal old ways. 'Their laws of war are certainly most barbarous', writes Elphinstone.[101] Renowned for their exertions in predatory war, the Uzbeks gave no quarter to any enemies except Shi^{c}as and infidels whom they could sell in Bukhara like cattle.[102] Even the Aymaqs, according to Elphinstone's information, although generally more quiet and orderly than the Afghans because of their despotic government, 'in their wars, where they are released from this restraint (...) show a degree of ferocity never heard of among the Afghans'.[103] There were authentic accounts of Aymaqs throwing their prisoners from precipices and shooting them to death with arrows in just the same way that the Mongols treated their prisoners, and of Aymaqs drinking the warm blood of their victims,

---

[99] *Ibidem*, 147-8, 150b, 158, 203, 213b, 218-218b, 221-221b, 238, 305.

[100] R.C. Temple (ed.), *The Travels of Peter Mundy in Europe and Asia, 1608-1667*, 5 vols. (London, 1914-24), II, pp. 90, 185-6, 207.

[101] Elphinstone, *An Account of the Kingdom of Caubul*, II, p. 194.

[102] *Ibidem*, pp. 193-4.

[103] *Ibidem*, p. 206.

and rubbing it over their faces and beards.[104] According to a fable common in both India and Khurasan, the Hazaras could eat out the liver of any person on whom they fixed their eyes.[105] Abu 'l-Fazl says about the Hazaras that 'their conventions of amity savor of the wolf'.[106] By contrast, the Afghans were regarded as relatively mild in their disposition. They were 'devils', but 'good devils', whereas the Uzbeks were 'devils altogether'.[107] They did not torture their prisoners to death, built no towers of skulls of vanquished opponents, and did not customarily enslave the latter's wives and children. Although there were foreign slaves among the Afghans (mostly descendants of Hindu captives taken in early campaigns, as well as some Kafirs purchased from their own nation and some Abyssinians brought back from Arabia), carrying off slaves was a practice the Afghans held in horror – at least outside the subcontinent.[108] They reviled the Uzbeks for this practice and applied to them with disgust the appellation of *ādam-faroš* or 'sellers of men'.[109]

The failure of empire

Like tribal people generally, the Afghans developed myths about their origins. The Afghan origin myths, however, are remarkable for two reasons. First, they provide evidence that the Afghans have no memory of a Hindu-Buddhist or 'pagan' past; in other words, that they do not claim to have been the mythic builders of

[104] *Ibidem*, p. 207.

[105] *Ibidem*, p. 210.

[106] Blochmann, *The Ā'īn-i Akbarī*, II, p. 406.

[107] Masson, *Narrative of Various Journeys*, II, p. 293.

[108] Afghans born and raised in the Indian subcontinent sold women and children of their opponents into slavery without much scruple (cf. S.M. Imām ad-Dīn (ed. and transl.), *The Tārīkh-i-Sher Shāhī of 'Abbas Khān Sarwānī, Volume I (Persian text) and II (English translation)* (Dacca, 1964) (henceforward *TSS*), I, p. 29 (II, p. 21), p. 185 (II, p. 141)).

[109] Elphinstone, *An Account of the Kingdom of Caubul*, I, pp. 318-20; Masson, *Narrative of Various Journeys*, I, p. 295 supports this: '(...) if Afghans were to be encountered, he might hope to pass through them, but that with Baloches and Turkomans he had little chance; while he had no wish to be consigned to slavery'.

the gigantic Buddha statues on the ancient trade route through Bamiyan, to the west of the capital of Kabul. Second, the Afghans claim descent from Qais, a Companion of the Prophet and a direct descendant of King Saul, the first king of the Israelites, and thus proclaim not only their essential unity as a people but to have been Muslims since the very beginnings of Islam.[110]

As already indicated, the real ethnogenesis of the Afghans is quite murky.[111] Linguistic evidence does not corroborate the origin myths. Pashto – which the Prophet declared to be a language from Hell – is not a Semitic language but appears to have evolved from an eastern Iranian 'Saka' dialect introduced from the north, and this makes it plausible that nomadic Sakas ('Scythians') or remnants of the Hephthalites formed an important segment of the evolving Afghan nation in ancient times. The historical record of this stage of the evolution of the Afghans as an ethnic group is extremely thin. What we have is no more than some vague references in Sanskrit and Chinese from the decades immediately preceding the rise of Islam. These appear to point at 'Afghans' by that name although the latter's exact location cannot be gauged from them.[112]

It is the Afghan legends that point at the semi-arid, mountainous country astride the Sulayman mountains or Kase Ghar, i.e. the Toba and Kakar ranges and the mountains of Zurmat, or 'Roh', as the original 'Afghanistan'. The Arab geographers, from about the tenth century on, confirm this view and identify the Zhob district, on an important route from India to the west, and the Koh Sulayman – which in its most extended sense comprehends all the southern mountains of present-day Afghanistan – as the habitat of the 'Abghān'. The Arab geographers also indicate that in Roh the Afghans had become involved in mercantile rela-

[110] Wink, *Al-Hind*, I, pp. 95, 167; Elphinstone, *An Account of the Kingdom of Caubul*, I, pp. 205-6; Arlinghaus, *Transformation of Afghan Tribal Society*, pp. 109-10.

[111] See above, p. 271.

[112] Wink, *Al-Hind*, II, p. 115.

tionships with the Banī Isrā'īl or 'Israelites', although they do not yet identify them as Muslims.[113]

Ferishta is the only Indo-Muslim historian who insists that the Afghans were Muslims as early as the seventh century AD, when they invaded areas north of Multan as far as Peshawar, effected an alliance with the Ghakkars in the Salt Range and erected a fort in the Khyber hills from where they subdued an area from Swat and Bajaur in the north to Sibi and Bhakkar in Sind, and from Hasan Abdal in the east to Kabul and Qandahar in the west – most of which they held on to through Samanid times.[114] Ferishta also maintains that many Arabs who came to Sind during Muhammad bin Qasim's campaign chose to stay with the Afghans.[115] If Ferishta's account is correct, it is not clear what this earliest Afghan expansion really amounted to, or whether it was permanent, and how many Afghans were involved in it. Ferishta may well have confused these events with later ones of the fifteenth and sixteenth centuries. What is generally not doubted is that Islam came to what is now eastern Afghanistan at an early stage, although at first it was not widely disseminated, and that it gained momentum under the early Saffarids and by the end of the tenth century the Afghans were expanding their range of activities in every direction but southwards, while also gradually becoming the primary carriers of merchandise between India and Central Asia.[116] The Afghans were a tribal people, but they were never isolated and, from the beginning, took note of the wider world. The marginality of the mountainous environment of their medieval homeland of Afghanistan made the Afghans more, not less, sensitive to larger commercial practices.[117]

---

[113] *Ibidem*, I, p. 167; II, p. 115; Elphinstone, *An Account of the Kingdom of Caubul*, I, p. 201.

[114] Wink, *Al-Hind*, I, p. 168.

[115] *Ibidem*, II, pp. 115-16.

[116] *Ibidem*, I, p. 201; II, p. 129; Arlinghaus, *Transformation of Afghan Tribal Society*, pp. 39, 69, 134.

[117] For this observation, with reference to the Appennines, see C. Wickham, *The Mountains and the City: The Tuscan Appennines in the Early Middle Ages* (Oxford, 1988), p. 359.

The Afghans' attempts at empire building, however, in sharp contrast to those of the Turko-Mongols, were always thwarted sooner or later by their inability to overcome their tribal ways. The historical record shows that at first the Afghans were auxiliaries in the Turkish-led *jihād* campaigns in India and that as such their role was by no means insignificant, even though Afghan historians of the seventeenth and eighteenth centuries are prone to exaggerate it, particularly in the earliest stages of Islamic expansion under the Ghaznavids, and often proclaim the Afghans to have been a crucial element in these campaigns, but they do not argue that the Afghans built their own empires at that stage.[118] From the thirteenth century they at times provided military support to the Mongols, and they were often deployed in frontier warfare by the Delhi Sultanate, or as infantry in especially treacherous mountain terrain, or as garrisons of hilltop fortresses. Afghan conversion to Islam definitely accelerated in this context of imperial expansion, even though it was far from complete by the twelfth and thirteenth centuries. By then the area of Afghan nomadic activity was also expanding beyond the Sulayman mountains, and we begin to see Afghan nomads occupying new lands in places like Binban and Ghur, while later in the thirteenth century they also began moving towards the Khyber pass and Peshawar, towards Qandahar, and into Mastung, northern Baluchistan.[119] With the advent of the Mongols, large areas of the Panjab – including the Sind Sagar Doab, the Potwar plateau, and the Jech and Rechna Doabs up to the Ravi river – began to suffer significant population losses and here too nomadic Afghans, with numerous other ethnic groups, including Turks, began to move in.[120] In the wake of Timur's withdrawal there was again a gen-

[118] Wink, *Al-Hind*, I, p. 169; II, pp. 113, 115-18, 137, 160, 193-4, 207, 210.

[119] Wink, *Al-Hind*, II, pp. 137, 169; III, pp. 128-9, 207; I.H. Siddiqui, 'The Afghans and their emergence in India as ruling elite during the Delhi Sultanate period', *Central Asiatic Journal*, 1982, nr. 26 (3-4), p. 246; Elphinstone, *An Account of the Kingdom of Caubul*, II, p. 9.

[120] H.G. Raverty, *Notes on Afghanistan and Parts of Baluchistan, Geographical, Ethnological, and Historical* (London, 1888), p. 222.

eral movement of all kinds of nomadic tribes seeking new lands on both sides of the Indus.

There was thus a number of generations of Afghans who achieved a modest measure of prominence within the context of the emerging Indo-Islamic states, and there is evidence of some intermarriage between Afghans, Turks, Mongols, Khalaj, as well as Indians.[121] In India, the Afghans were often bracketed with the Khalaj, and in the late thirteenth and early fourteenth centuries it was especially the Khalaji dynasty (1290-1320) that promoted the Afghans. Afghans played a substantial but still auxiliary military role under the Tughluq dynasty of Delhi (1320-1414) as well as under some of the regional Indo-Islamic dynasties that emerged in the second half of the fourteenth century, in Gujarat, Malwa, Bengal, Jaunpur, Multan, as well as in the Panjab, parts of the Doab, and possibly elsewhere.[122] Up to the mid-fifteenth century, however, there was no independent Afghan dynasty that made an attempt to build an empire of its own.

The Lodi Sultanate

The reason no such attempt was made is that up to the mid-fifteenth century there were no significant changes in Afghan society that had the potential to undermine its tribal structures. Ultimately such change could only be brought about by the increase of commercial traffic through their territories. This is where the roots of Afghan empire building can be found.

For centuries Afghans of various tribes had been migrating in autumn from their mountains and plateaus to the valley of the Indus, spent the winter in what are now the North-West Frontier Province, the adjacent tribal agencies or FATA territories of Pakistan, the Panjab, and Baluchistan, and had been returning in the spring. Known throughout these regions as either *kūčī*-s, *pūyanda*-s or *māldār*-s ('wealth-owners'), the great advantage these Afghans enjoyed over other pastoral nomads was that their annual pastoral migrations coincided with important trade routes between India, Persia and Turan. Afghan pastoral nomads drove

121 Wink, *Al-Hind*, I, p. 116; II, p. 120; III, pp. 127 n. 37, 128.

122 *Ibidem*, III, pp. 129-35, 138-48.

flocks of sheep and goats, rented out camels, guarded caravans, and engaged in trade, particularly trade in imported horses – an ever more crucial commodity on the Indian markets.[123] While all Afghans were alike in the sense that they shared the same tribal culture, spoke Pashto, and were Sunni Muslims of the Hanafi school, subtle but in the long term significant differences existed or could arise between the purely pastoral nomads and the pastoral nomads who were engaged in trade.[124] The tribes whose country enabled them to raise camels were more likely to gain ascendancy in some of the trade and thus had an initial advantage over those who did not have that ability. The trading nomads would travel in caravans of camels, and sometimes of mules, donkeys, and bullocks, mostly carrying the goods of others and only sometimes their own, and they would travel greater distances than the purely pastoral tribes. While the purely pastoralist nomads would remain in the hilly tracts or along the skirt of the hills, the trading nomads would more commonly pitch their tents in the plains and sometimes leave their families in Afghanistan. With or without their families, the trading nomads reached into the furthest regions of the subcontinent (as far as Bihar, Bengal, the Deccan, and Gujarat), and in the other direction travelled to Qandahar and from there as far as Persia, and, with horses and ponies, across the Hindu Kush, to Bukhara. The caravans, often traveling at night, did not encamp in the country at the end of their journeys, like those of the pastoral tribes, but put up in caravanserais in towns – large square structures, surrounded by apartments, with a mosque and often a bath in the middle, and a common gateway.

By the fourteenth and fifteenth centuries, Afghan pastoral--nomadic tribesmen had become the primary carriers of a huge volume of trade goods of all kinds (textiles, spices, horses, and many others), operating in caravans of ten, fifteen, or twenty thousand pack animals. It was a very extensive trading network. The roads travelled by the Afghan caravans, at about 8 to 10 miles per twenty-four hour day, were among the most discourag-

[123] *Ibidem*, p. 89.

[124] J.A. Robinson, *Notes on Nomad Tribes of Eastern Afghanistan* (1934; Lahore, 1978), pp. 2-25.

ing imaginable, leading northwards from Kabul through the Panjshir, Parwan and Ghurband valleys, on to the passes of the Hindu Kush, to Qunduz and Baglan, and eastwards through Nangrahar, the Khyber pass and then the Peshawar plain, crossing the Indus at Hazro, 15 miles above Atak, or at Nilab, 10 miles below Atak; or they went through the Logar valley towards Ghazna or Gardiz, and through the Gomal, Tochi and Kurram river valleys, to the Derajat and Bannu. In general the *pūyanda*-s or trading nomads were even more democratic in their internal government than the purely pastoral tribes of the Afghans.[125] The hereditary maliks of the Afghan trading nomads were often chiefs in name only, possessing nothing more than a shadow of influence, and even that only during the annual migration, or when fighting was imminent, and the trading nomads were far more impatient of being controlled by their own maliks or any government than other Afghan tribes. The trade as such did not bring any fundamental changes to the Afghans' tribal politics. But the horse trade, like nothing else, gave Afghan trading nomads access to the courts of the Indo-Muslim kings, providing extraordinary influence and privileges, and, as importantly, political intelligence as well as an initiation to a more sophisticated courtly life style that the purely pastoral tribes missed out on.[126] The horse trade was also the one and uniquely important way for Afghans to accumulate wealth, and therefore one of the few sources of inequality in the pastoral and semi-pastoral tribal economy, since tolls and booty obtained in raids were always divided in equal shares among the tribesmen but not the profits made in the horse trade. When nomadic Afghan tribesmen engaged in the horse trade, discrepancies in wealth could become pronounced, and these did have the potential of breaking down the tribal social structure predicated on the kinship of equals.

It is therefore significant that the Lodi nomad tribes living along the trading routes of the Tochi and Gomal valleys were the first Afghans to combine nomadism and the horse trade in a major way. The immediate ancestors of Bahlul Lodi, the founder of the first Afghan empire of Delhi in the second half of the fif-

[125] *Ibidem*, p. 8.
[126] Wink, *Al-Hind*, III, p. 135.

teenth century, were associated with the horse trade and had frequented Hind for many years.[127] In addition, under pressure from the growing power of the Ghilzais on the Ghazna plateau, some maliks of the Lodis had come out of Roh and, on the banks of the Indus, took the opportunity to join Timur, providing him with contingents of horse-mounted warriors as well as supplies of horses for his expedition to Delhi in 1398.[128] The Lodis' rise to political and military ascendancy continued during the first half of the fifteenth century, when numerous members of their tribe (together with other Afghans) were recruited by the Sayyid dynasty of Delhi (1414-51). By the 1440s the Lodis were really the prop of the Sayyids' power.[129] But it was with the support of his fellow tribesmen that Bahlul Lodi subjected the Panjab and was able to seize the throne of Delhi in 1451.

In that year the Lodis became the first Afghan royal dynasty in history, and as such it held on to power until 1526. The dynasty was able to assert its authority over much of north-western and northern India, absorb the territories of the Jaunpur rulers to the east, and, to a degree, succeeded in transforming its initial tribal constituency into a more hierarchically structured and even 'imperial' monarchy. It did so gradually, after severing the tribesmen from their homeland.

Sultan Bahlul Lodi still recruited Lodi Afghan tribesmen from Roh by appealing primarily to their sense of honour and to kinship solidarity. Enlisting on an individual basis, many Lodis desired to return to Roh after each campaign season, even though the Sultan offered them every possible incentive to stay in the form of revenue assignments (*iqṭaᶜ*-s) and governorships. In due course, however, a majority of the Lodi Afghans, together with members of smaller tribes such as the Sarvanis, Jalwanis and Kakars as well as neighbouring non-Afghan peoples such as the Farmulis and Barkis, migrated to India and became separated from the Afghan tribes west of the Indus. The first Lodi Sultan continued to assure his fellow tribesmen that he was a king in

127 *Ibidem*; Arlinghaus, *Transformation of Afghan Tribal Society*, pp. 61, 69.

128 Raverty, *Notes on Afghanistan*, Appendix, p. 22.

129 Wink, *Al-Hind*, III, pp. 134-8.

name only and that their joint conquests in Hind were going to be held by all Lodi tribesmen together, under a sharing arrangement. Loyalty to tribe or clan and kinship thus remained, for some time, the main organizing principle, and the revenue assignments and governorships enjoyed almost complete autonomy, while other Afghan tribes, such as the Niazis and Surs, were excluded from all important posts on a tribal basis. Before his death, Sultan Bahlul Lodi divided the Afghan dominion among his sons and relatives, with only Delhi and some districts in the Doab going to his heir and successor Sultan Sikandar Lodi (r. 1489-1517).

This Afghan tribal organization, however, came under increasing pressure from non-Afghan elements that entered the empire on different terms. Already Sultan Bahlul Lodi employed nearly 20,000 Mongols in his service, and he had begun to increasingly involve the Farmulis in his government. The latter were a Tajik ethnic group named after its district of origin, southeast of Ghazna, whom the Lodis had become associated with during their annual migrations through the Tochi and Gomal valleys.[130] To the Afghan king the Farmulis were useful because they allowed him to have non-Afghan amirs who were loyal and subordinate to him personally rather than 'sharers' of his power. Sultan Sikandar Lodi, himself born of an Indian mother, expanded the policy of absorbing non-Afghan elements, and subsequently, after destroying the Sharqi Sultanate of Jaunpur in 1479, invited a large influx of Tajiks, Mongols, and especially Rajputs into his realm. During Sikandar Lodi's reign, after repeated but half-hearted experiments with dual kingship, it became clear that in Hind tribal sharing arrangements were not going to work. Although not yet abandoning tribal politics altogether, he attempted to do away with the autonomy of the revenue assignments, promoted more and more Rajputs to high positions in his government, and introduced a more intrusive form of supervision throughout the provinces of his realm. Sikandar's son Ibrahim Lodi (r. 1517-26) abandoned tribal politics altogether and attempted to reduce all Afghans to servants of the state, introduc-

130 *Ibidem*, p. 137; on the Farmulis, see Arlinghaus, *Transformation of Afghan Tribal Society*, p. 142.

ing a ranking system of *manṣab*-s among his nobles, and in the end even keeping his own brothers out of any sharing arrangements – although not without briefly reviving dual kingship one final time.[131] Their tribal sense of independence threatened, the Lodi Afghan nobility revolted and then solicited Babur to assist them in regaining their power. Babur, however, terminated the Lodi dynasty and dispersed its Afghan followers to Bihar and Bengal, and to Gujarat.

The Battle of Panipat of 1526, in which a numerically superior Afghan army was defeated by Babur's Mughals, was a historical battle in the sense that it was the first major engagement in Hindustan that was decided by the use of fire arms and artillery in combination with cavalry by the Mughals.[132] It is not certain that the Mughals still entirely monopolized such weapons at that time. In the lengthy description which the *Bāburnāma* devotes to the battle there is no mention of the use of such weapons by the Afghans.[133] A chronicle of Akbar's time does mention the use of artillery and even the Afghan camel gun (*gola zambūrak*) in the Lodi empire, but these references seem anachronistic.[134] Whatever the case may be, the effective use of artillery and matchlocks by the Mughals was one major factor in the defeat of the Afghans. The other major factor was the disunity that prevailed among the Afghans. At Panipat, as one chronicler explains, 'although the Afghan army (*sipāh-i afġānī*) greatly outnumbered its opponents, yet the soldiers were dispirited and disheartened due to the Sultan's ill-treatment [of them] and because the nobles were offended'.[135]

Nomadic expansion in Qandahar

Among the expanding population of pastoral-nomadic Afghan tribes to the west of the Indus, those who lost out in the competi-

131 Wink, *Al-Hind*, III, p. 138.

132 N. Roy (transl.), *Niamatullah's History of the Afghans (Makhzan-i--Afghānī)*, Part I (Santiniketan, 1958), pp. 203-9 (Appendix II).

133 *BN*, 264-8.

134 M. Hidayat Hosain (ed.), *Tārīkh-i-Shāhī of Ahmad Yādgār* (Calcutta, 1939), pp. 22, 84.

135 *Ibidem*, p. 96.

tion for land moved in every direction except south into Baluchi territory. Like the Lodi migrations to India, such migrations of pastoral-nomadic Afghan tribes are especially in evidence in the aftermath of the Mongol-Timurid conquests in the region. But here the Afghan tribal structure was not compromised, and no attempt was made to create an empire.

Beginning in the thirteenth century, the Ghazna plateau and the province of Kabul up to the frontier of Sind, like other parts of Khurasan, suffered much from the devastations of the Mongols.[136] For about seventy years after the defeat of Sultan Jalal ad-Din Mingubirni, the Khwarazm Shah, this region remained under the occupation of various Mongol noyons, as did the greater part of the north-western portion of the Panjab. From here the Mongols were able to make constant raids on the districts on the Indus which belonged to the Delhi Sultanate. Subsequently these same regions came under the Kurats of Herat, a dynasty of Shansabani Tajik Ghurids which also held sovereignty in Khurasan and Ghur and which was under the subjection of the Mongols.[137] The third malik of the Kurat dynasty, Rukn ad-Din Muhammad, in 1281 obtained possession of Qandahar and its dependencies and this area continued in his dynasty's possession until it was brought to submission by Timur in 1383. Qandahar, together with Qunduz, Baqlan, Ghazna, and Kabul were conferred by Timur upon his grandson Mirza Pir Muhammad, who raided the Afghans 'dwelling in the Sulayman mountains'.[138] After the latter's death in 1407, Timur's son and successor Sultan Shah Rukh conferred these territories on Pir Muhammad's son Mirza Qaidu, and Qandahar became his capital.

It was due to the latter's misgovernment that disturbances broke out in Qandahar in 1417 and the Afghan tribes dwelling near the frontier of the province, and others from as far as the Indus valley, seized the opportunity to carry their raids into the Garmsir, causing great damage.[139] In 1418 Sultan Shah Rukh bestowed the government of 'the whole of the territories of

---

136 Raverty, *Notes on Afghanistan*, p. 577.

137 *Ibidem.*

138 *Ibidem*, Appendix, p. 22.

139 *Ibidem*, p. 577.

Qandahar, Ghazna, Kabul, Afghanistan, Sind, and parts of Hind' upon his eldest son Mirza Bae-Sunkar Bahadur and despatched him to Qandahar.[140] The Abdali branch of the Tarin Afghans then came southwards from their homeland in Kase Ghar and obtained grants of land in the south-eastern portion of the province of Qandahar, where they still dwell.[141] Another son and a grandson of Shah Rukh ruled these territories, until Shah Rukh's death in 1447, when great divisions arose in the family of Amir Timur. Sultan Abu-Said Bahadur became for a time all powerful over Timur's empire and in 1468-9 conferred the territories bordering the Indus as far as the frontier of Hind and Afghanistan, i.e. Kabul, Ghazna and their dependencies, upon his son Mirza Ulugh Beg, who held them until his death in 1501.[142] Throughout this time, Afghan tribes continued to expand their power in the arid and semi-arid subregions of Qandahar and Ghazna from their original homeland in Afghanistan. These Afghans maintained their nomadic way of life and in most cases became even more dependent on it. They retained the same tribal organization they had always had and essentially made Qandahar and extension of Afghanistan.

The Afghan conquest of the Kabul Wilayat

Afghan migration and conquest in the northern direction, in the Kabul river basin, the Lamghanat and the Peshawar subregion largely took place in three waves between the late fourteenth century and 1580.[143] For the Afghan nomads these regions, with their intensively irrigated agriculture in many river valleys, were difficult to penetrate. There were no unclaimed or sparsely settled lands here, the limited grazing land that existed was jealously guarded by Turkish and Mongol nomads, while Kabul and the tributary valleys of the Kabul river were well fortified and able to defend themselves against nomads.[144] The Afghans moved into these northern regions in tribal formations and, encountering

140 *Ibidem*, pp. 577-8.
141 *Ibidem*, p. 578.
142 *Ibidem*, p. 579.
143 Arlinghaus, *Transformation of Afghan Tribal Society*, pp. 126-269.
144 *Ibidem*, p. 144.

stratified, agricultural societies of an 'Indian' type, transformed their tribal structure while doing so. But they never abandoned it. In the Kabul river basin and the Peshawar subregion the Afghans again failed to create an imperial structure that transcended their tribal ties and, in the end, they too lost their independence to the Mughals.

When exactly the first Afghan nomads began to make Kabul and surrounding tumans their primary *yailāq*-s or 'summer pastures' is not easy to make out. Perhaps as early as Ghaznavid times they made parts of Nangrahar their *qišlāq*-s or 'winter pastures', while retaining their *yailāq*-s in the Sulayman mountains or on the Ghazna plateau. The first Afghan tribe to be forced to move northwards in the widespread *Völkerwanderung* that occurred during the Mongol invasions and down to the time of Timur were the Dilazaks. In the second half of the fourteenth century, the Dilazak Afghans abandoned their *yailāq*-s in the Sulayman mountains, seized lands along the Kabul river in Nangrahar, in the valley of Peshawar, occupied the valley of Jandol, and then began to cross the river into what is today Hazara district around 1400.[145] This first wave of Afghan migration was followed by a second wave of Khashi Khel or Yusufzai Afghans who reached the Kabul river basin from Ghazna and Qandahar in the first half of the fifteenth century.[146] By the second half of the fifteenth century the Yusufzai were in Kabulistan; there they increased their power and became quite overbearing until the Timurid ruler Ulugh Beg Kabuli (1460-1501) drove them out 'on foot' towards Peshawar between 1470 and 1480.

Thus, in the Kabul and Peshawar areas, Afghan expansion is above all associated with the reign of Ulugh Beg Kabuli, and subsequently with that of his nephew Babur. The latter's concerns with Central Asia and India left the process of Afghan tribal migration and conquests in the Peshawar subregion, especially in the isolated valleys in the north, relatively unchecked. This was a region where Babur had little control. The *Bābur-nāma* mentions the Afghans for the first time in 1504-5, the year Babur 'took Kabul and Ghazna and overran Kohat, Bannu, Dasht

[145] *Ibidem*, pp. 143-4, 169.

[146] *Ibidem*, pp. 145, 148-9, 155.

and Afghanistan'.[147] Between that year and 1508-9, and again from 1518-19 onwards, Babur frequently assaulted Afghans in almost every district, taking many sheep.[148] The tribesmen would withdraw into the hills for safety, or would appear with grass between their teeth, pretending to be cows – a token of surrender that Babur regarded as pathetic but which may have originated as a defense mechanism against Hindu attack.[149] Defeat would often result in a temporary alliance, and Babur went so far as to marry the daughter of a khan of the Yusufzai to seal one such alliance. Complicating the picture further, Babur pressured many Afghan tribesmen to enlist in his army. In the campaigns in Hindustan against the Lodis, there were Afghans and Hazaras, next to Arabs, Baluchis, Turks and Mongols in Babur's army.[150] After 1526, the Khalil and Mohmand tribes living on both sides of the road from Kabul to the Indus via the Khyber pass were generally more loyal to the Timurids than the Yusufzai tribes who lived north of this road in the isolated valleys of Swat, Bajaur, Panjkorah, and Buner, and who often continued to oppose the Timurids from their mountain fastnesses and fortresses. Between 1526 and 1530 Babur's main concern was not the Yusufzai Afghans but the suppression of about 'one hundred thousand' Afghans who, after the defeat of Sultan Ibrahim Lodi, still held out in the region east of Kanauj and the Ganges, seeking to restore a Lodi to the throne.[151] It was this preoccupation with the 'eastern Afghans' that gave a free hand to the Yusufzai in Swat, allowing them to expand their tribal dominion.

---

[147] *BN*, 138.

[148] *Ibidem*, 138, 146-154b, 158b, 203-203b, 213b-215b, 216b, 219-219b, 220b, 221-221b.

[149] Babur observed, without offering an explanation, that 'If Afghans are unable to fight they come before their enemies with grass in their teeth, as if to say «I am your cow»' (*BN*, 147). But Masson, observing the same custom, writes: 'The miserable hunted [Afghan] wretches threw themselves on the ground, and placing a blade or tuft of grass in their mouths, cried out, "I am your cow". This act and exclamation, which would have saved them from an orthodox Hindu, had no effect with the infuriated Sikhs' (Masson, *Narrative of Various Journeys*, I, p. 141).

[150] *BN*, 251b ff, 293b.

[151] *Ibidem*, 294, 296 ff, 299, 301, 303 ff, 362b.

After Babur's death in 1530, Afghan tribal expansion and rivalry in the Peshawar subregion took place within the broader context of the competition for power in the Kabul Wilayat between his sons and the struggle between the Afghans and Mughals for empire in Hindustan. Especially in the decade of struggle between Humayun and Mirza Kamran between 1545 and 1555 there was little to restrain the Afghans from consolidating their conquests in the Peshawar subregion. Such latitude continued to prevail between 1556, when Akbar ascended the Mughal throne in Hindustan, and 1580, when the government of the Kabul Wilayat was in the hands of Akbar's younger brother Mirza Hakim as an autonomous domain. It was during these decades that the Yusufzai became the dominant Afghan tribal confederation of the Peshawar subregion – at the time potentially the most prosperous and well populated district in all of the Indo-Khurasanian borderlands. By about 1540 the Yusufzai had successfully conquered the most productive lands in the Lamghanat and Peshawar subregion, including Swat, the Samah or Plain, Bajaur, Panjkorah, and Buner, expelling the Dilazaks from all of these lands.

In the sixteenth century there was still a third wave of Afghans moving into Nangrahar and the Peshawar valley in tribal formation. Most of these belonged to the Mohmand, Khalil and Daudzai tribes and were part of the Ghoriya Khel confederation. Allying themselves with the Mughals under Mirza Kamran, they were able to seize and hold lands in Nangrahar, the Khyber area, and around Peshawar town, but they could not match the military power of the Yusufzai.[152] The Yusufzai were still growing in strength. Between 1510 and 1530 they wrested the valley of Swat, a formerly fairly prominent centre of Buddhism with extensive ancient ruins and more populous and agriculturally productive in the late medieval period than Peshawar, from the Swatis and their Arab overlords, the Jahangiri Sultans, who ruled

---

[152] Arlinghaus, *Transformation of Afghan Tribal Society*, pp. 170, 227-8.

from the medieval capital of Manglaur.[153] After the conquest of Swat, in the battle of Shaykh Tapur (1550) the Yusufzai tribal confederation under Khan Kaju defeated the Ghoriya Khel tribes, ensuring their continued dominance in Peshawar and setting in place a more or less permanent division and encapsulation of tribal lands. Yusufzai military and political power then reached its peak, but even Khan Kaju never became more than a powerful leader of a tribal confederation, unable to found a dynasty, or a state, or even issue coins and read the *xuṭbah* in his own name. The segmentary lineage system was too ingrained, and expansion came to an end. The northern boundary of Afghan tribal expansion, which was reached by 1580, became the ecological boundary between double and single cropping at an altitude of about 5,000 feet. The Indus became the boundary to the east.[154]

As a result of sedentarization and changes in the patterns of transhumance, land-use, and settlement, Afghan tribal society in these northern, agricultural regions was not abandoned but transformed, or, as in Swat, 'feudalized'.[155] Initially, as Babur describes it, in places like Bajaur, the nomadic Afghan clans (*qaum-i afğān*) were held in check by the fortified towns. The Afghans began by taking possession of the grazing lands, while laying waste (*vīrān*) the agricultural lands, and only after a long test of strength possessed themselves of the fertile lands of the valleys.[156] By the early sixteenth century Babur observed that the Afghans and 'Afghan-like' people of Bajaur, Bangash, Bannu, Logar, Zurmat, Peshawar, and nearby regions were generally engaged in a mixture of pastoral and agricultural activities – being in the process of sedentarization – and that 'infidel customs' (*rusūm-i kuffār*) had spread among them.[157] What happened next is hidden from our view. But, by the early nineteenth century, the

---

[153] *Ibidem*, pp. 187, 189-93, 207; Wink, *Al-Hind*, I, s.v.; II, s.v.; F. Barth, *Political Leadership among Swat Pathans* (London, 1959), p. 7; W. R. Rai, 'The Usufzai State of Swat', *Geographical Journal*, 1934, nr. 84 (3).

[154] Arlinghaus, *Transformation of Afghan Tribal Society*, p. 18.

[155] *Ibidem*, pp. 3-4, 19, 42-3.

[156] *BN*, 131b.

[157] *Ibidem*, 137, 139b, 146b, 147-9, 153, 203-4, 216b, 218, 243b, 244b, 245.

process of sedentarization had advanced much further. Elphinstone wrote that 'the eastern Afghans appear to have received their civilization from India' and that they were virtually all 'agricultural' and lived in houses and villages.[158]

For tribes like the Yusufzai, even when sedentarized, the ideal of kinship solidarity remained vital, as did their 'peculiar patriarchal form of government', even though the inadequacies of this situation became painfully obvious and later induced them, at times, to invite outsiders among themselves and put themselves under receivership.[159] It did not allow them to fend off the Mughals in the sixteenth and seventeenth centuries, nor the Sikhs in the nineteenth.[160] They and other Afghans superimposed their tribal society on the pre-existing stratified peasant societies of Lamghanat, the Peshawar area, Swat, Bajaur, Buner, and Panjkorah, by replacing their landholding elites and by integrating the peasant societies. Over the subsequent centuries this resulted in the peculiar tribal patron-client or tribal 'caste' societies which are still found in the region today. What prevented the evolution of a state structure in Swat and Peshawar was the characteristically tribal system of land holding of *veš*.[161] Based on a periodic redistribution of land (itself not of nomadic origin), this system ensured tribal cohesion throughout the sixteenth century, and in the Peshawar plains for three and in Swat for as much as four centuries afterwards. Elphinstone wrote about the territories of the Yusufzai and other tribes in Swat, Bangash, Khyber, and the Peshawar plain, that most of the labour was done by the so-called Faqirs (called *ra*ᶜ*āyā* in other parts of South Asia), and that the Yusufzai merely superintended the cultivation, while spending the greater part of the day in conversing and smoking around a fire, with none but the poorest Yusufzai being obliged to work.[162] Striking in appearance, with their fair complexions, grey eyes, red beards, and the military affectation of their car-

[158] Elphinstone, *An Account of the Kingdom of Caubul*, II, pp. 2-3, 30, 32, 42. See also note 22.

[159] Cf. Masson, *Narrative of Various Journeys*, I, pp. 139-42.

[160] *Ibidem*, p. 429.

[161] Arlinghaus, *Transformation of Afghan Tribal Society*, pp. 233-7.

[162] Elphinstone, *An Account of the Kingdom of Caubul*, II, p. 32.

riage, the Yusufzai lived among a much more numerous conquered, humble and unwarlike people 'like Spartans among Helots' and, enjoying independence all around, were filled with the idea of their own dignity and importance.[163] The Faqirs had no land and were not allowed to participate in the tribal jirgas; but the treatment they received from their masters was generally mild.[164]

The Sur Empire of the sixteenth century

As the foregoing has shown, to the west of the Indus the Afghans were unable to overcome the limitations of their tribal institutions and create states or empires. In Hind, to the east of the Indus, Afghan empire building was aborted. The empire of the Lodis had ceased to exist after 1526, leaving many Afghans adrift. 'These Afghans', wrote Ahmad Yadgar, 'after being absolute rulers for seventy years, left their habitations, their goods, and their wealth behind, and proceeded to Bengal, and [there] they were completely dispersed'.[165]

One of them, a soldier named Dattu Sarvani, wrote a unique account of his dreams and reminiscences. This account is telling evidence that after the demise of the Lodi empire the Afghans left behind in Hind reverted to their tribal and migratory life style of old.[166] Dattu provides a vivid picture of the tribal hordes of Lodis, Luhanis, Surs, Niazis, as well as his own tribe of Sarvanis, moving incessantly across the plains with their women, children, and even some sheep, and how they did so in considerable numbers, setting up temporary tribal camping grounds (*maydān-i bāšiš*), and still speaking Pashto among themselves. The symbolism of the account is still entirely pastoral nomadic. Dattu describes a vision of the world spread out before him which was

[163] *Ibidem*, pp. 29, 33.

[164] *Ibidem*, pp. 27-8.

[165] Hidayat Hosain, *Tārīkh-i-Shāhī*, p. 99.

[166] S. Digby, 'Dreams and reminiscences of Dattu Sarvani, a sixteenth--century Indo-Afghan soldier', *The Indian Economic and Social History Review*, 1965 (January), nr. 2 (1), pp. 52-80 & 1965 (April), nr. 2 (2), pp. 178-94.

not one of a city but of a great encampment with many tents on a broad plain – an encampment from which one day one must pack up and go away. The portable darbar tent or *barga* was the visible symbol of sovereignty for this Afghan soldier, not the monumental mosques, tombs, fortresses, and caravanserais left behind by the Lodi emperors.

Dattu dreamt of Babur's invasion as a 'fierce wind with much dust and darkness from the west'. 'When I saw that dream', he writes, 'I was very much afraid whether (...) we would be preserved from that wind of wrath, and I was still awed by this when I learnt (...) that the wind had descended on account of the weakness of spirit of the Afghans, and that the battle line of the Afghans would be curled up, and that of the Turks stretched out, and there would be a crowding together'.[167] When Babur killed Sultan Ibrahim Lodi and took the province of Delhi, the Afghan tribes 'set off towards the east', crossing the river Saru in boats and then going in 'whatever direction each thought fit', with Dattu and the Sarvanis moving into Bihar.[168] Dattu's Pir and helper appeared in a dream. 'Dattu', he said, 'you really have cause to worry. Although the Afghans have gathered together in great numbers, they are prisoners of the demoralization of their spirits and are not yet firm. Victory is Babur's and the Afghans will be defeated'.[169]

What Dattu Sarvani did not know is that there would be a remarkable resurgence of Afghan power soon after his account was written. After defeating the Mughals in battle, a second and final attempt to transform the Afghan tribal structure into an early modern empire was undertaken in Hindustan by the formidable Sher Shah Sur between 1540 and 1545. Determined to overcome the deficiencies of his Lodi predecessors, Sher Shah Sur introduced important changes in the constitution of the Afghan polity, followed by fiscal and revenue reforms, and he might have succeeded in his aim to keep the Mughals out of Hindustan if he had not died prematurely from a gunpowder explosion in his own arsenal. As it happened, the Sur empire did

167 *Ibidem*, p. 62.
168 *Ibidem*, p. 64.
169 *Ibidem*.

not survive Sher Shah very long and fell prey, like its Lodi predecessor, to the customary Afghan tribal disunion, thus creating the conditions for the Mughal re-conquest of 1555-6 under Babur's successors Humayun (r. 1530-56) and Akbar (r. 1556-1605). Under his son Islam Shah (1545-54) and the latter's bickering successors the second Afghan empire quickly unraveled. Ironically, Sher Shah left an important legacy of state building efforts and administrative measures to his long-term rivals the Mughals not to his Afghan fellow countrymen.

The events of Sher Shah's reign are narrated by Abbas Khan Sarvani, an Indo-Muslim historian of Afghan origin who wrote about 1580. As a witness to Akbar's success, Abbas Khan Sarvani, like no other historian of his time, was concerned with the historic failure of the Afghans. An almost Gibbonian sense of melancholy pervades the pages of his *Tàrīx-i Šer Šāhī* as it belabors the decline and fall of the Afghan empire. Tracing the origins of Afghan migration from the earliest centuries, Sarvani begins by observing that the Afghans ruled Hindustan from 1451 to 1555, with an interruption of only fourteen years between 1526 to 1540 during the early conquests of the Mughal emperors Babur and Humayun. Success and failure during this Afghan century, he says, depended on unity and disunity. The Afghans succeeded in Hindustan under Sultan Bahlul Lodi, because they were cooperating together and were unified in their endeavours. They lost their empire under Sultan Ibrahim Lodi because of their internal dissensions. According to Sarvani, 'the Mughals did not conquer the country from Sultan Ibrahim [Lodi] by the sword but due to the discord of the Afghans (*muxālafat-i-afġānān*)'.[170] This observation about 'discord' among the Afghans – which is attributed to the great Sher Shah himself – is repeated throughout Sarvani's work. 'The Afghans lost the country of Hind on account of their internal strife...';[171] 'The greatest cause of the defeat of the Afghans has been the disunity in their own army...';[172] 'We lost every battle against the Mughals be-

[170] *TSS*, I, p. 68 (II, p. 50).
[171] *Ibidem*, I, p. 54 (II, p. 41).
[172] *Ibidem*, I, p. 72 (II, p. 52).

cause of our disunity'[173] – statements to this effect culminate in the author's major insight that discord and quarrelsomeness were part of the very temper of the Afghans as a people.[174] It is this theme that sets the stage for the narration of the events of Sher Shah Sur's reign.

Sher Shah's reign was exceptional in Afghan history, according to Sarvani, for several reasons. Firstly because Sher Shah, born Farid and known merely as Sher Khan until 1539, was an exceptional personality.'From his childhood he bore the sign of greatness on his forehead', Sarvani writes, 'and he possessed the qualities of learning, wisdom and prudence like no-one else of the Sur tribe'.[175] Secondly, Sher Shah's tribal genealogy made him a relatively marginal figure, and therefore less interested in a potential restoration of Lodi authority and more inclined to overhaul the very fundamentals of the tribal constitution. Sher Shah belonged to the minor Afghan tribe of the Surs from his father's side and this made him an outsider among the leading Lodi Afghans of his time.[176] His grandfather and father had been horse dealers when together they migrated to Hind from the Sulayman mountains during the reign of Bahlul Lodi, but 'had no distinction among the crowd of tradesmen'.[177] Thirdly, Sher Shah was born and raised in Hind, and, like most Indo-Afghans, was relatively unaware of 'Afghan custom' (*raviš-i afġānī*) and the notions of tribe and clanship that informed the sense of honour among the inhabitants of Roh or, as Sarvani calls them, the 'Rohillas'.[178] An assimilated Afghan, Sher Shah's genealogy from his mother's side is under dispute. Most Afghan historians hold that his mother was a Sarvani Afghan; but the bardic traditions of Hind surmise that his mother had been a

173 *Ibidem*, I, p. 127 (II, p. 91).

174 *Ibidem*, I, p. 116 (II, p. 81), p. 135 (II, p. 96), pp. 148-9 (II, p. 109).

175 *Ibidem*, I, p. 15 (II, p. 10).

176 *Ibidem*, I, pp. 39-40 (II, p. 29).

177 *AN*, I, 147; *TSS*, I, p. 8 (II, p. 5).

178 *TSS*, I, pp. 232, 234 (II, pp. 186-8).

daughter of the Qaimkhani Rajput family of Shekhawat and thus regard him as half-Indian.[179]

Long before he became Sultan in 1539, probably as early as the second decade of the sixteenth century, Sher Shah began building a power base for himself in Sahsaram, in what are now the Rohtas and Bhojpur districts of southern Bihar. One of eight sons, Farid, the later Sher Shah, began his career by challenging the established Afghan custom (*qā^cida-i rasm-i afġānān*) of inheritance sharing among brothers. Invoking a rule introduced by Sultan Sikandar Lodi that the normal laws of inheritance did not obtain in public affairs, he lost no time eliminating his brothers from the management of the two parganas of his father's *jāgīr*. 'This is not the country of Roh that we should divide it equally like brothers among us', he argued, 'for the country of Hind is completely at the disposal of the king, and, as Sultan Sikandar Lodi decided, nobody has any share in it and there is no consideration for seniority and kinship; if an Afghan noble dies, whatever he leaves behind in cash or kind should be divided among his heirs in accordance with the law of inheritance, but his parganas and military retinue he confers on any of his sons whom he regards as the most able, without allowing the others a share in it'.[180] From these early beginnings until 1529 Sher Khan was a successful commander who divided his time and energies between administering his father's parganas in southern Bihar and service with a variety of warlords in Awadh as well as with Sultan Ibrahim Lodi and the Mughal emperor Babur. It was probably in Babur's service that Sher Khan became acquainted with the use of artillery and muskets. Gunpowder technology was now quickly spreading eastwards, and we find not only Sher Khan but other Afghans in Bihar as well as the rulers of Bengal equipped with an artillery park (*topxāna*) soon after Babur's arrival in Hindustan, while in Gujarat it spread even earlier due to Portu-

[179] K. Qanungo, *Sher Shah and his Times: An Old Story Retold* (Bombay, 1965), p. xi.

[180] *TSS*, I, pp. 49-50 (II, p. 37); and see N. Roy, 'New Light on Sher Shah's Early Career', *Journal of the Asiatic Society, Letters*, 1952, nr. 18, pp. 53-62.

guese influence.[181] Sher Khan was just one of many Afghans who entered Babur's service and thereby obtained an opportunity to study Mughal methods of warfare and military organization firsthand. As Abbas Khan Sarvani put it, 'remaining for a time amongst the Mughals he acquainted himself with their military tactics and mode of government and the character of their pillars of state (nobles) (*atvār-i jang-o-tadbīr-i mulkdārī-o-raviš-i arkān-i daulat*)'.[182] He was the only Afghan, however, who already then conceived of the possibility of undermining Mughal rule in Hind and bringing it to an end. He thought it a potentially fatal weakness of the Mughal emperors that they did not personally attend to all affairs of state and were dependent on the support of their nobles and courtiers.[183] Among the Mughals, he observed, corruption and venality were rife and greed, 'the lust for gold', prevailed at all levels of the officialdom, so that friendship and enmity were decided by money more than anything else. If only he could unify the Afghans the Mughals would not be able to withstand him.[184]

Accordingly, it became Sher Khan's overriding goal and ambition in life to bring together the Afghans and undertake a joint effort to expel the Mughals from Hind and re-establish Afghan rule. In 1529 he resolutely left the Mughal camp and entered the service of the newly established Luhani Sultanate of southern Bihar. The Luhanis or Nuhanis were a tribe more numerous and stronger than the Surs at that time, trader nomads who had been in the possession of extensive *jāgīr*-s for three generations under the Lodis, but the Luhani Sultanate was a tribal and short-lived affair.[185] When the Luhani Sultan died in 1529, the entire management of southern Bihar devolved upon Sher Khan, giving him a measure of independence for the first time, but still essentially leaving him a servant of the Luhani clan and in modest circumstances. The following decade between

[181] *MT*, I, pp. 461, 470, 482.

[182] *TSS*, I, p. 54 (II, p. 40).

[183] *Ibidem*, I, pp. 55-6 (II, pp. 41-2).

[184] *Ibidem*, I, p. 72 (II, p. 52).

[185] On Luhani trade, see Masson, *Narrative of Various Journeys*, I, pp. 48, 52, 58, 67, 72.

1529 and 1539 – which preceded his successful overthrow of Babur's successor Humayun – is noteworthy for his dogged pursuit of independent wealth by a series of successful efforts, including multiple marriages with wealthy widows of the Luhani, Sarangkhani and Farmuli clans, to possess himself of the hoarded wealth and treasure of some of the most important remaining amirs of the defunct Lodi Sultanate, the acquisition of booty and spoils in many places, especially in Bengal, and even subsidies from Sultan Bahadur Shah of Gujarat who hoped to use him against their common Mughal enemy.[186] Characteristically, Sher Khan did not share these resources with the Luhanis but used them to increase his own power, recruit men into his service, train them, and thus, again, to attack the tribal basis of the realm. Demoralized Afghan soldiers who had gone into mendicancy were pressured back into service'.[187] All Afghans who served Sultan Bahadur Shah at the time of his defeat by Humayun came over to Sher Khan, together with many volunteers from elsewhere, including powerful chiefs who, observing Sher Khan's daily increasing power, 'put their pride aside'.[188] 'Laying aside every bond of friendship and respect for the honor of the Afghans (*nāmūs-i afğānān*), they all bowed down without hesitation and delay before his irresistible farman'.[189] Fixed salaries, equal opportunity employment, and discipline replaced clan loyalty. As a result, by the end of the 1530s, says Abbas Khan Sarvani, 'Sher Khan was known for his qualities of generosity and benevolence; throughout the day he was occupied in scattering gold like the sun and shedding pearls like clouds and this was the reason that the Afghans gathered around him and the kingdom of Hind fell into his hands'.[190] Most Afghans, including his own Sur tribesmen, continued to live in mobile camps, and many were still commuting on an annual basis, with their wives and chil-

[186] *Ibidem*, I, pp. 72-9, 95-126 (II, pp. 53-62, 69-90); D.H.A. Kolff, *Naukar, Rajput & Sepoy: The Ethnohistory of the Military Labour Market in Hindustan, 1450-1850* (Cambridge, 1990), pp. 43-54.

[187] *TSS*, I, p. 96 (II, p. 69).

[188] *Ibidem*.

[189] *Ibidem*, I, p. 231.

[190] *Ibidem, I*, pp. 224-5 (*II*, p. 178).

dren. As Abbas Khan Sarvani writes: 'Every Afghan who came from the country of Afghanistan to his presence, was given an amount of money beyond his calculation and expectation and was told, «This is your share in the country of Hind, which has fallen into my hands. This is your allowance, come every year to receive it». To the tribe and people of Sur who lived in the country of Roh he gave an annual stipend in money in proportion to the number of members and retainers of each family. On account of his wealth there was no Afghan in Hind or Roh who was left in poverty; rather they all became [like] merchants (*sāhib-i tijārat*)'.[191] When Sher Khan became convinced that all the Afghans had united with him and were eager to fight the Mughals, he came out of the hills of Rohtas and marched to engage Humayun, routing the latter at Chausa in 1539, and at Kanauj in 1540. This was the time Sher Khan ascended to the throne as Sher Shah.[192] Like Bahlul and Sikandar Lodi, he did so after overcoming considerable hesitation. He almost had to be dragged to the throne, if we can believe Abbas Khan Sarvani. It was pointed out to him by some of his followers that the early Lodi rulers had acted against the principles of kingship. Having defeated the Mughal Badshah, he – Sher Khan – was entitled to disregard the claims of other Afghan chiefs and become king in his turn. In the end, Sher Khan was ceremoniously enthroned amidst tribal dancing festivities that went on for seven days. The *xuṭbah* was read in his name, coins were issued, and he was given the title of Shah Alam.

The flight of the Mughal emperor left Sher Shah the unchallenged ruler at Agra between 1540 and his death in 1545. During these years his sustained attempt at imperial centralization and military reform went well beyond the measures taken by his Lodi predecessors. Extending his policies of the preceding decade, Sher Shah emphasized hierarchical subordination to and direct employment by the centre instead of horizontal linkages with tribal leaders and warlords. A whole new political economy was devised and implemented to recruit, pay, train and discipline a professional army. Making the most methodical and productive use of his time, Sher Shah supervised all campaigns and affairs

[191] *Ibidem*, I, p. 227 (II, p. 180).
[192] *Ibidem*, I, pp. 140-4 (II, pp. 101-4).

of state, no matter how great or small, in person.[193] Reliance on courtiers was avoided as much as possible, while none was allowed to do anything without his consent.[194] Sher Shah everywhere set spies on his nobles. The ranking system of mansabs that the Lodis had introduced was again implemented among Sher Shah's nobility, but much more systematically, and in combination with more closely audited revenue assignments or *jāgīr*-s.[195] After 1540, instead of hoarded wealth and booty the regularly assessed land revenue became the major source of income of the imperial state, while rules regulating the payment of soldiers' salaries and the branding of horses (*dāġ*) were implemented with great rigour. 'In every country that came into his possession', writes Abbas Khan Sarvani, 'he [Sher Shah] exerted himself in its development and agricultural improvement (...) he personally looked into all its affairs (...) and paid its soldiers regularly without oppressing the peasants'.[196] The Afghan army swelled to unprecedented proportions.[197] He built an alleged 1,700 caravanserais throughout the empire and introduced an improved system of news transmission.[198] Showing none of the customary Afghan contempt for fortification, Sher Shah built especially massive stone fortresses, in Delhi and elsewhere, and even introduced a novel system of earthen entrenchments to protect his mobile camp sites.[199] He protected peasants and agriculture against moving armies, and cast artillery.[200] Like his Lodi predecessors but even more so, Sher Shah associated himself with Turks, Farmulis, and Rajputs in order to expand the non-Afghan base of his empire.[201] Making use of more or less power-

[193] *Ibidem*, I, p. 205 (II, p. 158), p. 206 (II, p. 159).
[194] *Ibidem*, I, p. 172 (II, p. 129).
[195] *Ibidem*, I, p. 182 (II, p. 137), p. 188 (II, p. 144).
[196] *Ibidem*, I, p. 79 (II, p. 58).
[197] *Ibidem*, I, pp. 211-12 (II, p. 165).
[198] *Ibidem*, I, p. 218 (II, pp. 170-1).
[199] According to Masson, 'the Afghans affect to despise fortresses, and it may be observed, in all important cities once under their government, that the bulwarks have been neglected' (Masson, *Narrative of Various Journeys*, I, p. 356).
[200] *TSS*, I, p. 188 (II, p. 144), and *passim*.
[201] Kolff, *Naukar, Rajput & Sepoy*, esp. pp. 56, 63, 65, 67.

ful non-Afghan middlemen, he recruited substantial zamindari contingents and peasant soldiers in his military. These too were accommodated within the new Afghan imperial system under his own aggressive leadership. The second Afghan empire, thus, owed little to ethnic and tribal loyalties and segmentary politics but founded itself on direct recruitment and individual enterprise.

Islam Shah, succeeding to the imperial throne in 1545, resembled his father in his desire for dominion and conquest, and began his reign by bringing the entire country under his personal control by perpetuating many of his civil and military regulations, including the branding system and the mansabs.[202] Like his father, he assembled an immense army, together with horses, elephants, and possibly as many as sixty large guns.[203] However, having garrisoned the entire country between Kabul and Bengal with his own troops, he soon set about destroying his father's nobles. The latter were more or less faithful servants of the Sur empire when Sher Shah was still alive but had now become an independent and entrenched interest group. Islam Shah executed their leaders with uncommon cruelty and ruthlessness (some were blown up with explosives, as in his father's accident), dishonored their women, and deprived other Afghans of all dignities.[204] While becoming more and more addicted to opium and wine himself, for two years he forced his Afghan soldiers to do manual work, carrying stone and lime, building yet more forts.[205] Opposition against Islam Shah intensified as a result of these ill-calculated and perverse measures, while tribal factionalism and the intemperate Afghan blood feuds and revenge killings re-surfaced with a vengeance.[206] An epidemic of bubonic plague ravaged the whole of Hindustan in 1550. Two

---

[202] *MT*, I, p. 384; H.M. Elliot and J. Dowson, *The History of India as told by its own Historians*, 8 vols. (London, 1867-77), IV (*Tarikh-i-Daudi*), p. 479.

[203] Elliot and Dowson, *The History of India*, IV, pp. 479, 499.

[204] *Ibidem*, pp. 486-8, 480, 504; *MT*, I, 386, 388, 403, 406.

[205] *MT*, I, p. 387.

[206] Elliot and Dowson, *The History of India*, IV, p. 489; *MT*, I, pp. 378-80.

years later Islam Shah followed his father to the family grave in Sahsaram.

The fall of the second Afghan empire was now at hand. Immediately after Islam Shah's death, the Sur domains were partitioned among several sons and relatives of Sher Shah. By 1554 three different *xuṭbah*-s were read in Hindustan and three kings, openly declaring war on each other, issued their own sikka coinage.[207] This was the time of the 'kings of the clans'.[208] In the ensuing free-for-all, some two hundred aspiring Afghan amirs obtained royal tents, standards and kettle drums, while any Afghan who brought with him ten or fifteen horsemen was given a makeshift flagstaff with a bit of red rag wrapped around it, with some other dignities and a *jāgīr*.[209] Among the old Afghan nobility of Lodi times extreme demoralization set in, in 1555 aggravated by the outbreak of severe famine conditions (caused by drought) in eastern Hindustan.[210] When Humayun 'received intelligence of the dissensions of the [Afghan] nobles, and the partition of the territories of Hind, he felt persuaded that the discordance of the Afghans (*nāsāzīʾ afġānān*) would enable him to take easy possession of the country'.[211] And thus, as one Mughal historian, Badauni, put it, 'the kingdom fell away from the race of the Afghans and returned to its original holders'.[212]

Waiting for the millennium

With the Mughals re-establishing their hegemony in Hindustan, a second dispersal of Afghans occurred not unlike the one following the Lodi defeat thirty years earlier. Many Afghans and other men of Roh returned to their ancestral homelands, either to settle down or resume a nomadic or trading existence.[213]

---

207 Hidayat Hosain, *Tārīkh-i-Shāhī*, p. 300.
208 *MT*, I, p. 422.
209 *Ibidem*, pp. 422-3.
210 *Ibidem*, p. 428.
211 Hidayat Hosain, *Tārīkh-i-Shāhī*, p. 301.
212 *MT*, I, p. 436.
213 Arlinghaus, *Transformation of Afghan Tribal Society*, p. 277.

A great variety of Afghan clans profitably turned themselves into zamindars or landlords and agrarian colonizers, like the Yusufzai had in Swat and the Peshawar plain. Under Akbar dozens of such Afghan zamindars, not uncommonly identified by their tribal denominations, arose in the provinces of the Panjab, Sind, Agra, Allahabad, Delhi, and Bihar.[214] The Mughal emperor appears to have encouraged such colonizing pursuits among destitute Afghans preying on peasants in the Panjab.[215] Everywhere in Mughal India we see Afghan colonies of traders-cum-mercenaries spring up along the traditional routes of the horse trade. Tribal bands of Fuladis, Shirwanis, and Lodis also took up service with the Sultans of Gujarat.[216] Perhaps the majority of Afghans retreated eastwards. There were remnants of Indo-Afghan power in southeastern Bihar, and the Karrani Afghans were holding out in Gaur. By 1568 the Karrani and Luhani Afghans had brought large parts of Bengal and Orissa under their control. Bengal, because of its fragmented geography of waterways and jungles, was their best last hope. Fighting tenaciously, these 'eastern Afghans' were driven ever further towards the sea, in a long drawn and checkered confrontation with Mughal imperialism that took up all of Akbar's reign and did not come to an end until the seventh year of Jahangir's reign (AD 1611).[217] Over the course of these decades, many 'eastern Afghans' surrendered and took up service with the Mughals, as they did with the Sultans of Gujarat, or the Deccan, or Arakan.[218] It appears that Akbar absorbed the Afghans in his armies but mostly excluded the Afghans from the

---

[214] I. Husain, 'Pattern of Afghan Settlements in India in the 17th Century', *Proceedings of the Thirty-Ninth Session of the Indian History Congress* (Osmania University, Hyderabad, 1978), pp. 327-36.

[215] *AN*, III, 247.

[216] E.C. Bayley (ed. and transl.), *Mirʾāt-i Sikandarī* (London, 1886), pp. 367, 454.

[217] A large part of the third volume of the *Akbarnāma* is devoted to a narrative description of the Mughal struggle with the ill-fated 'eastern Afghans'. The final confrontation of 1611 is described at length by Jahangir in his memoirs [A. Rogers (transl.), *Tūzuk-i-Jahāngīrī* (Delhi, 1989), I, pp. 207-13].

[218] For Arakan, see *Manucci*, I, p. 354.

higher ranks of power.[219] Manucci wrote that 'recollecting what Shera [Sher Shah] had done to his father Humayun – that is, he rebelled because he found himself very wealthy – Akbar left it as a law to his descendants that the Pathans should never receive higher pay than four hundred thousand rupees a year, that they were not to be appointed governors, and should only be employed as soldiers'.[220] The Afghans of Mughal India thus stood apart from all other ethnic groups. Scattered across the subcontinent, their leaders employed their own tribal followings and maintained a volatile presence everywhere. They continued to speak Pashto and, in spite of their quarrelsomeness and dissensions, displayed a remarkably strong 'national sentiment' and sense of being 'all of one race'.[221] They were 'very jealous about their women'.[222] During birthdays and festivals, when the Mughal emperor and princes had themselves weighed, the chief ladies of the court were obliged to attend at the palace to make their compliments to the queens and princesses but 'from this ceremony the wives of Pathan captains were exempted'.[223] Only the Afghans continued to cherish hope for a return to power. Ever since the death of Sher Shah they had refused to bind on turbans, wearing in their place a fragment of cloth – a custom, they said, that was to endure until there would again be an Afghan king.[224] Resentful, and recognizing neither benefit nor obligation, 'it was the rule in the Mogul realm not to trust that race'.[225] Scattered as they were, it was feared that 'the Pathans might collect eighty thousand horse and much infantry'.[226] The Afghans were never allowed to hold any of the hundreds of for-

---

219 A. Rahim, 'The Position of the Afghans under the Mughals, 1526-1605 A.D.', *Journal of the Pakistan Historical Society* 1958, nr. 6, p. 126; F. Anwar, *Nobility under the Mughals (1628-1658)* (Delhi, 2001), p. 32.

220 *Manucci*, I, p. 144.

221 *Ibidem*, II, p. 131, 426; J. Sarkar (transl.), *Tarikh-i-Dilkasha (Memoirs of Bhimsen relating to Aurangzeb's Deccan Campaigns* (Bombay, 1972), p. 110.

222 *Manucci*, II, p. 426.

223 *Ibidem*, p. 241.

224 *Ibidem*, p. 188.

225 Sarkar, *Tarikh-i-Dilkasha*, p. 143; *Manucci*, I, p. 330.

226 *Manucci*, I, p. 425.

tresses, for fear that they would plot some treason, as they did to Humayun.[227] 'These [the Pathans] for the greater part serve as soldiers; others are merchants; and they resort to no other occupations', observed Manucci. 'They are very avaricious and foolhardy. When they come to court they are well-clad and well-armed, caracoling on fine horses richly caparisoned, posing as persons of some consideration, and followed by several servants borrowed or hired for the day. On reaching their house they divest themselves of all this finery and, tying a scanty cloth round their loins and wrapping a rag around their head, they take their seat on a mat, and live on kichri, i.e. rice and lentils, or badly cooked cow's flesh of low quality, which is very abundant in the Mogul country and very cheap. (...) They hate the Moguls so much that they will not intermarry with them; they are extremely pretentious, each one thinking himself greater than the rest, and decline to concede to others any superiority'.[228]

Beginning in the 1580s, Akbar stepped up efforts to increase imperial control among the tribal Afghans beyond the Indus river. Since these efforts coincided with the beginning of the second Islamic millennium in the year AH 1000 / AD 1591-2 and since their imperial prospects in Hindustan were in irreversible decline, the Afghan tribes turned to millennarian Islam.[229] Millenarian expectations of a new social order and the restoration of

---

[227] *Ibidem*, p. 419.

[228] *Ibidem*, pp. 425-6.

[229] Arlinghaus, *Transformation of Afghan Tribal Society*, pp. 270-330; idem, 'Varieties of Islamic Expression in the Mughal province of Kabul in the 16th century', in: A.L. Dallapiccola & S. Zingel-Avé Lallemant (eds.), *Islam and Indian Regions*, 2 vols. (Stuttgart, 1993), I, pp. 7-29; Jamal Malik, '16th century Mahdism: the Rawshaniya movement among the Pakhtun tribes', [in:] *ibidem*, pp. 31-59; Akbar S. Ahmed, *Millennium and Charisma among Pathans: An Essay in Social Anthropology* (London, 1976); J. Leyden, 'On the Raushanian Sect and its Founder, Bayazid Ansari', *Asiatick Researches*, 1810, nr. 11, pp. 363-428; S.A.A. Rizvi, 'Rawshaniyya Movement', *Abr-Nahrain*, 1965-6, nr. 6, pp. 63-91 & 1967-8, nr. 7, pp. 62-98; B. Dharma, 'The Raushania Movement and the Mughals', *Islamic Culture*, 1952, nr. 26, pp. 57-67; Ahmed Tariq, *Religio-Political Ferment in the North West Frontier during the Mughal Period* (Delhi, 1982).

piety by a Mahdi or 'Messiah' fueled a tribal insurrection against Mughal imperialism under the leadership of Bayazid Ansari, the Pir-i-Roshan ('Saint of Light'), and his sons and successors. The resulting Roshaniyya movement did succeed in unifying some of the most important and numerous Afghan tribes against the Mughals. But such unity, again, did not last.

Prior to the rise of the Roshaniyya movement, the Afghan tribes' commitment to Islam, in spite of their claim to be descendants of the patriarchs of ancient Israel and a Companion of the Prophet, had generally been weak. Among the Afghans entering the Kabul Wilayat and the Peshawar plain around the turn of the fifteenth century the tribal ethos clearly took precedence over Islamic belief and practice. To some extent this was a question of rustic ignorance. Many Afghan tribesmen were simply unaware of the precise nature of Islamic piety. The earliest Muslim commentators on the religion of the Afghan tribesmen refer to their rudimentary knowledge and crude understanding of Islam. Since the *ᶜulamā* among the nomads in the mountains and deserts of Afghanistan were few in number, so they observed, all kinds of unbelief (*kufr*), heresy (*ilḥād*), dualism (*zandaqa*), errors and deviation (*ẓalālat*), and innovation (*bidᶜa*) were rife. These same commentators, however, make it clear that from the outset there was a deep conflict between Afghan tribalism and Islamic belief and practice and that the Afghans were conscious of being 'bad Muslims' but considered upholding their tribal order of higher importance than being 'good Muslims'.[230] Ostensibly followers of Abu Hanifa, in practice the Afghans did not follow many precepts of the Sharia. They demanded a high bride price, did not allow women to inherit property, refused to intermarry with non-Afghans, killed fellow Muslims, and refused to pay *zakat* ('alms') and *ᶜušr* ('tithe'). Moreover, Afghan tribesmen generally mistrusted *pīr*-s and religious professionals from outside the tribe as a threat to social solidarity because religious loyalties between *pīr*-s and *murīd*-s cut across kinship lines and thus corroded the basic organizing principle of Afghan society.

---

[230] Arlinghaus, *Transformation of Afghan Tribal Society*, pp. 111-12, 115-16.

The major reason Bayazid Ansari succeeded where other pirs had failed was that he customized the Islamic religion for Afghan usage. Downplaying the importance of the Sharia, the Prophet Muhammad, and the entire religious establishment of Islam, his message was made to appeal to the tribesmen in all sorts of unprecedented ways. By its emphasis on mysticism, prayer, fasting, and poverty in preparation for the Day of Judgement, it was made especially attractive for poor or disadvantaged individuals, lineages and tribes – all those who were losing out in the competition for power and wealth. Bayazid Ansari was the Pir-i-Kamil or 'Perfect Saint' and Hadi, the guide and mystical Messiah who in the fulness of time would lead men along his superior path to salvation, and hence the Mahdi (although this was a claim he officially shunned). As such, he allowed nearly everything Afghans were wont to do without scruple, including the right to dispose of the lives and properties of all who did not adhere to his sect, in effect treating the latter as infidels, and dignifying brigandage as *jihād*. Writing and preaching in Pashto as well as in Arabic, Persian, and Hindi, he advocated free mingling of the sexes, while his assemblies were accompanied by music, singing and dancing. In short, the Roshaniyya message proved a uniting force in the 'ordered anarchical' society of the Afghan tribesmen while it also served as an important channel of cultural articulation and provided a new Islamic identity to the Afghans which was very much their own.

It is doubtful however that Bayazid Ansari's message would have developed mass appeal if it had not, through the exploitation of its millennarian qualities, been turned into the legitimation of an anti-Mughal insurrection. In other words, it succeeded because it served as a rallying force among the tribesmen with both millennarian and social revolutionary implications. Supra-tribal, and including Afghans as well as non-Afghans, the Roshaniyya movement was an Afghan millennarian response to the tightening of imperial control under Akbar. For this reason, the phases it went through, and the different reactions it solicited among the tribesmen, corresponded to the changing patterns of Mughal administration in the Kabul Wilayat.

Founded in 1565 by Bayazid Ansari (himself not an Afghan but of a family of Barkis with a *silsila* indicating Arab origins),[231] the Roshaniyya movement took the from of a localized but armed insurrection against the Mughals within a decade. After his death in 1575 or 1576, the insurrection continued to gain momentum. Bayazid Ansari's son and successor Shaykh Umar acquired such a large following among the Afghan tribes that he began to refer to himself as the Badshah of the Afghans. Aiming to integrate all Afghan tribes in a federation under his own leadership, he based his nascent state in the Samah, i.e. the plain of the Yusufzai and Muhammadzai Afghans. Predictably perhaps, Shaykh Umar's untimely demand of *ᶜušr* and *xaraj* ('tribute') at first caused a violent rupture with the Yusufzai, who felt threatened in their tribal autonomy. But the movement recovered under Shaykh Umar's son Jalal ad-Din or 'Jalala' after 1585, when Akbar initiated a massive offensive on the North-West Frontier, simultaneously sending his armies to the Khyber area, Baluchistan, Kashmir, and Swat and Bajaur.[232] The prime target here were the Yusufzai and their confederate Afghan tribes. 'From the days of Ulugh Beg', recalls Abu 'l-Fazl, 'the Yusufzai tribe, which was more than 100,000 strong, had, by the help of their difficult mountains, practiced highway robbery. (…) The Kabul rulers had not the strength to chastise them and the rulers of Hind were preoccupied with other business'.[233] Yusufzai resistance was as tenacious as that of the 'eastern Afghans'. The Mughals suffered one of their worst military reversals while campaigning in the difficult terrain of Swat. Most significantly, the Yusufzai now turned to the Roshaniyyas for leadership. A full-scale tribal insurrection followed that temporarily rallied the normally pro-Mughal Khalil and Mohmand tribes along the Peshawar-Jalalabad road as well. Subsequent defeats again caused the tribesmen to abandon Roshaniyya leadership. The Mughals, by building numerous fortresses, and enlisting the aid of the Kafirs in the neighboring mountains, ultimately achieved a measure of

---

[231] *Ibidem*, p. 274; Malik, '16th century Mahdism…', pp. 34, 40 n. 47, 41.

[232] *AN*, III, 472-6.

[233] *Ibidem*, 475, 481, 485-6.

control in the area, undermining the Roshaniyya movement, and causing Jalala to flee to the Uzbeks. Many Yusufzai were sold as slaves to Turan and Persia or died of disease.[234] But Jalala was again leading the Roshaniyyas in 1596, attacking caravans, and causing considerable trouble for the Mughals in the Khyber area, until he was finally killed by the Hazaras in 1601. Jalala's successor Ahad-Dad, the son of Shaykh Umar, again mobilized the Afghan tribes of Tirah and Bangash to oppose the Mughals and became a major concern for emperor Jahangir. The last Roshaniyya leader was Abd al-Qadir, a son of Ahad-Dad, who entered the service of Shah Jahan but was later executed on the latter's orders. The Roshaniyya movement thus came to an end in AD 1632, in the sixth year of Shah Jahan's reign. Afghan tribal rebellions in Aurangzeb's reign were no less ferocious than the earlier ones but they were no longer inspired by the Roshaniyya teachings.

Largely as the result of their rejection of the Roshaniyya doctrines in the late sixteenth and early seventeenth centuries and their identification with the teachings of a different kind of Islamic reformer, Sayyid ^{c}Ali Tirmizi, and his disciple Akhund Darveza, virtually all Afghans eventually returned to Sunni Islam. The only exceptions are the Turi tribe in the Kurram valley and certain sections of the Orakzai.[235] But the role of Islam continued to be minor wherever Afghans remained pastoral nomads and increased but slowly in importance among Afghans who were settled among a numerous non-Afghan population. It can plausibly be argued that in the subsequent centuries Afghans have continued putting their tribal customs above their adherence to Islam. Charles Masson, in the early nineteenth century, presented as common knowledge that 'Mogals and Patans were irreligious' and that 'no Patan ever kept fast or repeated prayers'.[236] He noted 'an unextinguishable rancour to exist between the two leading sects of Mahomedanism, the Shia and the Sunni', but otherwise found the people of Kabul 'entirely free of religious

[234] *Ibidem*, 518-25.

[235] Arlinghaus, 'Varieties of Islamic Expression', p. 28; idem, *Transformation of Afghan Tribal Society*, pp. 109, 113, 117.

[236] Masson, *Narrative of Various Journeys*, I, p. 386.

prejudices and antipathies'.[237] 'I soon observed there was very little religion among them', he writes elsewhere.[238] The mosques of Kabul were spacious and utilitarian rather than 'splendid edifices', and in the entire city there was but one madrasa – without endowment or scholars.[239] Elphinstone's picture of Afghan religion does not fundamentally contradict this, although he correctly observed a rather less lax attitude among the Durrani ruling elites of his time, particularly in Peshawar.[240] Until the rise of the Durranis in the mid-eighteenth century and the concomitant establishment of Sharia courts in the urban centers, however, the Afghans' religious prospects in general proved to be as dim as their imperial prospects. Afghan tribalism was ineradicable even by millennarian Islam.

Durrani imperialism and the origins of modern Afghanistan

A century after Babur, Jahangir describes in his own memoirs the Mughal armies' efforts at beating back the Afghan tribes athwart the Khyber pass – 'the Afghans who are full of darkness (...) black-faced and black-hearted' – in Bangash, Tirah, Kabul, Swat, and Bajaur.[241] Like Babur's, Jahangir's success in these efforts was inconclusive. The Afghans continued fighting from hill tops, shooting arrows and throwing down stones. Again many were being killed. Pillars of Afghans' skulls were on display in Peshawar. Afghan crops were destroyed, camps and villages raided and plundered. If the Afghans were not defeated by degrees, reconciliation attempts were made – equally inconclusive.

In the wake of the demise of Roshaniyya millennarianism, the Afghans once again made a remarkable come-back. Akbar's policy of exclusion proved unsustainable, and, already under

---

237 *Ibidem*, II, pp. 244, 297.
238 *Ibidem*, p. 245.
239 *Ibidem*, p. 263.
240 Elphinstone, *An Account of the Kingdom of Caubul*, I, pp. 262, 278, 282-4; II, p. 122.
241 Rogers, *Tūzuk-i-Jahāngīrī*, I, pp. 105, 111, 128, 197, 253, 263, 311-12; II, pp. 85-6, 99, 120, 153, 160.

Jahangir, the Afghans successfully began to claim their rightful place among the Mughal nobility and rose to the higher levels of the *manṣabdārī* system in significant numbers – a trend that continued, with the inevitable ups and downs, after the emperor's death.[242] Under Jahangir's successor Shah Jahan, major military setbacks in Central Asia and the loss of Qandahar to the Safawids in 1648 enhanced the Mughal empire's dependence on Afghan support, boosting the involvement of Afghans in its military campaigns and the protection of its supply routes, and boosting aspirations of autonomy among the Afghan tribes in the Mughal *ṣūba* of Kabul. Aurangzeb lived in constant fear that someone would mobilize the Afghans against him and take Kabul. In the 1670s, covert encouragement by Mahabat Khan, the Mughal governor of Kabul, led to a large-scale Yusufzai revolt against the Mughal strongholds in the area, prompting the emperor to intervene in person and set up camp in Hasan Abdal (between Rawalpindi and Peshawar).[243] At the close of a campaign which lasted twenty-six months and did not bring the emperor the least advantage, a new governor, Amir Khan, was installed for twenty years. The latter had to conciliate the tribes by cash handouts from the Kabul treasury and further concessions of privileges. 'Since the Pathans were strong', observes Manucci, 'there was no army sufficient to reduce the fury of these men who once claimed the crown of Hindustan and the lordship of Delhi'.[244] Aurangzeb's son Shah Alam, holding the governorship of Kabul from 1700 to 1707, was also forced to send presents 'to allay the fury of this barbarous people, in order that they might leave the routes open and that the great caravans might be allowed to pass'.[245] Meanwhile, the Afghans were gaining strength in the Deccan, raising private armies of thousands of horse-

[242] A. Rahim, 'Jahangir's Policy towards the Afghans', *Journal of the Pakistan Historical Society* 1959, nr. 7 (3), pp. 205-20; Anwar, *Nobility under the Mughals*, pp. 32, 51-2, 59-62, 86-7; M. Athar Ali, *The Mughal Nobility under Aurangzeb* (Bombay, 1970), pp. 20-1.

[243] *Manucci*, II, pp. 29, 186-211; Sarkar, *Tarikh-i-Dilkasha*, p. 98.

[244] *Manucci*, II, pp. 189-90.

[245] *Ibidem*, III, p. 468.

men.[246] Here they greatly facilitated the Mughal conquests by sowing dissension among the Afghan nobles serving the Sultanates of Ahmadnagar and Bijapur and bringing them over to the Mughal side. Newly recruited Deccani Afghans brought the frontier zone of Rayalseema under Mughal control.

Afghan migration to Hind also picked up again. Some of this migration was stimulated, and even forced, by the Mughal emperors themselves. Jahangir, for instance, marched 7,000 or 8,000 households of Khaturs and Dalazaks from the Hazara district to Lahore in order to put an end to their highway robbery and marauding in the Atak and Beas river areas; eventually he compelled them to move to the Deccan, where they became part of the Mughal conquest army.[247] Most of the Afghan migration of these centuries was however motivated again by economic opportunities.[248] As in the earlier centuries, many of the new Indo-Afghan leaders pursued careers as horse traders, acted as frontier wardens and colonists on the fringes of settled cultivation, or served as mercenaries in one or another army in the subcontinent. Almost all Indo-Afghan colonies and small states emerged along the routes of the horse trade; characteristically, such colonies retained links with the tribes remaining in their homelands and encouraged or facilitated further immigration.

Two distinct migration flows are in evidence. One was that of the Tarins, Pannis and Kakars from south-eastern Afghanistan to Bianah (south-west of Agra), Sind, Gujarat, Malwa, the Deccan, and South India. The exact number of migrants caught up in this flow is unknown but it clearly was large. So many Afghans settled down around Sarangpur, Bhilsa and Ujjain, for instance, that the zamindars of the neighboring regions could raise an exclusively Afghan army of 25,000 to 50,000. Further south, along the routes of the Deccan, Afghan settlement was vigorously

---

[246] *Ibidem*, I, p. 325; II, pp. 131, 241; Sarkar, *Tarikh-i-Dilkasha*, pp. 104, 111, 143.

[247] Rogers, *Tūzuk-i-Jahāngīrī*, I, pp. 100, 127, 299.

[248] J.J.L. Gommans, *The Rise of the Indo-Afghan Empire, c. 1710-1780* (Leiden, 1995), p. 101 & *passim*; *Manucci*, IV, p. 248; Elphinstone, *An Account of the Kingdom of Caubul*, II, pp. 164-5; Husain, 'Pattern of Afghan Settlements', pp. 327-31.

stimulated by Daud Khan Panni (d. 1715), a middleman and military entrepreneur who used his extensive Mughal connections to build an important military and commercial network to link Hindustan and the Deccan via the new Indo-Afghan trading principalities of Tonk, Bhopal, Kurnool (Karnul-Qamarnagar), Cuddapah (Kharappa), and the Indian Ocean port of Sao Thomé. The second, northern, migration flow was that of the Yusufzai, Bangash, Lodis, and other Afghan tribes from beyond Atak, the area between Bajaur, Tirah and Swat, across the length and breadth of Hindustan and as far as Bhatta in southern Bihar and Bhati in eastern Bengal. In the seventeenth century this flow of migrants gave rise to a large and compact new Afghan population center close to Delhi.[249] The newcomers occupied an almost solid block bounded by the Ganges in the west and the Garra river in the east, separating the *ṣūba*-s of Delhi and Agra from Awadh and Allahabad, and growing into a serious menace to the Mughal government by the middle of the eighteenth century. This area of Afghan immigration was formerly known as Katahr and part of the *iqṭa*ᶜ of Badaʾun under the Sultans of Delhi – renowned for its exceptionally good pasture land on the strips of swampy soil and loose sand which ran parallel to the numerous rivers of the area – and now renamed as Rohilkhand, after its newly dominant Rohilla immigrants.[250] Afghan settlement in Katahr/Rohilkhand was initially encouraged by Shah Jahan to keep the local Rajputs under control. Shahjahanpur, to the south-east of Rohilkhand, became a military colony of some 9,000 Yusufzai Afghan immigrants. The Afghan occupation of the fort of Shahabad, 20 miles south of Shahjahanpur, began in the same period and was directed against the turbulent Pandes of Agni district, in Hardoi. Immediately to the south of Rohilkhand proper, in Farrukhabad, another hereditary Afghan principality was carved out by Muhammad Khan Bangash in the early eighteenth century. Like their southern counterparts, these expanding Rohilla principalities were administered by town-based military entrepreneurs and their tribal retinues, in combination with Hindu bureaucrats and

---

[249] Sarkar, *Fall of the Mughal Empire*, 4 vols. (Bombay, 1971), I, pp. 26-41; Gommans, *Rise of the Indo-Afghan Empire*, pp. 144-59.

[250] Wink, *Al-Hind*, II, pp. 220-4.

bankers. The Rohillas presided over a productive countryside, cultivated by a largely Hindu peasantry, and they constituted a landed gentry not unlike the Yusufzai of Swat and Peshawar. In most cases, the tribes of these settlements were assigned separate *maḥalla*-s to live in. In Shahjahanpur, for example, there were fifty-two tribal *xail*-s (which are in evidence today) with their own lands; and in Shahabad and its satellite settlements, too, a strictly tribal division of residential space was maintained. This was never abandoned. The Rohilla settlements remained fundamentally tribal, although some Rohilla chiefs resorted to personal slave retainers (*čela*-s) to counteract the fissiparous tribal politics. Flourishing though they were, on their own the Afghans of Hind would have been incapable of yet another imperial revival in the eighteenth century. But Rohilkhand, Shahjahanpur, Shahabad, Farrukhabad, and the other Afghan-Rohilla settlements in Hind benefitted from the process of regional centralization that accompanied the decline of Mughal power in the eighteenth century and from the repeated invasions, in which innumerable Afghans were swept up, of the Persian emperor Nadir Shah in 1739 and of his Durrani Afghan successors in 1748 and afterwards.

By the early eighteenth century the Afghans had begun to play a prominent role not only in Mughal India but in Safawid Persia as well. In Persia, the Afghans made their presence felt in the declining years of the Safawid dynasty and it was here that Afghan imperial aspirations were kindled again. The first to rise in this context were the Ghilzai, a large western tribe with many subdivisions.[251] In 1707 Mir Vays, the leader of the Ghilzai of Qandahar, revolted against the Persians, killed the local governor, and declared his independence. His son Mahmud captured Kirman in 1720 and the Safawid capital Isfahan in 1722. Mahmud and his successor Ashraf ruled Persia, routing the Ottomans, until the rise of the great Persian conqueror Nadir Shah around 1728, and then melted away (although some of the tribe remained in Kirman and elsewhere).

After the third Ghilzai ruler Ashraf was expelled from Persia by Nadir Shah, the Abdali Afghans, led by Ahmad Khan, became

---

[251] *Encyclopaedia of Islam* (Leiden, 1986), s.v. Ghilzai & Abdali.

the principal Afghan tribe. Entirely nomadic, and scattered between Qandahar and Herat, the Abdali tribe had maintained close relations with Mughal India – especially with the Multan area, where some of its members made a living as camel traders – but its early rise to prominence was to a large extent the result of the intense Mughal-Safawid competition for Qandahar.[252] The Safawid monarch Shah Abbas I (1588-1629) brought large numbers of nomadic Abdali tribesmen under his control by moving them from Qandahar to Herat and making Sado, of the Popalzai clan, the head of the Abdali tribe, with the title of *Mīr-i Afāġina.* The Abdali tribe subsequently played off the two imperial parties against each other, and as a consequence gained in power, status and wealth, while competing for land with the Ghilzai. During the days of Ghilzai power in Persia they were ousted by them from Qandahar. But, with the help of their Multani fellow tribesmen, they were able to take Herat from the Ghilzai in 1716, and their power rapidly increased after that, until they were forced, like the Ghilzai, to submit to Nadir Shah in 1728. The Abdalis then served as mercenaries in Nadir Shah's numerous campaigns. With their aid he took Herat in 1731, Qandahar in the next six years, Delhi in 1739, and soon afterwards the *ṣūba* of Kabul with all parts of the Panjab and Sind west of the Indus (down to the sea), as well as Tatta province and its ports.[253] Nadir Shah removed the Abdalis from Herat and gave them back, in reward for their good services, their territory of Qandahar. He numbered the tribe, when he was fixing their lands and the proportion of men they were to furnish for military service, and found 60,000 families.[254] During the remainder of his life, Nadir Shah was incessantly campaigning in western and central Asia, with the aid of his Uzbek and Afghan supporters, while keeping up friendly relations with the Mughal emperor Muhammad Shah. Plotting the destruction of the Qizilbash (the former military supporters of the Safawid dynasty), he was murdered in 1747 and thus left the field open for Ahmad Khan Abdali.

---

252 Gommans, *Rise of the Indo-Afghan Empire*, p. 35.
253 Sarkar, *Fall of the Mughal Empire*, I, pp. 121-3.
254 Elphinstone, *An Account of the Kingdom of Caubul*, II, pp. 99-100.

Immediately upon Nadir Shah's assassination, Ahmad Khan Abdali crowned himself 'Shah' or 'King' of the Afghans. Ahmad Shah gave himself the title of *Durr-i Durrānī*, 'Pearl of Pearls,' after which the Abdalis, as the dominant tribe of the new monarchy, changed their name to Durranis. He made Qandahar his new capital, surrounding it with a wall, and from there expanded his empire from the west of Khurasan to Sirhind, and from the Amu Darya to the sea. It was the first time the Afghans were united under a native king in their own homeland. Notably, the forms of his royal government and court, as well as the organization of his army, were exactly the same as those of Nadir Shah. But whereas the Persians had long assented to the conventions of an absolute monarchy, Ahmad Shah founded his over a warlike and tribal people that had no attachment to that form of government.[255] Affecting a strong attachment to his nation, he adopted a policy of conciliation among Afghans. He treated mullahs with great respect; and he became known for few acts of cruelty and injustice. Showing dignity on occasion, at other times he was plain and familiar, and with the Durranis he kept up the same equal and open demeanor which was usual among khans before he assumed the title of king.[256] To minimize jealousy among his own tribe he distributed all the great offices of his new state among the leading Durranis, thus making his own tribe the main political and military support of the monarchy, and leaving the hereditary chiefs in the undisturbed possession of their privileges and rarely interfering with the internal government of the clans. Even the capital city of Qandahar, which grew greatly in size, was divided into many *maḥalla*-s or quarters, each of which belonged to one of the numerous tribes and ethnic groups, most of whom were Afghans, which inhabited the city.[257]

Ahmad Shah took great effort to improve the advantage he derived from the veneration in which the Durranis held the house of Suddozai to which he himself belonged.[258] The small division of the Suddozai had long been the Khankhail or head family of

[255] *Ibidem*, p. 104.
[256] *Ibidem*, pp. 298-9.
[257] *Ibidem*, pp. 129-45.
[258] *Ibidem*, pp. 95-105.

the Popalzai (a numerous clan) and all the Durranis, and was already recognized as such by the Safawid emperor Shah Abbas I when he made the hereditary chief of the clan the *Mīr-i Afāġina*. The royal family, on this account, was regarded as sacred, and no retaliation or punishment could be inflicted on any of them except by other members of the royal family. Most importantly perhaps, Ahmad Shah restored the Durranis to all their ancestral lands, with a large part of the lands of the Ghilzai as well, requiring in return only military service and exempting them from all payment of revenue. The lands of the Durranis were thus given to them on condition of military service, and this again set the Durranis apart from the other tribes, for whom military service to the crown was an innovation introduced after they had occupied their lands. Care was taken, however, that the military divisions were made to correspond to those of the tribes and that the authority of the latter's hereditary chiefs was preserved, in other words that the tribal chiefs commanded the troops. The power of the great officers of the Durrani empire, known as Sirdars, was thus checked by the influence which the tribal chiefs had over their *ūlūs*.[259] Foreign wars to a large extent supplied the means of consolidating power at home, providing the funds to maintain the army, for favours and rewards to Afghan chiefs, and hopes for plunder for the tribes, while at the same time raising the king's reputation and preventing the chiefs from unduly increasing their power among their own tribes. Outside the Afghan-dominated lands Ahmad Shah relied more on force than on conciliation. Among the Baluchis, he merely turned to the chiefs. In Khurasan he relied on the cooperation of some chiefs, took hostages from others, and used force against all others. In Turkistan he relied on force alone.

If, then, among Afghans the legitimacy of the Durrani empire to a large extent derived from a compromise with tribal authority on all levels, it was based on different premises everywhere else.[260] Under Ahmad Shah, the Afghans advanced a specifically Durrani form of Perso-Islamic universalism which superseded the imperial claims of all the older empires of Persia,

[259] *Ibidem*, p. 104.

[260] Gommans, *Rise of the Indo-Afghan Empire*, pp. 45-67.

Central Asia and India. In places like Herat and Qandahar, both of which were part of Persia, the Durranis avoided a clear commitment to fight Shiᶜism and, like Nadir Shah, attempted to incorporate the national Persian strand of Shiᶜism into their own more universalistic mainstream Sunnism, seeking the Ottoman Sultan's recognition of Twelver Shiᶜism as the fifth Sunni school of law. Khurasan and the whole of Persia were clearly seen as a Durrani client state. By contrast, in Turkistan Ahmad Shah tried to legitimize his activities by taking up the cause of Muslims endangered by the Chinese annexation of its eastern territories. While in India, Ahmad Shah defied Mughal authority by reclaiming all the Indian provinces previously handed over to Nadir Shah, even though, in the end, the Durrani territories extended well beyond those of Nadir Shah and came to include Sirhind, Lahore, Multan, Kashmir, Thatta, Sind, and the Derajat. In a letter written to the Ottoman Sultan after the defeat of the Marathas at Panipat in 1761, Ahmad Shah commemorated the Afghan legacy in Hindustan, pointing out that its conquest by Amir Timur had been facilitated by numerous Afghans and that since then it had prospered and had been well governed by twenty-nine Afghan rulers.[261] Now, however, Islam was in danger in India, prompting Ahmad Shah to declare a *jihād* against the Marathas and Sikhs in order to re-establish Mughal rule. Consistent with these stated aims, a few years earlier, during his fourth invasion of Hindustan, the Durrani emperor read the *xuṭbah* and issued coins (*sikka*) in his own name, while solemnly re-investing Shah Alamgir II with the Sultanate of Hindustan in return for a considerable tributary payment. Ahmad Shah also repeatedly gave out he came to India in order to support the Indo-Afghans whose territories were threatened by infidel Marathas and Jats. His Indo-Afghan Rohilla and Bangash allies were given new imperial titles and extensive territories in the Mian Doab in return for crucial military and financial support during the invasions. In effect, the Durranis and the Indo-Afghans shared, apart from their common ethnicity, a powerful interest in the preservation of the extensive Afghan trading network which linked Central Asia

[261] *Ibidem*, p. 56.

and India and which was one of the foundations of Durrani imperialism around the middle of the eighteenth century.

This new imperial system of Afghan states of the eighteenth century straddling India, Persia and Central Asia was remarkable because it successfully deployed the resources of a mixed pastoral-nomadic and agricultural-sedentary economy. Combining stock breeding, raiding, trading and agrarian management, it was the Afghans, above all others, who benefitted from the dual process of Chinese and Russian expansion which opened up new outlets for the Central-Asian economy.[262] The Durrani incorporation of Makran Baluchistan and Sind connected Central Asia with the Persian Gulf and its main port Masqat.[263] Emerging maritime trading links between the Makran, and Sind ports of Karachi, Gwalior, Sonmiani, and Chah Bahar and Kacch, Kathiawar and the Malabar coast increasingly reduced the role of the once dominant Mughal port of Surat. In the wake of Durrani expansion towards India, the overland trade of the Persian Gulf and Khurasan was almost entirely redirected via Qandahar and Multan to Sind. Great numbers of Hindu bankers and merchants were drawn to Shikarpur, Multan, Dera Ghazi Khan, Qandahar and Kabul.[264] Shikarpuri financial agents, carrying bills of exchange, moved across an area from Astrakhan to Calcutta and from Masqat to Samarkand. As Charles Masson put it, 'from Shikarpur were supplied the funds which set on foot those successive [Durrani] inroads into, and invasions of the neighbouring countries…'.[265] In Hindustan itself the traditional Mughal route from Bengal to the capitals of Agra and Delhi and, via Sirhind and Lahore, to Kabul, was also completely redirected.[266] The eastern leg of this route shifted northward, entering Rohilkhand via central Awadh and Farrukhabad, and from there could bypass

[262] *Ibidem*, pp. 1, 7, 33-4.

[263] *Ibidem*, p. 36.

[264] *Ibidem*, pp. 38-9; S.C. Levi, *The Indian Diaspora in Central Asia and its Trade, 1550-1900* (Leiden, 2002), esp. pp. 27, 55, 59, 114-17, 147-8, 161-3, 176-8, 207; C. Markovits, *The Global World of Indian Merchants, 1750-1947: Traders of Sind from Bukhara to Panama* (Cambridge, 2000).

[265] Masson, *Narrative of Various Journeys*, I, p. 355.

[266] Gommans, *Rise of the Indo-Afghan Empire*, p. 42.

Delhi (and the Sikh territories) altogether and continue south to Jaipur and the other cities of Rajasthan, or through Bareilly, along the hills, via Najibabad, Hardwar and Laldong, to Jammu and Kashmir, and from there to Peshawar and Kabul. Rohilkhand thus became the new crossroads of trade from the north, north-west and east, while the Rajput states commanded the route from the north towards the Deccan and Sind and Afghanistan. Food grains, sheep, horses, and camels moved through the Thar desert routes to Bahawalpur, Multan and Shikarpur. It was a configuration of imperial and commercial relations, in which the horse trade remained central, which lasted far into the second half of the eighteenth century and which exceeded in value the total of Bengal exports by the Dutch and English East India Companies combined.[267] In the Durrani territories to the north of the Hindu Kush it even led to increased nomadic penetration in some areas and a shift away from crop cultivation to pasturage.

As was to be expected, Durrani expansion did put the tribal institutions of Afghan society under severe strain. After Ahmad Shah's death in 1773, his son and successor Timur Shah, like all earlier Afghan monarchs, was tempted to reduce, if not outright abolish, the power of his tribal constituency.[268] Born in Meshed in 1746 and educated at his father's court and on expeditions, then stationed in the Panjab and appointed governor of Herat, a city with an overwhelmingly Persian population, Timur Shah was quite out of touch with Afghan tribal culture from the beginning, and unable even to speak Pashto. Mistrustful of the Durranis, he moved his capital from Qandahar to Kabul. Although leaving the great dignities of the state in the hands of the same Durrani families on which Ahmad Shah had conferred them, he introduced new offices and changed the nature of the old ones, thereby in practice thrusting the entire government into the hands of his own dependents. Ensconced in his capital of Kabul, he relied on his own guard troops, the *ġulām-i šāh*, who were mostly Persian and Tajik and entirely devoted to him. Timur Shah attempted to set his finances on a new footing and make himself independent of military expeditions. But the result was a

[267] *Ibidem*, pp. 89-90.

[268] Elphinstone, *An Account of the Kingdom of Caubul*, II, p. 297-352.

rapid reversal to the usual Afghan tribal fragmentation of power and a concomitant decline of the power of the monarchy. The remote provinces withdrew, and insurrections followed. Upon Timur Shah's death in Kabul in 1793, his successor Zaman Shah widened the breach between the Durranis and his court even further, and made no serious effort to safeguard Khurasan, while his efforts to invade India were generally thwarted by the dangers which he had failed to attend to in the west. Since Ahmad Shah's time, India had changed as much as Persia. There were no longer any treasuries in India to be raided.

From about 1800 onwards, then, the Afghan monarchy became more and more isolated. Afghan officials of the early nineteenth century were aware that the Mughal empire had declined, but they had, as Elphinstone put it, 'a very imperfect knowledge of the numerous states that have been erected on its ruins'.[269] Having been on the road to failure for centuries, Afghanistan now became a failed state, increasingly condemned to play a passive role in the Great Game between imperial Russia and Britain.

Not until the reign of Abdur Rahman, the Iron Amir, between 1880 and 1901, was the power of the Afghan tribal aristocracy totally reshaped.[270] At that juncture of Afghan history, a form of Islam came into being that had very little in common with what passed as Islam before it, and served as justification for the centralizing policies of the Amir, above all his right to collect taxes.[271] By then, however, it was too late to turn Afghanistan into a success. Failure would continue to haunt the Afghans. Successful modernization has eluded them to this day.

---

[269] *Ibidem*, p. 249.

[270] A. Ghani, 'Islam and State-Building in a Tribal Society: Afghanistan, 1880-1901', *Modern Asian Studies*, 1978, nr. 12 (2), pp. 269-84.

[271] *Ibidem*, pp. 277, 281.

Persian lexicography in South Asia

Kinga Maciuszak

For more than two centuries after the Arab Muslim conquest of Iran the Persian language had not appeared in any literary form. During the tenth century, the Samanid dynasty had established the dialect of it, known as Dari (*dar* 'court') as the court and literary language of their empire centred on Bukhara.[1] This dialect included elements of other northern Iranian languages (Parthian, Sogdian, Khoresmian) and differed noticeably from the variant of Persian (*Pārsī*) spoken in south-western Iran. The linguistic situation in the country at that time was even more complicated as the official language in the west was Arabic (e.g. at the Buvayhid court) and the Persian intellectuals of the region also wrote in that language. During the eleventh century the prestigious Dari, the language of original poetry and prose started to expand its domain westward. Such famous poets of the east as Abu Hafs Sogdi and particularly Asadi Tusi (b. *c.* 999-1000, d. 1072-3) composed the first lexicons to explain the unfamiliar words and phrases of the chic Dari poetry for the people of Azerbaijan, who were less fortunate because they "could not speak

[1] Cf. Perry, 1993: 250.

Persian very well".[2] Thus the earliest Persian monolingual dictionaries were compiled by poets of the east for poets and readers of the west; those lexicons arranged their vocabulary in alphabetical order of the final letter, i.e. by rhyme. The concept of a rhyming dictionary (Arabic methodological influence) often bearing an Arabic title[3] (fashionable convention) had also been developed by lexicographers in South Asia, who were the most active from the thirteenth century onwards.

From the very beginning of the Muslim invasion of northern India, Persian as the language of local administration and literature gradually achieved the rank of the most prominent language. The courts, first Ghaznavid (in Lahore – often called "little Ghazna"), then Ghurid (since 1192: Multan, Delhi) and Mughal (since 1525) became real literary and cultural centers. After 1206 (the foundation of the Delhi Sultanate), the generosity of their rulers attracted many poets and scholars from Persia. In fact emigration of Iranian scholars and artists to South Asia was quite common in the eleventh-seventeenth centuries. In particular, a province of Avadh (Oudh) in North India was a fertile area, where elites from Iran settled (Belgram, Hardoi, Kakori) and developed their intellectual activities. Since 1327, i.e. the transfer of Delhi's cultural elite to its second capital Daulatabad, the influence and prestige of Persian culture spread further south. Under open-minded sovereigns and governors the Muslim courts that flourished in the Deccan between the fourteenth and seventeenth centuries became prosperous centers of cultural produc-

[2] *Ibidem.*

[3] Persian dictionaries besides standard titles, e.g.: *Jāme᾽ al-loġāt* ('Collection of words'), *Karīm al-loġāt* ('Noble vocabulary'), *Kašf al-loġāt* ('Explanation of vocabulary'), *Majmaᶜ al-fors* ('Persian collection') and *Mojmal al-ᶜajam* ('Persian compendium'), also boast of pretentious ones as: *Baḥr al-fāẓil* ('The sea of the learned'), *Farā᾽id al-favā᾽id* ('Unique pearls of profits'), *Anīs ál-šo᾽arā* ('Garden of poets'), *Kaṣīr al-favā᾽id* ('Numerous profits'), *Laṭā᾽if al-loġāt* ('The elegance of words'), *Lesān al-šo᾽arā* ('The language of poets'), *Malāẕ al-kalemāt* ('Delights of words'), *Miftāḥ al-foẓalā᾽* ('The key of learned men'), *Me᾽yār al-loġāt* ('The mirror of words'), *Mozīl al-aġlāṭ* ('Remover of errors'), *Nafāyes al-loġāt* ('Precious words'), *Qisṭās al-loġāt* ('Balance of words'), *Xazānat al-loġāt* ('Treasure of words'), etc.

tion in Persian. The age of the first six Mughal rulers (1525-1707) represented the zenith of Indo-Persian literature and lexicography. In this period fresh waves of gifted emigrants from Safavid Persia came to South Asia. Moreover, with the advent of Lodi rule (1451-1526) the knowledge of Persian language and literature began to filter through to the Hindu administrative class. In the seventeenth century a lack of patronage led to the weakening of Indo-Persian cultural contacts. However, after the decline of Delhi in the early eighteenth century, in Avadh still ruled by Iranian Shiᶜites from Nishapur a new stream of Persian poets, scholars and painters appeared. This province then became the main centre for literary creativity and artistic activity in Persian. Despite the growing status of Urdu, the Persian language remained the medium of government, high culture and the court language until the mid-nineteenth century.

The Persian lexicographical tradition, which can be traced back to the eleventh century, began to be developed intensively in South Asia at the end of the thirteenth century. The influence of the Persian language and literature and the need for manuals and lexicons led both Persian emigrants and Indian men of letters to compile monolingual dictionaries. Many scholars maintain, that particularly the production of dictionaries was the greatest legacy of South Asia in the field of linguistic inquiry into Persian.

According to S.I. Baevski, the leading authority on this subject, the history of Persian lexicography in South Asia can be divided into 3 periods[4]:

13th-15th CE (8-9th H) – the early period
16th-17th CE (10-11th H) – the most flourishing period
18th-19th CE (12-13th H) – continuation and decline of tradition.

I. 13th-15th c. – early lexicographical works

Almost every dictionary of this period has a conventional introduction: its author declares that he was asked by his friends to compile a dictionary (*farhang* or *farhang-nāme*) of the unknown Dari words and phrases so that they could easily read Ferdousi's

[4] Baevski, 1989: 49.

Šāhnāme (most frequently) and other outstanding works of Persian literature (e.g. Nezami Ganjavi's *Eskandar-nāme*). For that reason some of those lexicons were also referred to as: *Farhang-e Šāhnāme* or *Farhang-e Sekandar-nāme.*[5] In the preface their authors usually claimed to have defined words from the works of Persian poets, but some of them also meant their dictionary to be useful to those reading academic works: "I have made a key that will unlock the treasures of scholars and poets" (*Dāneš-nāme-ye Qadar Xān*, fol. 4b). The majority of them included corroborative citations from many Persian poets to illustrate the definition of a given entry (only some of them offered simple one-word definitions) and listed the authors whose prose or poetry they had used. Many words were accompanied by two or three examples from poets from Transoxania, Khorasan, and Azerbaijan. There were also many anonymous stanzas, introduced with the words: *bozorg-i goft* 'a great one said' or *qāʾel guyad* 'the bard says'.

Entries were rather short, did not include all the meanings of a defined word, consisted only of the word and an equivalent (a synonym), usually without indication of pronunciation (with the exception of e.g. *Farhang-e zafānguyā* and *Šarafnāme-ye Monyarī*, where a descriptive characterization of the reading of the word was explained, sometimes noting variant readings, and marking *maᶜrūf* and *majhūl* vowels). Textual evidence (e.g. application of the same examples, repetitions and certain errors) shows that the lexicographers in South Asia used the first Persian dictionary by Asadi Tusi, i.e. *Loġāt al-fors* as a major source, and then exploited the works of their predecessors (often listed in the preface to their own works).

---

[5] Cf. *Farhang-e Sekandar-nāme* compiled by Seyyed b. Hasan in the middle of the eighteenth century. Lexicographers of that time also continued this tradition and composed dictionaries compirsing lexica of one book, e.g.: *Farhang-e Golestān* by Joneyd Abdallah Musavi, *Farhang-e Jaᶜfarī* by Jaᶜfar ᶜAli Khan (*Šāhnāme*), *Farhang-e nāyāb* (*Šabnom šādāb* of *Ẓahīrā-ye Tofrašī*) by Mohammad Hadi. Of these works one of the most interesting is *Farhang-e Dasātir* – a book, written in an invented language, about supposedly ancient Iranian prophets. Some of the fabricated words of the *Dasātir* found acceptance as genuine Persian vocabulary. From 1062/1652, when *Borhān-e qāṭeᶜ* was compiled, until very recently they were included in Persian dictionaries published in both Persia and India.

The first extant Persian dictionary in South Asia, entitled ***Farhang-e Qavvās***[6] ('The Qavvas' Dictionary') was composed no earlier than 695/1295 and no later than 716/1315[7] by a famous poet of the Alauddin Khalji's (695-715/1295-1316) court, Fakhr--al-Din Mobarakshah Qavvas of Ghazna (thus considered as a founder of Persian lexicography in India), also known as Kamangar ('a bone-setter'). He dedicated it to Dastur Roushanshah, of whom no information has been left. In the preface Qavvas wrote that he had composed it to facilitate reading the Ferdousi's *Šāhnāme*, however he cited the examples from some sixty other Persian and Indian poets (e.g. Rudaki, Adib Saber, Suzani, Nezami, Khaqani, Taj Rize, Shehab Mahmara and Naseri).

The dictionary included *c.* 1050-1341 entries. The words were arranged not alphabetically, like the majority of the later lexicons, but thematically, like Persian dictionaries of pre-Islamic times, which were exegetical in motivation and belonged to an entirely separate tradition of religious scholarship.[8] The contents – only native Persian simple nouns – is divided into five chapters (*baxš*) – also referred to as *Farhang-e panj baxš* (The dictionary of five chapters); each chapter is divided into sections (*guna*) comprised of a number of sub-sections (*bahra*), again on thematic principles: *Baxš* I: Names of the phenomena of the upper world: (*Guna* 1. names of God, who is the most important; *Guna* 2. names of the angels, the prophets, the religions and their holy books; *Guna* 3. names of the heavens, stars and months; *Guna* 4. names of fire, wind, water and earth; *Guna* 5. names of the phenomena that occur between heaven and earth); *Baxš* II: Names of minerals and inanimate objects (soil, mountain, stone, clay, mud, dust etc.); *Baxš* III: Names of things which grow, i.e. of the vegetable kingdom (*Guna* 1. names of grasses; *Guna* 2.

[6] The only known manuscript of this work written in the early sixteenth century is preserved in the library of the Asiatic Society of Bengal (Ivanov, no. 516; 68 folios). Persian edition by N. Ahmad appeared in Tehran in 1353/1974.

[7] According to *An Encyclopaedia of Persian Literature* (II: 1402) it was compiled earlier i.e. *c.* 690.

[8] Like the *Frahang-i oim* and the *Frahang-i pahlavik*. Cf. Perry, 1993: 251.

names of flowers and flower gardens; *Guna* 3. names of trees; *Guna* 4. names of crops and grains); *Baxš* IV: Names of animals (*Guna* 1. names of birds; *Bahr* 1. large birds, *Bahr* 2. small birds; *Guna* 2. aquatic animals; *Guna* 3. creeping animals (reptiles); *Guna* 4. quadrupeds; *Guna* 5. humans: *Bahr* 1. body parts, *Bahr* 2. human qualities); *Baxš* V: Names of things people produce and use (*Guna* 1. dwellings and houses; *Guna* 2. vessels, dishes; *Guna* 3. food; *Guna* 4. clothes; *Guna* 5. illnesses; *Guna* 6. war, warriors and weapons; *Guna* 7. tools, equipment, occupations; *Guna* 8. miscellaneous nouns; *Guna* 9. infinitives (*masdar*-s).

This dictionary played an important part in the development of Persian lexicography in South Asia, for it set the example for later *farhang*-s and influenced many of them, e.g. ***Dastūr al--afāẓel fī loġāt al-faẓāʾel***[9] ('Guidance of the learned for learned words') compiled in 743/1342, during the reign of Mohammad ben Tughlaq Shah (725-52/1325-52) by a poet Hajeb Kheyrat Rafi of Delhi for his patron Shams-al-Din Mohammad Ahmad ben ᶜAli Jajniri. This lexicon contains mostly nouns and proper names, with only a few infinitives, adjectives, and adverbs. There are many Arabic and a few Turkish words. It is the first Persian dictionary known to have been arranged alphabetically by initial letters, though words beginning with the same letter occur in no particular order. There is occasional evidence of dialectal or local lexical peculiarities, for example: Transoxanian *dādar* (= *barādar*) 'brother' and Deylamite *kīā* (= *pahlavān*) 'hero' (pp. 127, 208).[10]

One should also mention here a peculiar lexicon ***Maṭbūʾ as--ṣobyān*** ('Created with a disposition for youths')[11] also known as ***Xāleq-bārī***[12] ('Creator God') composed in verse (*maṡnavī*; 192

[9] Only one manuscript of this work is known to have survived; it was copied *c.* 900/1600 and is now kept in the library of The Asiatic Society in Calcutta (Ivanov, no. 517). It was published for the first time in Persia by Nazir Ahmad (Tehran, 1352/1973).

[10] Cf. Baevski, 1989: 56.

[11] Only in lithographic edition: cf. *Majmūᶜe-ye fārsī*, Bombay, 1887.

[12] In the eighteenth century an Indo-Persian poet and lexicographer Mohammad Azfari Gurgani (Mirza-ye Kalan) composed *Tengrī tārī*, a Turkish-Hindi imitation of the *Xāleq-bārī*.

bait-s) and ascribed to a famous poet, "a Parrot of India", Amir Khusrow Dehlavi (651-725/1253-1352). As we know, his profound knowledge of Arabic, Persian, Turkish, and Hindi enabled him to produce puns, wordplays, and stunning literary tricks. This work, in fact the first Persian-Arabic-Indian dictionary for children, is such a trick: the first *meṣrāᶜ* includes a Persian word, its synonym and an Arabic equivalent, while the second one – its translation into Hindustani. In South Asia it was used as a manual for children who learned Persian, that is why it contains only simple words, like: creator, prophet, soul, father, mother, brother, bread, salt, fire, mountain, horse, hare, lion, mouse, etc.

The admirable activity in compiling Persian lexicons was flourishing already during the fifteenth century. At that time many of the most valuable works appeared. The first of them dedicated to Qadar Khan, a son of Delavar Khan Quri, the ruler of Malva (794-809/1392-1405) entitled ***Dāneš-nāme-ye Qadar Xān***[13] ('Book of wisdom [dedicated] to Qadar Khan') was compiled in 807/1405[14] by Ashraf ben Sharaf al-Mozakker al-Faruqi, a native of the Chandiri district. In the preface medical terms and the old Persian names of months and days and of Persian calendar holidays were listed and defined. The dictionary included 2,419 definitions ranging over a broad general vocabulary, as well as names of flora and fauna. Arabic lexical elements and words of Greek and Syriac origin were included, though usually without indication of the original languages. Sometimes instead of Persian definitions the author offered only the Urdu equivalents.

Adāt al-foẓalāʾ[15] ('Tools of learned men') compiled in 822/1419 (or 812/1409) by Qazi Khan Badr-al-Din Mohammad (or Hoseyn). Born in Delhi, he studied there under two leading

---

[13] The existence of this text became known only in the twentieth century, and it still remains unpublished. The only manuscript – complete and well preserved – is kept in the Institute of Manuscripts at the Academy of Sciences of Azerbaijan in Baku.

[14] The colophon on fol. 227a includes the date when it was copied, i.e. the 21st of ẕū 'l-ḥejja 807 (20 June 1405), and the name of the copyist, Ešāq ben Ebrāhīm Boxārāʾī.

[15] Rare manuscripts of this dictionary are listed in catalogues: Blochet 1912: no 972; Rieu 1881, t. 2: 491; and Monzavi 1350, vol. 3: 1919. One of them is kept in the Punjab Public Library, Lahore (no. 473).

philologists of the time, Qazi Borhan-al-Din of Bodhana and Sheykh-zada Asheq. From Delhi he went to Jaunpur, the capital of the Sharqid kingdom (796-881/1394-1477), and then to the city of Dhar, the capital of the Ghurid principality of Malva which was an important centre of patronage for scholars. He took the pen-name Dharval and dedicated his dictionary to the sovereigns of Dhar (i.e. Qadr Khan, the scholarly brother of the Ghurid ruler Hushang-shah). Dharval was one of the first Indian, not Persian scholars who compiled a Persian dictionary. The *Adāt al-foẓalā᾽* is small book divided into two parts, the first an alphabetical list of Persian words and the second a list alphabetized by first and last letter of compounds and poetical phrases.

In the early ninth/fifteenth century (*c.* 837/1433) the dictionary ***Farhang-e zafāngūyā va jahānpūyā***[16] ('Dictionary of eloquent speakers and those, who study the world') by Badr-al-Din Ebrahimi appeared. It is one of the first Persian dictionaries to cover a comparatively large lexicographical field (5,170 words), the first to use the unparalleled so far principle of arrangment (seven individually titled parts – *baxš*, alphabetically arranged chapters – *guna* – containing explanations of words beginning with the same letter and divided into sections – *bahra* according to the last letter of the word explained), and the earliest attempt in Persian lexicography at compiling a multilingual dictionary.

[16] For a long time the *Farhang-e zafāngūyā* was counted as lost, but at the beginning of the 1960s the discovery of two manuscripts was reported: one, in the Orientalist Library of Patna (India), was a complete copy of the dictionary, but defective at the edges, written in the ninth/fifteenth century. The second manuscript was identified by S.I. Baevski in an incomplete copy of an unidentified dictionary in the library of the State University of Tashkent, written in 1123/1711. Baevski used this copy as the basis for an edition of the dictionary, comparing the Indian manuscript. In 1978, he published a report of the discovery of a third (incomplete) manuscript of the dictionary (wr. 998/1590) in the catalogue of the Ketāb-xāna-ye Senā (the Senate Library; no. 527), Tehran, which had until then been known in scholarly literature as the *Farhang-e panj-baxšī*. In 1986 Baevski identified a fourth manuscript. The manuscript, described in W. Pertsch, 1888: 142, no. 74 is dated 921/1515 but does not name itself. It contains a complete copy of the *Farhang-e zafāngūyā*, closely resembling the Tehran copy in its redaction. Cf. Baevski, 1989: 68-77.

The first three parts are devoted to the Persian lexicon and are arranged according to the formation of the words: 1. simple words (Pahlavi and Dari); 2. complex words (Dari); 3. Pahlavi and Dari words, mostly old, infinitives (rare in earlier dictionaries). In an appendix to the dictionary, the author has gathered Persian expressions and compounds with metaphorical meanings; 4. Arabic (*tāzī*) loanwords in Persian; 5. Arabic, Nabatean and Persian words; 6. "Roman" (*rumī*) lexicon (i.e. words of Greek, Latin, or Syriac provenience); 7. Turkic words.

In the preface to the dictionary Ebrahimi explained the tasks of his lexicographical work and the principles for the presentation of the material. He introduced an innovation into the very composition of a lexical article (marked short and long vowels). To a greater extent than his predecessors he quoted dialectal vocabulary, mentioning words from Shiraz, Gilan, Bukhara, Fergana, and Transoxiana. He also strives to adapt his dictionary to the reading of a variety of written texts, and to a certain degree for direct dealings with the foreign-speaking population.

In 837/1433 ***Baḥr al-faẓāʾel (fī manāfeʾ al-afāẓel)***[17] ('Sea of wisdom as a valuable profit for the learned') by Mohammad ben Qavam ben Rostam ben Ahmad Balkhi Keraʾi was compiled. It was divided into two volumes (*kist*); the first of them "Words of the learned man: Persian, Pahlavi, Arabic and Greek" (28 chapters – *bāb*) was arranged according to the initial and second letter of the word. The second *kist* "On various things" consisted of 14 *bāb*-s and was arranged thematically: 1. names of cities; 2. names of drugs and medicines; 3. nicknames; 4. names of months and days; 5. names of stars and constellations; 6. names of climates and famous towns; 7. names of human features; 8. names of measures of weight; 9. names of crafts; 10. names of various things; 11. names of wines; 12. names of tunes and musical instruments; 13. names of nations; 14. Indian words(!).

During the second half of the fifteenth century another four important *farhang*-s were composed: in 859/1455 ***Ommān al-***

---

[17] Not published; survived only in manuscripts, mentioned in the catalogues of the libraries in Iran, Pakistan, Georgia and France; cf. Ethé, 1903: no. 2512, 2967; Blochet, 1912: no. 960; and S.A. Abulandze, 1969: no. 78/114.

-maʾānī[18] ('Sea of senses') by Seyyed Ebrahim Mohammad Saʾad-o-Saʾud Amirak Balkhi (dictionary consists of rare vocabulary loaned into Persian from Arabic, Hebrew, Pahlavi, Syriac and Turkish, no quotations from literature; rare indications to pronunciation); in 873/1468 ***Meftāḥ al-fożalā***[19] ('Key of the learned') by Moula Mohammad ben Daud ben Mahmud Shadi Abadi ("a book for those, who love Persian poetry"; included many rare Persian words, archaisms, personal names); in 878/1473 appeared a wide-ranging ***Šaraf-nāma-ye Aḥmad Monyarī/Ebrāhīmī***[20] (also known as: ***Farhang-e Mirzā Ebrāhīm***) by Sheykh Ebrahim Qavam-ad-Din Faruqi Monyari Bihari-ye Hendi for the king of Bengal, Ruknuddin Barbak Shah (1457-74), dedicated to and named after the author's spiritual mentor Sharaf-ad-Din Ahmad ben Yahya of Monyar (the Bihar province). In the introduction the author explains a few grammatical points as well as some Turkish suffixes. At the end of the tenth/sixteenth century, Mirza Ebrahim ben Shah Hoseyn Esfahani abridged this dictionary and renamed it *Farhang-e Mirzā Ebrāhīm*. *Šaraf-nāma* was the source of many later dictionaries. The last dictionary of this period was ***Mojmal al-ᶜajam***[21] ('Persian compendium') composed in 899/1493 by Asem Shoʾayeb ᶜAbdusi for the vazir ᶜAli Akbar Davud Khan, the son of Emad al-Molk (many Indian equivalents for Persian words, citations from poetry).

II. 16th-17th c. – most flourishing period

In the sixteenth century increasing Hindu interest in Persian under the Lodi reign led to the realization of some important new dictionaries. At that time the most prestigious works were com-

---

[18] Not published; rare manuscripts in: the Institut for Eastern Studies, Tajik Academy of Sciences and India Office in London; cf. Ethé, 1903, no. 2960: 1605.

[19] Not published; only in manuscripts (e.g. in the British Museum). Cf. Rieu, 1879-83: 116.

[20] Not published; only in manuscripts (e.g. Iran, India, Pakistan, Egypt).

[21] Not published; only in manuscripts (e.g. in the British Museum).

piled, e.g. in 1510 ***Toḥfat al-saᶜādat***[22] ('Gift of happiness') (also known as ***Farhang-e Sekandarī***[23]), a work of Mahmud ben Sheykh Ziaᵓ-al-Din Mohammad, which registered many compounds for the first time and ten years later the famous ***Muᵓayyid al-foẓalāᵓ*** ('Great event of learned men') by Mohammad ben Sheykh Lad Dehlavi, which was divided according to the derivation of words from Arabic, Persian, and Turkish, contained an appendix of numerals, arithmetical notation, and elementary grammar. The last lexicon of the sixteenth century was ***Madār al-afāẓil*** by Allahdad Feyzi ben ᶜAli Shir Serhendi, compiled in 1001/1592.

At the beginning of the seventeenth century ***Farhang-e Jahāngīrī***[24] ('Dictionary in honour of Jahangir'), a dictionary of pure Persian words, preceded by an outline of Persian grammar was completed. Its compiler, a native of Shiraz, Mir Jamal-al-Din Hosayn ben Fakr-al-Din Hasan Enju served at the Mughal court and rose to a high position under Akbar and Jahangir. According to Baevski this work represents one of the earliest serious attempts to discuss the grammatical structure of Persian and to classify its lexicon.

By the middle of the seventeenth century, having finished his studies in Tabriz, Mohammad Hosayn ben Khalaf Tabrizi (who used the pen-name Borhan, also referred to as: Borhan-e Tabrizi, Molla Borhan) came to India and joined the court of ᶜAbd-Allah Qutb Shah (r. 1036-83/1626-72), the seventh sultan of the Shiᵓite dynasty of Golconda in the Deccan. Unfortunately the dates of Borhan's birth and death have not been recorded. The only thing we know is that in Persia he had studied under a great scholar of Safavid Iran Shaikh Bahaᵓ-al-Din Ameli (953-1031/1546-1622) and mastered the techniques of verse composition. He was a famous poet – Nezami quoted his poems and also

---

[22] Manuscripts of the *Toḥfat al-saᶜādat* are rare. One of them is kept in the Institute of Oriental Studies in St. Petersburg (C313).

[23] It was compiled in honour of Sultan Sekandar (Eskandar) II Nezam Khan (r. 1489-1517), hence its collateral title *Farhang-e Sekandarī* or *Eskandarī.*

[24] Completed only in 1017/1608 (2nd edn. 1032/1622). Numerous manuscripts.

admired him as a polymath (*jāme᾽ al-fonūn*) – but he did not leave a *dīvān*. In 1062/1651 he compiled the ***Borhān-e qāṯe**ᶜ*[25] ('Conclusive proof') and dedicated it to ᶜAbd-Allah Qutb Shah. He combined the materials of other dictionaries in one volume, saving users the trouble of consulting several different books. The work includes a large number of new words and compounds in various fields, particularly medical terms and a number of words from Iranian dialects, as well as Arabic, Turkish, Syriac, Greek, Latin and Indian words. He cites 274 Pahlavi heterograms, labeling them as *Zand* and *Pā-zand* and treating them as Persian, even though they have never been used in Persian verse or prose. Frequently reproduced in manuscripts, it became the real basis of subsequent Persian dictionaries. The spread of printing further enhanced its popularity, and editions were repeatedly brought out in South Asia and Iran. More than any other Persian dictionary, the *Borhān-e qāṯe*ᶜ was used by writers and linguists (e.g. J.A. Vullers, F. Johnson and F. Steingass).

Another noted lexicographer, Molla ᶜAbd-al-Rashid ben ᶜAbd-al-Ghafur Hoseyni, born in Tatta, Sind, was attached to the court of the Mughal ruler Shah Jahan. He was the author of the Arabic-Persian dictionary *Montaxab al-loġāt-e Šāh Jahānī*[26] (1046/1636-7), a short tract on arabicized Persian vocabulary *Resāle-ye moarrabat* and the most famous ***Farhang-e Rašīdī***[27] or ***Rašīdī-ye pārsī*** (1064/1653-4). According to many scholars it "constitutes the first essay of a critical nature in Persian philology" (Tauer, p. 431). It includes an introduction (one of the earli-

---

[25] This dictionary was aslo translated into Turkish (*Tebyān-e nāfe᾽*) by Seyyed Ahmad Asem Antabi and published in Constantinopole 1214/1799 and Cairo 1215/1800. A supplement to the *Borhān-e qāṯe*ᶜ titled *Molḥaqāt-e borhān* was compiled by Abd-al-Majid Qa᾽emmaqami and others and printed in Calcutta in 1250/1834 (rpt. 1274/1858). *Tebyān-e nāfe᾽* by Seyyed Ahmad Asem Antabi (into Turkish), Constantinopole 1214/1799, Cairo, 1215/1800.

[26] The most popular Arabic-Persian dictionary in South Asia, printed many times; including a rearranged version, published in Calcutta, 1816 by J.H. Taylor.

[27] Ed. M. Zulfaqar Ali, M. Aziz ur-Rahman as *The Farhang i Rashidi, a Persian dictionary*, 2 vols., Calcutta, 1875; ed. M. Abbasi, 2 vols., Tehran 1337/1958.

est attempts at describing the grammar of the Persian language[28]), 24 chapters (*bāb*) subdivided into sections (*faṣl*), where words with the same second letter are grouped together, and finally a conclusion. Entries are arranged in alphabetical order. Words are listed according to their first letter. Many of the sections have additions devoted to compound words and idiomatic expressions. The pronunciation of the word is indicated by giving the sequence of vowels. Sometimes the author provides Indian equivalents for listed words. The entries include quotations from many early Persian poets. This *farhang* is in fact an abridgement of *Farhang-e Jahāngīrī* and *Majma*ᶜ *al-fors* of Soruri, correcting some of their errors and omitting the corrupt forms as well as Arabic and Turkish words found in them. Mistakes and corrupt forms in *Farhang-e Rašīdī* are mentioned by ᶜAli Khan Arzu in his *Serāj al-loġāt*. This dictionary is highly valued as one of the most authoritative, reliable and complete Persian dictionaries. It was used by European compilers J.A. Vullers and F. Steingass for their own works.

III. 18-19th c. – continuation and decline of tradition

In the later Mughal period, some lexicographers made attempts to improve the falling standard of Persian in South Asia. One of the most successful ones was Anand Ram Mokhles (1111-64/1699-1750), chronicler and poet, a native of Sodhra, Sialkot district (now in Pakistan). He held a high position of a *vakīl* of the Qamar al-Din, the prime minister of Mohammad Shah (1131-61/1719-48) the governor of Lahore and Multan during the period of Nader Shah's invasion of India (1152/1739). His work ***Mer***ʾ***āt al-eṣṭelāḥ***[29] was a compendium of contemporary Persian usage based on standard works and conversations with newly

---

[28] Also published separately in Europe as *Grammaticae Persicae praecepta ac regulae quas lexico Persico Ferhengi Reshidi praefixas e duobus cod. uno Roedigeri altero bibliothecae R. Beroliensis scripsit et ed. Dr. Splieth*, Halis (Halle), 1846.

[29] MSS: Rieu, *Pers. Man.* III, 997; *Cat. Bankipore* IX, 810. The MS of the book in possession of Sayyed Azhar Ali has a sixteen-page index of its contents in Mokhles's own handwriting.

arrived Iranians. It explains official terms and procedures, idioms, and proverbs and gives the pay scale of Mughal officials and the privy purses of the nobility. It also provides information on such varied subjects as the glass industry, well-known calligraphers, and the cost of the Peacock Throne.

Among Mokhles' friends was Seraj-al-Din ᶜAli Khan Arzu, a major Indo-Muslim poet and lexicographer, born at Gwalior or Agra 1099/1687-8 or 1101/1689-90.[30] In 1132/1719-20, after finishing his early education at Agra, he went to Delhi, where he found generous patrons in Navab Eshaq Khan, the *xān-sāmān* of Mohammad Shah, and the *navvāb*'s sons, Najm al-Daula and Salar Jang. Of his dictionaries ***Serāj al-loġāt*** is the best known. Completed in 1147/1734-5, it lists the non-Arabic words used by classical Persian poets (*motaqaddemīn*) with definitions from the *Borhān-e qāṭeᶜ* of Mohammad Tabrizi (compl. 1062/1652), together with lengthy and often critical remarks.[31] *Čerāġ-e hedāyat*, a dictionary of words used by later Persian poets (*motaʾaxxerīn*), is in fact the second volume of the *Serāj*. Arzu wrote two other dictionaries: ***Zāʾed al-favāʾed***, a compilation of Persian verbs and abstract nouns based on ᶜAbd-al-Vaseʾ Hansavi's *Zavāʾed al-favāʾed*, and ***Qarāʾeb al-loġāt***, a corrected edition of Hansavi's *Qarāʾeb al-loġat*.[32]

In the eighteenth century, the increasingly complicated poetical style made new lexicographic works necessary, like the enormous work, Tik Chand Bahar's ***Bahār-e ᶜajam*** (1152/1739), which included a considerable number of idioms and expressions. In the introduction its author mentions as his source about 100 *dīvāns* and correspondence collections of the Persian and Indian poets of the Safavid period.

By the early nineteenth century South Asia had been the leading center of Persian lexicography. The accumulation of Persian-language sources: belletristic works, and treatises on medicine, astronomy, mathematics, philosophy, and poetics, necessitated

---

[30] Storey, I/2: 834.

[31] According to Blochmann: "the *Borhān* should never have been printed without the notes of the *Serāʾ*". Cf. "Contributions to Persian Lexicography", *Journal of the Asiatic Society of Bengal*, 1868, vol. 37/1: 25.

[32] Storey, I/2: 837.

the compilation of new comprehensive, encyclopedic dictionaries.

First dictionary published in this period was anonymous ***Šams al-loġāt*** (1219/1805) compiled by the order of Joseph Barretto (known as: Mestar Jozef Englisi, *sāken-e Hendustān*). The dictionary contained simple words, idioms, expressions and proverbs; examples are at times provided for illustration. As it was already mentioned, the majority of Persian monolingual dictionaries compiled in earlier periods included old, rare or unknown lexica. In the nineteenth century the main lexicographers' aim was to compile huge, more normative works. Such was the great *farhang* (27,709 entries) titled ***Haft qolzom*** ('The seven seas', i.e. seven volumes) by Shah Zaman Abu 'l-Mozaffar Ghazi-al--Din Haydar Padshah-e Ghazi, the king of Oudh, compiled in 1229-30/1813-14. Its editor was Moulavi Qabul Muhammad. The work was published by the Maṯbaᶜ-e Šāhī or Royal Press in the Daulat-khana on the Gomti river, founded by Ghazi-al-Din Haydar (r. 1814-27). The first six volumes were devoted to Persian words and idioms, arranged according to their first and final letters respectively. The last volume discussed Persian alphabet, morphology, prosody, rhyme, figures of speech, etc. A half of this size (17,000 entries) was ***Ġiyāṯ al-loġāt*** ('Aid in [the explication of] vocabulary') by the linguist, philologist, and poet Mohammad Ghiyas-al-Din ben Jamal-al-Din ben Sharaf-al-Din Rampuri Mostafa-abadi, compiled in 1242/1826. Besides Persian, Arabic and Turkish words, it recorded also determinative and attributive compounds, but without mentioning their figurative application or examples. However, this *farhang*, being in fact a critical comprehensive, encyclopedic dictionary superseded in importance the older works. Moreover it is still widely used, especially in Central Asia.

By the end of the nineteenth century in South India, at the court of the Maharaja Pusapati Ananda Gajapati Raju, the ruler of Vijayanagar, a chief secretary (*mīr monšī*), a poet and lexicographer Mohammad Padshah ben Gholam Mohi-al-Din, known by the pen-name Shad, composed for his patron two great works:

Farhang-e motarādefāt va eṣṭelāḥāt[33] (1294/1877) and ***Farhang-e Ānandrāj***[34] (1306/1888-9), which was a huge compilation of the articles from earlier dictionaries and contained about 50 thousand word-entries. It included Persian vocabulary, Arabic loan-words as well as some words of Turkic, Indian, Greek, and Latin origin. Shad's apparent interest in grammar is also worth mentioning as he includes grammatical material in his lexicon with relevant explanations and examples of metaphors and allegorical expressions. Shad's dictionary thus epitomizes the achievements of the centuries-old Persian tradition in lexicon compilation and marks a transition to the use of European methods of lexicography.[35] A European dictionary – *farhang-e farang* – is also mentioned by Shad as one of his sources. This might have been the large Persian-English dictionary of Francis Johnson (*Persian, Arabic, and English Dictionary*, London, 1852), which included many Arabic words.

One should also mention here the first European scholars working in South Asia, who contributed enormously to diffusion of the knowledge of Persian. One of them was Francis Gladwin (d. *c.* 1813), lexicographer and prolific translator of Persian literature into English, who served in the Bengal Army and later, owing to his linguistic ability, became one of the three professors of Persian at Fort William College in Calcutta in 1800. He was also a founding member of the Asiatic Society of Bengal and carried out his scholarly works and translations under the patronage of Warren Hastings. He published several dictionaries, including *The Persian Guide, Exhibiting the Arabic Derivatives* (Calcutta, 1800) and *A Dictionary, Persian, Hindoostanee and English, including Synonyma* (Calcutta, 1809), which was based on John Richardson's *Dictionary, Persian, Arabic, English...* (2 vols, Oxford, 1777). The compilers' apparent interest in grammar is also worth mentioning: the *farhang*-s of the nineteenth century besides lexicon with relevant explanations and examples included grammatical material. This attention lead them to com-

---

[33] Ed. Tehrān, 1967.

[34] 3 vols., Lucknow, 1889-92; ed. M. Dabirsiaqi, 7 vols., Tehrān, 1956-8.

[35] Baevski, *EI*.

pile the first grammars of the Persian language: e.g. W.C. Smith, *Three Persian Moonshee, containing a copious grammar and a series of entertaining stories, also the pand-nama of sheykh Sadee*, Calcutta, 1796, M. Lumsden, *A Grammar of the Persian Language*, comprising a portion of the elements of arabic inflection, vols. I-II, Calcutta, 1810; Th. Roebuck, *The Persian Primer: an easy introduction to the Persan language*, Calcutta, 1819; A. Faulkner, *The Orientalist's grammatical vademecum; being easy introduction to the rules and principles of the Hindustani, Persian, and Gujarati languages*, Bombay, 1853.

Since the beginning of the twentieth century, Persian lexicography has been influenced to some degree by Western methodology. The most important dictionary written in this period is ***Farhang-e neẕām***. Its author Sayyed Mohammad ᶜAli Daʾi-al--Eslam (1295/1878-1330/1951), was a Persian scholar, preacher, and lexicographer, a native of Larijan. In 1324/1906 he went on pilgrimage and wanted to return home via Bombay but stayed there for several years. Daʾi-al-Eslam learned Urdu, founded the Anjoman Daʾvat-al-Eslām and the Majalla Daʾvat-al-Eslām (October 1906), and preached so actively that he soon became known all over South Asia. During the third year of his stay in Bombay he was appointed professor of Persian in the Nezam college in Hyderabad, an ideal forum for his preaching. His greatest achievement was his *Farhang-e neẕām*, the first Persian etymological work that approximated in format and range of information comparable dictionaries in European languages and thus marked a watershed in the evolution of Persian lexicography. Unlike its predecessors, *Farhang-e neẕām* is not a mere compendium of archaic terms found mainly in poetic contexts; it includes words from Persian, Arabic, Turkish, and European languages that were likely to be required by those who spoke Persian, each classified according to a part of speech, as well as to whether it was colloquial, slang, literary, obsolete, and so on. Words confined to specific dialects or associated with different social groups were also clearly identified. When appropriate he illustrated correct usage by means of illustrative couplets, phrases, and the like. Daʾi-al-Eslam also compiled a Sanskrit grammar, which he included in *Farhang-e neẕām* (IV, pp. v--xcvi).[36]

The knowledge and analysis of Persian lexicographical works compiled in South Asia is still severely limited by the difficulties of access to the manuscripts conserved in many Asiatic libraries (in India, Pakistan, Tajikistan, Azerbaijan and Georgia). Only a relatively small number of studies have been devoted to this subject, in fact the work of S.I. Baevski on early Persian lexicography (in Russian, Moscov, 1989) remains the only monograph. However, the originality and importance of Indian contribution to the history of Persian lexicography as well as Indian lexicology (for many of the words lexicographers quoted Indian equivalents, labelled as *hendovī*) deserves further and more thorough researches.

PERSIAN DICTIONARIES COMPILED IN INDIA (CHRONOLOGICAL ORDER)

Date H/CE	Title	Author	Arrangement[37]
no later than 716/1315	*Farhang-e Qavvās* or: *Farhang-e panj baxš* *Farhang-e Šāhnāme* *Farhang-nāme*	Faxr-al-Dīn Mobārakšāh Qavvās Ġaznavī	E: 1,341 T: 5BX
743/1342	*Dastūr al-afāẕel fī loġāt al-faẕāʾel*	Ḥājeb Xeyrāt Rafīᶜ Dehlavī	E: 2,155 AI: 27B
807/1405	*Dāneš-nāme-ye Qadar Xān*	Ašrāf ben Šaraf al-Moẕakker al-Fārūqī	E: 2,419 AL: 22B

[36] Cf. the entry: DĀʾĪ-AL-ESLĀM, SAYYED MOḤAMMAD-ᶜALĪ, by M. Salim Akhtar in *EI*.

[37] Arrangement: E – (number of entries); T – thematical, A – alphabetical, AI – according to the initial letter; AL – according to the last letter; BX – *baxš* (part), G – *guna* (chapter), BH – *bahr* (sub-chapter); B – *bāb* (part); F – *faṣl* (chapter).

822/1419	*Adāt al-foẓalā'*	Qāẓī Xān Badr--al-Dīn Moḥammad Dehlavī (Dhārvāl)	AI: 2K: 25B (AL)
before 837/1433	*Farhang-e zafāngūyā va jahānpūyā* or: *Haftbaxšī/Panjbaxšī*	Badr-al-Dīn Ebrāhīmī	E: 5,170 T: 7BX G (AI) BH (AL)
837/1433	*Baḥr al-faẓā'el (fī manāfe' al-afāẓel)*	Moḥammad ben Qavām ben Rostam ben Aḥmad Balxī Kera'ī	1) 28B (AI) 2) 14B (T) (36F)
859/1455	*Ommān al-ma'ānī*	Seyyed Ebrāhīm Moḥammad Sa'ad-o-Sa'ud Amīrak Balxī	B (AI) F (AL)
873/1468	*Meftāḥ al-foẓalā*	Moḥammad ben Dā'ud ben Maḥmud Šādī--Ābādī	22B (AI) F (AL)
878/1474	*Šaraf-nāma-ye Aḥmad Monyarī (Ebrāhīmī)* or: *Farhang-e Mirzā Ebrāhīm*	Šeyx Ebrāhīm Qavām-al-Dīn Fārūqī Monyarī Bihārī-ye Hendī	E: 11,000 31B (AI) F (AL)
899/1493	*Mojmal al-ᶜajam*	Āsem Šo'ayeb ᶜAbdūsī	B (AI) F (AL)
916/1510	*Toḥfat al-saᶜādat* or: *Farhang-e Sekandarī*	Maḥmud ben Šeyx Ẓiā'-al-Dīn Moḥammad	E: 14,000 29B (AI) 2F (AL)
925/1519	*Mu'ayyid al-foẓalā'*	Moḥammad ben Šeyx Lād Dehlavī	E: 20 000 AI
1001/1592	*Madār al-afāẓil*	Allāhdād Feyẓī ben ᶜAlī Šir Serhendī	E: 12,000 AI

1017/1608	*Farhang-e Jahāngīrī*	Mīr Jamāl-al-Dīn Ḥosayn ben Fakr--al-Dīn Ḥasan Enjū Šīrāzī	E: 10,000 AI: 24B (F)
1147/1735	*Serāj al-loġāt* or: *Čerāġ-e hedāyat*	Serāj-al-Dīn ᶜAlī Xān Ārzū Motavaffī	E: 20,000
1046/1636	*Montaxab al-loġāt*	ᶜAbd-al-Rašīd ben ᶜAbd-al--Ġafūr Ḥoseynī Tattavī	
1062/1651	*Borhān-e qāṯeᶜ*	Moḥammad Ḥosayn ben Xalaf al-Tabrīzī (Borhān)	E: 20,215 5 VOLS.
1064/1654	*Farhang-e Rašīdī*	ᶜAbd-al-Rašīd ben ᶜAbd-al-Ġafūr Ḥoseynī Tattavī	E: 8-9,000 AI: 24B
1111-64 1699-750	*Merʾāt al-eṣṯelāḥ*	Ānand Rām Moxleṣ	
1152/1739	*Bahār-e ᶜajam*	Rāʾī Lāle Ṯīk Čand Bahār	E: 10,000
1189	*Taḥqīq al-eṣṯelāḥāt*	Amīr-e Ḥeydar	
1180	*Mostalehāt al-šoʾarā*	Vāraste-ye Siyālkutī Lāhurī	E: 2,000
1205/1790	*Montaxab al-loġāt denkeynī*	Moḥammad Sādiq Bihbahāni	
1209/1794	*Armaġān-e āṣafī*	Moḥammad ᶜAbd-al-Ġanī-Xān Ġanī	
1219/1805	*Šams al-loġāt*	anonymous (comp. by the Joseph Barretto's order)	

1229-30/ 1813-14	*Haft qolzom*	Šāh Zamān Abu 'l-Moẓaffar Ġāzī- -al-Dīn Ḥaydar Pādšāh-e Ġāzī	E: 27,709
?	*Farhang-e Sekandar-nāme*	Mīr Seyyed ben Ḥasan ben Seyyed Qāsem	
?	*Farhang-e Golestān*	Joneyd ben ᶜAbdallāh Musavī	
?	*Maẓhar al-ajāyeb*	Mirzā Moḥammad Ḥasan Qatīl	
1231/1816	*Farhang-e loġāt-e Dasātir*		
1237	*Farhang-e Ḥoseynī*	Seyyed Qalām Ḥoseyn Rezavī	
1242/1827	*Ġiyāṯ al-loġāt*	Moḥammad Ġiyāṯ-al-Dīn ben Jamāl-al-Dīn ben Šaraf-al-Dīn Moṣṭafā-ābādī Rāmpūrī	E: 17,000 AI
1250/1834	*Molḥaqāt-e Borhān*	ᶜAbd-al-Majīd Qāᵓemmaqāmī	
?	*Xāleq-bāri Maṭbuᶜ as-ṣobyān*	Amīr Xosrou Dehlavī	E: 192 BAYTS 36BX
1253/1837	*Nafāyes al-loġāt*	Ouḥad al-Dīn Balgerāmī	
1259/1843	*Farhang-e Jaᶜfarī*	Jaᶜfar ᶜAlī Xān ben Navvāb Moᵓin al-Doula	
1264/1848	*Taḥqīq al-vazān*	ᶜAbdallāh Ṣādeqī	
1265/1849	*Farhang-e nāyāb*	Moḥammad Hādī	
1268/1852	*Baḥr-e ᶜajam*	Moḥammad Ḥoseyn Qāderī (Rāqem)	

1268/1852	*Goldaste-ye goftār*	Ānandī Baršād	
1280/1863	*Xiyābān-e Golšan*	Šeyx Moulavī Moḥammad ᶜAlī	
1288/1871	*Ẓarūr al-mobtadī*	Saif-al-Dīn ben Qāyem-Allāh ᶜAẕīm Ābādī	
1291/1874	*Majmuᵓ-e motarādefāt*	Raḥīm-al-Dīn ben Karīm-al-Dīn	
1292/1875	*Farhang-e moḥtašamī*	Moḥammad Vazīr-al-Dīn Xān Sabeqat Jang Moḥtašam al-Doula	
1292/1875	*Armaġān-e āṣfā*	Moḥammad ᶜAbd-al-Ġanī Xān Ġanī	
1293/1876	*Malāẕẕ al-kalemāt*	Vājed ᶜAlišāh Pādšāh-e Oud	
1294/1877	*Laṭaᵓif al-loġāt*	ᶜAbd-al-Laṭīf ben ᶜAbdallah Niruᵓī	
1294/1877	*Farhang-e motarādefāt va esṭelāḥāt*	Moḥammad Pādšāh ben Ġo-lām Moḥī-al-Dīn (Šād)	
1298/1881	*Arbeᵓ ᶜanāṣer*	Moḥammad Nāser ᶜAlī Qiyās Purī	
1306/1888	*Farhang-e Ānandrāj*	Moḥammad Pādšāh ben Ġo-lām Moḥī-al-Dīn (Šād)	E: 50,000 AI: 32B
1308/1890	*Fīrūz al-loġāt fārsī* or: *Loġāt-e Fīrozī*	Ḥāj Moulavī ᶜAlī Moḥammad, Moḥammad Fīrūz al-Dīn	
1309/1891	*Jāmeᵓ al-loġāt*	Monšī Qalām Sorūr Lāhurī	

1316/1898	*Zobdat al-loġāt*	Monšī Qalām Sorūr Lāhurī	
1325-40 1907-22	*Āṣaf al-loġāt*	Aḥmad al-ᶜAzīz al-Nāʾeṯī Šams al-ᶜolamāʾ Navvāb ᶜAzīz Jang Bahādor	E: 17 VOLS. AI
1346/1927	*Farhang-e neẓām*	Seyyed Moḥammad Alī Dāʾī-al-Eslām	E: 30,000 5 VOLS. AI

PRINTED EDITIONS OF THE *FARHANG*-S (ALPHABETICAL ORDER):

Armaġān-e āṣafī: A dictionary of poetical quotations illustrating some usages of grammar and syntax, ed. M. ᶜAbd ul-Hamid Khan, 4 vols., Agra, 1904-6.

Āṣaf al-loġāt, 1325-40/1907-22, Hyderabad.

Bahār-e ᶜajam: A dictionary of Persian words and idioms employed both by ancient and modern poets, ed. Maulavi Hadi ᶜAli, 2 vols., pp. 480, 512, lith., Lucknow, 1879.

Borhān-e qāṭeᶜ: A dictionary of the Persian language explained in Persian; alphabetically arranged according to the system of European lexicons: comprising the whole of the words, phrases, and metaphors, in the Furhungi Juhangeeree, the Mujmuool Poors (...) the Soormu o Sooluemanee, and the Suhah ool Udwiyu (...) with a short grammar prefixed, by Moohummad Hoosuen Ibni Khuluf Oot-Tabreezee (...) to which is added an Appendix, consisting of the Molhuqat of the Boorhani Qafciu, the Khatimu or Appendix to the Furhungi Juhangeeree, together with a collection of words, phrases, metaphors, and proper names extracted from the Buhari Ujum, and (...) other authorities. The whole arranged (...) corrected, revised, and (...) illustrated with Persian notes by T. Roebuck et al., Calcutta, 1234/1818; 2 vols., Calcutta, 1238/1822; ed. H.M. ᶜAbd-al-Mujeed, pp. 797, 80, Calcutta, 1250/1834; Bombay (1259/1834, 1274/1858); ed. M. Azim Ullah, 2 vols., lith.,

Lucknow, 1871; Tehran (1278/1862, 1300/1883, 1304-1305/1887, 1317/1938).

Borhān-e qāṯe[c], a critical edition by M. Mo'in, 4 vols., Tehran (1330/1951), rpt. in 5 vols., Tehran, 1342/1963.

The Dasātir, ed. Sheriarji D. Bharucha, Bombay, 1907.

Dastūr al-afāẓel..., ed. N. Ahmad, Tehran, 1352/1973.

Farhang-e Ānandrāj, 3 vols., Lucknow, 1889-92; ed. M. Dabirsiaqi, 7 vols., Tehran, 1335/1956-8.

Farhang-e Jahāngīrī, ed. Sadiq [c]Ali (Ghalib), 2 vols., lith., Lucknow, 1876; ed. R. Afifi, 3 vols., Mashad, 1351/1972; 2nd edn. Mashad, 1980.

Farhang-e motarādefāt va eṣṭelāḥāt, Benares, 1294/1877; ed. Tehran, 1967.

Farhang-e Qavvās, ed. N. Ahmad, Tehran, 1353/1974.

The Farhang i Rashidi: A Persian dictionary by Sayyid Abdurrashid of Thatta…, ed. M. Zulfaqar [c]Ali, M. Aziz-ur-Rahman, 2 vols., Calcutta, 1875.

Farhang-e Rašidi, ed. M. Abbāsi, 2 vols., Tehran, 1337/1958.

Farhang-e zafāngūyā va jahānpūyā, ed. S.I. Baevski, Moscow, 1974.

Haft qolzom. The Seven Seas. A dictionary and grammar of the Persian language by His Majesty King of Oudh. In seven parts [with prefatory notices by Qabul Muhammad], 2 vols., Lucknow, 1822 (1879).

Haft qolzom. Grammatik, Poetik und Rhetorik der Perser. Nach dem siebenten Bande des Heft Kolzum dargestellt [in translation] von F. Rückert. Neu herausgegeben von W. Pertsch, Gotha, 1874.

Laṭa'if al-loġāt. A dictionary of words in Rumi's Masnavi, in the alphabetical order of their first and last letters, Lucknow, 1877.

Loġāt-e Fīrozī. A Persian dictionary, containing the meanings of words from the Arabic, Persian, Turkish, and other languages used in Urdu, Lahore, 1890.

Madār al-afāẓil, Lahore, 1337.

Majma[c] *al-šo'arā-ye Jahāngīršāhī*, ed. Mohammad Salim Akhtar, Karachi, 1979.

Molhaqāt-e Borhān, [c]Abd-al-Majīd Qā'emmaqāmī (a supplement to *Borhān-e qāṯe*[c]), Calcutta, 1250/1834 (rpt. 1274/1858).

Montaxab al-loġāt, or A dictionary of Arabic words, with a Persian translation, according to the authority of the Kamoos, the Sehauh, the Kunz, the Mohuzzub, and other Arabic lexicons (…) originally compiled by Abd-or-Rasheed-e Thattavee; and now revised, corrected and published by Molovee Allah Daud, [with English preface by M. Lumsden], Calcutta, 1808; Bombay, 1862.

Mu'ayyid al-fożalā': A Persian dictionary, containing also the Turkish and Arabic words in general use in the language, arranged throughout in separate groups. With an appendix of numerals, arithmetical notation, and elementary grammar, Lucknow, 1884; and in 2 vols., Cawnpore, 1899.

Ġiyāṣ al-loġāt: A dictionary of standard Persian, 2 vols., Lucknow, 1863-4; Kanpur, 1874, 1878, 1882, 1912; ed. M. Dabir-Siaqi, Tehran, 1958; Dushanbe, 2 vols., 1987-8 (in Cyrillic).

Ġiyāṣ al-loġāt, with *Čirāġ-i hidāyat*, a glossary of modern poetry by Siraj-al-Din ᶜAli Khān (Ārzu), on the margin, Cawnpore, 1874 (1878); Lucknow, 1879.

Ġiyāṣ al-loġāt, with the *Čirāġ-i hidāyat*, ed. M.M. Mangaluri, M. ᶜAbd al-Rahman Faizabadi, lith., Bombay 1880-1.

Ġiyāṣ al-loġāt, with *Montaxab al-loġāt*, a dictionary of Arabic words in common use, by ᶜAbd al-Rashid Husaini, in parallel columns, lith., Cawnpore, 1912.

Šams al-loġāt: A dictionary of Arabic, Persian, and common Turkish words, explained in Persian. Compiled under the direction of Joseph Barretto, 2 vols., Calcutta, 1806.

Majmu'-e motrādafāt. A collection of synonyms, forming an Idiomatic Persian Dictionary. Compiled by order of H.H. the Maharajah of Vizianagram (...) by Moonshee Mohammud Padsha, Benares, 1877; 2nd edn. with index, Benares, 1878.

Żarūr al-mobtadī. A Persian dictionary, lith., Lucknow, 1871.

LITERATURE

Abbāsī, M.A., *Tafṣīlī fehrest-e maxṭuṭāt-e fārsiya-ye Panjāb Public Library*, Lahore, 1966.

Abuladze, C'.A., et al., *Katalog arabskikh, tiurkskikh i persidskikh rukopisey Instituta Rukopisey im. K.S. Kekelidze* [Catalogue of Arabic, Turkish and Persian manuscripts in the K.S. Kekelidze's Manuscript Institute], Tbilisi, 1969.

Ahmad, A., *Studies in Islamic Culture in the Indian Environment*, London, 1964.

____, *An Intellectual History of Islam in India*, Edinburgh, 1969.

Alam, M., F. 'Nalini' Delvoye, M. Gaborieau, *The Making of Indo--Persian Culture: Indian and French Studies*, Delhi, 2000.

Baevski, S.I., *Opisanie persidskikh i tadzhikskikh rukopisey Instituta narodov Azii* [Description of the Persian manuscripts in the Institute of the Peoples of Asia], fasc. 4, Moscow, 1962.

____, *Predmetno-tematicheskiy slovaŕ persidskogo iazyka – Farhang-i Faxr-i Qawwās, konec XIII – načalo XIV vv.* [Subject-thematic Dictionary of the Persian Language – Farhang-i Faxr-i Qawwās, end of 13th – beginning of the 14th cents.], [in:] *Pismennye pamiatniki i problemy istorii kuľtury narodov Vostoka*, I, Moscow, 1986, pp. 14-17.

____, *Rannyaya persidskaya leksikografiya XI-XV v.* [Early Persian Lexicography, 11th-15th cents.], Moskow, 1989.

____, *Sposoby podtverditeľnogo citirovaniya v rannikh persidskikh slovariakh* [Methods of corroborative citation in early Persian dictionaries], [in:] *Pis'mennye pamiatniki i problemy istorii kuľtury narodov Vostoka* [Written scurces and cultural history of the peoples of the Orient], 8th Annual Scientific Conference, Leningrad section, Institute of Oriental Studies, Academy of Sciences of the S.S.S.R., Moscow, 1972, pp. 3-8.

____, *Redkaia rukopis rannego persidskogo tolkovago slovaria 'Tuhfat as-sa^c^adat' v rukopisnom sobranii Instituta Nazodov Azii* [A rare manuscript of the early Persian explanatory dictionary *Toḥfat al-sa^c^āda* in the collection of the Institute of the Peoples of Asia], [in:] *Tezisy dokladov nauchnoy konferentsii po iranskoy filologii*, Leningrad, 1962, pp. 44-5.

Blochet, E., *Catalogue des manuscrits persans de la Bibliothèque Nationale*, t. 2, Paris, 1912.

Blochmann, H., "Contributions to the Persian Lexicography", *Journal of the Asiatic Society of Bengal* (Calcutta) 1868, vol. 37, part 1, p. 20.

Borah, M.I., "The Nature of Persian Language Written and Spoken in India During the 13th and 14th centuries", *BSOS*, 1934, vol. 7, part 2.

Casari, M., Speziale, F., *La scienza islamica in India*, [in:] *Storia della Scienza* II, ed. S. Petruccioli, Rome, 2001, pp. 908-28.

____, *Persian literature in India*, [in:] *Encyclopaedia Iranica*, ed. E. Yarshater (www.iranica.com).

Conermann, S., *Historiographie als Sinnstiftung Indo-persische Geschichtschreibung waerhend der Mogulzeit (932-1118/1516-1707)*, Wiesbaden, 2002.

Dabīrān, Ḥ., *Šaraf-nāma-ye Monyarī*, [in:] *Pažuheš-nāme-ye Farhangestān-e zabān-e Irān*, 2, 1356/1977, pp. 97-122.

Dabīrsīāqī, M., *Farhanghā-ye fārsī va farhang-gunahā*, Tehrān, 1368/1989.

____, *Farhanghā-ye fārsī ba fārsī*, Tehrān, 1996.
Dā'ī-al-Eslām, M.A., *Farhang-nevisī-ye fārsī*, Hyderābād, 1347/1968.
____, *Farhang-e neẕām*, Hyderābād, 1362/1983.
Dehxodā, A.A., *Loġātnāme*, Tehrān, 1325-51/1946-72.
Ethé, H., *Catalogue of the Persian Manuscripts in the library of the India Office*, vol. 1, Oxford, 1903.
Ghani, M.A., *A History of Persian Language and Literature at the Mughal Court*, 3 vols., Allahabad, 1929-30.
____, *Pre-Mughal Persian in Hindustan: A Critical Survey of the Growth of Persian Language and Literature in India...*, Allahabad, 1941 (rpt. Gurgaon, 1994).
Gorekar, N.S., *Indo-Iran Relations: Cultural Aspects*, Bombay, 1970.
Hadi, N., *Dictionary of Indo-Persian Literature*, New Delhi, 1995.
Ḥekmat, A.-A., *Sarzamīn-e Hend*, Tehrān, 1337/1958.
Hosayni, A.H., *Al-Hend fi'l-ᶜahd al-eslāmī*, Hyderabad, 1392/1972.
Husaini, A.K., *Persian Language in the Deccan*, Hyderabad, 1934.
Ivanov, V., *Concise Descriptive Catalogue of the Persian Manuscripts in the Curzon Collection Asiatic Society of Bengal*, Calcutta, 1926.
Jaᶜfarī, Y., ed., *Armaġān-e adabī: pažuhešhā-ye adabī dar adabiyāt-e fārsī-e Hend*, Tehrān, 1997.
Kapranov, V., *Tadzhiksko-persidskaia leksikografia v Indii XVI-XIX v.* [Tajik-Persian Lexicography in India 16th-19th cents.], Dushanbe, 1987.
Lazard, G., 'The Rise of the New Persian Language', [in:] *The Cambridge History of Iran*, vol. IV, Cambridge, 1975, pp. 595-632.
MacKenzie, D.N., 'Persian Lexicography', [in:] *Encyclopaedia Iranica* IV, pp. 525-7 (www.iranica.com).
Marek, J., 'Persian Literature in India', [in:] *History of Iranian literature*, ed. J. Rypka, Dordrecht 1968, pp. 711-34, 832-8.
Marshall, D.N., *Mughals in India: A Bibliographical Survey*, I, *Manuscripts*, Bombay, 1967.
Momin, M., *The Chancellery and Persian Epistolography under the Mughals: Babur to Shah Jahan*, Calcutta, 1970.
Monzavī, A., *Fehrest-e nosxehā-ye xaṯṯī-ye fārsī*, Tehrān, 1350.
Mostafavi Sabzevari, R., "A Seminar on the compilation of Persian dictionaries in the Indian Subcontinent", *Nāme-ye Farhangestān, The Quarterly Journal of The Academy of Persian Language and Literature*, 1999, vol. 4, no. 1 (Ser. No. 13), pp. 193-6.
Nafīsī, S., 'Farhanghā-ye fārsī', [in:] *Loġātnāme-ye Dehhodā*, moqaddame (fasc. 40, preface), Tehrān, 1958, pp. 178-226.
Naqavī, Š., *Farhang-nevisi-ye fārsī dar Hend-o-Pākestān*, Tehrān, 1341/1962.

Nežād, Q., *Vāže-nāme*, [in:] *Farhang-nāme-ye adabi-ye fārsī* [An Encyclopaedia of Persian Literature], ed. H. Anuša, vol. 2, Tehrān, 1324/1997, pp. 1400-10.

Panāhī, S., "Rade-šenāsī va raveš-šenāsi-ye farhanghā-ye fārsi-ye qarn-e 13 hejrī dar Hend va Pākestān" [Categorization and Methodology in the Persian Dictionaries of the 13th cent. A.H./18th C.E. in India and Pakistan], *Nāme-ye Farhangestān, The Quarterly Journal of The Academy of Persian Language and Literature* 1999, vol. 4, no. 1 (Ser. No. 13), pp. 152-7.

Perry, J.R., 'Early Arabic-Persian Lexicography: the asāmī and masādir genres', [in:] *Proceedings of the Colloquium on Arabic Lexicology and Lexicography* (C.A.L.L.), *Budapest 1-7 September 1993*, Part 1, ed. K. Dévényi, T. Iványi, A. Shivtiel, pp. 247-59.

Pertsch, W., *Verzeichnis der persischen Handschriften*, Berlin, 1888.

Piemontese, A.M., *Amir Khusrau da Delhi. Le otto novelle del paradiso*, Rome, 1996.

Rahman, M.L., *Persian Literature in India During the Time of Jahangir and Shah Jahan*, Baroda, 1970.

Rāmpūrī, Ġ.M., *Ġiyāṣ al-loġāt*, ed. M. Dabīrsīāqī, 2 vols., Tehrān, 1337/1958.

Rieu, Ch., *Catalogue of the Persian Manuscripts in the British Museum*, London, 1881.

Robinson, F., 'Perso-Islamic Culture in India from the Seventeenth to the early Twentieth Century', [in:] *Turko-Persia in Historical Perspective*, ed. R.L. Canfield, Cambridge, 1991.

Rypka, J. ed., *History of Iranian literature*, Dordrecht, 1968.

Ṣādeqī, A.A., 'Persian dictionaries', [in:] *Encyclopaedia Iranica*, ed. E. Yarshater, pp. 387-90 (www.iranica.com).

Ṣāfī, Q., *Bahār-e adab, tārīx-e moxtaṣar-e zabān o adbiyāt-e fārsī dar šebh-e qāra-ye Hend o Pākestān*, Tehrān, 2003.

Salemann, C., 'Chronologisches Verzeichnis der Farhange', [in:] *Mélanges asiatiques* 1880-1881, vol. 9, pp. 531-5.

Schimmel, A., *Islamic Literatures of India*, Wiesbaden, 1973.

Shivtiel, A., 'Root-dictionary or Alphabetical Dictionary, a Methodological Dilemma', [in:] *Proceedings of the Colloquium on Arabic Lexicology and Lexicography* (C.A.L.L.), *Budapest 1-7 September 1993*, part 1, ed. K. Dévényi, T. Iványi, A. Shivtiel, pp. 13-25.

Siddiqui, I. H., "Historical Significance of the Farhang Literature of Delhi Sultanate Period", *Indo-Iranica*, 1979, vol. 32/3-4, pp. 9-21.

Storey, C. A., *Persian Literature, a bio-bibliographical survey*, vol. III, part I: *Lexicography, Grammar, Prosody and Poetics*, ed. V.M. Shepherd, Leiden, 1984.

Ṭabīb Zāde Qamṣarī, A., 'Šivehā-ye āvāngarī dar loġāt-nāmehā-ye fārsī va ẓarūrat-e taqyir-e ānhā', [in:] *Majale-ye zabān-šenāsī*, sāl-e 6, 1368, no. 1, pp. 74-8.

Tauer, F., 'Persian learned literature from its beginning up to the end of the 18th century', [in:] *History of Iranian literature*, ed. J. Rypka, Dordrecht 1968, pp. 419-82.

The learning of Persian in South Asia: the curricula and educational institutions for teaching Persian in South Asia

Tariq Rahman

South Asia came into contact with Persian in the late ninth century (Ghani 1941: 74-5). However, it was established as a prestigious literary language in the eleventh century as a consequence of Ghaznavide rule over the Punjab. Indeed, by the thirteenth century, it was established in the centres of Muslim power in other parts of India. The literature of these centres of Persian in pre-Mughal times has been discussed most recently and synoptically by Muzaffar Alam (2003: 131-59). It has also been discussed in detail along with Persian writing during the Mughal period, by Ghani (1929: 30) in English as well as in the three volumes of *Tārīx-e adabiyāt* (vols. 3, 4 and 5 abbreviated as *Tārīx* 1971-2) and Aḥmed (1974) in Urdu.

There is also some work on special aspects of Persian in India: the debate over Indian Persian (summed up by Alam 2003: 177-86); the contribution of Hindus to Persian literature (ᶜAbdullāh 1962); letter writing (Momin 1971); bureaucratic norms and conventions, especially those of the Mughals (Khan 1994). While the poets mentioned by Sufi (d. *c.* 1252) in his anthology of poets, *Lubāb al-albāb* may have needed little formal instruction in Persian – though presumably they too may have got lessons in prosody from the contemporary masters of the art – children born and brought up in India, surrounded by languages other than Persian, needed formal schooling in this powerful language. The theme of curricula in Persian has been recorded by G.M.D. Sufi in *Al-Minhaj* (1941) from Muhammad Tughlaq's time (r. 1325-51). There are many scattered references to the teaching of Persian in several sources. The present author too has studied the learning of Persian among the Muslims of north India and present-day Pakistan and connected it to world view and power (Rahman 2002: 121-60).

The present article focuses only on the curricula of Persian and the ways (privately or in institutions of learning) in which the language was learned in South Asia. It also provides some information to the teaching of Persian to females.

Pedagogical material

Most pedagogical material meant to teach children how to read Persian dates from a period when children seem to have known an Indian language better than the spoken language. One of the most well known of these primers, or lexicons, is the *Xāliq bārī* which is widely attributed to Amir Khusrau (Mirza 1934: 232). However, Hafiz Shirani, a painstaking researcher, attributes it to Ziauddin Khusro (written around 1621-2) (Šīrānī n.d.: 7). A number of such primers came on the scene during the fifteenth century and were certainly used for teaching Persian through Hindvi (the predecessor of Hindi and Urdu) while others, like Abu Nasr Farahi's *Nisāb ul Sabiyān* (1661) taught Arabic through the medium of Persian (Šīrānī n.d.: 7). The *Xulāṣatu 'l makātīb* (written in 1688) tells us that students were taught the alphabet, then the primers, and then they graduated to middle level books (*Gulistān* and *Bustān* of Sheikh Musleh al-Din Sa^{c}di (d. 1292) and then the more advanced books. The other books were about prose and composition, poetry, history and ethics (for details see

Annexure 1). A boy was supposed to be four years, four months and four days of age when he began his studies. The ceremony, called *bismillāh* (in the name of God), was, however, often postponed till the child was seven years old. The child was taught the Persian alphabet, the primers, the middle level books and then, if he undertook further studies, the more advanced books (Reid 1852: para 153, p. 52). Sir Syed Ahmad Khan (1817-98), the great reformer of education in India, was also educated in the same way by a private teacher (Hali 1901: 35).

The primers were not only meant for teaching the alphabet and the rudiments of the Persian language. They also disseminated the world view on which the civilization using that language was dependent. The moral values endorsed in the *Pand nāma* and the *Karīma* are patriarchal and hierarchical. Hospitality and silence are approved of; miserliness and talkativeness condemned. Women are considered inferior and untrustworthy. The advice given to the young student, presumably male and often addressed as *pisar* (son, boy), is to shun women and not get emotionally involved with them. The *Nām-e ḥaq* is a guidebook on ritual worship and cleanliness.

The most important part of letter writing was the knowledge of the form of address, tiles and honorifics (*alqāb* or *adab*) (for other constituents see Alam and Alavi 2001: 16) These were elaborate and calibrated according to the respective power differential (be it because of disparity in age, rank, wealth, religion, gender or whatever) of the addresser and the addressee. Then the language of the letter had to show deference or authority, coupled always with courtesy, according to circumstances. A copious vocabulary, knowledge of literature and stylistic graces were highly appreciated. In short, a successful letter writer upheld the values of hierarchy, conservatism (by adhering to conventions) and intellectual brilliance without heterodox analysis (by spending one's mental energy and learning on memorization and stylistic gymnastics).

What to say of the Muslims who benefited from Mughal rule, if the Hindus too upheld the same power structure. The Mughal king Akbar (r. 1556-1605) won their loyalty through marriage alliances and employment and they became Muslimized in culture (ᶜAbdullāh 1930). *Madrasa*-s, which were institutions for education rather than only Islamic education, took in and trained Hindus through Persian which was the instrument of this cultural Muslimization. The graduating Hindus became the *munšī*-s of the empire. Among the best known among them are people like Chandra Bhan Brahman (d. 1045 AH), Harkaran Das Kambuh (*c.* 1031 AH) and Madhu Ram (*c.* 1120). Chandra Bhan's letter to his son has a passage which gives useful insights into the educational values of that period.

Beginning by emphasizing the value of good calligraphy, he says:

> Although the science of Persian is vast, and almost beyond human grasp, in order to open the gates of language one should read the *Gulistān*, *Bustān*, and the letters of Mullā Jāmi, to start with.

This is followed by a long list of books on history and ethics. Then comes an even longer list of poets – forty four among the 'earlier' ones and twenty four among the 'modern' ones – which is cut short only because of the brevity of the communication (ᶜAbdullāh 1962: 240-2. Available in English [in:] Alam 2004: 130-2). What is more important for us is that throughout Chandra Bhan Brahman advises his son to be loyal to the social order. The author is impressed by Persian and the elite culture it represents. This makes him a fitting symbol and tool for spreading Mughal cultural hegemony (as defined by Gramsci 1978: 12) over the ruled which, I argue elsewhere, is one of the effects of Persian education during Muslim rule over India (Rahman 2002: 495-502).

Brief description of Persian literature and its world view

Persian literature was not theological. It was mostly poetic and the world view of this poetry was not Islamic as interpreted by the *ᶜulemā*. Its best works were in the Sufi tradition where love stood for divine love; the beloved, often symbolized as a beautiful boy, stood for an immanent deity and wine was a metaphor of mystic distraction. At another level, this literature celebrated romantic love, dwelt upon boyish and female beauty, mentioned drinking as a matter of course and with a certain iconoclastic, heterodox pride and had several erotic passages.

One of the most popular textbooks of Persian, *Bahār-e dāniš* written by Shaikh [c]Inayatullah Kumboh (1608-71) sometime in 1650-1?, was used in all the Persian schools in Mughal India. During British rule too, according to the education reports, it was taught in nearly all the schools and its 'style and idiom' were 'regarded as the best models of composition' (Reid 1852: 54).

The stories in it belong to the magical, medieval world view to which the *Alf laila* and other medieval tales belong. The moral values are unashamedly in the male chauvinist tradition. Women are cunning, lustful, unfaithful, unchaste and inconstant. This is especially driven home by the tale of four women who vow to deceive their husbands by fornicating with a handsome youth in the very presence of their husbands in such a way that the husbands are completely fooled.

Another textbook, written in the Punjab and mentioned as part of the curricula of Persian schools in that province (Leitner 1882: 63), was Maulana Muhammad Ghanimat's (b. 1688) *Maṣ̤navī nairang-e [c]išq* (called *Maṣ̤navī Ġanīmat*). The story is about Shahid, a poor boy whose beauty captivates men and women alike. The ruler's son, infatuated with Shahid, starts living with him. Later, Shahid falls in love with a girl. The theme of boy-love (*amrad-parastī*) is a recurrent one in Persian poetry and one which is found even in the basic course books of students such as the *Gulistān* and *Bustān.*

Rhymed tales, or *dāstān*-s, were also part of the traditional course of Persian studies. *Yūsuf-Zulaixā*, *Šīrīn-Xusrau* and *Lailā--Majnūn* were taught by famous teachers, sometimes but not always, attached to educational institutions. Bairam Khan, for instance, was taught a version of the *Yūsuf-Zulaixā* legend by Abdul Ghafur Lari (Badaoni 1595: 588). The tales are always formulaic. The hero and the heroine are beautiful beyond description. They fall in love but there are circumstances which prevent legal cohabitation. In the end they generally die. The passion they depict is so intense that it makes the lovers oblivious of social hierarchies, norms of society, societal taboos, material well-being, and even pain and death. Interpreted in a mystic way the love passion served as a metaphor for the mystic's (Sufi's) quest for an immanent deity.

The value system this literature supports was hierarchical, male dominating and supportive of Muslim ascendancy politically and their hegemony intellectually and culturally. Likewise it strengthened the common belief in the arbitrariness of life and in fate which all led to political quietism and acceptance of the prevalent gender roles and power structure.

The learning of Persian by foreigners

When Muslim kings of India were powerful, foreigners who visited their realm – especially those connected with the court itself – learned Persian. Ibn Battuta (1303-8 or 9), the Moroccan traveller who came to India in 1333, learned it so well that he conducted all his business in it. One of the earliest European travellers, John Mildenhall (visited during 1599-1606), wrote an application (he calls it 'Ars' which is a corrupted form of *ᶜarẓī*) to the king asking him for trade concessions for the British. He learned the language in six months with the help of a 'schoolmaster' (Foster 1921: 57).

Another traveller, Nicholas Withington (1612-16) reports that Jesuits preached 'first in the Persian tongue, that the Armenians and Moores may understand' (Foster 1921: 223). Thomas Coryat (1612-17) learned Persian and it helped him immensely in his travels across the Great Mughal's empire (*ibidem*, p. 284). The Jesuits, whose purpose was conversion, translated the Bible into Persian. Father Jerome Xavier, who did one translation, wrote in 1604 that an earlier translation, 'more than 300 years old', had been far from Rome (Maclagen 1932: 214). They presented a translated copy to Jahangir (r. 1605-27) in 1606 (Guerreiro 1930: 30-1) as well a Persian version of the lives of the Apostles (*ibidem*, pp. 43-4).

The early British officers of the East India Company corresponded with Indian princes and notables in Persian. Although Persian was abolished as the court language in 1834, the Persian Interpreter – an official who interpreted Persian correspondence to high functionaries of the company and wrote letters in that language to outsiders – was attached to the personal staff of high-ranking officials. Thus the C-in-C (Sir Henry Fane between 1835-8) had an interpreter on his staff during this period as his daughter, Miss Isabella Fane, testifies (Pemble 1985: 55).

Although political power was with the British, the cultural hegemony of the Muslim elite was still intact in the early period of British rule. Thus we find British officers becoming 'White Mughals' speaking Urdu, writing in Persian, wearing oriental clothes in private and, of course, marrying Indian women or keeping concubines (Dalrymple 2002). Some of them actually wrote Persian poetry as Ram Babu Saksena has described. Notable among them are: Edward Henry Palmer (1840-87); John Thomas (served with Begum Sumru in 1782); Lt. Col. Shadwell Plough (1858-1903); and Lt. Col. James Skinner (1778-1841) (Saksena 1943). Another example of Europeans taking pride in writing letters in Persian is Antoine-Louis Henri Polier, a Frenchman, who collected his Persian letters in two volumes called the *Iᶜjāz-i arsalānī* (1773-9) (Alam and Alavi 2001). It was only slowly that the British asserted their cultural and intellectual hegemony and English, rather than Persian, became the language which carried it throughout India.

The British learned Persian in formal institutions of learning and informally from private tutors. Among the formal institutions were the Fort William College in Calcutta which started functioning in 1801 (Fort William Vol. 1), and Haileybury College established at Hertford in 1806. At both places they taught the well known classics – *Ṭūṭī-nāma*, *Iyār-e dāniš*, *Bahār-e dāniš*, *Qiṣṣa Ḥātim Tāʾī* and *Gulistān* – changing one or two books here and there (Fort William Vol. 1 and Haileybury 1925). In India the young officers (writers) hired *munšī*-s as did H.T. Prinsep (1792-1878) when he came to India in 1809 and as did even John Beames who came in 1857 when Persian had officially been replaced by English (Prinsep 1904: 59 and Beames 1961: 80-1). Even in 1909, a report attributes the significance of Persian for British rule in India because of the 'political position' of Iran and because of the cultural prestige of the language among Indian and Afghan Muslims (Treasury 1909: 117).

Although Indians had been visiting England from the 1600s onwards, a certain Munshi Isma'il seems to have been recorded as a teacher of Persian in 1772. Others were Abdul Azim Isfahani (1775-6 and d. 1790); Munshi Muhammad Sami (*c.* 1785) and others (Fisher 2004: 104). I'tisam al Din visited England between 1767 and 1769 and taught students. He also helped William Jones with his Persian studies (Khan 1998: 76). Mahomet Saeed of Bengal advertised in the London newspapers for British pupils to whom he could teach Persian (Fisher 2004: 105). Abu Talib, who visited in 1799, tried to set up an institution to teach Persian but did not succeed. He reports, however, that an offer was made to him but by then he had resolved to return to India (Talib, vol. 1: 1810: 164). Indian instructors of Persian did not regard Britain with a sense of inferiority in the eighteenth and even up to the middle of the nineteenth century. They claimed they 'offered accurate and authentic language and cultural training' (Fisher 2004: 107). They were very few, of course, taught both to the civil servants (Haileybury) and the military officers (Addiscombe) who would rule India. However, Addiscombe's cadets were even less interested in Persian, taught to them by Hassan ᶜAli who joined the faculty in 1810, than Haileybury's civil servants (Fisher 2004: 126). By 1826 attitudes had changed as the British developed contempt for Indians and the Indian faculty was phased out (*ibidem*, pp. 132-3). Soon Persian too was phased out.

British officials kept up private correspondence with eminent Indians in Persian. Asadullah Khan Ghalib, the famous Urdu poet, tells his friend in a letter of 1858 that John Jacob discouraged people from writing in Urdu while encouraging them to write in Persian (Ġālib 1858). The poet himself wrote to the British Chief Secretary in Persian even in 1863 (Ġālib 1863) though he wrote to his Indian friends (except Tipu Sultan's maternal grandson) in Urdu (Ġālib 1866).

Even in 1872 British officials were encouraged to learn Persian. Indeed, while the reward for passing an examination in Persian was Rs. 1,200, it was only Rs. 750 for Urdu (Home 1872: 575). This importance decreased but Persian, as one of the classical languages of (Muslim) India, remained a subject in the prestigious civil service examination.

Persian in the educational institutions

Records of *madrasa*-s, meant for training functionaries of the state and the religious establishment, exist from the tenth century. Mansoora (Sindh), for instance, had the *madrasa* of Qazi Abu Muhammad Mansoori (*c.* tenth century); Lahore; Ajmer, Delhi, Uchh, Multan, Deccan, Jaunpur, Badayun and Bengal all had *madrasa*-s. Minhaj Uddin Siraj, the author of the history book *Ṭabaqāt-e nāṣirī* (*c.* 1260) was the administrator of Madrasa-e Ferozi in 1227 at the orders of Nasir Uddin Qabacha (r. 1205-28) at Uchh (Mehr 1975: 13). They existed when Ibn Battuta visited India in the fourteenth century (Battuta 1929: 230). In these *madrasa*-s the medium of instruction was Persian and books on Arabic grammar, such as the *Mīzān us ṣarf*, probably by Siraj Uddin al-Awadhi (d. 1372), had explanations in Persian (Baloč 1971: 69). Later, during the Mughal period, the number of *madrasa*-s increased.

There is much historical evidence about royalty learning Persian. They were generally given instruction by private tutors engaged for this purpose. Sher Khan (d. 1545), who began life as a landlord's son and not a prince, however, studied at a *madrasa* in Narnaul (between Hisar and Jaipur) which had been built in 1520. Here, among other things, he studied Nizami's *Sikandar nāma* and, of course, the inevitable *Gulistān* and *Bustān* (Sufi 1941: 52). The legend of *Hīr Rānjhā*, as narrated by Varis Shah (1722-98), mentions the *Nām-e ḥaq*, *Xāliq bārī* as primers and the usual canonical works of literature prose and ethics numbering thirteen as part of the curriculum in the Punjab (Sufi 1941: 109; also see Šāh 1986). This curriculum did not change much since the British found it much the same when they arrived (Leitner 1882: 55-57). Indeed, the *madrasa*-s of the Bengal and Behar (Adam 1836: in Long 1868: 199-215) as well as present-day U.P. also taught the same with some minor variations (Reid 1852: para 153, p. 52).

Reports during the British period, such as Fisher's Report (1832), Leitner's Report (1882) etc. provide lists of schools functioning from pre-British times. Those called *maktab*-s taught rudimentary Persian while *madrasa*-s went on to teach more Persian books. The British themselves established government educational institutions where Persian was an important subject in the beginning of their rule.

The British divided schools into several categories. The two relevant for our purposes are the Arabic and the Persian schools. The British officers made tours of towns in order to find out the condition of schools. Out of a sample of sixteen tours the information about thirty-one schools of North-Western Provinces (part of U.P. today) is as follows: there were 903 Persian schools and 150 Arabic ones in 1850 (Edn. NWP 1850: 25). Also see Rahman 2002: 81). In the Punjab there were 458 Persian schools in the early 1880s. They taught 4,015 students and, according to W.R.M. Holroyd, only 95 contained more than twelve while 247 has six or less students (Edn. P 1883: para 26, p. 10).

The British also promoted Persian studies in the Calcutta Madrasah established in 1781 (Fisher 1832: 2). They also established the Agra (1822) and Delhi (1826) colleges where Persian was taught (Fisher 1832: 24-5). Private entrepreneurs, such as a philanthropist named Fraser, opened a school in Delhi to teach Persian to 80 Indian boys in 1814 (Fisher 1832: 25). Later, when the universities were established from 1858 onwards, Persian was a subject of study.

As Persian was not used in the domains of power, the demand for it decreased. In 1877 some members of the Punjab University senate complained that the study of Persian only creates paper *munšī*-s and hence English should be taught in its place (Nobin et al. 1871: 89; Khan R. 1872: 283-4). Even the Anjuman-e Punjab agreed with this idea. Holroyd, the Director of Public Instruction, suspected that such demands had been inspired by rich people who could afford to teach their sons at home (Holroyd 1871: 117-18). However, other British officers agreed that Persian be phased out of the school curricula: The Governor General omitted it from the Persian courses in the

Bengal (Madrasah 1941). It was also omitted in the Punjab (Edn. P 1914: 12) and in Sindh (Younghusband 1908).

Another change introduced by the British was the gradual introduction of modern texts in place of the classical ones. One reason why this was done was because they, as well as the Indian reformers, began to find the classics embarrassingly erotic (Rahman 2002: 506). Thus, Maulana Muhammad Hussain Azad wrote *Fārsī kī pahlī kitāb* in 1870 in Lahore; Shibli Nomani wrote *Niṣāb-e fārsī* (1894) and so on. There were books for matriculation, intermediate, BA and so on. This happened in the high tide of Victorian prudery, but even as early as 1830 the Calcutta Book Society reported new books: Roebuck's Persian Primer and a grammar (Fisher 1832: 90). The shift from things Indian to British, modern products of the intellect, had begun in the early part of the nineteenth century.

On the whole, Persian lost its importance and is taught in the educational institutions of Pakistan and India as an optional subject. Students take it because it is taught through the memorization and translation of selected passages from simple textbooks which are so easy that they get high marks with little effort. They also take it, at least in Pakistan, in the competitive examinations for state services for the same reason. Some *madrasa*-s in South Asia also teach Persian more as a symbol of continuity than for giving actual competence in the language. Some Shiᶜa *madrasa*-s teach it, however, to show their affiliation with Iran, the only Shiᶜa state in the world. Both *madrasa* students and students from secular institutions lack knowledge of modern, spoken Persian and are unable to function in real life situations either in Afghanistan or Iran. Some modern language-teaching institutions are trying to remedy this shortcoming in order to create interpreters for state and business purposes (Rahman 2002: 152-7).

Female education in Persian

Although some Muslim women always had some education, mostly the Qurᶜan which was read without understanding (*naẕra*), reading and writing was not always considered appropriate for women. The *Qābūs nāma*, a manual of appropriate behaviour dating from the eleventh century advises that a daughter need not be taught how to read and write though she may be instructed in the rudiments of religion (Iskandar 1951: 125). The *Axlāq-e nāṣirī*, a widely read book of *adab* in Mughal India, is equally mistrustful of womens' education (Naim 1987: 112-13). As education at that time was in Persian it appears that men, while enjoying the aesthetic, amorous and erotic appeal of this literature, were uncomfortable about their women getting exposed to it. This became very clear during Victorian India when the Indian reformers of education spoke out strongly against it.

Nazir Ahmad (1833?-1912), the didactic novelist, recommends the study of Urdu and simple arithmetic besides the Qurᶜan and religious books, in his novels. However, his character Nusuh in *Taūbat un-Nuṣūḥ* (1874) teaches the *Gulistān* to his wife but censors one fourth of it by blackening its lines. These, he explains to her, were obscene (Axtar 1994: 410-11). In *Fasāna-e Mubtilā* (1885) the protagonist Mubtila learns Persian in school and the eroticism of this literature makes him conscious of his beauty and wayward in behaviour thus ruining his life (*ibidem*, p. 630). However, Persian could be safely studied under good supervision. Thus in *Majālis un-nissā* (1874) Khwaja Altaf Husain Hali (1837-1914), another reformer, shows his character Zubaida Khatun being taught at home, first by an *ustānī* (female teacher) and then by her father. Besides the inevitable *Gulistān* and *Bustān*, she also reads the *Iyār-e dāniš* (Minault 1998: 36).

However, despite this bias women were educated in Persian. Ibn Battuta found in a town in Malabar (Hinawr) 'thirteen schools for girls and twenty-three for boys'. This was unusual because he remarks that it is 'a thing which I have never seen elsewhere' (Battuta 1929: 230). The women of this town knew the Qurᶜan by heart and, Persian being the language used by Muslim educated people, this language was certainly taught in these schools.

Women from the most powerful families, not having to conform to public opinion, did get educated. The names of such women are found in many historical sources and are as follows: Gulbadan Begum (born 1523), author of the *Humāyūn nāma*; Salima Sultana, niece of Humayun; Nur Jahan; Mumtaz Mahal;

Raziya Sultana; Chand Bibi and several Mughal princesses (Sufi 1941: 81-2; Rafīq 1982: 196-211; for Mughal princesses also see Badaxšānī 1971: 95-8). Although details of their education are seldom provided, it appears that princesses and women from eminent families were instructed at home by women teachers. For instance, Inayatullah Khan's mother Hafiza Maryam, had been commissioned to teach Aurangzeb's (r. 1658-1707) accomplished daughter, Zebunnissa Begum (1639-89)[1] (Xān 1969: 821). The princess Jahan Ara, daughter of Shah Jahan, wrote a letter and couplets in Persian to a *ṣūfī* called Mulla Shah (Aḥmed 1974: 132-3). Minor royalty of the latter period, such as the Begums of Bhopal, seem to have regarded education as an accomplishment in women of their stature. Sultan Jahan Begum, the third woman ruler of the state, learnt Persian as well as English (Minault 1998: 25). Her granddaughter, Abida Sultaan, also studied Persian for less than an hour daily (Sultaan 2004: 23).

Women from the *ašrāf* classes were educated if their fathers taught them or kept teachers to do so. For instance, Azizunnissa Begum (1780?-1857), Sir Syed's mother, read elementary Persian and the Qurᶜan (quoted from Minault 1998: 14). There is evidence that some of the women of the Hindu *Kāyasth* class, which had taken to Persian, also knew the language (Durgā Prašād in *Tazkirat un-nissā* as quoted by ᶜAbdullāh 1962: 233). But, ironically enough, society also gave enough autonomy to courtesans who lived in surrogate families run by women (*gharānā*-s), to enable them to control their education. And some of the best of them were taught Persian. According to Leitner, who must have conversed with *ašrāf* men of the Punjab, the 'superior class of *Hetairai* are known to have received an education in Persian poetry and in calligraphy' and this is the reason, he claims, that Persian poetry, 'which has an almost intoxicating effect on the native mind, is sternly prohibited to be heard or read by most respectable females' (Leitner 1882: 98). Umrao Jan Ada, the protagonist of Mirza Hadi Rusva's novel of the same name,

---

[1] A collection of poems called *Dīvān-i Maxfī* collected in 1724, is credited to Zeb un-Nissa. However, some ascribe it to another Makhfi. For the English translation of the first fifty *ġazāl*-s see Magan Lal and Jessie Duncan Westbrook, *The Diwan of Zeb-un-Nissa*, London: John Murray, 1913.

says she was taught the *Karīmā*, *Amad nāma*, *Gulistān* and other books of Persian (Rusvā 2000: 54-5). While the courtesans needed the language to entertain gentlemanly customers, this was precisely the reason the middle class mistrusted it.

It appears, however, that in the primary schools (*maktab*-s) boys and girls Hindus as well as Muslims, studied together (ᶜAbd ul-Laṭīf 1971: 34 and Leitner 1882: 105). This has been reported as the normal practice in Pakistan's rural areas by people in their seventies (Malik 2005). There were also female indigenous schools which admitted small boys in various districts of the Punjab (Leitner 1882: 98). This was also true of other parts of India. According to the testimony of Badruddin Tyabji before the Hunter Commission of 1882: 'There are some Koris [*Qārī*-s] or Mullas in the chief centres of Muhammadan population who teach the Koran and perhaps a little Hindustani and Persian to the girls' (Tyabji 1882: 501). Though these schools taught the Qurᶜan (*naẓra*), some of them taught the primers of Persian also. In the Punjab, according to Leitner, 'some of the ladies are good Persian scholars, and in a distinguished Muhammadan family that I know, I have been given to understand that several of the ladies are excellent poets' (Leitner 1882: 104). This was the condition of the Punjab in the 1880s when Leitner collected his data. However, even today, curiously enough, some women, otherwise illiterate, know the *Karīmā* by heart and narrate it in women's gatherings even now in the Pakistani Punjab. It is possible that, like the Qurᶜan, they also memorize the primer (personal communication).

Modernity brought ideas of womens' emancipation, especially through education. Mumtaz ᶜAli (1860-1935), a reformer, expressed them in his book *Ḥaqūq un-nisvān.* He launched the paper 'Tahẕīb un-nisvān' in Urdu from Lahore in 1898. He commends books of good Urdu style as well as the *Gulistān* and *Bustān* (Minault 1998: 83). His wife Muhammadi Begum (1878?-1908) learned Urdu on her own (Minault 1998: 111-12). Mumtaz ᶜAlī taught her Persian (*ibidem*, p. 112). The Anjuman-i Ḥimāyat-i Islām made five primary schools for girls in 1885 and increased them to fifteen by 1894. The curriculum included Persian (Minault 1998: 176). At this time, indigenous schools did sometimes teach Persian to girls. Although Persian was being phased out of the domains of power, it had such prestige that it was considered too much of an accomplishment to be denied altogether to young ladies. Thus, when Syed Karamat Husain (1854-1917) founded the Lucknow Girls' School, Persian was taught along with Arabic, Urdu and English (Minault 1998: 223). Another educationist, Rokeya Sakhavat Hossain (1880-1932), who was a Bengali also established a school in Calcutta where Persian was taught in the beginning (Hossain 1988: 41-2). It was phased out, like it was in the boys' schools, but because it could not empower the learner and not because of gender discrimination.

Conclusion

Persian was learned by the Muslim elite as well as its subordinate allies among the Hindus (such as *Kāyasth*-s) because it was used in the domains of power. The purpose of the learners was to empower themselves individually and collectively. However, by doing so, they helped in maintaining the cultural and intellectual hegemony of the Indian Persianized Muslim elite. This hegemony made Muslim (Mughal) political supremacy acceptable to Indians.

The studying of Muslims and Hindus in the same schools and the courses of study – primers, composition and epistolography, literature and ethics – created a consensus of values among the educated elite which, in the last analysis, supported Muslim values and perceptions of reality. Hierarchy – the superiority of males over females, the elite over the masses, Muslims over Hindus etc – was one of these values. Arbitrariness was another. It promoted belief in fate and, therefore, political quietism. The magical universe of Persian literature, disconnecting cause and effect and creating a world in which things happened arbitrarily, helped one reconcile oneself to the arbitrariness of political authorities and blame their excesses on one's fate (*kismat* or *karma*). Yet another attitude, again connected with Persian literature, was the idea that literature was an aesthetic device completely alienated from real life. Thus stories of love, disregard of the norms of society, revolt against one's socio-economic class (by falling in love with persons from another class), disregard of gender (boy-love) lost their heterodox force because they were consumed as aesthetic products and put on a pedestal which separated them from life. Thus, the unconventional was conventionalized and the subversive potential of Persian texts neutralized and, indeed, recruited into supporting the power structure. But because this subversive potential existed, women were generally kept away from it. Women powerful in their own right or autonomous, or being on the fringes of society (courtesans), did, however, study Persian. Middle class women too were taught the language under strict supervision and generally at home but sometimes in schools. The demand for learning Persian decreased when Persian was no longer useful for obtaining jobs in the state or the private sector. It is now studied either for the few jobs where it is still used, by scholars or by students who find it easy to get high marks in it.

ANNEXURE 1

Books of Persian taught in the educational institutions of South Asia[2]

Books in bold are taught even now in Pakistan's *madrasa*-s (religious seminaries)

Primers

ᶜAṭṭār, Farīduddīn (*c.* 12-13 cent.), 1959, ***Pand nāma***, Multān: Maktaba Širkat-e ᶜIlmiyat, 1959 [Urdu meanings in margins by Sajjād Ḥusain].

Buxarī, Šarfuddīn (*c.* 14 cent.), ***Nām-e Ḥaq***, Karachi: H.M. Saeed Company.

[2] Details are given in Sufi 1941: 77-8. Only the most commonly studied books of Persian language and literature are given above.

Sa[c]dī, Muṣleḥuddīn (*c.* 13 cent.), ***Karīmā***, Multan: Bairoon Bohar Gate [Urdu words in margins by Qāẓī Sajjād Ḥusain].

Prose and Composition

1. *Badā[ɔ]i[c] ul-inšā[ɔ]* (or *Inšā[ɔ]-i Yūsufī*).
2. Prose works of Mullā Jāmī and Mullā Munīr.
3. Letters of Abū 'l-Faẓl.
4. Handbook of Šaix [c]Ināyatullāh, secretary to Šāh Jahān.
5. *Bahār-i suxan* by Šaix Muḥammad Ṣāliḥ.
6. Letters of Mullā Munīr.
7. Epistles of Šaidā and Mullā Ṯuġrā.
8. Story of Lāl Čand.
9. *Līlāvatī* translated by Šaix Faiẓī.

Literature

1. ***Gulistān*** and ***Bustān*** (beginners) by Sa[c]dī
2. *Yūsuf-Zulaixā* by [c]Abd ur-Raḥmān
3. *Tuḥfat-ul-aḥrār* by Jāmī (d. 1494)
4. *Nuzhat-ul-abrār* by Jāmī
5. *Sikandar nāma* by Niẓāmī Ganjavī (d. 1209)
6. *Maxzan-ul-asrār* by Niẓāmī Ganjavī
7. *Haft paikar* by Niẓāmī Ganjavī
8. *Šīrīn Xusrau* by Niẓāmī Ganjavī
9. *Lailā-Majnūn* by Niẓāmī Ganjavī
10. *Qirān us-Sa[c]dain* by Amīr Xusrau (d. 1325)
11. *Maṯla[c]-ul-anwār* by Amīr Xusrau
12. *I[c]jāz-e Xusravī* by Amīr Xusrau
13. Works of many poets including Sa[c]di, Ḥāfiẓ Šīrāzī (d. 1389/90) and Ṣā[ɔ]ib Tabrīzī (d. 1651). Also the *Qaṣā[ɔ]id* of Badr-i-Čač, Anvarī, Xāqānī, [c]Urfī (d. 1592), and Faiẓī (d. 1595).
14. Fiction: *Ṯūṯī-nāma* by Nakšābī; *Anvār-e suhailī* by Ḥusain Va[ɔ]iẓ Kāšifī (d. 1504); *Iyār-e dāniš* by Šaix Abū 'l-Faẓl (d. 1602), and *Bahār-e dāniš*.

REFERENCES

ᶜAbdullāh, S.M., 1930, 'Fārsī taᶜlim kā aṣar Hinduon par' [The effect of Persian education on the Hindus], *Xyālistān* (April), pp. 33-8.

____, 1962, *Adabiyāt-i Fārsī main Hinduon kā hīssā* [The contribution of the Hindus to Persian Literature], Lahore: Majlis-i Taraqqī-e Adab, 1967.

ᶜAbd ul-Laṭīf, Muḥammad, 1971, Chapter 1, [in:] *Tārīx*, vol. 4.

Aḥmad, Naẕīr, 1874, 'Taubat un-Nusūh', [in:] Axtar, 1994.

Aḥmed, Zahur ud-din, 1974, *Pākistān main Farsī adab kī tārīx: Ahed-e Jahāngīr se Aurangzeb tak* [The history of Persian literature in Pakistan: from the reign of Jahangir to Aurangzeb], Lahore: Majlis Taraqqī Adab.

Alam, Muzaffar, 2003, 'The Culture and Politics of Persian in Precolonial Hindustan', [in:] Sheldon Pollock (ed.), 2003, *Literary Cultures in History: Reconstructions from South Asia*, Berkeley and Los Angeles: University of California Press, pp. 131-98.

____, 2004, *The Languages of Political Islam: India 1200-1800*, Chicago: The University of Chicago Press.

Alam, Muzaffar and Seema Alavi, Transl. from Persian and Intro., 2001, *A European Experience of the Mughal Orient: The I'jaz-i Arsalani (Persian Letters, 1773-1779) of Antoine-Louis Henri Polier*, New Delhi: Oxford University Press. This edn. 2002.

Axtar, Salīm, 1994, *Majmūᶜa Deputy Naẕīr Aḥmad* [Urdu: The Collected Works], Lahore: Sang-e Mīl.

Badaxšānī, Mirzā Maqbūl Beg, 1971, 'Adabī Manzar', [in:] *Tārīx*, vol. 3, pp. 42-122.

Badaoni, Abdul-Qadir Ibn-i-Muluk Shah, 1595, *A History of India: Muntakhabu-t-Tawarikh*, vol. 1, trans. from Persian by George S. A. Ranking, Calcutta, 1884. Edition used: Patna: Academica Asiatica, 1973.

Baloč, Nabī Baxš, 1971, 'Maẕhab', [in:] *Tārīx*, vol. 3, pp. 60-8.

Battuta, Ibn, 1929, *Travels in Asia and Africa 1325-1354*, transl. from Arabic by H.A.R. Gibb, London: Routledge and Kegan Paul Ltd.

Beames, John, 1961, *Memoirs of a Bengal Civilian*, London: Chatto and Windus.

Dalrymple, William, 2002, *White Mughals: Love and Betrayal in Eighteenth-Century India*, London: HarperCollins.

Edn. NWP, 1850, *Memoir on the Statiṣtics of Indigenous Education Within the North Western Provinces of the Bengal Presidency*,

(Comp.) Reginald Thornton, Calcutta: Printed by J. Thomas, Baptist Mission Press.

Edn. P, 1883, *Report on the State of Education in the Punjab and its Dependencies for the Year 1882-83*, by Lt. Col. William R.M. Holroyd, Director Public Instruction Punjab, Lahore: Printed at the Central Jail Press.

____, 1914, *Report on Progress of Education in the Punjab for the Year 1913-14*, Lahore: Superintendent, Government Printing.

Fisher, 1832, 'Memoir compiled from the records of the India Governments at the East India House, in pursuance of a Minute of the Committee of Correspondence of the 7th February 1826, «showing the extent to which aid has been afforded by the local Governments in India, towards the establishment of Native schools in that country»', [in:] Anath Nath Basu (ed.), 1952, *Indian Education in Parliamentary Papers: Part I (1832)*, Bombay: Asia Publishing House, pp. 1-143.

Fisher, Michael H., 2004, *Counterflows to Colonialism: Indian Travelers and Settlers in Britain 1600-1857*, New Delhi: Permanent Black.

Foster, William, 1921, *Early Travels in India 1583-1619*, London: Oxford University Press.

Ġālib, Asadullāh Xān, 1858, Letter of 5 March to Ḥātim ᶜAlī Beg, [in:] Mehr, 1982, p. 180.

____, 1863, Letter of 12 May to Mirzā ᶜAbbās Beg, [in:] Mehr, 1982, p. 543.

____, 1866, Letter of 6 October to Nomān Aḥmad, [in:] Mehr, 1982, p. 519.

Ghani, Muhammad Abdul, 1929-30, *A History of Persian Language and Literature at the Mughal Court (Babur to Akbar)*, in three parts, Allahabad: Indian Press.

____, 1941, *Pre-Mughal Persian in Hindustan*, Allahabad: The Allahabad Law Journal Press.

Gramsci, Antonio, 1978, *Selections from the Prison Notebooks*, Hoare, Quintin and Nowell-Smith, Geoffrey (eds and trans.), London: Lawrence and Wishart.

Guerreiro, Father Fernao, 1930, *Jahangir and the Jesuits: From the Relations of FFG, S.J.*, trans. from the Portuguese by C.H. Payne, New Delhi: Munshiram Manoharlal, 1977.

Haileybury, 1825, Yearly Report 1824-1825. IOR Haileybury Records (1749-1923) J/2/1 (OIOC).

Hali, Altaf Husain, 1901, *Hayat-i-Javed (A Biography of Sir Sayyid)*, transl. by David J. Matthews, New Delhi: Rupa and Company, 1994.

Holroyd, 1871, Letter from Captain W.R.M. Holroyd, DPI, to the Officiating Secretary, Punjab No. 85, Lahore, 13 May 1871, [in:] *Extracts from Punjab Records (Education): Home Department June 1871*, ACC No. 799 (NDC).

Home, 1872, *Rewards to Educational Officers for Passing in Vernacular Languages: Home Dept.*, 8 July 1872, ACC No. 1686 (NDC).

Hossain, Rokeya Sakhavat, 1988, *Sultana's Dream and Selections From the Secluded Ones*, transl. from Urdu and ed. Roushan Jahān, New York: Feminist Press.

Iskandar, Kai Ka'us ibn, 1951, *A Mirror for Princes: the Qābūs Nāma of Kai Kaus ibn Iskandar*, transl. Reuben Levy, London: Cresset Press.

Khan, Gulfishan, 1998, *Indian Muslim Perceptions of the West During the Eighteenth Century*, Karachi: Oxford University Press.

Khan, Rahim, 1872, 'Memorandum on Muhammadan Education in India', 17 April 1872, [in:] Senate, 1872.

Khan, A.D., 1994, *Diplomatics of the Soyurghal Farman of the Great Mughals, 1556-1707*, Allahabad: Quemer Publications.

Leitner, G.W., 1882, *History of Indigenous Education in the Punjab since Annexation and in 1882*, rpt. Lahore: Republican Books, 1991.

Long, J., 1868. *Adam's Reports on vernacular Education in Bengal and Behar, Submitted to Government in 1835, 1836 and 1838*, Calcutta: Printed at the Home Secretariat Press.

Maclagen, Edward, 1932, *The Jesuits and the Great Mogul*, London: Burns Oats and Washbourne Ltd.

Madrasah, 1941, *Report of the Madrasah Education Committee*, Alipore: Superintendent of Govt. Printing.

Malik, Fateh Muhammad, 2005, Personal information, 12 September, Islamabad.

Mehr, Ġulām Rasūl (trans.), 1975, 'Introduction' to the Urdu translation of *Ṭabaqāt-e Nāṣirī* (*c.* 1260) (from Persian), Lahore: Markazī Urdu Board.

____ (comp.), 1982, *Xuṭūṭ-e Ġālib* [Urdu: The Letters of Ghalib], Lahore: Šeix Ġulām ᶜAlī.

Minault, Gail, 1998, *Secluded Scholars: Women's Education and Muslim Social Reform in Colonial India*, New Delhi: Oxford University Press.

Mirza, Mohammad Wahid, 1934, *The Life and Works of Amir Khusrau*, Lahore: Punjab University Press, 1962.

Mohiuddin, Momin, 1971, *The Chancellery and Persian Epistolography under the Mughals: from Babur to Shah Jahan, 1526-1658*, Calcutta: Iran Society.

Naim, C.M., 1987, 'How Bibi Ashraf Learned to Read and Write', *Annual of Urdu Studies*, No. 6, pp. 99-115.

Naqvī, Sayyid ᶜAlī Raẓā, 1972, 'Šuᶜarā ke taẕkire', [in:] *Tārīx*, vol. 5, pp. 165-262.

Nobin, Chandra Rai; Raja Harbans; Rai Mul Sing etc., 1871, 'Opinion with reference to the Resolution of the Government of India, no. 300, 7 August 1871', [in:] Senate, 1873.

Pemble, John (ed.), 1985, *Miss Fane in India*, Gloucester: Alan Sutton.

Prinsep, 1904, 'Three Generations in India 1770-1904' by Sir Henry Thoby Prinsep. MSS. Eur. C. 97/2 (OIOC).

Rafīq, Sayyid Aḥmad, 1982, *Musalmānon kā Niẕām-e Taᶜlīm*, Karachi: Academy of Educational Research.

Rahman, Tariq, 2002, *Language, Ideology and Power, Language Learning Among the Muslims of Pakistan and North India*, Karachi: Oxford University Press.

Reid, H.S., 1852, *Report on the Indigenous Education and Vernacular Schools in Agra, Aligarh, Bareli, Etawah, Farrukhabad, Mainpuri, Mathura, Shahjahanpur for the Year 1850-1851*, Agra: Printed at the Secundra Orphan Press.

Rusvā, Mirzā Muḥammad Hādi, 2000, *Umrāʾo Jān Adā*, Islamabad: Alhamra Publishing.

Saksena, Ram Babu, 1943, *European and Indo-European Poets of Urdu and Persian*, rpt. Lahore: Book Traders, n.d.

Senate, 1872, *Proceedings of the Senate of the Punjab University College*, April 1872, ACC No. 799 (NDC).

____, 1873, *Proceedings of the Senate of the Punjab University College*, February 1873, ACC. No. 799 (NDC).

Sufi, G.M.D., 1941, *Al-Minhaj: Being the Evolution of Curriculum in the Muslim Educational Institutions of India*, Delhi: Idārah-i Adabiyāt-i Dillī. Edition used: 1977 rpt.

Sultaan, Abida, 2004, *Memoirs of a Rebel Princess*, Karachi: Oxford University Press.

Šāh, M. Akram, 1971, 'Dāstānen; Chapter 17' [Urdu: Tales], [in:] *Tārīx*, vol. 4.

Šāh, Vāriṣ̤, 1986, *Hīr Vāriṣ̤ Šāh*, (Comp.) Ṣābir, Moḥammad Šarīf, Lahore: Vāriṣ̤ Šāh Memorial Committee.

Šīrānī, Ḥāfiẓ Maḥmūd, n.d., *Ḥifẓ ʾul-Lisān Maᶜrūf ba Xāliq Bārī*, Delhi: Anjuman Taraqqī-e Urdū.

Talib, Abu, 1810, *The Travels of Mirza abu Talib Khan in Asia, Africa, and Europe During the years 1799, 1800, 1801, 1802 and 1803. Written by Himself, in the Persian Language*, Trans. Charles Stewart, vols. 1 & 2, London: Longman, Hurst, Rees & Orme.

Tārīx, 1971 and 1972, *Tārīx-e Adabiyāt-e-Musalmān-e Pākistān-o--Hind*, General editor Mahmud, S.F., *Fārsī Adab*: vols. 3 and 4 (1971) and vol. 5 (1972).

Tyabji, Badruddin, 1882, 'Testimony Before the Hunter Commission', [in:] *Report of the Bombay Provincial Committee: Appendix of the Education Commission Report*, Calcutta: Superintendent of Government Printing.

Treasury, 1909, *Report of the Committee Appointed by Lords Commissioners of His Majesty's Treasury Organization of Oriental Studies in London*, London: His Majesty's Stationery Office.

Xān, Ṣamṣām-ud Daulah Šāh Nawāz, 1969, *Maʾāṣir ul-Ūmarā*, Lahore: Markazī Urdu Board. [The author lived between 1700-58].

Younghusband, A.D., 1908, Letter of the Commissioner of Sind to the Governor of Bombay, 27 July 1908, SA.

ABBREVIATIONS

NDC = National Documentation Centre, Cabinet Division, Islamabad
OIOC = Oriental and India Office Collection, British Library, London
SA = Sindh Archives, Clifton, Karachi

Index of names

List of contributors

Daniela Bredi is Associate Professor of History and Institutions of Islam in South Asia in the Department of Oriental Studies in the Faculty of FiLeSUSO of University Sapienza of Rome (Italy), where she also teaches Muslim Law. From 1993 to 2011 she taught Urdu Language and Literature as well, and from 2007 through 2010 served as Coordinator of the Doctorate in Civilizations, Cultures and Societies of Asia and Africa of the University Sapienza of Rome (Italy). During Fall 2011 she has been Visiting Fellow at the South Asian Studies Council of the Whitney and Betty MacMillan Center for International and Areas Studies at Yale (USA). Author of *Storia della cultura indo-musulmana*, Roma: Carocci, 2006, she has several publications on historical, political and literary subject to her credit.

Renata Czekalska is Assistant Professor at the Institute of the Middle and Far East at the Jagiellonian University, Krakow, Poland. She specializes in South Asian culture, twentieth century Hindi literature, modern history of South Asia, and intercultural communication. Dr. Czekalska's recent publications include two books, *Rodowody nowoczesnej poezji hindi* (Origins of modern Hindi poetry, Krakow, 2008) and *Traktat o sztuce celebracji* (Treatise on the art of celebration, Krakow, 2009). She has also published several book-length translations of Hindi poetry into Polish and Polish poetry into Hindi.

Rahul Peter Das heads the Department of South Asian Studies (Südasien-Seminar) of the Martin-Luther-Universität Halle-Wittenberg, Germany, where he is also Dean of Studies of the Faculty of Philosophy I. He studied Indology, Islamic Studies and Tamil Studies at Cologne and Hamburg. He has published widely on diverse topics relevant to South Asia both traditional and contemporary, and is the editor or co-editor of various scholarly series and journals.

Mehr Afshan Farooqi is Assistant Professor of Urdu and South Asian Studies at the Department of Middle Eastern and South Asian Languages and Cultures (MESALC), University of Virginia. Her research interests lie in the general area of cultural studies with a special focus on Urdu literary culture. Her most recent work is the two volume *The Oxford India Anthology of Modern Urdu Literature*, New Delhi: Oxford University Press, 2008. She is presently working on completing her book on Muhammad Hasan Askari, arguably Urdu's greatest literary-cultural critic.

Kamila Junik is an Indologist conducting research on modern Hindi literature, teaching at the Department of Indian Studies, Jagiellonian University, Krakow. She also translates Hindi literature into Polish. In 2009, she published a translation of a Hindi novel *Nīlā* (by Teji Grover). Presently, she is concluding her PhD thesis dedicated to the so-called "Bhopal School".

Agnieszka Kuczkiewicz-Fraś is Assistant Professor at the Jagiellonian University, Krakow. Her main field of research is Hindi-Urdu linguistics as well as the Islamicate traditions and culture in South Asia and intercultural communication. She also translates from Hindi and Urdu into Polish. She published *Perso-Arabic Hybrids in Hindi. The Socio-linguistic and Structural Analysis* (New Delhi: Manohar, 2003) and *Perso-Arabic Loanwords in Hindustani. Part I: Dictionary* (Krakow: Księgarnia Akademicka, 2008).

David Lelyveld is the author of *Aligarh's First Generation: Muslim Solidarity in British India* (1978, rpt. 2003) and co-editor of *A Wilderness of Possibilities: Urdu Studies in Transnational Perspective* (2005). His most recent publications deal with the social and political history of Urdu and its differentiation from Hindi. His current project is *Sir Syed and Macaulay's Curse*, a study of Sir Sayyid Ahmad Khan, Justice Sayyid Mahmud, and Sir Sayyid Ross Masood. He has held faculty and administrative positions at the University of Minnesota, Columbia and Cornell. He is now Professor of History at William Paterson University in New Jersey.

Kinga Maciuszak is Professor of Iranian Studies in the Institute of Oriental Philology, Jagiellonian University, Krakow; doctorate Jagiellonian University, 1999 ("Irańskie nomina agentis z sufiksem -tar" [Iranian nomina agentis in -tar]). She specialises in Iranian and Indo-European linguistics. The author of: *Średnioperski poemat Drzewo asyryjskie i jego partyjska geneza* [*Middle Persian Epic "The Assyrian Tree" and its Parthian Genesis*, Krakow: Księgarnia Akademicka, 2007].

Gail Minault is Professor of History and Asian Studies at the University of Texas in Austin, Texas, USA. She is the author of numerous works including, most recently: *Gender, Language, and Learning: Essays in Indo-Muslim Cultural History* (New Delhi: Permanent Black, 2009).

Christina Oesterheld, Heidelberg, Germany: PhD in Indology, doctoral thesis on three novels by Urdu writer Qurratulain Hyder; main research interest: Urdu fiction from the nineteenth century to the present; has translated Urdu short stories and poetry into German; presently teaches Urdu at the South Asia Institute, Heidelberg University.

Tariq Rahman (Ph.D.) is presently Dean of the School of Education at the Beaconhouse National University, Lahore. He is also HEC Distinguished National Professor and Professor Emeritus at the National Institute of Pakistan Studies, Quaid-i-Azam University, Islamabad. From June 2007 till June 2011 he was also the Director of NIPS. He is a highly published scholar with over 93 articles in scholarly journals; 18 books; 6 encyclopedia articles; 32 contributions to books and several book reviews. Among his books are: *Language and Politics in Pakistan* (OUP, 1996), *Language, Ideology and Power* (OUP, 2002), *Denizens of Alien Worlds* (OUP, 2004). His latest book *From Hindi to Urdu: A Social and Political History* has been published simultaneously by Oxford (Pakistan) and Orient (India) in 2011.

Harish Trivedi is Professor of English, University of Delhi, and has been visiting Professor at the universities of Chicago and London. He is the author of *Colonial Transactions: English Literature and India* (Calcutta, 1993; Manchester, 1995), and has co-edited *The Nation across the World: Postcolonial Literary Representations* (New Delhi, 2007), *Literature and Nation: Britain and India 1800-1990* (London, 2000), *Post-colonial Translation: Theory and Practice* (London, 1999), and *Interrogating Post-colonialism: Theory, Text and Context* (Shimla, 1996; rpt. 2000). He guest-edited a special issue of *New Comparison* (U.K.) on "Comparative Literature in India" (Spring 1997), and co-edited an issue of the postcolonial journal *Wasafiri* with "Focus on Translation" (London: Winter 2003).

Ashok Vajpeyi is a Hindi poet, literary and art critic, editor and translator. He is the author of thirteen books of poetry, eight of criticism (three of which are on visual arts), and co-author of four bilingual volumes of translations of poems by W. Szymborska, C. Miłosz, Z. Herbert and T. Różewicz. He won the Sahitya Akademi Award, Kabir Samman, Dayavati Modi Kavi Shekhar Samman and has been decorated by the governments of France and Poland for his cultural contributions. Book-length translations of his poetry have been published in English, French, Polish, Bengali, Marathi, and Urdu. Till the beginning of 2012 he was Chairman of the Lalit Kala Akademi (National Academy of Art).

André Wink (PhD Leiden, 1984) is Professor of History at the University of Wisconsin-Madison and Senior Fellow at the Institute for Research in the Humanities. He is the author of *Al-Hind: The Making of the Indo-Islamic World*, 3 vols. (1990-2004), and most recently *Akbar* (2009).